D0071853

HUBERT H. HUMPHREY

HUBERT H. HUMPHREY

The Politics of Joy

Charles Lloyd Garrettson III

With a foreword by
William Lee Miller

Transaction Publishers
New Brunswick (U.S.A.) and London (U.K.)

Copyright © 1993 by Transaction Publishers,
New Brunswick, New Jersey 08903

All rights reserved under International and Pan-American Copyright Conventions. No part of this book may be reproduced or transmitted in any form or by any means, electronic or mechanical, including photocopy, recording, or any information storage and retrieval system, without prior permission in writing from the publisher. All inquiries should be addressed to Transaction Publishers, Rutgers-The State University, New Brunswick, New Jersey 08903.

Library of Congress Catalog Number: 91-29601
ISBN: 1-56000-029-5
Printed in the United States of America

Library of Congress Cataloging-in-Publication Data

Garrettson, Charles Lloyd, 1953–
Hubert H. Humphrey : the politics of joy / Charles Lloyd Garrettson.

p. cm.
Includes bibliographical references and index.
ISBN 1-56000-029-5
1. Humphrey, Hubert H. (Hubert Horatio), 1911–1978—Ethics.
2. Humphrey, Hubert H. (Hubert Horatio), 1911–1978—Religion.
3. Legislators—United States—Biography. 4. United States.
Congress. Senate—Biography. I. Title.
E748.H945G37 1992
973.923′092—dc20 91-29601
[B] CIP

For Jamie and for Hadley

Where joy most revels, grief doth most lament;
Grief joys, joy grieves, on slender accident.

—Shakespeare, *Hamlet*

It is not a sacrifice to give to the suffering and the needy. It is a privilege worthy of a true American. Our greatness is not in our military might alone, our greatness springs from the generous heart of a generous people. Our reward will be eternal gratitude from the plain and humble folk of a war-torn world. Our "reservoir of goodwill" will again be our biggest asset.

—Note found in Hubert Humphrey's handwriting, circa 1946, Humphrey Collection.

Contents

Foreword

Here is an opportunity to reassess Hubert H. Humphrey. Humphrey was once the most beloved and celebrated of liberal Democrats on the national scene. From the moment he made his speech, as the young mayor of Minneapolis, to the 1948 Democratic Convention, at least until he accepted the nomination for the office of vice president under Lyndon Johnson, he held a special place in the hearts of those whose spiritual home in politics was an inheritance from the New Deal.

Harry Truman in the White House certainly won over many who had had reservations about him, and eggheads might fall madly for Adlai for a time, and a segment of the Democracy might be caught up in the brief moment of Camelot, and inconsolable at its end, and the complex giant Lyndon Johnson would, on one of his many sides, claim his due from that inheritance, but no one represented the moral legacy of American progressive politics in mid-century in so pure and consistent a way, with so warm an appreciation from those who shared those political purposes, as Hubert Humphrey.

At least until the middle 1960s, Humphrey lost altitude, in the view of many, when he became Lyndon Johnson's vice president. The imperious Texan was not one to treat his vice president with a great deal of respect, and Humphrey, already beholden to Johnson, and perhaps also accustomed to submission to Johnson, from their days in the Senate, seemed much diminished in that role. And as the war in Vietnam came to be the main preoccupation of national politics, and as Humphrey, in his dependent role, supported it with his customary vigor, he came to represent something quite different to a new generation from what he had been to their elders.

In the maelstrom of the 1960s a new political configuration arose, whose consequences are not yet quite played out. A new left, youthful, bred on the simplicities of the television set, unacquainted with the economic issues of the Great Depression, infuriated both by the moral dubiety and by the personal threat of the war in Vietnam, distinguishing itself sharply in cultural terms from its elders, came to be as hostile to the old liberalism as were the established opponents in the right wing of the Republican party and in the conservative movement. The conservative movement also took on a new life and a new form in the vortex of the 1960s. These two movements, taking shape in that turbulent decade—a new left, with a penumbra of cultural acolytes around it, and a new and newly invigorated conservatism, operated a kind of pincer movement on the moral redoubts of the older liberalism. Lyndon Johnson's presidency fell victim to the Vietnam War. Hubert Humphrey's standing in the nation's memory fell victim not only to the war but to that attack from two sides.

Ironically this movement of repudiation and rebuke to Humphrey's older liberalism came at the moment of its greatest achievement, or just afterward. The Democratic presidencies of the 1960s—as this book indicates—are replete with projects and ideas of which Humphrey was the originator, or a major proponent, or legislative leader, often while allowing the chief credit to go to someone else. The Civil Rights Act of 1964 is by no means the only, although it is the most important, of those accomplishments. The peak of Humphrey's career came in that moment in June of 1964 when the vote was cast that enacted cloture in the Senate on the Civil Rights bill, thus preventing a filibuster and guaranteeing the bill's passage, and Humphrey sitting in the front row as floor leader raised his arms in a moving gesture, at long last, of victory. That victory over the forces of resistance on a racial issue in the proud state-rights protecting institution of the United States Senate was unprecedented not only in modern times but in the whole of American history, and it was the work above all of Hubert Humphrey. And yet just four years later, Humphrey would be holed up in a Chicago hotel, besieged, while angry youthful "progressive" voices chanted endlessly, menacingly, over and over, "Dump the Hump! Dump the Hump!"

Mr. Garrettson tells the story of Humphrey's career, not as a historian, but as an interpreter of politics in their relation to morals, and of morals in their relation to religion. Mr. Humphrey's own religious convictions, as a reader can learn from this book, had a genial inclusiveness almost entirely lacking in specificity. But he was an authentic representative of the piety of the plains states as it intersected with prairie progressivism. He represented that utterly practical American, and particularly American Middle-Western, interpretation of religion that asked of it only practical questions, and found answers in social progress, social justice, social reform. What does religious belief mean—whatever your church or synagogue? For the HubertHumphreys of this world it means—making a better world. And making a better world means making better sociopolitical arrangements. It means helping justice to roll down as water, and righteousness as a mighty stream (this quotation does not come originally from Martin Luther King, Jr., as a memory-less generation seems to think, but from the prophet Amos).

Humphrey represented that prairie reformism, which often had religious origins, in the moment that it encountered larger problems than it had dealt with before: America as a dominant world power. That evoked some of Humphrey's most notable accomplishments, for which he has not received credit, as he endeavored to spread the moral outlook of American democratic progressivism around the world. But it also provoked his great trouble at the end.

He already knew the dark side of politics, especially the world politics of twentieth-century ideologies. This book relates how he had already had bruising encounters with the cynicism of the hard-line Communists in Minnesota as a young man. He already knew, as politicians always tell us, that politics is not a game of beanbag, and—particularly—that the clash of national egos and of closed and pretentious ideologies in the world require a harsher perspective than the politics of reform in the protected environment of America's stable republic. And so, like many others, he developed a rigorous Cold War conception that he carried through to the interpretation of the complex postwar events in Indochina. That, and his obligations and perhaps subordination to Lyndon Johnson produced for him what in the end many have viewed as not a politics of joy but as a tragedy.

Here is a book that opens new vistas on that story, and offers a chance to reconsider the meaning of Hubert Humphrey's career for moral and political thinking in the United States.

William Lee Miller

Acknowledgments

In our interview William Connell stated how "when you were involved with Humphrey it really made you feel good—you were caught up in something that made you feel good." The years that I have been caught up in this project have made me "feel good." The bottom line, for Humphrey, had to do with people. Perhaps the greatest source of the good feeling that I have enjoyed has had to do with the people with whom I have been associated because of this project. Whatever strength this work may have, much of it has surely come from them. I therefore wish to acknowledge their contribution—a contribution that has been as significant as it has been varied—especially the following:

As the bibliography indicates, certainly one key to my research effort lies in the time that I spent at the Research Center of the Minnesota Historical Society in St. Paul. The staff there made my stay in Minnesota tremendously worthwhile on both a personal and a professional level. The people with whom I worked closely at the Center include, Ruth Bauer, Dallas Lindgren, Steve Nielson—and especially Linda Fagen, who proved to be not only a pleasant hostess, but a good friend.

Roslea Coats not only showed that she is Doland's best tour guide but proved that she could make an Easterner feel quite at home amidst the endless but nevertheless beautifully black midwestern soil. I am grateful for the glimpses of "Pinky" that she provided me—glimpses that I am sure most researchers never would have had access to. I especially would like to remember her for a certain dinner down on Main Street . . .

One of HHH's campaign posters reads: "People care about Humphrey because Humphrey cares about people." People today still care about Humphrey. It has been my great pleasure (as well as good fortune) to have had a chance to meet with a number of those who knew HHH and, in most cases, knew him well. They include, in the order of their being interviewed, Dr. Julian Hartt, Norman Sherman, Ambassador Max Kampelman, the Reverend Richard Kozelka, the Reverend Calvin Didier, Ambassador Geraldine Joseph, David Gartner, William Connell, Joseph Rauh, Frances Humphrey Howard, Maj. Gen. Edward Lansdale, Arthur Naftalin, Bert Fraleigh, Rufus Phillips, Ernest Lefever, Douglas Cater, Theodore Van Dyk, Evron Kirkpatrick, Lt. Gen. Herbert Beckington, Senator Barry Goldwater, Bill Moyers, Dean Rusk, Ambassador Bui Diem, John Stewart, Senator Russell Long, and Victor Reuther.

Particular mention goes to a number of the above who assisted me in special ways. Frances Howard, Edward Lansdale, Bill Moyers, and John Stewart were all willing to read various chapters. William Connell and Julian Hartt read *all* of the chapters and offered generous encouragement. William Connell also provided access to his impressively done film, *Into the Bright Sunshine*, and permission to quote at length was granted by *Fortune* magazine and the University of Minnesota Press. Rufus Phillips provided a number of critically important materials, including his 25 November 1964 memorandum, from which he permitted me to quote liberally. Bill Moyers did the same and also showed genuine enthusiasm for the project through many stages. Frances Howard provided her own characteristically Humphreyesque enthusiasm, which has meant a great deal. Edward Lansdale was generous enough simply to allow a religion student—of all things—to take up his time on a number of occasions.

My family provided assistance that I truly depended on time and again. Perhaps now, for once, I will be able to return the favor. I have in mind especially a certain summer in a certain place: the summer of 1990 in Norfolk, Connecticut, which I was able to happily discover to be an ideal place to think and write, even under difficult circumstances, thanks to the supreme graciousness of my sister and brother-in-law, Linda and Frank Pizzica.

A number of teachers, colleagues, and friends provided varying degrees of support and helpful criticism. These include first and foremost David Little, William Lee Miller, Kenneth Thompson, and especially my mentor and HHH's "closest childhood friend," Julian Hartt. A true keeper of the flame and good friend was John Zuraw, who was part of a certain "bier gruppe" that also provided helpful encouragement, as well as an earnest challenge. My department chair, Darrell Jodock, also deserves special mention as someone who asked very hard questions and thus helped tremendously in terms of bringing about much of whatever focus this work might have. In that same regard, a number of other close friends also deserve special mention. Ashton and Kimberly Nichols always and will always come to mind. In this particular case, however, Richard Miller and Barbara Klinger must be mentioned for a special visit to the Midwest. Other such friends would also include Dr. John and Dr. Mary Voyatzis, Michael and Esty Koplen, Alan Mittleman, and others besides. Special mention deserves to go to Mary Sysak, another keeper of the flame, who, in her own particular way, greatly helped to make this project possible.

Last but hardly least, I am indebted to the staff of Musselman Advertising, Inc. Special thanks and recognition go to Eileen Detweiler for her always friendly assistance with such things as a project like this necessitates; Nancy Schneider and Caron Lane in like regard; Bertie and Jim Musselman, for their never-failing generosity in providing me with unlimited access to their impressive and much depended upon facilities.

They did so, of course, at least in part, at the bequest and in the interest of those to whom this book is dedicated.

Introduction

While the old convention has it that religion and politics are two of the three topics that are never to be discussed in polite company, this work intends to discuss both. It does so by focusing on a particular individual who, in his own way, conjoined them: Hubert Humphrey. For Humphrey, politics were to be "the politics of joy"—the joy of providing an equal opportunity for everyone—regardless of race, color, or creed (and later gender)—to pursue happiness. Though not overtly religious in the conventional sense, the above could still be described as Humphrey's vocation or calling. It was, at the very least, his ideal, and a very high one indeed. For many, it was too high. Yet Humphrey was quite aware of what was involved in effecting such an ideal—unusually so, in fact, for someone so often written off as an "idealist." Hence, the following graced his living room wall:

> The saint may dream and the philosopher construct his ideal world, but the man who wields power must live in the pit of reality, doing the very best he can and ever reconciled to the limited and the partial.

Humphrey's life and career was a striking amalgam of "the saint" and "the man who wields power." While he did "dream" and "construct his ideal world," he was also "ever reconciled to the limited and the partial." While he saw bringing joy as his vocation, he was committed to doing so in and by politics, and thus to living in the "pit of reality." As such, his story provides a dialectically poignant interface of the religiously ideal and the politically real, with "dialectical" understood to mean the critical examination into the truth via the poising of opposing viewpoints.

His background was something literally out of *The Music Man*: he was reared on the Main Street of the early twentieth-century American Midwest. Based on the values that he took from that time and place, he built a political career that brought him to the heights of political power. He happened to have done so, however, amidst one of the most significant, tumultuous, and challenging times in American history: the 1960s—a time *not* noted for its emphasis on Main Street values. His life, then, was one of profound irony: the very source of strength that brought him to his greatest triumph and joy—his role in the passage of the Civil Rights Act of 1964, and thus the vice presidency—ironically enough also brought him to his greatest failure and grief—the presidential campaign of 1968.

Talking of the source of strength and joy as also being the source of failure and grief is the stuff of drama—tragedy, to be specific. Yet this is a book on ethics. Wherein lies the connection? It lies within the fact that while nearly everyone has an opinion on what is right, politically speaking, it is rarer for people to base such an opinion squarely on what is involved in applying the "right" to politics. That is, thinking about what is "right" in regards to politics, all too often—certainly in the academic community for which this work is primarily written—becomes too much a theoretical exercise that lacks sufficient experiential content and consideration. "Academic" becomes all too often a pejorative term for just this reason. While this text does not dispute the critical importance of debating what ideals we *should* hold in regards to politics, it seeks to provide the term "academic" with more honor than it tends to hold by suggesting that perhaps such a debate should and could include more serious consideration of what is involved in actually *applying* such ideals, religious and otherwise, to the politically real. In other words, it tries to unite, or at least bring into more fruitful dialogue, the academic and the political communities—the "ideal" and the "real," if you will, and it does so by considering the story of Hubert Humphrey.

To conduct an ethical debate essentially by focusing on a story is to accept at least the premise of contemporary "narrative" approach to ethics, established primarily by Stanley Hauerwas and Alasdair MacIntyre. For them, narrative, whether literary or historical, is the more appropriate genre for ethical inquiry than traditional casuistry because it captures more thoroughly the complex texture of moral experience than did the traditional application of principles and rules to ethical cases. As with Hauerwas, and as already indicated, this work does not deny the critical importance of considering ethical principles in abstraction. Rather, it simply agrees with Hauerwas's contention that ethical reflection might remain incomplete when it is conducted solely as such an exercise. To that this work would also add that this may be particularly so when it comes to politics. Hence, its key point: knowing what is "right," politically speaking, must involve serious consideration of what it takes to effect it.

From that key point a comparable one follows: in pursuing ethics this way, not to say life itself, what can emerge is not just a sense of life involving *both* triumph *and* tragedy, but also of both oftentimes having a quite intimate interrelatedness. That is to say, what emerges is a profound sense of irony and of the sense already cited: what is at once the source of one's strength and thus joy can also prove to be the source of one's weakness and thus sorrow. And what is ethically significant in appreciating that? That no matter what our differences, religious, political or otherwise, if we would all recognize that we share life's irony together, perhaps we would be less quick to judge and thus less prone to perpetuate unnecessary and often enough unjust contention—contention that is suffering in itself, yet which can also lead to even greater suffering as well. In a word, we would be more humble, and as a consequence, hopefully, more virtuous.

Speaking of irony, while the method of such a lesson is new—the application of contemporary narrative theory—the lesson itself is ancient. When told that he was the wisest of men, Socrates's response was the famous: "I only know that I do not know." Perhaps if all of us would recognize that when it comes to something as extremely complex and vexingly difficult as applying religious-ethical ideals to political reality we really do not know as much as we thought, we might be a bit more humble and thus, presumably, better—perhaps, indeed, even wiser. Such, at any rate, is the zenith of aspiration of the work in hand.

It seeks to aspire to such a zenith via a three-way progression, beginning with "the Dream," to which is then juxtaposed "the Fact," and from which in turn follows a concluding "Analysis." Its overall methodology, then, is to be dialectical, in the sense already defined. "The Dream" provides a detailed account of the origins and content of Humphrey's religious-political outlook, culminating in its most idealistic application, the "Bright Sunshine" speech delivered to the 1948 Democratic National Convention. "The Fact" then demonstrates how such idealism, once fully immersed in the political realm, can yield results which are sometimes joyful, sometimes tragic, and very often ironic. "Analysis" then seeks a synthesis of the two by attempting to locate Humphrey in a religious-political category, concluding that, among other things, while he is to be associated with those that are considered, he is also distinct from them, and, furthermore, that the "answers" which an analysis of this kind can yield can also result in as many questions.

Religious-political categories are utilized because Humphrey's own ethics were, to use his term, "Judeo-Christian." That is to say, his is a case of someone with a specifically (though, as indicated, hardly conventional) religious vision who attempted to apply that vision to the world, and was *thus* put to the test. This particular study of that life seeks, therefore, to provide potential lessons for anyone seeking to achieve the good, religiously conceived, yet politically applied. Its appeal is not intended to be limited to a religious audience alone, nor to a strictly political audience either, but rather to anyone who wishes to reflect on what may be involved in applying principle to practice—on, in other words, what may be experienced by attempting to make one's dream fact somewhere within the "pit of reality."

Part One

The Dream

1

Idealism Born: Doland, South Dakota

In his autobiography, Hubert Humphrey proudly and tellingly declared that "the kind of public man I am has been overwhelmingly shaped by two influences: the land of South Dakota and an extraordinary relationship with an extraordinary man, my father."[1] For Humphrey, "the land of South Dakota" was essentially a reference to an ordinary and tiny portion of that land: the little town of Doland, the scene of his upbringing and, in many ways—though hardly in all—the quintessential American small town.

"During the twenties," wrote Julian Hartt, son of Doland's Methodist minister and Humphrey's high school chum,[2]

> Doland claimed a population of 600-plus; the old wheeze had it that the census must have been taken on a Saturday night in mid-July. There was nothing of singular charm in its appearance or memorable in its history, nothing whatever to set it apart from scores and scores of towns on the plains, almost all of them created by the railroad.[3]

Hartt went on to describe Doland in terms of having "had one schoolhouse. The primary grades occupied the first floor, the high school the second floor. The gymnasium was in the basement. And it had the lowest ceiling of any basketball court in Christendom. Our team was at a nearly irremediable disadvantage when they played in gyms where you could *arch* the ball."[4] Yet as Michael Amrine, one of Humphrey's biographers noted, "at almost any place in town one can stand on a front porch and in the sharp and brilliant light scan with perfect clarity the open country. The horizon lies around the town, very close and very far . . . the big questions seem very close in this small place."[5]

Certainly, in the twenties, "the big questions" *were* very close. This was unavoidable, but not only because of how the horizon seemed to surround the town. Contrary to popular belief, the Great Depression of the thirties had actually hit the American Midwest a number of years before the crash of '29. Banks had begun to close there as early as 1926. The drought, the dust, and the locusts were then to follow in about that order. Humphrey recalled the apocalyptic pall of those times by stating how, after watching the grasshoppers actually eat the paint off the houses, he "sometimes . . . thought it was the end of the world."[6]

Such an "end" in fact came much closer to home, in the most literal sense possible. It provided what was probably the most profound experience in shaping young Humphrey's life, and one which he himself referred to time and again:

> The first time I ever saw my father weep, I was sixteen years old and he was forty-five. It was something I have never forgotten, not just because it moved me deeply, but because what followed was so typical of my father's approach to life.
>
> The place we lived in was the kind of home every lucky child has in his life—not just a house but a warm nest for all the excitement and love of growing up.
>
> It wasn't a showplace but it was a pretty good house, as good as any in Doland. It was a two-story, squarish place with white siding and a big screened-in front porch, rooms with hardwood floors, a big basement and two bathrooms, beautiful shade trees on the front lawn, and a plum and apple orchard in the back. A cement driveway led up to a garage, and behind it was a tool shed we turned into a chicken house.
>
> When I came home from high school one day in 1927 [actually it was 1926], my mother was standing next to Dad and a stranger, under a big cottonwood on the front lawn. She was crying. Both men looked solemn, and I wondered what was wrong. Mother said, "Dad has to sell the house to pay our bills." My father talked to the man for a short time, signed a paper, and then the man went away. Afterward, Dad wept.
>
> He was a broad-shouldered man almost six feet tall, with big strong hands, a jutting chin, and that high forehead his children inherited. His rimless glasses sometimes gave him a professional look, but he was usually so jolly and

> vigorous that the most noticeable thing about him was seemingly inexhaustible zest. He just couldn't be passive about anything and was seldom sad. Seeing my father's tears shook me.
>
> At that moment, I began to have an adult's awareness of the possibilities for pain and tragedy in life. Other people in town suffered similar losses of home and happiness. One neighbor and close friend, the president of Security State Bank, Fred Gross, committed suicide.[7]

Despite such a terrible loss, however, the Humphreys remained undaunted:

> Our tears dried. We moved to a smaller house, which we rented. Distress in a small town like Doland had no protection of anonymity. It seemed then [like] such total and public humiliation, but my father never looked back.
>
> He showed not a discernible ounce of acrimony, apology, or defeatism, and I don't think he felt any. He plunged on. Some people who enjoy the sunshine of living are unprepared for the storms. When they are shocked or hurt, they withdraw and cover up. Not my father. Right up to the time he died, in November 1949, he had an undiminished appetite for life, accepting the bitter with the sweet.[8]

That example was to be the one that Humphrey himself would try to follow through all the "storms" that he would have to brave in his own life.

Beyond this deeply personal lesson, however, there was a political lesson to be learned in this as well, and one that would be equally instrumental in Humphrey's outlook:

> No matter how competent my father may have been, or how good my mother, or how fine my community . . . it could be wrenched by forces over which we had no control . . . this little secure world of my hometown just wasn't strong enough to fight off the powerful forces that seemed to be crowding in on us.[9]

One of the greatest of heroes in the Humphrey household was William Jennings Bryan. His insistence that East Coast money manipulators controlled and would ruin the lives of the rest of the country had now been driven home with a new and indelible force on a family in which the Cross of Gold speech was recited twice a year. Hence, "when I see tight money, and when I see the Federal Reserve Bank raising that discount rate, and the prime rate . . . I remember my daddy telling me what happened in 1922, and I remember 1926 and I remember 1928, and I am rightly suspicious of the manipulators of money."[10]

Another hero was FDR. This was "because I thought he was the first president in my lifetime to challenge the power of these moneychangers,"[11] and perhaps more important, "he was the man who saved our homes."[12] FDR *was* a hero because he acted on the basis of principles embedded in America's foundation to challenge the pernicious materialist evil that the Eastern financial establishment represented—an evil that violated those very principles. Given the circumstances, lionizing such efforts—and believing in the possibility of their eventual success—was easy for someone like Humphrey, coming, as he did, out of the midwestern prairie populist tradition of that time.

For Humphrey, that tradition began, literally at home. As great as Bryan and FDR were, Humphrey's greatest hero was his own father. Humphrey, Sr. was known as the druggist "who never sells you a pill without selling you an idea." In this, as in other things, he was something of an eccentric. He claimed that after he heard William Jennings Bryan speak for the first time he became a Democrat—and that was eccentric enough in a town that had only five such curiosities. Yet he proved to be both sufficiently personable and able as to gain a seat on the town's city council. In fact he eventually was to go on and become the town's mayor.[13] His tenure as town councilman is most vividly remembered in terms of his ardent (though ultimately unsuccessful) opposition to the takeover of the town's power plant by Northwest Public Electric, a sell-out that the town would later regret for the very reasons Humphrey, Sr. predicted, namely, higher rates and poorer service, when just the opposite had been promised, along with a fancy lighting system on Main Street.[14]

Both the Humphrey home and the Humphrey store were powerhouses of their own—they each produced scenes of intellectual probing and cultural richness that were striking for their locale.

Humphrey, Sr. used to say his closest friends were "first his children and then his books." His library consisted of such disparate texts as Bryce's *American Commonwealth*, Gibbon's *History of the Decline and Fall of the Roman Empire*, Joseph Tumulty's

Wilson [Woodrow] As I Knew Him, Wilson's own *New Freedom*, Henry S. Raymond's *The Life and Public Services of Abraham Lincoln*, Moncure D. Conway's *The Life of Thomas Paine*, Emil Ludwig's *Napolean*, Ortega Y. Gasset's *Revolt of the Masses*, Robert Ingersoll's *Why I Am an Agnostic*, and the Bible. There were volumes on nearly all the American presidents and founding fathers, especially Thomas Paine, Benjamin Franklin, Patrick Henry, and Andrew Jackson. There were also works by Kant, the mystic Henry Drummond, Harry Emerson Fosdick, Elbert Hubbard, Longfellow, the Romantics—Wordsworth, Keats, Shelley—and Edgar Guest. All of these books, and the ideas in them, were avidly discussed and expounded upon both within the Humphrey home and from behind the Humphrey counter. Humphrey, Jr. illustrates this by telling the story of how his mother would break in on late-night sessions of Humphrey, Sr. having all the children arrayed around him listening to him read. When the mother would protest the late hour, "he would give her an affectionate squeeze and urge her to 'sleep for all of us.'"[15] His affection for his books is illustrated by another story told by Frances Howard, Humphrey's sister. "In his will he very carefully divided between me and Hubert and Ralph and Fern—each one getting [their own volumes]—as if they were a portfolio stock."[16] The fact that such an "inheritance" was passed on to the children was evidenced in Humphrey's own statement that his father

> was the greatest influence in my life because he more than anyone else led me into the world of books. He had a profound appreciation for the value of knowledge and inspired me to read many, many authors. He was always interested in the affairs of his state and nation. I was brought up on political literature, Jefferson, Lincoln, Wilson, Washington, the early American patriots, and of course more recent figures of American history.[17]

"Dad" Humphrey's books were also involved in another eccentricity of his: his early agnosticism. For a time Humphrey, Sr. had provided Doland with its own village atheist. Frances Howard relates how her father would tell her, whenever more strait-laced members of the family came to visit, to go and hide his copies of Voltaire, Ingersoll, and Darwin's *Origin of Species* under the sofa.

Despite such eccentricities (eccentric certainly according to the prevailing order of the day), Humphrey, Sr. had an eager and receptive mind. He subscribed to *The Christian Science Monitor, The New York Times, The New York Herald Tribune, The Minneapolis Journal*, and *The St. Paul Dispatch*, as well as more local productions, such as the *Watertown Public Opinion*.* When he discovered classical music he drove to Minneapolis to hear its symphony orchestra, and bought a Victrola, along with piles of RCA Victor Red Seal records. That library was subsequently enlarged when he later discovered opera and another trip was inspired: "He got out of bed once in the middle of the night so that he could drive to New York and arrive at the proper time to attend a performance at the Metropolitan."[18] He offered to sell the tickets for traveling theatrical companies that periodically came through town, and then also offered the family furniture as props. The fact that the family received their tickets free was small consolation to Mrs. Humphrey's disconsolation at seeing the family home half-emptied of its earthly possessions. After discovering poetry, "Dad" Humphrey went so far as to read it on local radio to a perhaps bewildered, but perhaps also inspired audience.

Eventually, Humphrey, Sr. was to discover religion. His entrance into the church was made possible largely by the positive example set by the Reverend Albert Hartt. Reverend Hartt and Humphrey, Sr. became close friends soon after the Hartts moved to Doland from Groton. The extent to which this friendship had an influence on the elder Humphrey was testified to in a letter written to Albert Hartt years later by Humphrey, Jr.: "My dad loved you as if you were his own brother. He told me many times that your ministry had made his life truly meaningful."[19] Humphrey, Sr. plunged into religion just as he had into music, poetry, and anything else he happened to take an interest in: "Dad was soon on the church board and taught Sunday school, drawing the biggest, most enthusiastic adult classes in the county."[20] According to Humphrey, Jr.,

*Humphrey Sr. also had a reputation for his subscriptions to more radically minded publications as well.

the elder Humphrey taught the course "more like a social action class" by relating "the Bible to the contemporary scene."[21] In fact, "his own good works did not end when his class was over. In an evangelical spirit, he would bring home three or four or more people for Sunday dinner and more talk."[22] Of these same classes Julian Hartt amusingly stated how Humphrey's "evangelical spirit" could lead "somewhat to my father's annoyance on occasion, because with Humphrey leading the men's bible class, it was pretty hard for anyone else to get a word in."[23]

Beyond even his religious zeal, however, Dad Humphrey's real passion was for politics, and Humphrey Drug became his podium. "Just think of it, boys," Humphrey recalls his father saying, "here we are in the middle of this great big continent here in South Dakota, with the land stretching out for hundreds of miles, with people who can vote and govern their own lives, with riches enough for all if we will take care to do justice."[24] Such was the view of a true democrat and a true patriot. What some might see as a potentially forlorn and isolated existence, Humphrey saw as a remarkable and wonderful opportunity. This was the essential Humphrey, and it was a view propounded as steadily as it was vigorously, not only in those Sunday school classes, but also from the platform of the drugstore counter.

Humphrey, Jr. tells of how, even as a small boy, he would be imbued with that outlook while quite literally standing on that "platform":

> When I was ten, my father decided the time had come; I would wash dishes and make sodas. I was too short to reach the counter and pull the spigots, so he built a little ramp behind the fountain, and I worked—and listened—from there.
>
> In that ice-cream parlor atmosphere, I heard things that further shaped my life and attitudes toward people and ideas. At night, Dad would sit down with the local lawyer, the doctor, a minister, the bankers, and the postmaster, to discuss and argue the issues of the day. In his store, there was eager talk about politics, town affairs, and religion—just as there was around our dinner-table . . . I've attended several good universities, listened to some of the great parliamentary debates of our time, but have seldom heard better discussions of basic issues than I did as a boy standing on a wooden platform behind a soda fountain.[25]

Foes and friends alike would complain until his dying day of Humphrey's chronic penchant for overstatement. Yet he claimed that this was simply something that had been ingrained in him from early on: "I was infected then with the excitement of good discussions. Dialogue and conversation, as I listened and learned, meant having something to say but [also] drawing out others; being passionately concerned with the people and issues but tempering that passion with respect for those who thought differently."[26]

Talk in the Humphrey household was not simply a matter of passing the time. As stated, Humphrey, Sr. would regularly expostulate that, "Before the fact is the dream." Conversation for all the Humphreys became a way of building their dreams. In truth, it made all the world a possibility: "A druggist in a tiny town in the middle of the continent, American history and world affairs were as real to him as they were in Washington, D.C. 1,342 miles away"[27] (as a sign on Doland's Main Street had indicated throughout Humphrey's youth). In 1964, Michael Amrine described Doland as a town where all you are likely to see besides "a man, just loading a sack of feed onto a pickup truck" is "a dog, asleep—and a few dragonflies that are only pretending to be busy."[28] While that may or may not be a fair depiction of the Doland of the 1960s, the life lived in it during the twenties was surely grander than that, and all the more impressive for it. Furthermore, the Humphreys were without question key players in that "grandeur"—as it blossomed both in Doland and throughout the midwest during this period, providing the young Humphrey with his dream that would later become the basis of action for his life.

Foremost among those ideals was one cited by Julian Hartt: "the atmosphere clearly was egalitarian" in both Doland in particular and in the prairie at large, and it was an egalitarianism that was "all but universal."[29] Though pervasive, that was not to say therefore "that it was inclusive and coherent." There was no racial prejudice against blacks for the simple reason that there were none. "But now you raise the question about the *Indians*," Hartt went on, "and almost all the cliches entertained about the black were entertained about the Indian—even among the liberal people," namely, that "they were shiftless, immoral, and lazy and they are riddled with alcoholism and venereal disease etc. etc. etc. You see it is exactly the same pattern."[30]

Though incomplete, the egalitarianism of the prairie "was still an important thing as part of the frontier mentality."[31] "In our home," Humphrey, Jr. had written, "high-hatting anyone was strictly taboo. If anything, the children were taught to go out of their way in treating less fortunately situated children in the community with kindness and respect."[32] Such a stress on egalitarian virtue had made enough of an imprint on Humphrey, Jr. to have him joke, years afterward, regarding his high school years: "That class of '28 walloped everybody in football, and then we [the class of '29] had to take a beating from the teams next year just to get even. We were the sacrificial lamb. We had to be sacrificed on the altar of equality of treatment."[33]

The key concept was, "A person was what a person made himself to be." Twain's joke that people who are infatuated with their ancestors are like potatoes – the best parts are underground – may have reflected the aristocratic pretensions of easterners but it did not reflect the American Midwest of that time. Initiative and self-reliance counted for nearly everything. The prestige (or lack thereof) of one's origins counted for little. As Hartt drolly quipped: "Once in a while someone who had gone to school in the East would show up out there but he was always regarded as a freak – his parents had more money than they were entitled to, or . . . he had taken the wrong train somewhere and hadn't realized it until it was too late."[34] At the outset, everyone was treated as an equal, at least until they showed themselves unworthy of being treated in such manner. "So self-reliance, independence, doing an honest day's work for an honest day's dollar, taking care of yourself, provision for the future"[35] – these were the ingredients comprising the mix of values that flavored the prairie piety of that time. Coupled with that was a concept of the *deserving poor* – those upon whom economic hardship had been imposed by forces over which the individual or family had no control. That concept would be considerably liberalized in the prairie of the twenties and thirties by such "forces." Throughout the Depression, drifters looking for some lunch would become as much a fixture of the American

Midwest as the dust. "To be poor was not in itself a disgrace," Hartt insisted, "We were given every encouragement to believe that among the poor there were many admirable people, victims of circumstance rather than of defects of character."[36]

Humphrey tells two stories that illustrate how this distinction was acknowledged in the Humphrey home:

> One day, a friend of mine and I went into the drugstore. I said, "Dad, Jonathan here doesn't have any shoes, and his feet are so cold, they're blue." My father took one look, pushed the NO SALE key on the cash register, took out some money, and walked Jonathan down the street to buy him woolen socks and a pair of sturdy boots.
>
> My father did that kind of thing in a way that was not an act of charity—simply a matter of elemental justice and fairness. (Years later, during the depression, when he canceled thirteen thousand dollars' worth of debts at our drugstore—money we sorely needed to pay our own bills—he shrugged it off with the same humane attitude. He coupled it with a business rationalization: "Hubert, if they owe us money they can't pay, they'll be too embarrassed to come into the store. This way, at least they feel easier about coming in.")[37]

The persistence of such a charitable view of things was not due simply to the fact that so many were forced to suffer through the economic hard times of the Dustbowl period. It was also due to another civic virtue, related to egalitarianism, and equally engrained into the religious-political fabric of that era, namely, a sense of fair play.

Julian Hartt discussed how in Doland's Scout troop, of which both he and Humphrey were part, the sense of fair play was instilled by the insistence that when "we were playing games, everybody had to play—even the fat kid who couldn't run . . . no one was left out."[38] In the prairie of the twenties, "fair play was an ideal of transcendent importance. It ordained sympathy and help to any deserving underdog. It commanded one to detest and if possible actively oppose any kind of bullying. So it was a great thing to take on a bully and thrash him. Success in that was a vindication of the moral order."[39]

A third civic virtue woven into the religious-political outlook of that era, and related to the previous two, was "doing one's part." During that time,

> to do one's part was a clear and weighty imperative of the piety of the nation. True, there was a degree of tension between the vestigial spirit of the frontier, which urged us to be self-creators, and the doctrine of the covenanted nation which required everybody to contribute to the common good. But we did not feel that tension very keenly in Doland during the twenties. We understood that the idea required us to be hard workers; the immediate community which needed our concern for the common good was of course the family. By the time you had reached middle adolescence you were expected to earn the money to buy your clothes. For young Humphrey that meant long hours in the drugstore; for me it meant farm work during the summer months; and doing the janitor work in the church the rest of the time.
>
> The interests of the largest community, the nation, overrode all others in times of crisis. Then not to do one's part was a heinous offence. "Slacker," and "draft dodger!" were terms of severe obloquy during World War I; their taint lingered long after.[40]

Such a view can easily be seen as providing the basis for the tremendous emphasis on work that existed in Doland at that time. Humphrey once commented that "the worst sin [in Doland] was not to be a worker,"[41] and Frances Howard similarly spoke of how "everybody had to do their part . . . everybody had a task to do."[42]

And so egalitarianism, fair play, and doing one's part were the three predominant features of the moral landscape within which Humphrey grew up. In a sense, to use a Christian analogy, they formed a kind of moral "trinity," of which egalitarianism was the "Father," generating the consequent mutual responsibilities of guaranteeing the "Son" of an equal chance for all to participate, but also the "Spirit" of equally *requiring* all to contribute at the same time. Together they formed the moral kernel out of which the Doland community grew.

An additional characteristic of Doland life that also formed an important part of Humphrey's character was its sense of community. In his interview with Theodore White, Humphrey said of Doland: "I think what that little town taught me was community spirit."[43] When he also said, "I swear I never had a key to a house until I was mayor of Minneapolis,"[44] he was referring to the sense of interrelatedness (not to mention trust) that existed among the entire population of Doland—and of the Midwest in general. People lived with an understanding that they lived *together*, a genuine sense of familial closeness. There were, for instance, neighbors like the Wilkeys whose "house was real close—you just walked in one door and out the other when you wanted to save steps—that's the kind of folks they were."[45] Such easy familiarity was still evident forty-six years after Humphrey left Doland. On one of his many returns to the town, Humphrey was still able to recall

> the Riley family, and the home there where they now have the filling station on that corner—that's where 212 intersects down there. And I went by and I said, "Oh yes, that used to be Mrs. Gordon's, and that's where she used to live, and there was the LaBree family, that's where they used to live, and there was the Gothwraites, and there was the Scogmos and the Riskes, and so on down the line, and over there was the Jones family, and . . . there was the Shauf family, and my goodness, I could go on and on."[46]

Reflecting, in that same speech, on "the kind of community spirit that has characterized this community" he was led to argue that

> there needs to be a sense of community—for people to really belong—to feel that they are a part of a society, or, to put it another way, when you feel that you are a part of society there is a sense of community. Now one of the great tragedies of the great urban centers today is that their people don't feel they belong. They live there, but they're not really involved. It isn't their life. It's their residence. It's the place they work [in] or the place they sleep in, or the place they play in, but it isn't their life."[47]

Doland, in contrast,

> was like one big family. Lots of times troubles, but don't we have that in families? Sometimes bitter arguments, but we've had that in families. People very different, but isn't that true in families? But there was a sense of being, and a sense of belonging, and a sense of caring. Everybody knew everybody. There was really no place to hide. There was always a place to be. And you had the feeling that you were *wanted*.[48]

Humphrey wanted America as a whole to be that kind of place, and thus *there* was the inspiration for so many domestic programs—programs ranging from the school lunch program to NASA and the National Endowment for the Humanities—that Humphrey championed in his thirty-plus years of political life. When he stated, "Those fifteen years of my life [of growing up in

Doland] were very important, and they taught me things that I have never forgotten," he meant every word.

This is not to say, therefore, that life in Doland was easy. On the contrary, as Frances Howard made clear, life was "financially and physically very hard."[49] The point is that with all, and even *despite* the hardships, emotionally life was "very warm and very generous." There was, as Mrs. Howard went on, "no deprivation of the spirit or deprivation of affection . . . no one thought he was poor . . . in Doland because there was much more egalitarianism [than there is in the world today] . . . most people worked for a living and most people knew each other."[50] Everyone had a place. Everyone was made to feel important. The *Times Record* was the town newspaper, and its editor, Mrs. Dody, saw to it that "everything that was done in the school, or in the churches or in the community or in the farm community was put in that paper—*everything*."[51] The sense of belonging that this kind of community fostered gave a sense "to every individual [of] having the right of assertion, of his own sense of righteousness—of what he thinks is right for him."[52] Mrs. Howard even told of how this communal regard helped foster a sense of ecumenism when, for instance, the children of a nearby Russian Mennonite church would come to sing in a four-part choral performance hosted by the other churches in Doland. As such there was a "sense of community, a brightness of spirit that was rare."[53]

Of religious matters Humphrey once defined a Christian as someone who is "interested in good living. In living a good life. In doing that which he can as Jesus said in the Lord's Prayer, of trying somehow to arrive at heaven on earth."[54] "Trying somehow to arrive at heaven on earth" was the clarion call of the great American religious-political movement of the late nineteenth and early twentieth centuries, the Social Gospel. Its main features could be listed as follows: (1) as just stated, a sense of religious mission in bringing the heavenly city to earth; (2) doing so in a highly "enthusiastic" manner, which is to say, to unreflectively emphasize action over thought, specifically action for the needy; (3) a belief that democracy represents the closest thing in the political order to the Kingdom yet attained; and (4) a belief that private wealth, not government, represented the greatest threat to individual integrity, with the consequence that government was the crucial (though not the only) institution by which this threat was to be thwarted. Such an intervention would result in a balance between capitalism and socialism that would provide the most just form of political-economic order possible.

While the above summarizes the "call" of the Social Gospel, it also details the "call" that was consistently heard in the Humphrey household as well. This is indicated in many statements of Humphrey's that clearly represent Social Gospel themes. For example: "My father brought me up to believe that there was worth in every person. My religion tells me that there is worth in every person. That's what it is all about."[55] Humphrey noted that in his upbringing, the emphasis "was on the social imperatives of religion. A heavenly city, according to Dad, could be created on earth through good works."[56]

It only followed, then, that if one's religion did not directly—and effectively—involve you in righting social wrongs, then it was not a religion worthy of the name. Such was not a viewpoint indigenous to the Humphrey household alone—it was in fact the message received at church regularly as well.

Humphrey declared the Reverend Albert Hartt to have been the man who, "more than any other outside of my father had an influence on my life."[57] He described that influence largely in terms of what were also familiar Social Gospel themes: "I was brought up to believe that religion was more than a Sunday experience, that the truly religious man was one who understood the meaning of love, compassion, and justice and these were the standards to which one should aspire."[58] Similarly, "the Reverend Albert Hartt," Humphrey wrote, "was not only a preacher of the gospel in terms of the strict religious and spiritual message, but also he was a man motivated by a sense of social justice, which I am sure came from his understanding and love of the precepts of Christianity."[59] These precepts included "social responsibility . . . community leadership in the Christian spirit of decency, wholesomeness, friendliness, compassion, forgiveness and yet the stern requirements of morality."[60] True understanding of Christianity, then—real spiritual insight—consisted in understanding one's social responsibility and meeting it.

Such requirements were stern, but that is not to say that Christianity in the Humphrey home was simply a sober and rigid discipline. Humphrey explained his early churchgoing as being "primarily at Mother's insistence, but also because I liked it and because Julian Hartt, the minister's son, was a close friend."[61] The religion that young Hubert grew up in was "full and rich with joy. It was not the cold, stern, forbidding existence that is often pictured of some early Christians, but rather, the outgoing, the full, the rich, the joyous experience of the full life."[62] As "the joyous experience of the full life," it provided the stuff of a religious viewpoint that would be characterized by its "enthusiasm for humanity"—one of the great slogans of the Social Gospel. It obviously also provided the kind of religious soil out of which the politics of joy could easily (and eagerly) grow.

In line with the Social Gospel's emphasis on "The deed, not the creed" (another of its great slogans) there was an additional feature of Humphrey's upbringing that is important to mention as well. Focus in life in both the Humphrey home in particular, and in the Doland community of the twenties at large, was on work—on *doing*. Talking was certainly (and constantly) important. Yet *action* was always given the predominant emphasis of the two. Amrine recounts how Grandfather Sannes (Humphrey's maternal grandfather) "preached a doctrine in which work was about the equal of life and life meant work."[63] Frances Howard similarly talked of "this tremendous emphasis on the work ethic." For her, "Everybody had to do his part . . . 'work for the night is coming'—the work ethic—that was our religion."[64] This only parallels a comparable emphasis within the Social Gospel, as stated by its principal proponent, Walter Rauschenbusch: "In the long run the only true way to gain moral insight, self-discipline, humility, love, and a consciousness of coherence and dependence, is to take our place among those who serve one another by useful labor. Parasitism blinds; work reveals."[65]

In terms of religious obligation this meant honoring the Social Gospel characteristic that social justice was the primary feature of one's religion. That is, it was mostly in "deeds" and not in "creeds" that Humphrey was taught to express his religious convictions. Hays Gorey, another Humphrey biographer, recalls Humphrey as saying that he "had been taught that the way you treat people is the way you treat God. I was taught that religion should have something to do with your daily life—not just with Sunday."[66] Similarly Humphrey himself wrote, "When I was a young boy, one of the first Bible verses taught to me by my parents was: 'Let your light shine so that men may see your good works and glorify your father which is in heaven.'"[67] Thus, for life in Doland, the epistle of James was hardly "an epistle of straw," as Luther had labelled it. Its 1:22 injunction to *do* the word and not hear it only can be found in Humphrey materials covering the course of his entire career. It and the idea it evoked were both engrained in him from early on; one idle moment in his childhood was abruptly ended by his father tapping on young Hubert's shoulder and saying, "Activity!"*

Even if the Social Gospel emphasis on social justice was the predominant religious theme in Humphrey's upbringing, evangelism, too, played its part. As an example, in his seminal *Religious History of the American People*, Sidney Ahlstrom talked of the joint evangelical-humanitarian cast to America's frontier religion. Though a product of the First and Second Great Awakenings in an earlier moment of American history, evangelism's mark was still clearly stamped on Humphrey's own religious experience. Doland was the stopping place, for example, of various revivalistic entourages. Julian Hartt provides a description of one of them, and one in which Humphrey actually took part:

> I am quite sure it was Easter Sunday that the whole family came forward to be received into the church. . . . No one was baptized at the evangelistic services. . . . [Instead there] was confession of sin and acceptance of Jesus as your saviour, all with the appropriate music . . . banging in your ears.
>
> Now I don't know what sins he [Humphrey] confessed, but you see public confession of sin wasn't required, that is, in particular. It was just assumed, that you [were] "under conviction"—the phrase was that—"came under conviction"—and then you accepted Jesus as your savior, often with tears both of remorse and of joy etc., and it . . . was really emotionally very, very excit-

*Such an experience evidently made quite an impression on the young Humphrey, for he would later honor such an injunction with a vengeance. See Appendix A for several illustrations of this.

> ing. The whole group would get caught up in these feelings, and then people would gather around you and extend the right hand of fellowship and all this. It was sort of like . . . like a pep meeting.[68]

That reveals something of the religious piety of the time. So does another such story involving an evangelist from Cincinnati whose official name was the Reverend Joseph Knapp, but whom the people of Doland knew better as "Cryin' Joe":

> You called him Cryin' Joe because he was not a hell-fire and damnation preacher, but he would tell these sad, sad stories—children on their death beds, pleading for Momma and Poppa to accept Jesus. Momma and Poppa accept Jesus and the child dies and goes to heaven, of course, radiant. And Joe used to cry telling his own stories. He would cry gracefully—wipe his eyes and so on.

"Cryin'," however, was not the only part of the performance:

> [Joe] also had a young man on the trumpet. A lot of these evangelists had their own musicians, and that was memorable because this guy had what [in] later years we would have identified as a "hot trumpet." Later on we came to recognize some of this stuff very quickly—it was about the time . . . [that] we were discovering Louis Armstrong in his early years.[69]

As was often typical of such performances,

> occasionally this guy would feel inspired to preach. Well he was a terrible preacher . . . he would go on for a while, and then Cryin' Joe [would say], "Well, now let's hear . . . you on the horn," and this guy would cut loose. He would indeed. That of course went over great, quite apart from the fact that it was the only show in town—that's why a lot of people came to it.
>
> Well Humphrey was converted—that is to say, he trotted off to the altar when the altar [call] came.[70]

Hartt, however, discounts the idea that because of the above Humphrey was therefore an evangelical. As Humphrey's pastor, Albert Hartt "had severe reservations about such [evangelical fervor]." He followed the lead set by Jonathan Edwards, who "found things that were profoundly spiritual about the Great Awakening" but who was suspicious about the ephemeral nature of its ministry, which would, often enough, quite literally pack up and leave town once the revival was over, "and nothing ever happened thereafter."[71]

For Hartt, then, the moral essence of Doland's piety was "the will to press a relentless attack on the social evils which deprive multitudes of their rightful inheritance as children of God and Americans."[72] In his view, "such a faith is sublimely optimistic: what God demands is something that can and must be done. To delay is bad faith; to lose hope is to sell out to false gods."[73] Such a faith may indeed have been optimistic, but such was Doland's, and Humphrey's, faith nonetheless—the "faith" of the politics of joy.*

While the above may describe the religion of Hubert Humphrey as a *child*, in the eyes of some, he was *not* a religious person as an adult. Religion never struck them as a characterizing feature of his. If he was religious, and *that* was certainly open to question, it made a perceptible difference neither in the man nor in his policies. Yes, as already indicated, he quoted, or at least referred to Scripture, but any politician can and often will do that. Furthermore, he quoted the Constitution and the Declaration of Independence at least as often. They, along with dozens of other such references, were all just entries in his little black book—the stuff that political speeches are made of. They do not in themselves constitute a legitimate basis upon which to assert that Humphrey was a person significantly moved by religious conviction.

In opposition to this view, however, another opinion holds that Humphrey *was* religious, and that his religion had a genuine and substantial effect on his political outlook. Those who argue this way can differ in their testimony as to the *nature* of his religion, yet they agree that Humphrey was religious nonetheless. Humphrey himself, in addition, offers quite clear and consistent attestation to that same effect.

Beginning with the "nonreligious" extreme, Norman Sherman, a member of Humphrey's staff during the sixties (eventually to become Humphrey's press secretary during the vice-presidential years), "never heard him talk any kind of theology or self-conscious application of Christian principles to . . . what he was doing." For Sherman, "as best I can tell, his sense of justice, his

*For a more complete analysis of Doland's influence on Humphrey see Hartt's "Pieties," and Jeane Kirkpatrick's "The Celebration of HHH."

efforts in civil rights—were not particularly based [on religion] so much as they found roots in the Declaration of Independence, [the] Constitution—that sort of thing." His [that is, Humphrey's] outlook, in other words, was "more [a] secular humanism that may have been molded by Christian background" than it was a genuine religious faith. Yet, upon saying that Sherman added, "That is not to say that he did not love to go to church . . . he kind of liked it, and my sense of Humphrey was [that] what he most shared, as I think back, is a sense of hope which he thought churches gave people as much as it gave them moral guidance."[74]

While thus downplaying religion's influence on Humphrey's outlook, Sherman at least agreed that Humphrey drew "from the Christian traditions . . . very, very thoroughly. He was a man of immense tolerance, of [an] immense sense of justice."[75] Yet, for Sherman, if Humphrey had a religion it was not specifically Christianity: "He may have been a religious man," but only "in the broadest sense." Still, if justice "is a Christian consideration," Sherman went on, "Hubert Humphrey was quintessentially a man seeking justice for all men . . . he *was* moved by some things of a religious nature, especially . . . feeding the hungry, clothing the naked, healing the sick. [These things] really meant something to Humphrey."[76]

William Connell, one of Humphrey's chief and longest-serving assistants, similarly described Humphrey as religious, "not in the sense of a devout churchgoing man," but rather in the sense that "he had a strong ethical sense, and he would talk a great deal about the Judeo-Christian ethic. He was [religious] in that sense—rather than being narrowly Protestant. . . . He thought of himself as being in the compassionate tradition of the Judeo-Christian ethic—of justice and compassion for the weak and helpless.[77]

John Stewart, also a Humphrey aide throughout the sixties, stated that Humphrey "was not a terribly religious person in an institutional kind of way. He did belong to a church . . . and he would occasionally go to church, but it was not something he did with a kind of committed regularity." Yet, for Stewart, "there were certainly religious and humanist values that were essential parts of his being . . . that really motivated most of what he did, and I think he would have thought about it in those terms . . . would have recognized [that] there was some kind of religious dimension to those concerns."[78]

Bill Moyers, who had come to know Humphrey first in the Senate and then later in the White House, answered the question of Humphrey's religion by asking,

> What does one mean by "*religion*"? by a "*religious man*"? Does it mean one that actively, openly, and explicitly is a champion of a particular creed or faith? Or does it mean that one's life has been shaped consciously or unconsciously by the values of the faith? He [Humphrey] was a defender of the faith, in the sense that public officials often are, but he was not an apostle of the faith. I think he was, on the basis of my experience with him—and we had a lot of intimate times together—a religious man in the sense that he was a man shaped by religious values—aware of the infinite mystery of life—aware of ends and conscious that there was to life a sacred element, a sacred root. I have no question about that, if by that you define *relgion*.[79]

Arthur Naftalin, a friend from the early days in Minneapolis on, (and later to himself become mayor of Minneapolis), believed that Humphrey was religious by "two measures." First, in terms of religion in general, Humphrey "felt a family connection, he felt that he was home . . . he wasn't doing it just for cosmetic purposes," and, while he may not have gone to church every Sunday, "he went when he could." Second, beyond the outward symbol of faith, "he was really a believer . . . he believed in a divine being." For Naftalin, "he [Humphrey] certainly was no fundamentalist . . . he did not believe in the literal word of God, but he did accept in his whole kind of being the sense of a supreme being."[80]

Whatever the nature of his faith, it evidently was a faith that counted in some appreciable way. David Gartner, a staff member from 1961 until the day Humphrey died, said,

> I don't know that we ever sat down and had any lengthy discussions about it but I certainly observed him very closely and lived in their home on many occasions when I traveled with him and spent a lot of time with him. I can tell you that he was a deeply religious man—not necessarily in the traditional sense of every Sunday or everyday churchgoing, but he was very much a believer, and he was very much a Christian himself.[81]

To complete the "nonreligious vs. religious" spectrum, Max Kampelman,[82] one of Humphrey's longest and closest friends, felt not "the slightest doubt . . . that he was a deeply religious person, and not only that but he *looked* upon himself as [religious]. You know—there are people some may call deeply religious but do not like to be *identified* as [religious]—but that was not Hubert. He was not only deeply religious, but *looked* upon himself as a deeply religious person."[83] Humphrey, for Kampelman, "didn't go to church very often, but he always, when he did go, would feel that that was important to him. There was never any hesitancy about it."[82] According to Kampelman, "Hubert enjoyed being with religious people. He enjoyed speaking to them. He enjoyed going to their conventions. He enjoyed having them come to the office. He felt a kinship."[83]

In addition, Michael Amrine said, "no one who knows him, including opponents who have watched him for years, doubts that he is sincerely religious."[84] This only reflected a tradition that evidently stretched back to Humphrey's youth, for as Amrine also described: "Around Doland it was taken for granted that Pinky Humphrey would be religious."[85]

Carl Solberg, another of Humphrey's biographers, similarly concluded that "Humphrey remained essentially religious [throughout his life]—filled with faith in the brotherhood of man."[86]

Despite the mixed testimony as to the exact nature of Humphrey's religion, what is at least clear is that he was not a sectarian. Reinforcing this, Norman Sherman, for instance, described Humphrey to be "the first ecumenist."[87] Geri Joseph, a longtime friend and supporter[88] said, "I would not have called him a person of narrow sectarian views."[89] David Gartner said, "he didn't have any deep bond to any particular church. He would go to different churches on different occasions. And this pretty much runs the gamut—Protestant, Catholic, and Jew."[90] William Connell also described Humphrey as "an ecumenist—he used that term over and over again—Judeo-Christian ethic."[91]

Humphrey's lifelong religious affiliations certainly reflected this nondenominational, nondogmatic type of religious faith. Humphrey was baptized in the Norwegian Lutheran Church (Highland Lutheran Church, Lily, South Dakota, 27 May 1911). When his family moved to Doland in 1916 they became affiliated with the Methodist Church there, primarily because there simply was no Lutheran Church in town. Later in Huron he and Muriel were married in Union Presbyterian Church. While going to school, and then later as mayor in Minneapolis, he attended and was active in both the Hennepin Avenue Methodist Church and the First Congregationalist Church. In all the years of living in Washington the Humphrey family attended the First Methodist Church of Chevy Chase. All the while, however, they continued to maintain their membership in the First Congregational Church in Minneapolis. Yet, on weekends in their retreat home in Waverly, Minnesota, they attended St. Mary's Roman Catholic Church. He was introduced to at least one Jewish audience as "Rabbi Humphrey," and he declared to another, "I am a Jew." He was a friend of Billy Graham's and a devotee of John XXIII. His funeral was held in the House of Hope Presbyterian Church in St. Paul, and while presided over by its pastor, Calvin Didier, the clergy present included ministers, rabbis, and priests. To wit: Robert Schuler spoke; Rabbi Max Shapiro read the Old Testament lesson; Archbishop John Roach read from the New Testament.

For Humphrey, dwelling on distinctions between denominations, or even between different traditions as a whole was a misguided effort at best. As he said, "It is not the matter of sectarianism. Oftentimes church people use a good deal of their energy thinking only in terms of denomination rather than thinking in terms of the church of Jesus Christ and its full meaning."[92]

In 1955 the superintendent of the Methodist Church had inquired about Humphrey's simultaneous membership in the First Methodist Church of Chevy Chase and the First Congregationalist Church of Minneapolis. Humphrey responded by saying,

> Now, this may all sound very mixed up to you, but, frankly, when your family lives part of the time in Minnesota and part of the time in Washington, you don't have an exactly normal situation. Furthermore, I find that we like the First Congregational Church in Minnesota, and we like the Methodist Church here. Thus, I think we better leave it just as it is. We contribute rather substan-

tially to both churches, and frankly, I find their services and doctrine very much alike.

Now, I don't know how you are going to classify me because I am a Congregationalist and a Methodist, but I like it that way—and what is equally important, so do my wife and children. They love their church in Minnesota and they love this one here; yet they are different denominations.[93]

In his memorandum to Winthrop Griffith he stated that "the historic heritage of Congregationalism has played a rather important part in my church or religious experience." Yet the reason given for this is, "I like the democracy that is found in the Congregational Church. I like the freedom, the spiritual freedom that is there and yet the true Christian message that is to be found."[94] In other words, he identified with the Congregationalist Church because of its nondenominational character. The rubrics, the specifics of dogma are not what count—openness and denominational democracy are, so long as the "true Christian message" is to be found along with it.

In a speech before a church group in 1945 Humphrey responded to criticism of his multidenominational preference by saying,

Now some people may not think that's very good. They say "Where do your loyalties lie?" My loyalties lie with the church. And I'll be very candid with you. I find that there is the same message wherever you go. It may be dressed up a little differently here and there but it is very much the same message and we [the Humphrey family] not only are loyal to our church but we try to participate in any little way that we can wherever we find a home—a church home.[95]

Having a "church home," then, and being loyal to it were important. Which "house" you chose, however, was not. Humphrey clearly felt, and was willing to explicitly state his identification with the "Church," but only in the very broadest sense of the term. What might have been interpreted as lack of theological awareness or even religious indifference by those who did not note such an identification may have been simply a refusal to participate in denominational bickering. Such refusal—based on the conviction that "the specifics of dogma are not what count"—can be clearly linked to his Social Gospel background.

It is possible that his apparent reticence in regards to religion can be as well. Despite Humphrey's volubility in regards to nearly every other topic, he evidently did not discuss religion very much.

Max Kampelman recalled having "lots of conversations over the years about it,"[96] but he is one of the very few who claim that. William Connell offered a more characteristic view of the testimony given on this when he stated that Humphrey "was never one to be doing a lot of talking about religion in the times I knew him [and] I knew him from 1954 on, quite well."[97] Joseph Rauh, a friend and ADA colleague,[98] while believing that "Hubert had the greatest of personal ethics," that he, in fact, had "the highest ethical standards," never recalled religion "ever being the issue"[99] in conversations with Humphrey. For Orville Freeman,[100] "Humphrey did not wear religion on his sleeve and seldom spoke directly in terms of the Almighty," yet he was still "a devout man, a participating Christian."[101] Similarly, for David Gartner, "in terms of the Jimmy Carter type of religion, the sort of born-again type, wear your religion on your shirt cuffs—he [Humphrey] was just 180 degrees opposite of that."[102] Winthrop Griffith stated that

> His [Humphrey's] religious convictions are rarely flaunted, but they are deeply rooted in his personality and affect much of what he says and does. "I can never understand how one can be a Christian and not have a sacred regard for human dignity," he says. "When the New Testament tells us that we are all one in Jesus Christ, I can see no room for segregation, bigotry, or intolerance." His lifelong effort to champion the cause of civil and human rights did not evolve, to use his phrase, "from a bunch of books or economic charts."[103]

Likewise, for Bill Moyers, Humphrey

> was not an outwardly pious man, not a man who, like Jimmy Carter, carried his religion openly and admittedly. Humphrey was more a man shaped by his religious tradition rather than [one who] articulated it. But the constant compassion he felt for the victims of society, the casualties of society, would be reflected in conversations that invoked the prophets and the Judeo-Christian tradition. He was never obvious about that. It extruded at times that even he wasn't aware of.[104]

In Norman Sherman's words, "he [Humphrey] was not a man who mused on things . . . Humphrey did not have books on his shelves . . . he was not a man who sat and read his Bible or religious texts or anything else."[105]

Thus as Bill Moyers described it, Humphrey's faith was one "which he lived more than he paused to explain."[106] It could, in fact, be argued that Humphrey had moral, and even religious *reservations* about any such pausing. All too often, for Humphrey, "religious morality becomes the luxury of Sunday, not the solid substance of the work week."[107] Rather than languishing over protracted definitions of faith, Humphrey instead sought simply to enact it. By so doing he also revealed the unreflective, action-oriented nature of the Social Gospel—a nature represented in his own stated view of religion:

> My religious conviction is that the way you treat people is the way you treat God. Religious faith must be more than an exercise in theology, dogma, ritual or doctrine. It must be part of one's life. And the Christian faith, to be an effective force in the modern world, must have practical meaning in the lives of those who inherit the earth.[108]

Along with that he also included criticism of the institutionalized church—a kind of criticism that also rings with Social Gospel themes:

> Frankly, sometimes I am afraid the churches just don't reach out to the people. They reach out to their congregations, to be sure, but not to the people. Of all the people in the world who need and who would find comfort and inspiration in the teachings of Christianity, it is the working people, that is, the laboring people, the farmers, those who all too often are not too richly rewarded with material blessings. . . . In other words, the church is sometimes too socially and politically conservative. It refuses to translate into social action its moral doctrines.[109]

The evangelical imperative, for Humphrey, consisted simply in loving one another—in doing good works for our neighbor. Hence, "We did not wear religion on our arm or anything. It was part of our life."[110] Faith without these works was indeed "dead," and Humphrey always saw to it that his faith remained appropriately enlivened.

Beyond his hesitancy to indulge in theological speculation or denominational assertion at the expense of actively applying his religious faith, Humphrey's refusal to "wear religion on our arm or anything" may also have had to do with his belief in religious toleration. When asked whether she considered Humphrey to be a "devout" person, Geri Joseph responded by saying, "The word 'devout' has a connotation that to me is often not open or flexible—that was not Humphrey. . . . I don't think he was the kind of religious person who felt that everybody had to believe the way he believed. His religion was enormously tolerant and really encompassed everybody and everything."[111] In the Humphrey outlook, love for others included respect for opposite views, and opposite views in *belief*, as already indicated, were not critical so long as there was consensus on the course of *action*. As he said himself: "I am a Protestant but have never been of a mind that any one man had a monopoly on religious virtue and understanding."[112] For Humphrey, even

> our forefathers . . . believed that God fulfills His purposes in many different ways, and that it is presumptuous of any person or groups of people to claim to know God's ways with complete certainty. Indeed, they believed the best way to ascertain God's will is through civil and religious liberty and through the openness which this liberty would provide citizens to debate and discuss public policy.[113]

Such a statement only reflects his having held Roger Williams as a role model:

> I have been particularly impressed with Roger Williams. I always felt that the Puritans, while being very moral, were also very stern. But Roger Williams was a much more understanding, tolerant and considerate man. He was a forgiving person and one who practiced tolerance and fought against all forms of bigotry and intolerance.[114]

Because of Humphrey's view of religious tolerance, because of his emphasis on the social justice aspect of religion, and because of the broad cast of his religious outlook, the safest conclusion in regards to Humphrey's denominational orientation is that he was a "liberal Protestant."

In addition to all of the above, there is Humphrey himself on religion. There is evidence of his consistently articulating his religious views throughout his life. In 1945, for instance, he stated that "there is only one race, the human race. God would have all men saved—God has no favorites. He is the creator of all, hence every individual is precious to him."[115] He introduced a 1959 civil rights bill by arguing that "first of all . . . man has certain rights under the natural law; rights given to him not by the government, but rights given to him by God himself. As such these rights are unchangeable and everlasting and above the power of government to destroy or deny. . . . Human rights are inalienable rights. They are God's gift to man."[116] In his memorandum to Winthrop Griffith, Humphrey wrote of how, "When the Scripture tell us that God created man in his image it seems to me that this is the one compelling reason above all others why there is spiritual equality among all people and it is spiritual equality which is more important than any other kind."[117] In a 1965 speech to the Jewish Theological Seminary he stated that "the Prophets believed that, as a child of God, each man has inherent worth and infinite possibilities for moral growth."[118] In a letter to J. Oscar Lee, executive secretary of the Federal Council of Churches in Christ in America he wrote, "Christianity and equal rights go hand in hand. Equality—human rights—these are the themes of Christ's teachings. The church encourages the love of man for man—the love of all men for all men. This is the right—there can be no compromise."[119]

This theme, then, of being the children of God, of being created in His image, and thus of all being equally precious to Him, was one he did articulate throughout his life. If he had a theology, this was its essence. William Connell stated,

> I think [the] "all God's children" thing is . . . one of the . . . basic root beliefs that he [Humphrey] had. Every man and woman was equal in the sight of God and they had equal rights. . . . He believed—he was so passionate about it that obviously it was more than just an intellectual conviction . . . he really, in his *gut*, in his heart . . . believed those things, and he worked awfully hard for them."[120]

Humphrey did believe in, therefore, and publicly stated his belief in the existence of God. The point, however, is that making such a theological affirmation was not the real issue for him. There is no readily available public record of Hubert Humphrey going through a significant questioning of God's existence. Probing the historical development of the doctrine of the Trinity or pondering the hermeneutical issues involved in the use of Scripture were not the kinds of things that Hubert Humphrey ever apparently preoccupied himself with. His was hardly a sophisticated theology. Arthur Naftalin, for instance, recalls this illuminating theological incident:

> It was after the successful election of '45 and we had gone out to Big Stone where Muriel Humphrey's family had a cabin. This was to celebrate the victory. I remember that Bill Simms, who was his other administrative assistant, was there. We got into an argument—whether there was a God or not—but Hubert came on very firm and very strong insisting that there was a God. We demanded that he give us some evidence and he said, "The evidence is that all men are brothers, right? If all men are brothers, then they all must have a common father—and the common father is God." He was dead serious and he meant it all the way.[121]

Such an argument, based, as it is, on the above "evidence," is hardly compelling. Pointing that out, however, is not to therefore argue that Humphrey's religion was insignificant. It is simply to say that for Hubert Humphrey the concern was to be not so much with the *veracity* of religion as it was with the implications of affirming it *as* veracious. Humphrey's theology was almost entirely one of *response*, not of interpretation.

For Humphrey, therefore, if you *do* believe in Christ, then you must respond to the charge that He gives. In Humphrey's mind, the content of that charge was quite clear: feed the hungry, heal the sick, clothe the naked. The critical issue for faith was, *Will* you respond to this charge or not? It was *not*, Do you affirm this particular creed or dogma? Doing unto the least of these was *the* litmus test for Christian faith according to the Humphrey systema. As such it compared quite closely with Rauschenbusch's view that "the fundamental truth is that religion and ethics are inseparable, and that ethical conduct is the supreme and sufficient religious act."[122] Because this is so, Humphrey's religious outlook can be appropriately regarded as the near-perfect child of the Social Gospel.

Since this is the case, Humphrey's religious outlook is to be considered as one having direct and clear political implication. When Humphrey talked of how

> we liberal Americans tend to show deep concern for the welfare of *all* our fellow beings. We wince when any man—of any race, color or creed in any land—suffers hunger, poverty, fear or injustice. We look beyond our immediate, familiar surroundings and sympathize with those less fortunate. We seek to find solutions, not just to the broad problems of administration but to the basic problems of human need. We respect—yes, we welcome—differences of opinion and belief. We honor a man for his independence, for his unique personality, for his separate, personal identity."[123]

he was articulating a religious view as well as proposing a political program. "We cannot begin," Humphrey stated, "to define the character and purposes of America unless we understand our religious tradition as the foundation of our Nation, the fiber which has bound us together as a people, and the source of the repeated renewals and new horizons to which we have been called."[124] For Humphrey, we were indeed called to community by God, and this was as true in the international sphere as it was in the domestic. Indeed, the two were inextricably bound together and went down to the most fundamental of domestic levels—the level at which he first learned it in Doland:

> I believe that each of us has an obligation to serve God at each level of his existence and within each institution of his society—from doing honor to one's parents and children—to performing his work with dignity and honesty—to playing his role within his school, his neighborhood, his church, his community, and nation.
>
> The building of a better and more peaceful world will never come from any diplomat's ingenious plan. It will come only from the cumulative acts of men who live their lives in respect for their fellow men, and thus for God.
>
> I believe it is thus that all men may one day march proudly under the banner: Community.[125]

Humphrey often spoke fondly of the Judeo-Christian tradition. He was fond of that tradition because of what he saw as its central emphasis on the individual, which is to say, on the God-given worth of each and every person. It is certain that Humphrey never read Austin Farrer, the great twentieth-century Anglican philosopher-theologian, yet it is quite likely that he would have enjoyed using the following quotation of Farrer's as a particularly lucid expression of this emphasis: "for God is regarded by regard for what he regards, and what he regards is the man."[126] The likeliness of his enjoying such a quote is evidenced in his statement to the National Conference of Christians and Jews, where he described how people who act on their religious beliefs

> have truly understood that the way you treat people is the way you treat God, and I've never heard a more succinct and concise definition of my religion. If God created man in his own image, then, indeed the way you treat that which God created exemplifies your respect for your faith—for your religion—for your oneness in God and in the family of man.[127]

In conclusion, then, as the primary shaper of his religious-ethical outlook the overall Doland experience is to be summarized by the following points. First, as for religious principles, there was first the sense of mission—of establishing the Kingdom of God on earth. Second, this was to be done with great evangelical "enthusiasm," which is to say, with stress on activity, as opposed to reflection. Such "activity" had to do with the achievement of "great ends," namely, meeting the demands of social justice. "Understanding and love of the precepts of Christianity" led ineluctably to community responsibility. Churchgoing was also important in the Humphrey household, even enjoyable. Humphrey talked, for instance, about how much he enjoyed singing hymns, and he said that, "My feeling of being in church was one of comfort, and in a very real sense, an experience of happiness and joy."[128] And so, joy was also a prominent feature of the religion of Humphrey's upbringing. Yet, what was *crucial*? Hearing the message that "all men were created in the image of God"; that "in Christ there is neither Jew nor Gentile, neither slave nor free. Ye are all one"; that "faith without works is dead"; and that "whatever ye do unto the least of these ye do unto me also"—all religious expressions having direct political implications.

Secondly, as far as ethical principles go, there were egalitarianism, the sense of fair play, the responsibility to do one's part, and acknowledgment of the "deserving poor." All of these were understood to be the foundation for yet another feature of that time and place: a sense of community.

Third, and speaking of community, Doland itself, certainly in the time that Humphrey grew up there, represented quintessential small-town America, and thus was "ideal" as far as that Norman Rockwellian image is "ideal." That is not to say, however, that such an experience did not also provide its own truly sobering dose of reality. The Great Depression hit Doland in 1926 – fully three years before the stock market crash of '29, and, among other things, took with it the Humphrey home.

Fourth, despite its naive and provincial aspect, Doland in general, and the Humphrey home in particular, provided at that time a lively and impressive atmosphere for intellectual, cultural, and political debate and experience. This was largely due to the greatest influence on Humphrey's life other than Doland itself, namely, Hubert Humphrey, Sr. In both the Humphrey home and the Humphrey drugstore, young Hubert, from an early age on, was imbued with a fervor for involved debate about great issues – it was there that he learned, and was tested on the principles of his "dream." To wit: in a discussion about Doland, Mrs. Howard spoke of how "there were in Doland . . . only one or two Democratic families – the Reilly's – they were the only Catholic family there. And so we formed the first coalition – Protestant and Catholic – of the Democratic Party . . . the party of William Jennings Bryan and Woodrow Wilson . . . [to whom he, Dad Humphrey] adhered . . . [as] fervently as he did to believing in the Social Gospel and the social mission of the New Testament."[129]

The fact that Humphrey's father did so, and was at the same time one of two of Humphrey's most important influences holds the key to Humphrey's religious-political outlook. His religious upbringing *was* "believing in the Social Gospel and the social mission of the New Testament." But that same upbringing also included seeing the Democratic Party as the primary agency of fulfillment for that mission. Hence, it is to it, and the political philosophy that Humphrey saw it representing, that we now turn.

Notes

1. Hubert Humphrey, *The Education of a Public Man*, ed. Norman Sherman (Garden City, N.Y.: Doubleday, 1976), 19.
2. In his memorandum to Winthrop Griffith, for instance, Humphrey had described Hartt as "my closest boyhood friend and is today a very close and

dear friend." Hubert Humphrey, memorandum to Winthrop Griffith, 16 May 1962. From the Hubert H. Humphrey Jr. Papers, Minnesota Historical Society, hereafter cited as "Humphrey Collection."

3. Julian Hartt, "Hubert Humphrey and the Pieties of the Prairies," *Dialog* 23, 3 (Summer 1984): 174.
4. Ibid., 174.
5. Michael Amrine. *This Is Humphrey* (Garden City, N.Y.: Doubleday, 1960), 24.
6. Humphrey, *Education*, 56.
7. Ibid., 33–34.
8. Ibid.
9. Humphrey, as quoted in Albert Eisele, *Almost to the Presidency* (Blue Earth, Minn.: The Piper Company, 1972), 20.
10. Ibid., 22.
11. Ibid.
12. From *Into the Bright Sunshine*, a film documentary directed by William Connell, produced by Concept Associates, 1982.
13. Humphrey, Sr. would continue in political life to become South Dakota delegate to a number of Democratic National Conventions, including the 1948 convention in Philadelphia, and declined to run for governor only when Humphrey, Jr.'s return to the University of Minnesota forced the elder Humphrey to remain in the drugstore.
14. Of Northwest Public Electric, Julian Hartt once quipped: "How these monopolistic enterprises ever came [to be known] as 'public utilities' is an interesting hermeneutical question."
15. Humphrey, *Education*, 27.
16. Frances Humphrey Howard, interview, no. 1 with author, 27 October 1983.
17. Hubert Humphrey, letter, 18 March 1970, Humphrey Collection.
18. Hubert Humphrey, "My Father," *Atlantic Monthly* (November 1966): 84.
19. Hubert Humphrey, letter to the Reverend Albert Hartt, 19 December 1955, Humphrey Collection.
20. Humphrey, *Education*, 29.
21. Humphrey, from a transcript of an interview with Theodore White, Humphrey Collection.
22. Humphrey, *Education*, 29.
23. Julian Hartt, interview with author, 23 March 1983.
24. Hubert Humphrey, Sr., as quoted in *Education*, 23.
25. Ibid., 26.
26. Ibid.
27. Ibid., 27.
28. Amrine, *This Is Humphrey*, 24.
29. Hartt interview.
30. Ibid.
31. Ibid.
32. Humphrey, "My Father," 84.
33. Hubert Humphrey, speech to All-class reunion of Doland High School, 12 June 1976, Doland, South Dakota, author's collection.
34. Hartt interview. Hartt himself received his Ph.D. from Yale and went on to

teach there for nearly thirty years afterwards. He then left Yale to become William F. Kenan Professor of Religious Studies at the University of Virginia, later to retire as professor emeritus.

35. Ibid.
36. Hartt, "Pieties," 180.
37. Humphrey, *Education*, 26.
38. Hartt interview.
39. Hartt, "Pieties," 177.
40. Ibid.
41. Humphrey, White interview.
42. Howard interview, no. 1.
43. Humphrey, White interview.
44. Ibid.
45. Amrine, *This Is Humphrey*, 22.
46. Humphrey, Doland speech.
47. Ibid.
48. Ibid.
49. Howard interview, no. 1.
50. Ibid.
51. Ibid.
52. Ibid.
53. Humphrey, *Education*, 25.
54. Hubert Humphrey, speech to Emmanuel Lutheran Church, St. Paul, Minnesota, 9 November 1945, Humphrey Collection, mayoralty years.
55. Hubert Humphrey, as quoted in an interview with Caspar Nannes in *The Link* (November 1974), Humphrey Collection, post-vice presidential years.
56. Humphrey, *Education*, 29.
57. Humphrey, Griffith memorandum.
58. Ibid.
59. Ibid.
60. Ibid.
61. Humphrey, *Education*, 29.
62. Humphrey, Griffith memorandum.
63. Amrine, *This Is Humphrey*, 25.
64. Howard interview, no. 1.
65. Walter Rauschenbusch, as quoted in David Little, "Francis Greenwood Peabody," *Harvard Library Bulletin* 15, 3 (July 1967): 297.
66. Humphrey, as quoted in Hays Gorey, "I'm a Born Optimist," *American Heritage* (December 1977): 65.
67. Hubert Humphrey, letter to Mrs. Claudia Bailey, 7 July 1967, Humphrey Collection.
68. Hartt interview.
69. Ibid.
70. Ibid.
71. Ibid.
72. Hartt, "Pieties," 176.
73. Ibid.
74. Norman Sherman, interview with author, 28 June 1983.

75. Ibid.
76. Ibid.
77. William Connell, interview with author, 27 October 1983.
78. John Stewart, interview with author, 2 May 1985.
79. Bill Moyers, interview with author, 18 January 1985.
80. Arthur Naftalin, interview with author, 8 November 1983.
81. David Gartner, interview with author, 26 October 1983.
82. Max Kampelman was American ambassador to the Madrid talks, and eventually was to become chief American negotiator for the Geneva disarmament talks.
83. Max Kampelman, interview with author, 27 July 1983.
82. Ibid.
83. Ibid.
84. Amrine, *This Is Humphrey*, 72.
85. Ibid., 40.
86. Carl Solberg, *Hubert Humphrey: A Biography* (New York: W. W. Norton Company, 1984), 467.
87. Sherman interview.
88. Joseph was, among other things, co-chairperson of the Democratic National Committee and ambassador to the Netherlands.
89. Geraldine Joseph, interview with author, 16 September 1983.
90. Gartner interview.
91. Connell interview. John Stewart provides a story which helps to illustrate this: "The worst thing that could possibly happen to you was when you were trying to rush him around and get him someplace—since he was always late. . . . It happened once—you were just about to get him into a markup for the Appropriations Committee. If he was physically there he could offer some amendments and things and get some stuff for Minnesota. All he had to do . . . was physically get there. I was just about to push him through the door when he spotted a nun with a bunch of kids [that] she was shepherding along . . . in the new Senate office building. Humphrey just put on the brakes—you know—*stopped* . . . [and] down the hall [he] went . . . to say hello to the good sister and her charges. Then [he] proceeded to deliver a mini course on American government and the Senate and the marvels of democracy and the Constitution and the Pledge of Allegiance and four or five other topics . . . that he would specialize in. And you know he talked for about 25 minutes. I kept trying to get him to leave and . . . he finally said, "Stop it! I know I'm going to miss the markup! It's better I should miss the markup than I should miss these children! This is much more important—that they go away from their visit to Washington with a sense of what this democracy is all about and this is my opportunity to help them get that and that is more important than whatever you have cooked up in there with those people . . . " and went back to his lecture. And sure enough, they goddamned adjourned the subcommittee! But Humphrey was delighted, you know, and . . . I think that when he really put on the brakes and turned and streaked down the hall—was when he saw it was a nun. . . . If it had been just a group of kids he probably would have gone on through the door—that would be my guess." From the Stewart interview.

92. Humphrey, Emmanuel Lutheran speech.
93. Hubert Humphrey, letter to Paul G. Hayes, 9 November 1955, Humphrey Collection.
94. Humphrey, Griffith memorandum.
95. Humphrey, Emmanuel Lutheran speech.
96. Kampelman interview.
97. Connell interview.
98. Rauh, a longtime liberal activist, was, among other things, a law clerk to Felix Frankfurter, an ADA cofounder, and general counsel to the UAW, as well as a prominent civil rights activist.
99. Joseph Rauh, interview with author, 28 October 1983.
100. In addition to being one of Humphrey's closest friends and associates, Freeman was multiterm governor of Minnesota and Secretary of Agriculture for both the Kennedy and Johnson administrations.
101. Orville Freeman, letter to author, 31 May 1983.
102. Gartner interview.
103. Winthrop Griffith, *Humphrey: A Candid Biography* (New York: William Morrow, 1965), 42.
104. Moyers interview.
105. Sherman interview.
106. Bill Moyers, letter to author, 29 January 1985.
107. Humphrey, Griffith memorandum.
108. Hubert Humphrey, letter to the Reverend Theodore K. Pitt, 18 November 1977, Humphrey Collection.
109. Humphrey, Griffith memorandum.
110. Humphrey, *The Link* interview.
111. Joseph interview.
112. Hubert Humphrey, letter to R. C. Bolen, Charlotte, North Carolina, 28 July 1948, Humphrey Collection.
113. Hubert Humphrey, speech to the Christian Life Commission of the Southern Baptist Convention, as quoted in the *Congressional Record*, 94th Cong., 2nd sess., 24 March 1976. Vol. 122, 7865.
114. Humphrey, Griffith memorandum.
115. Humphrey, Emmanuel Lutheran speech.
116. Hubert Humphrey, *Congressional Record*, 88th Cong., 1st sess., 1959. Vol. 105, 8388.
117. Humphrey, Griffith memorandum.
118. Hubert Humphrey, speech to the Jewish Theological Seminary, New York City, 21 February 1965, Humphrey Collection.
119. Hubert Humphrey, letter to J. Oscar Lee, Humphrey Collection.
120. Connell interview.
121. Arthur Naftalin, as quoted in Dan Cohen, *Undefeated: The Life of Hubert H. Humphrey* (Minneapolis: Lerner Publications Company, 1978), 114.
122. Rauschenbusch, as quoted in Sidney Ahlstrom, *A Religious History of the American People* (New Haven and London: Yale University Press, 1972), 781.
123. Hubert Humphrey, "What is a Liberal?," *Think* (October 1960): 7.

124. Humphrey, "Baptist," 7864.
125. Hubert Humphrey, speech to The National Council of Churches, Miami, Florida, 7 December 1966, Humphrey Collection.
126. Austin Farrer, "A Moral Argument for the Existence of God," *Reflective Faith* (Grand Rapids: William B. Eerdmans Publishing Company, 1972), 124.
127. Hubert Humphrey, speech to the National Conference of Christians and Jews, 28 June 1966, Humphrey Collection.
128. Hubert Humphrey, "My Childhood," from a transcript of an interview of Hubert Humphrey and James Baldwin, Humphrey Collection.
129. Howard interview, no. 1.

2

Idealism Embodied: The New Deal as the Kingdom Nearly Come

Perhaps nowhere else did Humphrey reveal how the Democratic Party was the direct political expression of the Social Gospel than in his master's thesis, *The Political Philosophy of the New Deal*. The forward to that work, as it appeared in its published form, was written by Robert Harris, one of Humphrey's professors and examiners at Louisiana State University. In it (and as should come as no surprise, coming from someone who had known Humphrey well) Harris referred to Humphrey's "abiding faith in the inherent moral worth and dignity of the individual person," while at the same time mentioning Humphrey's "conviction that individual interests can and must be protected and promoted by community action."[1] Pointing to such things indicates the nature of Humphrey's overall thesis, tersely summarized as: respect for individual worth and dignity is the end; governmental action on behalf of that individual is the means. It is not a coincidence that this could be offered as a terse summation of the Social Gospel as well.

The authority for such is taken from a quotation that has been standard fare for American liberal speechwriters ever since it was first given by its author, Abraham Lincoln:

> The legitimate object of government is to do for a community of people whatever they need to have done, but cannot do at all, or cannot do so well, for themselves, in their separate and individual capacities.

For many, the New Deal was precisely a matter of the government "doing" the above. The common term used to describe such "doing" is "intervention," yet it is not the term Humphrey would have preferred. If "intervention" is to be used in such a context, it is done so appropriately only when associated with its positive connotation. That is, government *is* to intervene, yet only on *behalf* of people, not in spite of them. "Intervention," in other words, is not "imposition." Even with such a positive cast given to it, however, it still appears rather jejune. Nineteenth-century liberalism saw the role of government as one strictly of curbing the abuses of power and of restraining man's more sinister impulses—it was protection of the individual's interest, and that only. For Humphrey, the New Deal was to provide that role, but also to go beyond it: "Government was to be more than the protector and the regulator, it was to be a partner, a constructive force, in improving the nation and helping the individual."[2] It was, in other words, to *promote* the individual's interest, as well as protect it. In a democratic government pledged to promoting the general welfare, this was, in Humphrey's opinion, only proper.

Such a view of government developed within a specific historic context: once the "objective of business was no longer the seeking of legitimate economic expansion" but was instead exploitation "by stock market manipulation and monopoly price maintenance,"[3] it became the duty of government "to regain economic liberty for the average man."[4] In the 1920s "democratic processes were not functioning. Government was listening to [only] the voice of finance and industry, agriculture and labor dissipated their energies in dissension and political apathy."[5] There had to be, therefore, a "reordering of the profit system in order to provide economic security without sacrificing political liberty."[6] The goal of New Deal intervention was to provide such a balance between the freedom of large concentrations of economic power and the equality of the individual working person or entrepreneur. Such a balance was to foster an economic climate in which anyone who had the will could succeed in whatever pursuit they chose. As in nearly all things for Humphrey, achieving this balance was desirable as much out of ethical consideration as it was out of pragmatic: justice demanded it, yet failing to do so risked anarchy. As in all things as well, it echoed Social Gospel themes—in this case those of believing that an unregulated private sector represented the principal threat to individual liberty, not government, and that government interference, therefore, was necessary so that a just (and productive) balance between the extremes of capitalism and socialism might be maintained.

It was, then, the maintenance of precisely such a balance that the New Deal assumed as its object. As such, it was for Humphrey, "American democracy working within the political and economic limitations of established government and private enterprise,"[7] which is to say, it was as All-American as the Chamber of Commerce. Humphrey stressed how the New Deal liberal was a capitalist, but one who believed that certain checks on capitalism were necessary in order to prevent its own self-destruction. That is, while capitalists, liberals were so with a difference: they wanted to be fully aware of Lenin's famous rope and thus recognize that the achievement of social justice is crucial to capitalism's longevity, beyond simply being right.

It was to such longevity that the New Deal was primarily committed. Humphrey pointed to the fact that it was to banks and to productive enterprises that FDR's administration first extended "unprecedented financial assistance" as evidence for this. FDR was not interested in being an antagonist of business per se. He sought merely to curb its excesses, and did so, if for nothing else, so as to assure its own survival. It was understood, however, that so acting was simply part and parcel of the effort to better the lives of all Americans. As such, the New Deal was hardly a revolutionary movement. Its intention was to *preserve* the American system, not overturn it. Rather than leading us down the road to socialism, as many rightist critics have contended, its purpose expressly was to detour us from that road. It sought to do so in a way that would address the Marxist charge of capitalist domination, while at the same time avoid the Marxist pitfall of government domination. It was to be, in other words, a program of reform, not of revolution—both in the means employed and in the ends envisioned.

Humphrey looked to the Constitution itself for defense in this:

> The aspect of the Constitution of the United States as an *instrument* of popular government for the achievement of great ends of social growth is stamped on its opening words: "We the people of the United States, in order to form a more perfect union, establish justice, insure domestic tranquility, provide for the common defense, promote the general welfare, and secure the blessings of liberty to *ourselves* and our *posterity* do ordain and establish this Constitution for the United States of America."[8]

"It is this interpretation," Humphrey argued, "that has provided the basis for the New Deal philosophy of government."[9] "This interpretation" is that the Constitution is a document primarily *granting* power, not negating it. It is a document designating who is to have power, and for what purposes, and not a document merely denying power to specific groups or institutions, as conservatives have argued. It is therefore to be seen primarily as a "positive" statement regarding the role of government, not a "negative" one. As such, it is in accord with the Social Gospel view of the "positive," as well as activist nature of the role of governmental authority.

Humphrey agreed with Mill that government interference with the activities of the individual was "never justified except when manifestly necessary to prevent the activities of some individuals from injuring others."[10] The issue was, however, had such a situation in fact arisen? For Humphrey, the answer was unquestionably, "Yes." Furthermore, he believed that the warrant for acting as the New Deal did in order to rectify such a situation was clearly written into the very document upon which the country was founded. In Humphrey's view, then, the political philosophy of the New Deal was only to apply those principles, already implicit in the Constitution, to a situation where the Constitution was being threatened by forces acting contrary to the vision which originally inspired it.

Despite his clear and consistent praise for them, however, Humphrey did not regard the New Deal programs as a panacea. They were not quite the Kingdom come. Humphrey made sure that what FDR labelled as the "quarterback" model of the New Deal was emphasized: plays would be called only as the situation dictated. The pragmatic test was to be the deciding one. Programs were proposed and established with the understanding that they were strictly experimental. If they worked, well and good. If they did not, try something else—but at least try *something*. That was the point. The policies and programs of the past had failed. Classical economics could not account for, let alone correct, the tremendous problems, economic and social, that had resulted from the Great Depression. The New Deal was, therefore, to be just that—a *new* deal. It was not, however, to be a new *order*. It was simply to be a positive answer to the question: "Can the flagrant inequality of possessions and of opportunity now existing in a democratic state be corrected by democratic methods?"[11] While the means proposed may have been distinctive, the ends sought remained firmly fixed in the American charter.

For Humphrey, the idea of looking to new means for solving problems was a predominant characteristic of American liberalism. Examples of his holding such a view are many, and cover the range of years in which he held high political office. In a 1955 article for *American Scholar*, for instance, he wrote, "The liberal approach must be experimental, the solution tentative, the test pragmatic. Believing that no particular manifestation of our basic social institutions is sacrosanct or immutable, there should be a willingness to re-examine and reconstruct institutions in the light of new needs."[12] In an October 1960 article in *Think* magazine he said that "woven into the fabric of liberal philosophy and policy are the qualities of movement: imagination, experimentation, progress, initiative, and even daring . . . the liberal American seeks adventure and progress. He dares to try. He says 'yes' to life."[13] In his 1964 book, *The Cause Is Mankind*, he stated that "the enduring strength of American liberalism is that it recognizes and welcomes change as an essential part of life, and moves to seize rather than evade the challenges and opportunities that change presents. It is, basically, an attitude toward life rather than a dogma—characterized by a warm heart, an open mind, and willing hands."[14] In his biography of Humphrey, Griffith quotes as saying, "The key word which may be applied to the liberal viewpoint is 'change.' The liberal understands that life is not static, that anything—from a plant to a government—must change, or it will die. . . . The liberal welcomes change—not for its own sake, but as an inevitable force of life which must be captured and channeled toward the right direction."[15] In the 15 December 1975 issue of *Business Week*, Humphrey argued that "we have never before been confronted by inflation and recession at the same time, and we have to find new government tools for combating both."[16] In a 1984 interview, Evron Kirkpatrick related that "He said to me a number of times, 'you know if [New Deal policy] doesn't fit today . . . it is a different set of problems and we have to address them as a different set of problems.'"[17]

It was this commitment to facing new circumstances with new ideas that opened the door, in Humphrey's view, to the belief in governmental action on behalf of the individual that should characterize liberalism. For Humphrey, liberalism was a political philosophy "based on the assumption that freedom is essential for the full development of the human personality and that therefore [assuming the egalitarian creed] all men should be free."[18] For Humphrey this basic tenet of liberalism had its roots in classical Greek philosophy, in the Hebrew prophets, and in the Christian faith. Thus he would refer, for instance, to the prophets, to the Sermon on the Mount, and to Thomas Aquinas in such regard. As he saw it, though, this doctrine came into actual political effect only with the advent of the modern world, and with one specific and especially significant instance of that "world": the American revolution represented "the culmination, among Europeans transplanted to a new world, of centuries of struggle by their ancestors. . . . [It was] the beginning of a new era in history."[19] Man was now liberated from a hierarchical society and a political system that had prevented him from exercising his individual talents and abilities by categorizing him into distinct and rigidly maintained castes. Yet, with the advent of the modern age, feudalism's aristocracy was now giving way to modernity's democracy.

Certainly one of, and perhaps the key ingredient in this was the rise of the middle class. With the attainment of economic power on the part of the bourgeoisie, the way was opened to independence for all classes beneath the nobility. The Industrial Revolution, in Humphrey's view, had provided the final, culminating impetus for such a change.

The issue arises, however, of whether the Industrial Revolution, while culminating one struggle, did not at the same time inaugurate an entirely new and different one: "Intoxicated by the opportunities the machine offered to expand production and create wealth, orthodox European liberals tended to be ruthlessly indifferent to the suffering the machine caused."[20] For Humphrey, at any rate, one oppressive ruling class had simply been replaced by another. The liberals who had advocated and struggled for the liberation of the lower classes from the tyranny of the upper had now, having witnessed their own ascendance, become an oppressive ruling class themselves. Shocking working conditions, dismal slums, ignorance, poverty, disease, and abuse of child and female labor—these had all become characteristic of the industrial age. Yet, as is so often the wont of exploitive groups, attempts to alleviate the injustices caused by these new conditions were resisted, in this case in the name of individual liberty. It was this "name" that Leonard Trelawney Hobhouse criticized and that Humphrey echoed often as being of nothing more than "noble sound and squalid results."

It was at this juncture in the late nineteenth century that liberalism split into two more or less distinct camps—camps that represent the two generally predominant competing political options in the West today. The two camps agree that freedom is a virtue. They disagree, however, as to what degree it is a virtue, or, perhaps better, as to what precisely constitutes liberty's greatest threat. "Liberals" on the right continue to regard it as government itself, whereas "liberals" on the left view it as large concentrations of economic power in the hands of a private oligarchy. Government, in other words, is the oppressor for one and the liberator for the other.

American liberalism obviously developed along the lines of the latter view. For Humphrey, American liberalism was the movement that

> proved capable of coping with the problems of the new industrial society that came into being here in the latter part of the nineteenth century. Instead of uncritically welcoming the new concentrations of wealth and power that emerged, it recognized the danger that they would be used to control and cripple government, destroy competition, and increase the maldistribution of wealth. It saw in them the seeds of a new menace to freedom, as threat-

ening to the freedom of the individual as the power of a seventeenth century king.[21]

The phrase "destroy competition" deserves some attention. Humphrey again and again sought to distinguish American liberalism from its European counterpart. For Humphrey, American liberalism was the "authentic liberalism" because liberalism in Europe had fallen either to the extreme of Manchesterism on the right or to Marxism on the left. In America, on the other hand, the integrity of liberalism had been maintained. This was achieved by its consistently recognizing, on the one hand, "free competitive enterprise as the mainspring of economic life," as well as fully allowing for the "traditional freedoms of speech, of the press, of assembly, and the like"[22] on the other. Liberalism, in the characteristic American form in which Humphrey both practiced and preached it—a form of which he no doubt believed the Social Gospel was an integral part—was not, nor was ever understood to be an enemy of free enterprise. Rather, it was simply to be the guarantor of *truly* free enterprise, when that is understood to be *equal* freedom for *all*.

Hubert Humphrey was not a radical. The only significant departure from the nineteenth-century past that he championed was in the instrument of reform, namely, government: "The new liberalism . . . began to press government to intervene and restore a balance in society. It understood that the same forces which had released the productive energies of Western society now threatened to restrain them, and that the forces which had once demolished the power of despots now nourished a new despotism."[23]

Such a view of government did represent a change, yet, as Humphrey argued, and as has already been indicated, it was a change that had its roots in the same soil out of which America itself had grown. It was a change that was not only sanctioned, but actually stipulated by the documents by which the country was engendered. As such, this change marked the fulfillment of a duty rather than the imposition of a new revision of the Constitution or the Declaration of Independence. It was certainly no more of a change than that already imposed on Western culture by the Industrial Revolution. Given this line of reasoning it could, ironically enough, be argued that modern American liberalism has been more *conservative*. By that what is meant is that it has been the attempt to conserve the traditional humane values of the classical and medieval traditions now being threatened by the radical changes which the Industrial Age wrought on the modern world. The only novelty was that government—and not simply the religious institution—was to be responsible for seeing to it that fairness remain a viable societal virtue.

For Humphrey, this denoted a number of things: (1) "acceptance of collective responsibility for providing all individuals with equality of opportunity"; (2) acceptance of "responsibility for the basic economic security of those who are unable, through no fault of their own, to provide such security for themselves"; (3) acceptance of "responsibility for reducing great disparities in the distribution of wealth and bringing about a closer coincidence between the income of the individual and his contribution to society"; and (4) assuming the "responsibility for promoting the full employment of our manpower and the full utilization of our resources," or, in other words: "full production within the limits of an intelligent human and rational resources conservation and utilization program."[24]

Government is obviously critical in attaining such an objective, for Humphrey, and its crucialness was clearly *not* that of minimizing its own effect, as conservatives would have it, but rather, to be a constructive *partner* by "setting a general framework of growth in which private enterprise can flourish and in establishing minimum living standards for all people."[25]

By virtue of such an ideal, liberalism "stands generally committed to the qualified use of state power to achieve the values of freedom and human dignity."[26] It is, in other words, to be responsible for maintaining a balance between freedom and equality. As creatures created in the image of God, each individual is accorded an equal dignity. What this dignity entitles an individual to is the freedom to live as one chooses. Since all enjoy this same dignity, this freedom ought to be equally accorded to all.

In a letter to a grade school class that had inquired about the issue, Humphrey described the role of government with regard to liberty and equality this way:

> I said that the democrat believes in liberty. But the democrat must realize that in order to protect the liberty of all other people, he himself will have to give up a certain degree of liberty. That is only practical. For instance, if everybody took the liberty to drive down the streets and highways in whatever fashion he wished, all drivers would be in danger of losing their lives. In order to protect the liberty of all drivers to make their way to their destinations, each driver must agree to follow certain laws about driving. If everybody gives up the right to drive in whatever way he wants, and if every driver follows certain laws, then it turns out that there is the most liberty for all drivers. What each driver has gained is worth far more than the little bit of liberty he has lost by submitting to the laws.
>
> The same thing is true in a government like ours. When the majority of people in our country agree to live under certain laws that they have themselves passed through their representation in Congress, then we have an organized kind of life that will permit the greatest liberty for all people.[27]

In Hubert Humphrey's view of liberalism it is government's business to see to it that this equal liberty be maintained. It is of this maintenance that justice essentially consists, insofar as, according to the Constitution, justice is each person's due. But it must be again noted that justice, for Humphrey, is not simply the stern rebuke of wrongdoing—it is also the creative fostering and channeling of human growth and productivity. As William Penn said, it is much like

> a part of religion itself, a thing sacred in its institution and end. . . . They weakly err that think there is no other use of government than correction which is the coarsest part of it. Daily experience tells that the care and regulation of many other affairs, more soft and daily necessary, make up much of the greatest part of government.[28]

For Humphrey, justice demands that every individual have an equal opportunity to develop his or her talents, ambition, and character to the fullest extent possible. Justice forever carries with it this positive role. It is, furthermore, a role to be filled by government, for only government can provide a balance to the contemporary threat that private concentrations of economic power have posed to individual liberty.

It is important to stress the contemporaneousness of this particular historical depiction. Humphrey was not a statist in the sense that government is viewed as a guaranteed remedy for all of our ills. This can be illustrated by a number of passages taken, as a for instance, from his master's thesis regarding the potential threat that big government can pose: "The great danger of executive leadership and New Deal practices lies in the deadening influence it may have on individual initiative and responsiveness";[29] "The safety of democratic society rests in eternal vigilance on the part of its members, and this spirit of inquisitiveness must be nourished as much as the bodily security of the individual";[30] "The service state must not become the servile state"

> But it [centralized planning] may lead to an impersonal relationship between government and citizen that will be destructive of individual initiative and personal integrity (—the consecrated initiative of competent individuals that the Social Gospel had stood for). People may grow to regard government as something separate from and above them. A bureaucracy may find a firm foothold in our governmental system and cease to be responsive to the will of the people.[31]

It is important to note that these passages were written in *1938*. The New Deal was then at its height, and the young Hubert Humphrey was one of millions of young people enthralled by it. Given that, the astuteness of these passages—certainly in light of the criticism of the New Deal that arose half a century later—is all the more noteworthy. Humphrey's concern with "the deadening influence" of government on "individual initiative and personal integrity," however, was not limited to this one work or time alone. Eisele tells of how when Norman Sherman first joined Humphrey's staff in 1963, he told Sherman that "bureaucracy and big government are the enemy."[32] In his autobiography Humphrey wrote, "Some 'specialists' in the executive branch seem to think they not only know without question what is best for the people, but have a kind of subtle disdain and occasionally not-so-subtle contempt for both the private enterprise system on the one hand and the elected representatives of the people on the other."[33] In a response to Milton Friedman in a 1976 article in *Newsweek*, Humphrey wrote,

> I believe, I believe most Americans agree, that work is far better than the dole. . . . The choice is not between the public and the private sector, or between inflation and full employment; the true choice is between income support through welfare and unemployment compensation for an increasingly disaffected and pessimistic populace, and creating a climate in which Ameri-

> cans will have the dignity to earn their own incomes while contributing to a more prosperous society.
>
> The Humphrey-Hawkins Bill is based on the premise that the work ethic—a job for every American willing, able and seeking work—rather than the welfare ethic truly reflects America's aspirations for itself.[34]

Humphrey, in other words, was not blind to the problems commonly associated with liberalism by the 1980s. He was not a believer in the dole at home (nor, for that matter, in appeasement abroad). His liberalism was of the classical or European variety insofar as he placed individual liberty above all other rights. Yet by insisting that it was a right that all must be able to share *equally*, his liberalism was one that stood finally and squarely within the American version of that outlook. As he himself said,

> The genius of American democratic society is the belief that individual fulfillment and the attainment of individual goals can best be achieved in a community environment which provides for meeting common needs, and which establishes a security which allows for true freedom of action.[35]

In American liberalism, in other words, there is a balance between regard for the needs of the individual and regard for the needs of the community. Humphrey's freedom was a freedom *within* and *for* community, not one outside or despite it. Liberty may have been on a pedestal, but if so it was a pedestal named "Equality." Liberty's glory, in other words, was a shared one. For Humphrey, as for Locke, liberty was not license. Extremism in its name could, and most likely would indeed be a vice. Without equality its noble sound betokened only squalid results. Since the worth of each individual is a sacred one, any governmental/social structure that would guarantee respect for that worth would be just.

Government, when viewed in this light, is charged with a high calling indeed. It is to carry out the divine mandate "that ye shall all be one." As Humphrey stated,

> It is because of this basic respect of the individual, the fact that a man does have a soul, a spirit which is his identity with divine providence that government by the consent of the governed becomes more than a legal doctrine, it indeed becomes a moral imperative. Individual rights—those so-called inalienable rights are the God-given rights. They are the rights that man has because of his relationship to his God.[36]

Note here ought to be made of the phrase "consent of the governed." Government, for Humphrey, does not have the only high calling. Government is comprised of individuals. When a government exists by the free consent of the governed, the governed have a calling to see to it that their government honors its own calling, namely, to harbor individual dignity. Participation in government, then, is not simply a right, a possibility, or an opportunity. It is a moral duty. Prudence dictates that one act in one's own self-interest. That self-interest includes the protection of one's rights. Each American citizen is entitled to this. Yet, for Humphrey, as Americans we are to go beyond mere consideration of our own personal entitlements. We are to see to it that those entitlements are assured to *all*. God has commanded *all* of us to be "one." The state is to serve this divine fiat by being the main instrument through which this fiat is to be enacted. In a participatory democracy, it is the individual citizen who is responsible for seeing to it that government effectively fulfills this, its charge. Participation in government, therefore, can in this sense be seen as religious vocation, just as Calvin, and the Puritan tradition with him, (not to mention the Social Gospel) had advocated. That tradition, as Ahlstrom said, "strengthened the colonists' conception of his 'calling,' or vocation, making him more serious, purposeful and responsible in both his civic and economic roles."[37] This same tradition would find later expression in Humphrey's reference to the "sacred duty to take an active part in public life."[38] If loving one's divinely created neighbor consists chiefly in honoring the rights inherent in anyone of such origin, then participating in the institution chiefly responsible for and most capable of seeing to it that such honor is made becomes religious duty. It did, at any rate, for Hubert Humphrey.

Thus, when Norman Sherman said that "Hubert Humphrey was quintessentially a man seeking justice for all men," that "feeding the hungry, clothing the naked, healing the sick—really *meant* something to Humphrey," Sherman was asserting that it was an "injunction that was in him . . . that [it] really was a mission and it controlled most of what he did."[39] For William Connell,

> this [acting as if his politics were a vocation] was his whole life—it was his recreation—it was everything. He didn't golf, he didn't fish, to speak of, he

> didn't do anything other than this work. He was completely caught up in it. Yes, I think he saw it as a vocation . . . I think he felt he was on a ministry—he was in the world with special obligations, with special gifts, and they ought to be used.[40]

For Frances Howard, "His mission lasted until the end . . . a religious mission [that if] you serve man, you are serving God"[41]—the very "mission" that the Social Gospel had insisted upon.

That is not to say, therefore, that Humphrey necessarily understood his political career in the formal terms of a religious calling. It is, however, to assert that there was clear and consciously applied religious motivation on his part for the particular political point of view [liberal-Democratic] which his career represented—a career which he understood in itself to have religious content. For Humphrey, working for the poor, the sick, the aged *was* religion—and it was a religion that had clear and direct ties to, if not providing the foundation for his political outlook. Perhaps he stated it best himself by saying, "My religion and the teachings of the churches I have attended have brought me into a rich political philosophy and one that I hold very dear and one that is not subject to change on the matter of basic principle. There is no expediency in this philosophy. It is a way of life for me."[42]

Though hardly a theologian, that is not to say that Humphrey did not at times make quite specific religious references. In an early speech to a church group, for instance, Humphrey asked, "How many people of democratic faith have really understood that Jesus made great men out of little people and common men . . . ?" for this, "is, after all, the real significance of whatever political implication there happens to be in the philosophy of Jesus Christ."[43] Humphrey pointed to the fact that it was not the scribes and the Pharisees that Jesus associated with but rather, the blind, the lame, the publican, the adulterer: "But you know, Jesus Christ didn't go around selecting off all the best ones."[44]

Peter, for Humphrey, symbolized this common touch of Jesus best. Peter was the disciple closest to Jesus, yet he was "nothing but a fisherman—a very lowly occupation in those days."[45] Peter was not only lowly in terms of his former employment—he was also "the one who would deny in one moment and protest to high heaven in the next moment that he never denied"[46]; he was "the one who was the impetuous one who would stand up like everyone of us would and fight like a demon and slash off ears or whatever else it may be and then the next moment be very repentant. Isn't that quite human?"[47] For Humphrey, it was clearly those who *were* "quite human" that Jesus chose to be among—those who were just like "everyone of us." Griffith offers an example of Humphrey acting along these lines himself by telling of how "he stayed at the reception [given in his honor at Atlantic City's Hotel Dennis]—for which guests paid a thousand dollars each for the privilege of attending—for ten minutes. In the hotel kitchen on the way out he lingered for fifteen minutes, chatting with waitresses, cooks, busboys, and dishwashers."[48]

Being like "everyone of us," then, was a divine mandate for Humphrey. It was not simply a pleasant, let alone convenient political ploy. When he said, "The whole teachings of Jesus Christ are intimately associated with the lot of the poor, the sick, the hungry, the heavy laden, the worker, the needy, the whole message of the Christian faith is filled with consideration for, the love of, and the attention to ordinary people"[49] he meant it. This was not a casual reference for him. It was not simply a pious plucking at elective heartstrings. It was a consistent theme that Humphrey reiterated throughout his career.

Calvin Didier provides his own evidence for this:

> I remember one time [on a plane] going down to Washington. As I went through the first class section I noticed [George] McGovern . . . sitting in the first seat there. He had an aide with him, and . . . had taken . . . his shoes off—there were only the two of them. Nobody else really knew he was there.
>
> By contrast, [however], I saw Hubert come out two weeks later, and he just went up and down the aisles and shook hands with every person in the place.
>
> Now you say, "that's because he loved politics." Well, he wasn't running for office at the time—he just had so many friends. I mean it was really something to see . . . how much he enjoyed going up and down the aisles.[50]

There are other examples. Amrine describes how, "in defending the European aid program he said, 'I was taught in church that it was right to feed the starving; it is right to heal the sick; it is right to lead the blind; and it is right to teach the illiterate. This is what

Americans have been doing with their dollars abroad.'"[51] In introducing the Civil Rights Act of 1964 he argued that

> the Golden Rule exemplifies what we are attempting to do in this civil rights legislation. Chapter 7, verse 12 of Matthew reads as follows: "All things, therefore, whatsoever ye would that men should do unto you, even so also do ye unto them, for this is the law and the prophets."
>
> If I were to capsule what we are trying to do in this legislation, it is to fulfill this great admonition which is the guiding rule of human relations, if we are to have justice, tranquility, peace and freedom.[52]

For Humphrey, the *imitatio Christi* was literally to be "perfect" in this way.

In fact it went even further. Humphrey would actually look to features of Jesus' character for additional support for his own political outlook. He described the attempt to portray Jesus as "an ethereal body that just happened to stride along through the clouds."[53] He stressed the fact of Jesus being the son of a carpenter, and would often mention physical strength in the same regard: "He was an immensely strong person and a humble one. The son of a carpenter, a working man," whom Humphrey was sure "was strong physically."[54] Strength itself, both physical and moral, is the predominant characteristic for Humphrey's depiction of Jesus. Vitality and vibrancy are regularly juxtaposed beside humility as Humphrey's prime choices with which to limn Christ's figure: "He was a very vibrant and a very vital and strong person."[55] The focus is clearly on Jesus the *man*. Jesus was hardly "lamblike" in Humphrey's understanding of him. He was decidedly not to be just Sunday School pabulum. The stress, for Humphrey, was on charisma and dynamism, alongside of compassion.[56] At such a point, the question should be asked: Is it a coincidence that such features also happen to be the features of a political leader—one, in fact, who might very well "smite a pathway for the Almighty in human affairs"?

Given the egalitarian emphasis of Jesus' teachings—teachings that are boldly and dynamically confirmed in his character and behavior—his potential role for Humphrey as a model of political involvement was evident. It would only seem to follow, in addition, that a nation based on similar principles, and one committed to providing the opportunity for such involvement, would also serve as a model for Humphrey. In fact there was no doubt in his mind that such a "model" already did exist.

If Hubert Humphrey had a mission to make his "rich political philosophy" a "way of life," America was the context, both geographical and political, in which he would attempt to do so. Humphrey was always seen as a political figure committed to keeping the common touch. In Humphrey's eyes, America was the kind of place where such a commitment would only be appropriate. As he saw it, there was religious reason for this as well as political. The rightness of America's egalitarian creed, according to Humphrey, was made clear in Scripture, both by commandment and by example, as just illustrated. Though America, of which the New Deal was the political pinnacle, was not quite, in Humphrey's view, the kingdom come, it was nonetheless the closest to date: "We have," he wrote, "in America a democratic system which embodies the most advanced development in the application of the Christian (which is to say Social Gospel) ideal of the essential dignity of every individual."[57] "Isn't it thoroughly Christian" Humphrey asked,

> when you hear for example from the July 4, 1776 declaration that all men are created equal? That they were all endowed by their Creator with certain inalienable rights of life, liberty and the pursuit of happiness. That's as Christian as the Sermon on the Mount and that is the very creed of democratic government—that all men are created equal—that they're endowed by their Creator with certain inalienable rights of life, liberty and the pursuit of happiness. That's the very basis of our government because it merely states quite categorically that no power has the right, no power except God himself, has the right to take away from man his inalienable right, his right that was never given to him by government, his right that was never given to him by business or labor or anything else but came with him as a person . . . as a person created in the image of his Maker—the right of life and of liberty and of the pursuit of happiness.[58]

In many ways this one statement sums up Humphrey's entire religious-political outlook. It should thus come as no surprise that the first and foremost tenet mentioned is the equality of mankind. For Humphrey, this is fundamental to *both* Christianity *and* America: "Christianity holds that before God each man is equal. Democracy holds that before the Law each man is equal. This parallel is not a coincidence because the development of democracy grew out of the acceptance of Christian principles."[59] The Declaration of Independence is for this reason, "thoroughly Christian." The religious assertion of God's equal regard for all of his creatures is politically realized in the declaration of life, liberty, and the pursuit of happiness to be inalienable rights for all people. This is what is "as Christian as the Sermon on the Mount" and yet is at the same time the "very basis of our government." In that regard, following the credo of the Puritan fathers—and with them the Social Gospel leaders—America is something of the New Jerusalem. As Humphrey himself stated, "I have long believed that the ethical basis for democracy was to be found in the spiritual conception of man."[60] It should be noted here that by "spiritual conception of man" Humphrey undoubtedly meant the spiritual *worth* of the individual. He did not mean a sort of transcendental potential for mystical absorption into another world. For Humphrey the spiritual life had comparatively little to do with something practiced in silence. It had nearly everything to do with something practiced in voting booths and along the halls of Congress:

> Democracy is a spirit of government. Democracy is the spirit of human personality. It is something which may be classified as intangible. It is a basic, fundamental belief that every human being is worthy of respect and of dignified treatment. It is a basic realization that we are created in the image of our Maker, and that there is something very precious about human life, the human soul, the human mind, the human body. That is what we mean when we talk about the spirit of democracy. It means the dignity of the individual, and respect for his personality. It means the freedom of conscience to seek the truth, so that the truth may make us free.[61]

Spiritual worth was not, on the other hand, a concept by which everyone was seen to be the same. In the same letter written to the Baltimore class that had inquired about this issue he offered the following clarification:

> I do not mean that democracy believes that all men are born with equal talents and equal abilities and equal attractions. It is a fact that there are individual differences in people as far as abilities and talents go, and there are differences in the amount of skill and knowledge that people have. A democrat recognizes these differences, but at the same time he has a complete respect for every

person, just because that person is a human being. Because of that respect, a democrat treats every other human being as he would like to be treated himself. That is what I mean by equality. It is a mutual respect, one human being for another, and an equality of treatment.[62]

Evidence of Humphrey's consistent linkage of Christianity and democracy are readily available. In notes prepared for a speech that he gave as mayor of Minneapolis (clearly just following World War II) he marked the following as key points to be made:

Democracy & Christianity

1. Both *Goals*—both Guide Posts—Both are *Challenges*
   Man must be "born again"
2. Democracy—a social system based on
   A. Dignity of individual
   B. Freedom of conscience—"Seek ye the Truth"
   C. Brotherhood of Mankind "neither bond nor free, neither Jew nor Gentile" "Ye are all one in Jesus"
3. Democracy & Christianity depend on an *idealism*, on Humanitarianism
   . . . and we, the common people, just as *Peter*, are the rock on which faith must rest. "Seek ye first the kingdom of God & all these other things shall be added unto you"
   A. Love of common man
   B. Demand courage, self discipline, constant crusade "for Heaven on Earth"
      Jesus as crusader—an idealist
      Jesus died for *principle*
      Jesus—*for* and against—
      The Military Victory not Enough—
      The Peace must be recognized not as the answer,
      but as the hope for an answer
      We must become *Great* people, *Humble* people
      "I came not to be ministered unto, but to minister"
      "He who would be first, let him be last"
      "With malice toward none—with charity for all"[63]

These themes were put into more succinct form in an article he wrote at that same time and already cited entitled, "The Christian Student in Politics." In that article he said,

There is a striking parallel between the teachings of Christ and the fundamental philosophy of Democracy. Both stand foursquare in respect for the identity and individuality of each personality. Before God each man is equal; in the eyes of the law in a democratic state the same respect for individuality reigns supreme. Such attitudes of mind as sympathy for the unfortunate, hope to the unlucky, care for the weak and sick, and general moderation, understanding and tolerance come to us through the lessons of Jesus Christ and also by means of the democratic philosophy our country embraces.[64]

There are many other examples of this as well. In a speech he made in 1957 before the directors of CARE he asked,

Now, what is the motivating principle behind a democracy? It is service to the individual. And I say that every person who is elected to office, or holds office by appointment, in a free country under democratic institutions, should remind himself every hour of the day that his primary responsibility, duty, and purpose is to serve and not to be served. This is the Christian ethic too. "He who would be first, let him be last." "I came to minister, not to be ministered unto."[65]

In a speech, also already cited, to the Jewish Theological Seminary in 1965 he stated,

I have long believed that the *best* we have been able to create in this country—the most enduring aspects of our accomplishments—the noblest aspects of our aspirations—bear a striking kinship to the vision of the Prophets of ancient Israel.[66]

In a 1976 speech to the Christian Life Commission of the Southern Baptist Church he said that

the Declaration of Independence, in fact, put in words a tremendous political revolution springing from a spiritual emancipation. Men's minds and souls were to be free—free to build a new world. They were to be regarded as equal in the eyes of their Maker. The political literature of our early republic is permeated with a firm conviction of human dignity—dignity not achieved by man himself, but dignity because each human soul is part of the spirit of God.[67]

There is evidence, then, that this direct association of religious and political principles, just as the Social Gospel had advocated, remained a consistent theme throughout all of his life. For his sister Frances, this mix of religion and politics was thus like

a milkshake of politics and ethics—a part of this cauldron, this brew that my father created in the drugstore. It was a prescription made . . . there: ethical community values, serving your community, serving your state, serving your family, serving your church, and at the same time the Protestant ethic of believing in making a living—the enlightened form of capitalism.[68]

It was something, in other words, clearly instilled in Humphrey from early on.

As a result he would, for example, close his speech to the Emmanuel Lutheran Church by stating, "I mention these things to you because it's the thing, these are the thoughts that give me what I call my own political philosophy. I'm interested in human welfare not because it's politically expedient to be interested in good pensions for the aged people but because I believe that whatever ye do unto the least of these ye do unto me also."[69] It is also worth noting that he made these remarks in the same speech in which he mentioned that "I don't always [talk about such things in] every speech I give but it always motivates my thinking."

That was the young Humphrey speaking—in the ninth month of his first term in elected office. Yet these themes are virtually identical to those he reiterated nearly twenty years later, for instance, in the private memorandum to Winthrop Griffith, and then again over ten years after that in the published interview with Caspar Nannes in *The Link* magazine. His statements in these sources constitute (comparatively speaking) major texts. Minor references supporting the same themes are too numerous to list. The point overall is, as he stated himself, "I found in the New Testament for example—in the teaching of Jesus and his disciples—not only the justification for a liberal and progressive philosophy of politics, but indeed the moral imperative of such a philosophy."[70] Therefore, "when I've been interested in health programs, for example, the migratory worker, the person who was discriminated against because of his color, I didn't do this because I thought it was good politics. I was brought up this way."[71]

Neither Humphrey's religion, then, nor its relation to his political outlook can be simply regarded as incidental.

This can be confirmed not only by testimony gathered from Humphrey himself but from that given by numerous friends and associates as well. For Max Kampelman "there is no question" that Humphrey saw his life as a means of applying his religious principles. William Connell described Humphrey's mix of religious principle and political outlook as an "interlocking firm structure."[72] When Geri Joseph claimed that religion was a "very strong feeling in him," she insisted that that was not to be understood in the rigid sense of holding to specific denominational dogma, as already discussed, but rather in the sense of translating "itself into the everyday, practical kinds of things"—in the sense that "he really lived what he believed."[73] Ted Van Dyk, a member of Humphrey's staff during the vice presidential years, believed that "the whole basis of his life and public career was really built on the Christian ethic with which he grew up . . . it formed a basis for just about everything."[74] David Gartner argued that this had to have been so, since "you've got to figure that anybody . . . who did so much and who attempted to do even more for the poor and the hungry and the underprivileged . . . has got to have some kind of religious purpose in doing it."[75]

Accounts of Humphrey acting out of such purpose are legion. Geri Joseph tells one particularly illuminating tale:

> I remember one incident in Little Rock, Arkansas. We were running late—we were *always* running late . . . and he was giving a speech in an outdoor . . . park. There was a stand there, and there were a lot of people.
>
> He had [already] given a speech [that day] and a lot of his aides were really upset because . . . it must have been at *least* an hour and a half . . . to the next stop and it was going to take him a while to get there. . . .
>
> I had just been standing by the fence listening to him and . . . a woman came up to me and said, "You're with the Senator, aren't you? My daughter is over there in my station wagon. She works for the local radio station . . . she is in a wheelchair. She is handicapped. She can't get out easily, and it would be difficult for her in this crowd. Do you think there would be any chance that Senator Humphrey would let her have an interview?"
>
> Well, I knew the other aides would just *kill* me, but I knew that *he* would be furious if he knew that [there] was a situation [that] I hadn't told him [of]. So, he came off . . . the podium and I told him and he didn't hesitate. He walked over and got into the station wagon. And this young woman—I guess she must have been in her early '20s—was so flustered, so excited—and he said, "Take your time. It's alright, don't worry about [it]" . . . and she asked him a number of questions.
> It took maybe twenty minutes or so, and then she said, "Thank you so much." And he said, "Well, I'll tell you what. Why don't you check your tape recorder, just to be sure that this was working . . . and [that] it's just what you want?" So she fumbled around some more [and] sure enough it had not worked properly. Well, she was so upset and so flustered. He said, "Now you just take your time, because I am going to sit right here with you until you get it straight."
>
> . . . There was such a warmth about him, such a kindness about him. I must say, I was very moved.[76]

She went on to finish the story by saying that years later, after Humphrey's death, she received a letter from the same woman in which the latter recounted the experience of having met him, and of how she "would absolutely never forget him." At that point, Joseph stated that she "would bet that there are people all over this country who could tell you stories about Hubert."

Norman Sherman is one such person. He remembers, for instance,

> after the election of 1968, when depression and fatigue were constantly with you. Somehow or other I got a letter on my desk from a blind girl from Boston who said, "You may have lost and I am very sorry for you but I want you to know one good thing that came out of this election. I am blind. I went to the Humphrey office with my seeing eye dog and asked if I could be a volunteer and they were nervous about having the dog around, but I finally insisted and they let me fold . . . things to go into envelopes and seal [them]. . . . " And she said, "I then pointed out that I could dial telephones. I did it all the time, and people who heard me call did not know I was blind . . . and I would rather do [that] and [so] they let me do it . . . " and she just wrote about her growth in that period.
>
> I showed the letter to Humphrey, thinking, "Wasn't that nice?" He said, "Why don't you get her on the phone?" This is a guy who is down. He has just been beaten by Richard Nixon. Life has fallen about. No vacation really. . . . I went to the telephone and called . . . her, and said: "Just a minute" for the vice president, and I listened in as Humphrey said, "Mary, this is Hubert Humphrey. I just wanted to tell you how much that letter meant to me . . . " and the girl on the other end couldn't breathe . . . because here was Hubert Humphrey on [the phone]. . . . She and Humphrey to the day he died had a correspondence from time to time. Humphrey did things [like that] for people on a daily basis.[77]

Perhaps the greatest proof of his having done so was the line of thousands of people who waited for hours in sub-zero weather simply to have a chance to view his casket or to file by his graveside. It is possible that they, too, had their own stories to tell.

For Joseph these kinds of stories were highly illustrative of Humphrey's religious belief. They revealed his commitment, as understood in religious terms, to honoring the worth of each individual, as well as to believing that we are religiously *commanded* to put this into political practice—precisely as the Social Gospel had insisted. In Sherman's view such stories show how "ultimately, it is the accumulation of personal decencies that is subliminal, unattributable, unseen—acts of not even charity—of kindness, of reaching out, embracing" that best demonstrate that "he was really the most loving guy that you ever saw."[78] For Sherman, they proved that "Humphrey had a reservoir of decency, if you will—of just, just joy in other people's lives . . . I tell you it was a physical force, it was a power there that was just immense."[79] (See Appendix B for other such stories.)

For Humphrey America was a nation built on such power. It was the kind of place where the very existence of its political system would thereby automatically see that joy incorporated into people's lives—that is, into *all* people's lives. When Humphrey saw Jesus taking "little insignificant people that amounted to nothing in their day and making great men out of them," he saw direct political implication in it. For Humphrey, that "implication" was to teach that egalitarianism was the foundational principle for morality. The political tradition that he saw as having best learned this lesson was liberal-progressivism: "Liberal-progressivism is not just politics. It is morality, and it is in a very real sense, Christian morality."[80]

Thus, Humphrey was, quite literally, a devout believer in what the New Deal, that is, "liberal-progressivism," stood for. For him, that principally meant government intervention on behalf of the "least of these." That did not mean that there was simply religious justification for this: such "intervention" was, additionally, stipulated by the Constitution itself. Since it was, acting on the basis of this was *not* to act outside of the system, but rather fully within it. It was literally as American as Yankee Doodle Dandy. Furthermore, doing so was, on a personal note, not only Humphrey's intention: he saw it, in his own quite qualified sense of it, as his vocation. Doing so was hardly, however, a noteworthy, let alone extreme stand, for that was precisely what America was about: it was *the* political embodiment of what religion stipulated. We are all to regard each other as equals, for that is how God wishes and thus commands that each of us regard each other. Such a religious imperative was to be applied politically, yet that is not to say through any rigid ideology. As crucial as such political application of religious principle was, the results of such application must be forever understood to be "limited" and "partial," which is to say, tentative. Thus, no matter the depth and intensity of Humphrey's commitment to such application, part and parcel of it was also the commitment to the pragmatic—to whatever finally *worked*, as opposed to what sounded truly fine in moral tone, yet which was simply unfeasible when it came to application.

Such, at any rate, is a summary of the religious-political outlook of what Humphrey would refer to himself as being that "simple American kid from the prairie." As with every "child," however, there are important, and, often enough, painful steps that must be taken in order to achieve full "adulthood." Humphrey needed to take as many as anyone. For someone who was committed to achieving an effective balance between religious/moral idealism and political realism—someone who believed that faith was meaningful only when it was translated into action—deeds were in fact going to be at least as important as the creed. And so, after reaching a certain stage in his life, he began to act on precisely such a basis.

Notes

1. Robert Harris, forward to Hubert Humphrey, *The Political Philosophy of the New Deal* (Baton Rouge: Louisiana State University Press, 1970), vi–vii.
2. Humphrey, *New Deal*, x.
3. Ibid., 9.
4. Ibid., 5.
5. Ibid., 39.
6. Ibid., 6.
7. Ibid., 17.
8. Ibid., 66.
9. Ibid.
10. Ibid., 81.
11. Ibid., 80.
12. Hubert Humphrey, "Liberalism," *American Scholar* (Autumn 1955): 433.
13. Humphrey, *Think*, 7.
14. Hubert Humphrey, *The Cause Is Mankind* (New York: Frederick A. Praeger, 1964), 17.
15. Humphrey, as quoted in Griffith, *Candid*, 238.
16. Humphrey, as quoted in, "Hubert Humphrey's Springboard for '76," *Business Week* (15 December 1975): 68–70.
17. Evron Kirkpatrick, interview with author, 5 July 1984.
18. Humphrey, *American Scholar*, 419.
19. Humphrey, *Cause*, 9.
20. Ibid., 11.
21. Ibid., 12.
22. Ibid.
23. Ibid., 12–13.
24. Humphrey, *American Scholar*, 431.
25. Humphrey, *Cause*, 12.
26. Humphrey, *American Scholar*, 429–30.

27. Humphrey, letter to Class 6B-6A, Public School No. 112, Baltimore, Maryland, 28 March 1949, Humphrey Collection.
28. From Penn's "Preface to the Frame of Government of Pennsylvania," as quoted in Ahlstrom, *History*, 122.
29. Humphrey, *New Deal*, 53–54.
30. Ibid., 54.
31. Ibid., 77.
32. Eisele, *Almost*, 188.
33. Humphrey, *Education*, 47.
34. Hubert Humphrey, "Reply to Milton Friedman," *Newsweek* (11 October 1976): 7–8.
35. Hubert Humphrey, speech to Minneapolis Ministerial Association Breakfast, Minneapolis, Minnesota, 13 May 1974, Humphrey Collection.
36. Humphrey, Griffith memorandum.
37. Ahlstrom, *History*, 348.
38. Hubert Humphrey, "The Cristian Student in Politics," unpublished draft of an article prepared for the YMCA, second copy, Humphrey Collection, from the mayoralty years.
39. Sherman interview.
40. Connell interview.
41. Howard interview, no. 1.
42. Humphrey, Griffith memorandum.
43. Humphrey, Emmanuel Lutheran speech.
44. Ibid.
45. Ibid.
46. Ibid.
47. Ibid.
48. Griffith, *Candid*, 31.
49. Humphrey, Griffith memorandum.
50. Calvin Didier, interview with author, 15 September 1983.
51. Amrine, *This Is Humphrey*, 40.
52. Humphrey, *Congressional Record*, 88th Cong., 2nd sess., 1964. Vol. 110, 6529.
53. Humphrey, Emmanuel Lutheran speech.
54. Ibid.
55. Ibid.
56. In this Humphrey was very much like Francis Greenwood Peabody, the great Social Gospel leader, who regarded "power and life" as "words, not of opinion or definition, but of expansion, vitality, momentum, growth. They are symbols of a dynamic faith. . . . " Peabody, as quoted in Little, "Peabody," 290.
57. Humphrey, "Christian Student."
58. Humphrey, Emmanuel Lutheran speech.
59. Humphrey, "Christian Student."
60. Humphrey, Griffith memorandum.
61. Humphrey, *Congressional Record*, 81st Cong., 1st sess., 1949. Vol. 95, 4044.
62. Humphrey, letter to Class 6B-6A.
63. Hubert Humphrey, notes for a speech entitled, "A Time for Greatness," Humphrey Collection.

64. Humphrey, "Christian Student."
65. Humphrey, *Congressional Record*, 85th Cong., 1st sess., 1957. Vol. 103, 14641.
66. Hubert Humphrey, Jewish Theological speech.
67. Humphrey, "Baptist," 7865.
68. Howard interview, no. 1.
69. Humphrey, Emmanuel Lutheran speech.
70. Humphrey, Griffith memorandum.
71. Humphrey, *The Link* interview.
72. Connell interview.
73. Joseph interview.
74. Ted Van Dyk, interview with author, 5 July 1984.
75. Gartner interview.
76. Joseph interview.
77. Sherman interview.
78. Ibid.
79. Ibid.
80. Humphrey, Emmanuel Lutheran speech.

3

Idealism Triumphant: Into the Bright Sunshine

Hubert Humphrey's political career began with a Sunday stroll in April of 1943. As a Ph.D. candidate at the University of Minnesota, Humphrey at the time was very much a part of the ivory tower and could hardly be conceived as a veteran in political affairs. After receiving his B.A. from the University of Minnesota, he had gone on to Louisiana State University for his master's, largely because of a fellowship offered him by the chairman of the political science department there—Charles Hyneman—a friend and colleague of Humphrey's undergraduate professor at the University of Minnesota, Evron Kirkpatrick. After receiving his degree from LSU, he had entered the doctoral program in political science back at the University of Minnesota after turning down an offer from Princeton (mainly because he could not afford the tuition costs). While in the university he had been engaged in various politically related pursuits—giving speeches, debating in heated political discussion,[1] and working as both a WPA teacher and later as a director of the Worker's Education Program. He had discussed entering politics with friends, all of whom thought he would be well suited for the political trade, but had not seriously considered entering a specific race. Earlier in 1943, he had met a number of times with a group of Republicans who were interested in offering their support for a Humphrey mayoralty race, but that support evaporated when it was discovered that Humphrey had associations with a number of leftists, and that he was intent on ending Minneapolis's reputation as an "open city."

It was some time after that that he went on "an aimless walk," a walk which, as he described himself, "gave my life direction for the next twenty-five years."[2] He had wandered across the bridge in Minneapolis that spanned the Mississippi when he met George Phillips, president of the Minneapolis Central Labor Union, and George Murk, president of the Musician's Union, outside of the Nicollet Hotel in downtown Minneapolis. He knew both of them through his work in the Worker's Education Program. They began talking about the upcoming mayoral campaign. The question was soon raised about the possibility of a Humphrey candidacy. The potential, but not yet committed candidate replied that he might be interested, though he expressed doubt as to what kind of support he might be able to raise. It was one of the few doubts that he would ever again raise, at least publicly, regarding his becoming involved in the political process.

At the time Humphrey was "thirty-two years old, married, a father, on a new job (Assistant Director of the Minnesota War Manpower Commission), with an unfinished doctoral degree hanging in abeyance, and broke."[3] He had only lived in Minneapolis for a few years and then only as a student. Furthermore, he knew next to nothing about municipal politics. "A more objective person," he said, "might have considered it an unpropitious moment to launch a political career."[4] Nevertheless, after considering it for a few days, Humphrey decided to file as a candidate. There were nineteen days remaining before the primary elections. As Humphrey himself stated, "I was not an objective person"[5]—a rather euphemistic understatement for saying that his entrance into politics was wildly optimistic.

Remarkably and impressively enough, the wild optimist came comparatively close to winning. The primary in Minneapolis at that time was nonpartisan. All that was required to file was a $10 fee and the desire to enter. The top two finishers would then contend for the mayoralty in the general election.

Eight people filed that year. After filing himself Humphrey began his own "whirlwind campaign."[6] With the help of Evron Kirkpatrick and Arthur Naftalin he built a small but dedicated organization.

Characteristically he spoke "anywhere I could get an audience."[7] He would scrounge, for instance, for $26 for a fifteen-minute radio broadcast on one of the lesser-known radio stations in Minneapolis and speak on street corners or wherever else he could manage to attract a crowd.

After three weeks of precious little sleep and never-slackening attempts to reach potential voters, the results were satisfying, if not remarkable. He won one of the two runoff slots, having garnered 16,148 votes to the incumbent mayor's 29,752. Six weeks later, following the same schedule, he lost the general election by a mere 5,725 votes out of a total of 124,425 cast.

If nothing else, Hubert Humphrey, in this his premiere political experience, learned that he could speak to an audience—and that it was something he loved to do. Herbert McClosky, a fellow political science doctoral candidate, campaign chauffeur, speech writer, and friend claimed, for instance, that Humphrey gave his best speech ever in an impromptu performance in a garage on Minneapolis's Plymouth Avenue before a crowd of wildly applauding mechanics and passersby.

Despite such performances, however, Humphrey also learned that engendering enthusiasm for the democratic system was not all that there was to winning an election, let alone running a government. There were other "lessons" as well.

One such lesson was that politics unquestionably had its seamier side. In the early 1940s Minneapolis was a divided city: "During the day it was a vibrant regional center of finance and transportation, of milling and agriculture."[8] It was a daytime city dominated by "the New England Yankee families who had come early to Minnesota," who lived in distinct parts of the city, and who wanted a distinctive type of government: "primarily a conservative government—no radicals in office, police who stood on the 'right' side in labor disputes, and relatively low taxes."[9] Such was Minneapolis while the sun shone.

At night another group dominated. As Humphrey came to learn, Minneapolis at night was a "wide-open town"—wide open to gambling, prostitution, and racketeering. All were generally run by two groups, "The Syndicate" and "The Combination." In viewing the political scene, both saw this young, unowned university idealist as a threat to their interests and let their sentiments to that effect be known.

They were not alone in this. Though sympathetic to and supported by labor, Humphrey had also seen the effects of "bad" money being passed to certain hands within labor, ultimately affecting votes on city council. He saw then that that part of Minneapolis needed cleaning up as well.

Perhaps the most startling lesson of all, however, was that many of the "good people" of the community really did not seem to care. As long as their 9:00–5:00 status quo went unchallenged, they were content to allow the 5:00–9:00 status quo remain unchallenged.

The final lesson, though, and one which Humphrey stressed himself, was that of the premium to be placed on loyalty. A campaign attracts many different people for many different reasons. Many pledge their support and have genuine reason for doing so. Many, however, are more duplicitous in their rationale. Still others fail to come through at all. Two years after his election debut, Humphrey, in the midst of his 1945 campaign, came upon literature of his in a perennial and purportedly loyal political headquarters—literature from his 1943 campaign. The loyalty of those who could be counted on to make good their promises quickly came to be regarded as one of the most valuable assets of all—a fact that would be a critical factor in Humphrey's career later on.

A final asset that Humphrey learned the value of was the simple humanizing contact provided by friends and family—contact so badly needed by a politician otherwise emotionally exhausted by constant confrontation with unfamiliar and, often enough, hostile faces. As Humphrey himself said, "A political man must have at least one close friend he can be perfectly at ease with—someone with whom he can enjoy total relaxation, knowing there is full confidence and true feeling. Without that one the loneliness of politicians would be unbearable" (in this Humphrey had such a "close friend" in mind—the enigmatic, yet nevertheless utterly loyal Freddie Gates).[10]

One thing that was painfully clear to the whirlwind idealist as a result of his first political campaign was the $1,300 debt with which he was left afterwards. For a graduate student in 1943, only halfway through his degree program, and having no financial wherewithal to speak of,[11] this was a considerable blow. Such a blow only meant that the following encounter provided all the more temptation as a result.

After his defeat, Humphrey was approached by Gideon Seymour, then executive editor of the *Minneapolis Star and Tribune*. Humphrey liked Seymour and respected him as a "reasonably liberal," nondoctrinaire Republican. Seymour himself was similarly impressed with Humphrey; Seymour had been part of the original Republican group that had first broached the topic of a mayoralty race to Humphrey in the previous spring. Seymour's reason for wishing to see Humphrey now was to encourage him to switch to the Republican Party. There was nearly every good reason for doing so.

The Republicans held the majority of positions in Minnesota, and they were firmly in power, now that Floyd Olson, the long dominant left-wing leader in Minnesota politics, was dead. They had the means to provide for a well-run race for any candidate whom they might choose. Though the Democratic Party and the Farmer-Labor Party together represented the majority of registered voters in Minnesota, the Republicans had been able to divide and thus conquer for some time. Furthermore, the Republican Party in Minnesota was quite liberal. Harold Stassen was then governor and maintained a liberal reputation. So did, for instance, Representative Richard Gale of the 3rd District. Humphrey owed nothing to the Democratic Party, and clearly anyone who hoped for a political future in Minnesota could see how futile any Democratic candidacy would be. Why, then, not switch?

Humphrey considered the offer seriously, was in fact flattered by it, yet in the final run found that he simply could not accept it. As he told Herbert McClosky at the time: "I just can't do it."[12] The Democratic Party had been the party of his upbringing—the party to which his father had remained loyal despite quite similar prudentialist reasons for not doing so in South Dakota. Hubert Humphrey, Jr. would honor that tradition and remain a Democrat.

Doing so *was* honorable, and consistent with what would be expected from an idealist such as Humphrey, yet it—as will develop as a key point for this work overall—now posed a dilemma for him. He still had considerable political ambition, yet was loyal to a party which could guarantee him little other than defeat. It was this predicament that led him into the next step of his career—the famous political brouhaha known as the Democratic/Farmer-Labor merger.

Accounts of this "transaction" are varied. Alan Ryskind, a rightist critic of Humphrey's, contends that while Humphrey is "given great credit for having booted the Communists out of the Democratic Party in Minnesota in 1948, [he] appeared more than willing to let the Communists in via the merger route in 1944."[13] Ryskind goes on to accuse Humphrey of pandering to Communist interests, chiefly those "Stalinists and other assorted radicals who dominated the CIO in Minneapolis at this time."[14] Ryskind is perfectly willing to thereby give full credit to Humphrey, not only for having formed the DFL, but also for thereby allowing "Communists and extreme leftists to gain control of the party's nerve center."[15]

Two other critics of Humphrey, however, this time from the left, complete a rather odd juxtaposition of views on this. Robert Sherrill and Harry Ernst looked to Elmer Benson, the 1936 Farmer-Labor gubernatorial successor to Floyd Olson, for their account. Benson's recollection was as follows: "I don't recall he [Humphrey] played any role whatsoever in the merger. He was chosen chairman of the meeting at the time of the merger, but he had no part in the merger."[16] Benson, in fact, went on to claim that Humphrey was actually *against* the merger. This was so, according to Benson, because neither Humphrey nor any of his political friends had served in the armed forces during World War II and were now making up for it by being "especially belligerent towards the Communists; in fact, overwhelmingly so. It colored all they did. They were consumed, obsessed by anti-Communism."[17] (Orville Freeman, one such friend not noted by Sherrill and Ernst, was a decorated Marine hero who had been badly wounded during the war.)

Humphrey himself believed his role, and thus greatest contribution to Minnesota politics, to be his acting as a "catalyst for the amalgamation of the Democrats and the Farmer-Laborites."[18] Arthur Naftalin described him as having been "the swing person."[19] While Humphrey certainly was not alone in bringing the effort to a successful conclusion, it seems that he ought to at least be given credit for playing a crucial role. He was the one who scraped together what little money he had to go to Washington where he spent a week futilely trying to see Frank Walker, Postmaster General and chairman of the DNC. By chance he was able to see him only at the last minute through the intervention of an old family friend. It was because of this meeting that Oscar Ewing, an assistant national chairman of the Democratic Party and an expert in political organization, was sent to Minnesota where he played a pivotal role in seeing the merger through to completion. Humphrey had thus given the merger its original impetus (though there had been much talk of a merger before), and had also acted as an important moderator between the two contending factions—a role which he was to fulfill many times in future political confrontations.

Whatever the case, the now-welded Democratic-Farmer-Labor Party, or DFL, was thereafter (or at least up until the time of his death) to become a winning combination, often enough with Humphrey as its leading candidate.

After his defeat in the 1943 mayoralty contest, Humphrey took a summer teaching job at Macalester College. His students included ninety-day air force cadets who voted three times to have him give their commencement address. One of his students that summer was Walter Mondale.

Regardless of Benson's denial of any radical credentials on Humphrey's part, Humphrey continued to show such tendencies. During the summer of '44 he attended the Democratic National Convention in Chicago, where he was a staunch Henry Wallace supporter. He seized the Minnesota standard when Wallace's name was put up for the vice-presidential nomination, and then led a pro-Wallace demonstration on the convention floor.* Humphrey was subsequently chosen as Minnesota state chairman for the 1944 FDR-Truman ticket.

In a very short time, then, the University of Minnesota graduate student, though not yet a holder of political office, had nevertheless become a major player in Minnesota politics. The Humphrey emphasis on *doing*, and Humphrey's own energy, enthusiasm, and speaking ability had at least gained him a hopeful start. It was hopeful enough, in fact, as to have Humphrey form a small public relations firm with Art Naftalin, a firm which was to serve as a front for the next Humphrey for Mayor campaign.

The 1945 Minneapolis mayoralty race was one run largely on the issue of law and order. Under the [incumbent] Kline administration, Minneapolis's notorious reputation for racketeering had not been diminished. There were regular gangland-type murders, and Minneapolis was beginning to show signs of decline as a result of such prominent criminal activity. Humphrey decided to run a campaign intended to reverse all of this. This time he had solid labor support. Yet appeals for law and order—the promise of cleaning up Minneapolis—had tremendously impressed a number of business leaders as well. John Cowles, the owner of the *Minneapolis Star Journal and Tribune*, was one such leader. Others included John Pillsbury, of Pillsbury Mills; Peavey Heffelfinger, a prominent grain merchant; and Lucian Sprague, president of the Minneapolis and St. Louis Railroad. Church groups were impressed by Humphrey's active membership in Minneapolis's First Congregational Church, and by his "University of Life" classes at Minneapolis's leading Methodist church. Bradshaw Mintener, general counsel for Pillsbury, member of First Congregational Church, and trustee of Macalester College, was convinced that Humphrey was a "sound fellow" who would "choose a police chief who [would] clean up the city and drive out the racketeers,"[20] and said so to Rotary lunches and high school assemblies around the city.

*Humphrey later broke with Wallace following the latter's 1948 Madison Square Garden speech where he called for accommodation with the Soviets.

Humphrey by now had come into full stride as a candidate. Geri Joseph, for instance, recounts her first encounter with the still young but clearly able Humphrey of that time:

> I was one of the editors of the University newspaper at the time. . . . Some of my political science professors had been very active on his behalf—Kirk (Evron Kirkpatrick) and Herbie McClosky—and they brought him into The *Daily* [office]. It was very shortly after . . . World War II—and the housing situation for returning students was horrible, just horrible . . .
>
> He [Humphrey] came in and began to talk about what he saw as an editorial campaign that we could put together—the need for housing for these young men who were returning. I always remembered—he sat on a table in the corner of the room, and when he first started to talk there were just the staff members, you know—rather a few of us, but by the time he had finished everybody in Murphy Hall [was in that room]. . . . It really was an unbelievable experience. The word got around that building that he was there. He . . . was a tremendous speaker—he didn't have a single note—but it was such a compelling kind of statement that he was making in an informal way. He wasn't pontificating. It was absolutely marvelous. People were just spell-bound. The *Daily* office was not a huge room by any means. We had people poring out into the halls trying to hear him and to see him. . . . He sold me and I stayed sold for years after that.[21]

By generating this kind of appeal, Humphrey had put Mayor Kline on notice. Notice was fully served when, once the Cowles newspaper endorsed Humphrey, following his 2–1 victory in the primary, the Republican State committee refused Kline their support. The election confirmed the power of Humphrey's ability to attract widespread segments of the population: on 11 June 1945, he was elected mayor by a vote of 86,377 to Kline's 55,203. It was the greatest plurality in Minneapolis history.

Perhaps the most striking thing about the Humphrey mayoralty was that he was able to have any significant impact on life in Minneapolis at all. This was striking, given Minneapolis's weak mayoral system. Under this system the mayor had no budgetary control, and had no vote in city council. He or she did not even participate in the deliberations. He or she did, however, have the power to appoint the police chief—the power that Bradshaw Mintener had referred to in his campaign speeches supporting Humphrey. In addition to this one asset, the mayor also had the public spotlight which the office naturally afforded. Humphrey effectively utilized both.

Having run on a strong law-and-order platform, Humphrey was committed to finding a choice for police chief that would successfully implement that platform. His choice was a 6′4″, 220 lb. Irish neighbor named Ed Ryan. Ryan was the only member of the Minneapolis police force who had undergone training at the FBI academy. He was honest and he was free of corruption. He was the choice of Bradshaw Mintener, whom Humphrey had appointed as chairman of the advisory committee of business, labor, and public representatives to recommend a candidate. He was also Humphrey's friend, with whom he had often talked about Minneapolis's crime situation out on the front porch.

Ryan was a controversial choice for two reasons. First, his appointment was opposed by labor—an opposition that Humphrey would have to take extremely seriously. Second, while Ryan seemed like a safe bet to uphold Humphrey's pledge of a clean administration, the objects of that housecleaning knew it and therefore would do what they could to stop it.

The Ryan appointment had to be made specifically over the strenuous opposition of Humphrey's friend and political backer, Bob Wishart. Wishart was head of the then quite radical United Electrical Worker's Local, no. 1145, which he had built into the state's largest union. Wishart had been Humphrey's strongest CIO backer, had oftentimes been consulted by Humphrey on political matters, and had been appointed by the new mayor to the Board of Public Welfare. He was also on the board of business, labor, and public representatives that was to provide a candidate for police chief. When Mintener proposed Ryan for the position, Wishart was the one dissenting vote out of thirteen cast. As a result, in what was to become characteristic Humphrey fashion, the mayor took his friend into a corridor and, using a soft touch, convinced him that Ryan must be the man. Wishart agreed, yet nearly lost his position as head of the Hennepin County CIO council as a result.

In a sense this one incident, though small, would loom symbolically large in Humphrey's career. The reason is multifold. First, it would represent Humphrey's commitment to doing what he believed was right, even if it meant going against the very source of his political support. Here was an ostensibly "leftist" political figure backing an ostensibly "rightist" appointee, over and against his own leftist support. Second, it also demonstrated his commitment, and ability, to achieve results in the name of what he believed was right through a friendly chat and handshake, rather than through a twisted arm. His means, in other words, remained consistent with his end—an approach that would serve him admirably in his struggle to pass the Civil Rights Act of 1964. Above all else, however, what the Ryan appointment demonstrated was that Humphrey was not to be easily pinned down—not to be readily categorized as a "knee-jerk" political figure, whether from the left or from the right. Depending upon one's interpretation, he either had the strength of character to rise above his ideology, or was so weak in character that he failed to remain committed to it. In either case, the point remains that from the earliest stage of his career on, Humphrey was not ideologically rigid—something that worked in his favor in 1945, yet which would not work out quite so well in a later time parallel to it. The ostensible liberal candidate for president in 1968 risked his liberal support in that race, by, among other things, a strong stand on law and order—particularly when he refused to denounce outright the Chicago police at the '68 Democratic convention.

Speaking of law and order, Humphrey also held to a hard line against to Minneapolis's underworld. Solberg provides one such instance in a story told by Humphrey's aide, Bill Simms, during the time of Humphrey's inauguration.

Chickie Berman of the Syndicate had heard that Humphrey could be paid off, though not cheaply. He decided to take advantage of Humphrey's announced policy of being willing to see anyone as his means of testing the new waters. Simms provides the ensuing dialogue with Berman:

> Berman began by asking straight off: "What do you want?"
>
> "What do you mean, 'What do I want?'" asked Humphrey.
>
> Berman said: "Well, what do you want so we can operate like we used to? I don't mean absolutely—we don't mind getting knocked off once in a while so you can keep your record clear. But you're going to ruin our business."

Humphrey replied, "Well, what's your proposition, Berman?"

Berman said, "25% of the take."

Humphrey answered, "I don't think that's a good deal for me. Let's make it 75-25—my 75 and your 25."

Berman was shocked and cried: "My God, that would break us!"

Jumping to his feet Humphrey announced: "That's exactly right—and that's what's going to happen to you."[22]

Another such story is provided by Evron Kirkpatrick:

> One day I came into his [Humphrey's] office and he said, "Do you see that package?" And I said, "Sure I see the package." "You know what's in it?—Money," he said. "Oh?" I said. He said, "Yes it is. $10,000 cash." And he said, "I want you to take it and give it back to the fellow that sent it to me and tell him not to send me anything more, there is nothing he can buy from me." It was a very typical kind of action.[23]

One of the first law-and-order moves that the Mayor made was to raise the salaries of the entire police force. Another was to make Minneapolis become the first city in the country to take advantage of consultation services on police training and race relations when they were offered by the American Council on Race Relations. Humphrey had Ryan post the order, "We will enforce the law," where every member of the force could see it. The order was enforced. When yet another gangland murder occurred, Humphrey ordered Ryan to track down the offender, who had escaped to California following his conviction, and sent him to his term of life imprisonment. Afterwards, the gangland murders ceased. One night, however, when the mayor was returning home late from a meeting, a shot (or shots—the account varies) rang out in the Humphrey driveway. It was taken by many to be proof of the effectiveness of the Humphrey administration's commitment to "enforce the law."

If his doing so, however, was a sign of his "rightist" tendencies, as Sherrill and Ernst would have it, then another controversy might show how such an interpretation might be lacking in breadth. The Minnesota state labor code of that time forbade the blocking of entrances to buildings during a strike. Yet, in the midst of the 1947 telephone strike Humphrey refused to send in police to break the picketing lines. The Cowles' *Minneapolis Star* reported Humphrey to have said: "We will not use police to break a strike."[24]

Conservative adversaries took advantage of this opportunity to question the mayor's stated determination to enforce the law. Humphrey's answer to this charge was twofold. First, in a response to such an attack by *The Star* he wrote to Cowles that he "didn't send in police because it would have precipitated a police battle."[25] Second, he also claimed that

> the true test of whether the law has been enforced was whether or not service was maintained, whether or not property was destroyed, and whether or not personal injury and violence took place. Our balance sheet shows that in Minneapolis things went pretty well for a dispute of such magnitude. We don't ever recall that a window was broken or a door hinge removed. We have no record of anyone going to the hospital because of injury or of any riot or disturbance which affected the public welfare. Seems like it was handled pretty well.[26]

Such a positive balance was due in good measure to the successful personal intervention made by the mayor himself.

These arguments did not placate many conservative critics. They did, however, at least elicit this one favorable response from a constituent: "[I] am voting other than Republican for the first time in many years."[27]

Even more significant is the case where Humphrey's conscience led him, not to a conflict of whether or not to enforce a law he did not believe in, but rather to *create* a law where there had in fact been none to enforce. This is a reference to Minneapolis's FEPC (Fair Employment Practices Commission) bill.

In an article in *The New Republic* published at that time, Carey McWilliams had labeled Minneapolis as "the capital of anti-Semitism in America." Such a label had shaken the city. As a result, in his first week as mayor Humphrey made a trip to Chicago to study its own proposed "FEP" ordinance. Humphrey was impressed and set out to pass an even stronger bill for Minneapolis. In a 3–2 vote, however, the measure was turned down in city council subcommittee.

Given Minneapolis's weak mayoralty system, Humphrey was forced to resort to the only major strategic weapon at his disposal:

public support. He formed an advisory committee consisting of many of Minneapolis's leading citizens. He named Reuben Youngdahl, pastor of one of America's largest Protestant congregations (the size of which Youngdahl had himself been largely responsible for attaining), and brother of Luther Youngdahl, governor of Minnesota in 1946, to head the Mayor's Committee on Human Relations—a smaller central committee responsible for developing racial policy. It was out of this committee that the well-known "Self-Survey" was initiated.

The idea of the survey was to force a frank appraisal of discriminatory practices by all organizations and institutions within Minneapolis, including all if its churches. The goal was "to assure to all citizens the opportunity for full and equal participation in the affairs of the community" and do so by calling attention to "the destructive character of those forces which sow the seeds of disunity among us, and the undemocratic nature of all discriminatory practices which deny to any group such rights as are plainly intended under the American system to be the rights of everyone." One of the questions listed on its questionnaire was the blunt: "Do you believe in discrimination or not?"[29]

The survey was organized by Dr. Charles S. Johnson of Fisk University and utilized the help of over six hundred volunteers to act as interviewers. Meanwhile, the mayor, as well as Reverend Youngdahl and Bradshaw Mintener, maintained a highly visible publicity campaign.

The self-survey was a tremendous success. Blacks began to be hired in increasing numbers. For the first time black clerks began to appear in area department stores. Housing restrictions on race were deleted from deeds. Race and religion questions were eliminated from application forms. The level of anti-Semitism was clearly lowered. Where resistance was met from certain businessmen and others, Humphrey again employed a soft touch by having Reverend Youngdahl meet personally with them. Youngdahl proved himself to be consistently convincing. Another reason for its effectiveness was the fact that, as Geri Joseph recounted, "it involved so many plain ordinary citizens."[30] Humphrey's appeal, in other words, to the electorate at large had worked. College students, as well as business, labor, and church leaders, were all involved. A year following its 3–2 vote against the first proposed FEPC bill, city council reversed itself and passed the bill. It was the first municipal FEPC law in America. By the fact of its passage Humphrey had proved his ability to mobilize widespread public support from every tier of the social structure in a matter of social conscience. His rather pragmatic choice of building consensus as the means of attaining idealistic ends was also to serve as an example of things to come. As a result, the uninitiated idealist, in this early round, had proved to be effective in both recognizing political realities and in using them to his advantage. The result was, as Joseph stated, impressive: "It [the racial issue] was just completely turned around." It took the "efforts of many in order to ensure its success," she recounted, yet Humphrey himself "really started the ball rolling"[31] and did so without any semblance of a national movement to support him. An article by Sidney Goldish entitled, "We Are Less Hateful Now," appearing in *The American Jewish World*, attested to this change. Cecil Newman, then editor of a black weekly, had cautioned Humphrey in the midst of the struggle to soft-pedal FEPC: "It is not a popular issue," he told Humphrey, and he did not need to push the FEPC just in order to guarantee what little black vote there was. The following night, however, Mayor Humphrey made a stirring appeal on the radio—the kind of appeal that was eventually to ensure its success. The FEPC bill became, as a result, a clear victory for the kind of idealism that Humphrey sought to champion.

There were other more day-to-day ways by which Humphrey made stirring appeals for the sake of his populist-progressive idealism. He accompanied police on their night patrols. He read the comics—Fiorello LaGuardia style—over the radio to Minneapolis's children during a polio epidemic. He went to fires. He saw all visitors. He gave over one thousand speeches. When the members of the all-black Carmen Jones troupe planned to come to Minneapolis to give a performance, they were refused reservations at nearly all of Minneapolis's hotels. The mayor, in response, had the executive secretary of the Human Relations Council call hotels and say simply, "Set aside some rooms for guests of the mayor." Before the "guests" arrived she went to each hotel and handed the manager a copy of the anti-discrimination pamphlet "Outside the

Home." Once the hotel's managers discovered who these "guests" were they are angered and protested bitterly, but the color barrier had been broken.[32]

Word of this kind of thing apparently got out, for at that time an older cop was overheard to say to a younger: "And don't arrest too many negroes, the mayor doesn't like it."[33]

With this kind of personal-populist style Humphrey was able to win over large parts of the community and to effect policy which had either been opposed outright, or at least had originally engendered no apparent popular support.

The results of this winning style were clear: Humphrey was designated "Minneapolis Man of the Year" in 1946. He won the Annual Brotherhood Award from the National Conference of Christians and Jews. Minneapolis itself was designated as "Brotherhood City" by that same organization. The FBI gave Humphrey its top award for effective municipal law enforcement. The Junior Chamber of Commerce named Humphrey "Outstanding Young Man of Minnesota."

All of these awards naturally had telling political effect. In his reelection bid for 1947 Humphrey could count on not only the support of labor, but that of the president of the Chamber of Commerce, vice presidents of General Mills, Pillsbury, and Honeywell, and all of the city newspapers—still more early evidence of his growing commitment to consensus-building as the means for attaining political results. In the June 1947 mayoralty primary, he carried all thirteen wards. In the general election he won by a vote of 102,696 to 52,358. It set a new record for the greatest majority ever in Minneapolis city elections.

While Humphrey's star was clearly on the rise, he was still very much a naive political figure. He had indeed shown an ability, and even a dexterity for taking stock of the political realities that he faced and for dealing with them as he found them. There was one, however, that he was unprepared for. Once he *was* forced to deal with it, however, it would affect him deeply for ever-afterwards, and for some, brand him. It was that of his 1946–48 struggle with the Communists for control of the DFL.

Though the DFL's top political officeholder, and a tremendously successful one, Humphrey had, following his 1945 election, allowed his grip on the DFL to waver. He had begun to send representatives to DFL meetings rather than attend himself. He became too caught up in local municipal affairs to offer any leadership on the state and national, let alone international fronts. He simply dismissed rumors that the left wing was planning a major push.

The first consequences of such laxness was made clear in the 1946 caucuses. Leftists won 120 of the 160 Hennepin County delegate spots for the up-and-coming DFL state convention—and Hennepin County was Humphrey's own district. Humphrey himself was defeated and attained delegate status only when the Hennepin County convention elected him as a delegate at large. Devastating as this was, it was only a portent of worse to come.

At the convention, Humphrey, again as the party's highest officeholder, was expected to deliver the keynote address. Arriving at the convention, however, he was spat upon and subjected to sneers of "fascist" and "warmonger" (a scene that also presaged comparable scenes twenty years later). Humphrey's police chauffeur had to escort Muriel into the convention hall. When Humphrey rose to speak, a sergeant of arms yelled, "Sit down, you son of a bitch, or I'll knock you down."[34] He was never able to finish his speech.

During the war the radical left wing had been allied with the liberals in the so-called "Popular Front." The Popular Front had only become "popular" after invading German troops had breached the Soviet-Nazi Molotov-Ribbentrop nonaggression treaty of 1939. Nevertheless, in Minnesota, Humphrey had looked to the far left as friends, though always from a distance. They could often be, as he said himself, "on the right side of a good issue, even if for the wrong reasons."[35]

Following the war, however, and with the descent of the Iron Curtain, this friendship quickly dissolved. That the American Communist Party was subservient to Moscow's dictates Humphrey had realized for a long time. *How* subservient they were was now driven home with overwhelming clarity in the 1946 convention. It was shortly after the convention incident that Humphrey began to state publicly such things as: "You can be a liberal without being a Communist, and you can be a progressive without being a Communist sympathizer, and we're a liberal progressive party out here.

We're not going to let this left-wing Communist ideology be the prevailing force, because the people of this state won't accept it, and what's more, it's wrong."[36]

With that his resistance to communism became a crusade—another "characteristic" that was to persist and to affect his career profoundly. It was a crusade that was to flower in his association with the just-forming liberal, yet anti-communist ADA—Americans for Democratic Action—and in his determination to oust the communists from the DFL. Having not only witnessed these kinds of communist tactics first hand, but having also been victimized by them, Humphrey believed that he had been given a true picture of communism—one that he would look to for ever-afterwards as the genuine one. This picture was that of a political movement that would cynically, and, if needs be, violently usurp moral causes for its own ends. As such, they could be looked to as a group which might share views similar to liberalism's on certain specific issues, yet, because they would do so, finally, only for their own good and *not* for the good overall, they were never to be trusted. Though more nuanced than the extremist and reflexive anti-communism of the American right, represented in its most blatant form by Joseph McCarthy, among others, it was nonetheless not likely to be nuanced enough: Are therefore, *all* communists for *all* times and in *all* places to be so regarded? Such was certainly the charge from the left that was to haunt, not to say harass him for the rest of his life.

Though soundly beaten, and as was also becoming characteristic style, Humphrey managed to salvage something out of the otherwise hopeless situation in the DFL of 1946. Through Bob Wishart, he was able to keep two lieutenants, Orville Freeman and Eugenie Anderson,* on the executive committee. Through their leverage, and through considerable political struggle,[37] they were able eventually to gain back enough control of the party so that by the 1948 convention Orville Freeman became DFL state chairman, Eugenie Anderson became national committeewoman, and Humphrey himself was nominated as the DFL's candidate for the Senate of the United States.

*Eugenie Anderson was later to become America's first woman ambassador upon her appointment to Denmark. She would also serve as U.S. minister to Bulgaria and as U.S. delegate to the U.N. under President Truman.

In this an irony is to be found. It has to do with the fact that his candidacy was made *possible* by his strenuous and bitter opposition to the radical elements in his own party, yet that same candidacy would then be made *successful* by Humphrey himself now making the most radical move of his political career: his speech to the 1948 Democratic National convention.

Humphrey came in to the '48 convention at a time when the Democratic Party was in trouble. FDR was dead. The long term of his leadership was over. The Great Depression and the Second World War were behind us, and thus the Republicans were intent upon putting his legacy behind us as well. At the time they had good reason for believing that they would be able to do just that.

Harry Truman had generally been regarded as a weak choice for vice president. His ascendance to the White House had resulted only from a fluke of history. The British had recently ousted Churchill in a shocking post war electoral turnabout, and so the Republicans were restless for an equally dramatic turnabout on this side of the Atlantic as well. There was a sense in the air that one long era had passed and that a new and refreshingly different one was about to begin. In other words, they smelled blood.

The Democrats were nearly as convinced of the coming of such a change as were the Republicans. Truman himself enjoyed comparatively little support from the mainstream of the party, and there were major splits on both the left and the right flanks that threatened to erode even that support. Henry Wallace had broken with the party to form his own Progressive Party ticket on the left, and the "Solid South" was making equally threatening gestures on the right in response to pushes for a strong civil rights plank. The Republican candidate, Thomas Dewey, was an attractive and articulate opponent with the legacy of a successful New York governorship behind him—the same legacy that had helped propel Truman's predecessor into the White House. Dewey was poised to recoup his losses from his unsuccessful 1944 bid to occupy that same house, and the party of the New Deal appeared to be about to provide such a vacancy.

The Minnesota delegation came to the Democratic convention committed to one option only: "support anybody but Harry Truman."[38] There were any number of worthy alternatives to be considered. Dwight Eisenhower's party preference was then unknown, but James Roosevelt, as a leader in the ADA, had traveled across the country supporting his [Eisenhower's] nomination to the head of the Democratic ticket. William O. Douglas and Claude Pepper were other popular choices. In Philadelphia the ADA was leading a stop-Truman drive from its headquarters in a rented University of Pennsylvania fraternity house. It was quickly halted, however, when Dwight Eisenhower flatly squashed the nomination surge for him.

As a result, Humphrey began arguing for ADA support for Truman. He was, after all, the incumbent president, and, while no FDR, he had not clearly failed in a position of having been suddenly saddled with the presidency at a time of great historical portent—largely negative support, but support nevertheless.

In the next day or so a consensus throughout the Democratic Party gradually formed behind Truman. As it did attention began to focus on the one remaining decisive (not to say divisive) issue: the civil rights plank.

The New Deal had made gestures toward civil rights, chiefly in Executive Order 8802 (forbidding discrimination in hiring practices in defense industries and calling for the establishment of a federal FEPC), yet they were largely gestures only. No substantial change had taken place despite many pledges to provide it. The truth is that there was little that could have been done legislatively, given the South's control of the Senate and the lack of popular support for such measures.

In 1947 the Civil Rights Commission, which Truman had appointed, gave its report. The report, entitled "We Hold These Truths," urged legislative change in many civil rights areas. Humphrey read the report and wanted a plank reflecting its recommendations. So did most of the ADA contingent. They believed that the Democratic Party was morally committed to such a plank and that it ought to show its political commitment to it by incorporating it into its platform.

That was the idealist rationale for supporting such a plank, but there was pragmatic reason as well. In their earlier convention the Republicans had adopted a civil rights plank of their own. It was a fairly progressive piece for the time and could have easily upstaged the Democrats, should their own plank appear only lukewarm in comparison. Humphrey felt that that was "ideologically absurd and politically stupid," so he "came down hard on the side of a strong civil rights plank, both as a matter of conscience and as an imperative of political pragmatism."[39]

Humphrey was one of 119 members of the convention platform committee for that year. It was not his first national convention, but his was still very much a junior voice. Though "junior," it was nevertheless a voice that was to be heard and heard loudly—loudly enough as to make Scott Lucas of Illinois, the Senate Majority Leader, point to Humphrey amidst the debate and yell: "Who is this pipsqueak who wants to redo FDR's work and deny the wishes of the present President of the United States?"[40] The argument was that what was good enough for FDR's 1944 platform ought to be good enough for the Democratic platform of 1948. This was only a ploy, of course, to cover the concern over splitting an already split party in an already desperate race. Unfortunately for the Democrats, it was an all-too-legitimate concern.

Despite the persistent arguments that both Humphrey and Andrew Biemiller (then a congressman from Wisconsin) presented, the minority plank was voted down by a vote of about 70 to 30. As with the 1946 DFL debacle, however, Humphrey managed to salvage something out of the loss: he sustained the right to present the minority plank to the convention floor.

The minority plank itself, tame by later standards, yet radical enough for 1948, read as follows:

> We call upon Congress to support our president in guaranteeing these basic and fundamental rights:
> 1. the right of full and equal political participation;
> 2. the right to equal opportunity of employment;
> 3. the right of security of person;
> 4. the right of equal treatment in the service and defense of our nation.

Humphrey did not consider himself to be a radical, but he did consider the adoption of a strong civil rights plank to be *right*. Still, there were profoundly weighty reasons for not doing so. As already suggested, it was a foregone conclusion that a major part of the Southern contingent would walk out of the convention if any such plank were to be adopted. Humphrey knew he was only a "pipsqueak." What right did a pipsqueak have to split the already weak and vulnerable Democratic Party and thereby likely doom any chance it may have to pull out the 1948 election? Being responsible for such a disastrous move, in addition, would be disastrous for his own political future. Finally, the plank had little hope of passage at all, so why even bother?

And so, here was the idealist caught between the Scylla of his own principles, and the Charybdis of political realism. What issue, furthermore, could more clearly and pointedly elicit the very principles with which Humphrey was raised, and to which he was committed—principles such as, "All men were created in the image of God"; "In Christ there is neither Jew nor Gentile . . . ye are all one"; and, "Whatever ye do unto the least of these my brethren, ye do unto me also"? In addition, there was also the pledge that Humphrey had made to there being "no compromise" when it came to the political philosophy that "I hold very dear and one that is not subject to change on the matter of basic principle." And yet, in this situation there was manifest political, which is to say, overwhelmingly pragmatic reason *for* "changing" on "the matter of basic principle." Such poignancy was only sharpened by the fact that not only was Humphrey committed to such "principle"—he was also, of course, committed to *acting* on the basis of it, and had, in fact, established a very creditable record of doing so, so far as his career had gone. Yet, acting *now* as his principle dictated clearly meant only disaster for him, for his party, and for the very political future which he looked to as the means of putting his principles to practice. It was, shall it be said, a rather "striking" dilemma to have to face.

Humphrey consulted everyone he knew. At best he got mixed reactions. Lucas told him point blank that "you'll split the party wide open if you do this. You'll kill any chance we have of winning the election in November,"[41] and he was not alone in such sentiment. It was a view shared by, for instance, national party chairman J. Howard McGrath, who told Humphrey: "It will be the end of you."[42] Other figures of comparable stature felt precisely the same way—figures including convention chairman Sam Rayburn, the platform committee chairman Senator Francis Meyers of Pennsylvania, and even Harry Truman himself. These figures were, for

Humphrey, "not Southerners and they were not racists. They were moderates who wanted to keep the party together and elect Harry Truman president. So did I."[43]

The Minnesota delegation encouraged him to take the question to the floor. His labor friends, however, were only able to offer him conflicting advice. It reflected all too well the state of his own mind.

In despair, Humphrey turned to another source of advice, and one that proved to be finally decisive: the head of the South Dakota delegation, Hubert Humphrey, Sr. From this source Humphrey received rather different counsel: "This may tear the party apart, but if you feel strongly, then you've got to go with it. You can't run away from your conscience, son. You've got to go with it."[44] Though expressing concern for his party's future, Hubert Humphrey, Sr. pledged all of South Dakota's eight votes for the minority plank. The son decided to follow his father's advice.

The night before the speech was to be given there was yet another ADA meeting at the rented fraternity house. It ended up going all night—with a decision not being reached until 5:00 A.M. The decision was that a strong plank would be called for but, at Eugenie Anderson's suggestion, one short line was to be added to the report. The line read, "We highly commend President Harry Truman for his courageous stand on the issue of civil rights." Once that was settled Humphrey ended the meeting by announcing: "If there is one thing I believe in in this crazy business, it's civil rights. Regardless of what happens, we're going to do it. Now get the hell out of here and let me write a speech and get some sleep."[45]

Ten hours later Humphrey was sitting on the platform nervously awaiting his turn to speak before the convention on what he knew was now the central issue before the Democratic Party. His large yellow Truman button did not cover his anxiety. He turned to the Bronx's boss, Ed Flynn, for advice. After reading the plank, Flynn's counsel was "You go ahead, young man. We should have done this a long time ago. We've got to do it. Go ahead. We'll back you."[46]

This advice coincided with advice given Andrew Biemiller earlier by another boss: "You kids are dead right. This is the only way we can win the election—by stirring up the minorities and capturing the cities. And besides, I'd also like to kick those Southern bastards in the teeth for what they did to Al Smith in 1928."[47] Flynn promised New York, and said that he would try to bring in both Illinois, through Colonel Jack Arvey, and Pennsylvania, through David Lawrence. At this last moment Humphrey finally felt some solid encouragement.

The Southerners, of course, had been offering something less than encouragement. Richard Russell, the leader of the Southern contingent and acknowledged "Dean" of the Senate, was overheard to say: "Who the hell is that damned fool from Minneapolis who keeps talking about civil rights?" and led a discussion about pressuring convention chairman Rayburn to block Humphrey from giving the speech. In the end, however, they agreed to allow it, doing so on the basis of Russell's argument that "if he wants to make a damned fool of himself, let him."[48]

Many have said it was Humphrey's greatest speech, with the irony there being that it was also to be his shortest. Eisele contends that many believed it to be "the most electrifying convention speech since Bryan's celebrated 'Cross of Gold,'"[49] one that "would be remembered by millions of Americans as one of the most stirring moments of their lives."[50] Others called it "the greatest and most effective speech in politics in this century."[51] Its text reads as follows:

> I realize that I am dealing with a charged issue—with an issue which has been confused by emotionalism on all sides. I realize that there are those here—friends and colleagues of mine, many of them—who feel as deeply as I do about this issue and who are yet in complete disagreement with me.
>
> My respect and admiration for these men and their views was great when I came here.
>
> It is now far greater because of the sincerity, the courtesy and the forthrightness with which they have argued in our discussions.
>
> Because of this very respect—because of my profound belief that we have a challenging task to do here—because good conscience demands it—I feel I must rise at this time to support this report—a report that spells out our democracy, a report that the people will understand and enthusiastically acclaim.
>
> Let me say at the outset that this proposal is made with no single region, no single class, no single racial or religious group in mind.

All regions and all states have shared in the precious heritage of American freedom. All states and all regions have at least some infringements of that freedom—all people, all groups have been the victims of discrimination.

The masterly statement of our keynote speaker, the distinguished United States Senator from Kentucky, Alben Barkley, made that point with great force. Speaking of the founder of our party, Thomas Jefferson, he said:

"He did not proclaim that all white, or black, or red, or yellow men are equal; that all Christian or Jewish men are equal; that all Protestant and Catholic men are equal; that all rich or poor men are equal; that all good or bad men are equal.

What he declared was that all men are equal; and the equality which he proclaimed was equality in the right to enjoy the blessing of free government in which they may participate to which they have given their consent."

We are here as Democrats. But more important, as Americans—and I firmly believe that as men concerned with our country's future, we must specify in our platform the guarantees which I have mentioned.

Yes, this is far more than a party matter. Every citizen has a state in the emergence of the United States as the leader of the free world. That world is being challenged by the world of slavery. For us to play our part effectively, we must be in a morally sound position.

We cannot use a double standard for measuring our own and other people's policies. Our demands for democratic practices in other lands will be no more effective than the guarantees of those practiced in our own country.

We are God-fearing men and women. We place our faith in the brotherhood of man under the fatherhood of God.

I do not believe that there can be any compromise of the guarantees of civil rights which I have mentioned.

In spite of my desire for unanimous agreement on the platform there are some matters which I think must be stated without qualification. There can be no hedging—no watering down.

There are those who say to you—we are rushing this issue of civil rights. I say we are 172 years late.

There are those who say—this issue of civil rights is an infringement on states' rights. The time has arrived for the Democratic Party to get out of the shadow of states' rights and walk forthrightly into the bright sunshine of human rights.

People—human beings—this is the issue of the twentieth century. People—all kinds and sorts of people—look to America for leadership—for help—for guidance.

My friends—my fellow Democrats—I ask you for a calm consideration of our historic opportunity. Let us forget the evil passions, the blindness of the past. In these times of world economic, political, and spiritual—

> above all spiritual, crisis, we cannot—we must not, turn from the path so plainly before us.
>
> That path has already led us through many valleys of the shadow of death. Now is the time to recall those who were left on that path of American freedom.
>
> For all of us here, for the millions who have sent us, for the whole two billion members of the human family—our land is now, more than ever, the last best hope on earth. I know that we can—I know that we shall—begin here the fuller and richer realization of that hope—that promise of a land where all men are free and equal, and each man uses his freedom and equally wisely and well.[52]

Paul Douglas, as a member of the Illinois delegation, watched Humphrey deliver the speech. For Douglas, Humphrey appeared to be "on fire, just like the Bible speaks of Moses. His face was glowing and his sentiments were marvelous."[53] For a black who was not in attendance, but who was able to read the speech afterwards, "Humphrey's civil rights speech was the highlight of the convention. . . . It had a profound effect upon me when I read it in the newspaper the next day. Never had I heard a white politician say so many hopeful and powerful things in so few words."[54] The speech was interrupted many times by applause. When it was finished, the convention erupted into a roaring ovation that had everyone in the hall on their feet. As Griffith relates, the white-haired, professorial Douglas, soon to be elected senator himself, turned to the Illinois delegate chairman, Ed Kelly, and said, "I think we should lead the parade for this." Kelly hesitated for several seconds, glanced over the auditorium of cheering, applauding, standing delegates, and then answered, "Yes." Douglas grabbed the "Illinois standard* and led the delegation into the aisle. California followed Illinois. Wisconsin, New York, New Jersey, Ohio fell into the cheering line. The standards of Massachusetts, Michigan, Indiana, Connecticut, North Dakota, Kansas, West Virginia, Vermont bobbed above the parade."[55]

The ensuing demonstration lasted as long as had the speech. Once it finally died down the vote was taken. The roll was first called on an already proposed States' Rights report. It was overwhelmed in a 925 to 309 vote against. Then the roll was called on

*along with Richard Daley.

the Humphrey-Biemiller report. When it came his turn, Hubert Humphrey, Sr. proudly cast all eight South Dakota votes for it as promised. With Wisconsin's twenty-four votes shortly following them, it went over the top. The final tally was 651½ for, 582½ against. Again, the convention erupted into a tumultuous ovation. The Democratic Party had indeed finally walked into "the bright sunshine."

Yet, speaking of "walking," Strom Thurmond and thirty-five of his associates remained true to their word and walked out of the Democratic Party (and into a teeming downpour). Though their Dixiecrat Party was eventually to garner over one million votes in the November election, (as would Henry Wallace's Progressive Party), Truman would still shock the world by going on to defeat Dewey by more than two million votes.

Many argue that the civil rights plank played a crucial role in that victory. The argument is that the plank became a rallying point for the Democratic Party at a time when it badly needed a "cause." It acted as an injection of new blood. Not only did it embolden minorities to join it as a result, it also gave new life to the intellectuals as well. For Humphrey, of course, it was a tremendous personal triumph—it was his national debut, and one that could not have represented a more resounding success—"success" that would have direct and obvious political ramifications: when he returned home to Minnesota he was met by an enthusiastic crowd (organized by his friend, Freddie Gates) who bore him away on its shoulders from the train station. Quite literally, he had become a national figure overnight. When coupled with yet another characteristically whirlwind campaign (in which he traveled over 31,000 miles, giving 700 speeches), he bowled over Minnesota's senatorial incumbent, Joe Ball, by a vote of 729,494 to 485,801, winning eighty-five out of eighty-seven counties, thus becoming the first Democratic (Farmer-Laborite) senator in Minnesota's history—"idealism triumphant" indeed.

That it was was testified to by the 17 January 1949 cover of *Time*, which depicted a young Hubert Humphrey, newly elected to the United States Senate, with a prairie twister swirling in the background. His radical move at the convention had established a comparably radical reputation for him in the nation's eyes: in the article that followed, Humphrey was singled out as the most radically minded senator of his entire freshman class. Clearly his more conservative side—his commitment to consensus building, even when it meant violating ideological purity, his strong law-and-order stand, etc., had been overshadowed by the sensationalism of his convention triumph. This same article went on to describe him as a "glib, jaunty spellbinder" with "a listen-you-guys approach" who "has the cyclonic attack of an advertising salesman."[56] After so labelling him, however, it also went on to call him "the most articulate spokesman of the Fair Deal among the newcomers," and referred to him as a "hardworking, fast-talking fireball from the Midwest."[57] To the nation, then, in 1949, Hubert Humphrey was a wild-eyed radical—a cyclone just waiting to stir up whatever lay in his path.

Such was the "success" that his radical/idealistic side had provided him. In his own autobiography, Humphrey offered a somewhat more tempered view of it than *Time* had, stating the great lesson of the speech to be that "you *could* stand for a principle in politics and you could move an unwilling party toward a necessary goal."[58] It should be noted, however, that to that he added this rather quixotic qualification: "How slowly and with what difficulty you kept it moving I was yet to learn."[59] While "triumphant," Humphrey's idealism still had to learn how temporary political success could be. Indeed, it was to learn how "triumph" in its name could, ironically enough, in fact be the flip side of "defeat." The "dream," in other words, of Humphrey's idealism, was about to run into the "fact" of political realism.

Notes

1. Evron Kirkpatrick tells the following story in this regard: "I remember Bill Anderson, who was chairman at the time of the department, came and got me one day . . . and said, "Come here a minute. I want to know who that fellow is out [there]"—looking out the window from the first floor above the ground. Humphrey was out on the steps of Hurter Hall and there were, I suppose, twenty-five kids around him and he was letting them have it—arguing with them, answering questions and so on . . . [just as would often be the case while working] in a drugstore over on the other side of the campus." From the Kirkpatrick interview.
2. Humphrey, *Education*, 73.
3. Ibid., 74.

4. Ibid.
5. Ibid., 75.
6. Ibid., 77.
7. Ibid.
8. Ibid.
9. Ibid., 78.
10. Humphrey, as quoted in Edgar Berman, *Hubert* (New York: G. P. Putnam's Sons, 1979), 257.
11. In his autobiography, for instance, Humphrey told of how he had cleaned toilets while working as a janitor, and of how Muriel had sold homemade sandwiches—both in an effort to supplement their meager livelihood.
12. Humphrey, from *Sunshine*.
13. Alan Ryskind, *Hubert: An Unauthorized Biography* (New Rochelle, New York: Arlington House, 1968), 45–46.
14. Ibid., 45.
15. Ibid., 95.
16. Robert Sherrill and Harry W. Ernst, *The Drugstore Liberal* (New York: Grossman Publishers, 1968), 34.
17. Ibid., 29.
18. Solberg, *Humphrey*, 94.
19. Naftalin, from *Sunshine*.
20. Bradshaw Mintener, as quoted in Solberg, *Humphrey*, 102.
21. Joseph interview.
22. Solberg, *Humphrey*, 103.
23. Kirkpatrick interview.
24. Humphrey, as quoted in Ryskind, *Unauthorized*, 90.
25. Humphrey, as quoted in Solberg, *Humphrey*, 105.
26. Hubert Humphrey, press release from the mayor's office, Humphrey Collection, from the mayoralty years.
27. Letter to Hubert Humphrey, 9 May 1947, Humphrey Collection.
28.
29. "Self-Survey" literature, Humphrey Collection.
30. Joseph interview.
31. Ibid.
32. As recounted in Amrine, *This Is Humphrey*, 106.
33. Ibid.
34. As recounted in Solberg, *Humphrey*, 113.
35. Humphrey, *Education*, 104.
36. Ibid., 106.
37. Griffith quotes Humphrey to reveal the kind of struggle it was: "We just outmaneuvered, outworked, and outvoted the Communists. . . . We'd get forty or fifty people together and walk into a local DFL meeting run by the Communists, and just vote the old officers out and our people in. The Communists fought back hard. But if they stayed up until midnight, we stayed up until 3 am. If they issued five press releases, we put out ten. It was tough, and sometimes the fight got dirty. But we were just as tough as the Commies were—and sometimes just as mean." See Griffith, *Candid*, 148–49.
38. Humphrey, *Education*, 110.
39. Ibid., 111.

40. Scott Lucas, as quoted in Griffith, *Candid*, 152.
41. Ibid., 152–53.
42. J. Howard McCrath, as quoted in Richard Parker, *Capitol Hill in Black and White* (New York: Dodd, Mead & Company, 1986), 39.
43. Humphrey, *Education*, 112.
44. Ibid., 113.
45. Eisele, *Almost*, 67.
46. Ed Flynn, as quoted in Humphrey, *Education*, 114.
47. As recounted in Griffith, *Candid*, 154–55.
48. Richard Russell, as quoted in *Black and White*, 40.
49. Eisele, *Almost*, 68.
50. Ibid., 69.
51. Griffith, *Candid*, 156.
52. Text as given in *Education*, 458–59.
53. Paul Douglas, as quoted in Eisele, *Almost*, 68.
54. *Black and White*, 40.
55. As recounted in Griffith, *Candid*, 159.
56. "The Education of a Senator," *Time* (17 January 1949): 13.
57. Ibid.
58. Humphrey, *Education*, 116.
59. Ibid.

Part Two

The Fact

4

Idealism Tempered: "The Most Miserable Period of My Life . . . "

Though by now a victorious veteran of a number of significant political battles, Hubert Humphrey still came to Washington with a wide-eyed, mouth-agape outlook. In his own words, "I arrived in Washington with all the excitement of a kid in a new neighborhood."[1] The excitement, however, was to be short-lived.

Humphrey was shocked, for example, to find the same system of segregation in place in the nation's capitol in the late forties as he had seen in place in Louisiana as a graduate student in the thirties. He no longer had his own driver, and he had to learn the directions of a strange new town on his own. With help from Freddie Gates, he bought a house "for twenty-seven thousand dollars in a typical postwar development."[2] When the movers arrived with all of the Humphrey possessions, however, the senator-elect did not have enough money to pay them, and they refused to unload until he did. Though already in debt to his father for the down payment on the house, he had to call his father again for some additional cash.

By coming to Washington, Humphrey had fulfilled a prophecy made back in 1935. In a letter to Muriel, written from Washington while attending his sister Frances' graduation from George Washington University, he had said,

> Maybe I seem foolish to have such vain hopes and plans, but Bucky, I can see how someday, if you and I just apply ourselves and make up our minds to work for bigger things, how we can someday live here in Washington and probably be in government politics or service. I intend to set my aim at Congress.[3]

The fulfillment of that prophecy was now at hand. What "fulfillment" was to be gained from such a consummation, however, was not immediately clear. Though he had been a successful mayor of the sixteenth largest city in the United States, and had made a national name for himself by his convention triumph, Hubert Humphrey had suddenly become a small fish in a very big pond.

True to *Time*'s depiction of him, Humphrey was soon caught up in a whirlwind of controversy. Shortly after having been sworn in, Humphrey took a black member of his staff, Cyril King (later to become governor of the Virgin Islands), to lunch in the Senate Dining Room. He was stopped at the door by an embarrassed headwaiter, also black. The waitor told him that they could not be served. Humphrey responded angrily and loudly, stating that the color of a senator's guest was no one else's business. He insisted that they both be served immediately, which they were, but only by creating quite a stir. That "stir" became only more aggravated when Humphrey also joined in a demonstration against the then segregated National Theater.

And so, once again color barriers were falling as a result of Humphrey's ability to dramatize the race issue, but this time he was unaware of the fact that there were equally dramatic forces beginning to seek his own fall as a result.

On opening day of what in that year included a special session of Congress, Humphrey had to sit alone in the gallery to watch senior senators introduce their newly elected junior colleagues. One after another the freshman class was acknowledged before their senior associates. Minnesota's Ed Thye, however, ignored Humphrey completely, as did nearly everyone else.*

Because of the special session, outgoing senators were still using their offices. Newly elected senators awaiting their designated of-

*Except—of all people—Lister Hill of Alabama, who apparently went up to Humphrey and eventually brought him down to the floor.

fices were provided with temporary space somewhere on the Hill. Humphrey, however, of all the newly elected senators, was forced to find a space downtown, and was able to do so only through the gracious effort of an attorney who had worked for Harry Truman, Paul Porter.

Without realizing it, Humphrey's idealistic, yet nonetheless "radical," stand on the very sensitive topic of civil rights had generated tremendous bitterness beyond anything that he had expected. As he said, "I was prepared for the normal political opposition you could expect to encounter. But I was unprepared for what seemed to be a hostile personal reaction."[4] For someone who depended tremendously on, and believed so firmly in personal regard, no matter what the ideological difference, this was a tremendous blow.

Such incidents might have been written off as coincidence. The fact that they were not was confirmed soon enough. When leaving the Senate chamber one day, Humphrey strode past a contingent of Southern senators. They ignored him in passing, but, while still within earshot, Humphrey himself overheard Richard Russell, in an ominous repetition of the '48 Convention, state unmistakably, "Can you imagine the people of Minnesota sending that damn fool down here to represent them?"[5]

Humphrey was stung. He knew that he had taken a decisive stand on a highly charged and controversial issue, but he had fully believed—beyond the rightness of the cause—that a firm distinction between professional and personal regard would have been maintained. He had fully expected that he would at least be respected personally, even if professional differences existed between himself and other colleagues. What was worse, however, was that he simply wanted to be and needed to be well *liked*. Being singled out as the sole target of a universal freeze from the day he arrived was a shocking blow that he was not prepared for. Satirical letters, editorials, and cartoons soon followed, only making his outlook all the more bleak.

Humphrey had arrived in Washington after an exhilarating campaign in which he had buried the incumbent, and thereby more than fulfilled a dream of a lifetime. Yet here he was being greeted with nothing but scorn. It was not the kind of reception that he had expected. As a result, this became a gloomy time for someone unaccustomed to gloominess. The grimness of his frustration with this dilemma was revealed in his own assessment of the period: "My principles offended, my personality enraged, I wasn't going to change one and I didn't know how to change the other."[6]

There was, at least, one break in the clouds. Amidst a courtesy call to the White House, President Truman told Humphrey: "Senator, if there's ever anything I can do for you, will you let me know?"[7] Some time afterwards, Humphrey's parents came to town for a visit and Humphrey decided to take the president up on his offer. He asked to have his parents invited to the White House for a chance to meet with the chief executive. The response was that of genuine executive graciousness. Not only did President Truman agree to meet the Humphreys, he even gave them a personal tour of the White House. He talked about the 1948 campaign and the current Potsdam Conference. He also talked about Stalin and what difficulty he was having convincing him that America's intentions were honorable. He predicted that Russia would be the next trouble spot in the world and that therefore we would have to be strong and willing to face up to them. He finished by predicting that Hubert Humphrey, Jr. would prove to be a great senator, and then, finally, how being senator was to hold the greatest office in the land: the White House was only a prison in which you were cut off from the people.

Getting back into their car, the Humphreys glowed, not only with pride in their son, but with affection for Harry Truman as well. He had provided a balmy respite from an otherwise frosty season. Such respite, however, was to be only a brief thaw.

In 1949 Senator Harry Byrd was at the height of his career. The Byrd machine had run Virginia politics for a quarter of a century. In Humphrey's words, "there were two kinds of candidates in Virginia during this time: the Byrd candidates and the losers."[8] Byrd was a leader among the southern conservative Democrats. A constant critic of FDR, he had himself been considered as a possible presidential candidate. Among other things, he was chairman of the Joint Committee on Reduction of Non-Essential Federal Expenditures. From the liberal viewpoint, the amount of nonessential expenditures that this committee had eliminated was comparatively low to the number of jobs it had provided for Byrd friends and relations. Humphrey was convinced that the committee itself was the most nonessential expenditure of federal funds that he could think of. Prompted by liberal colleagues and advisers, he chose to make his conviction public by attacking its head in an ill-advised and ill-prepared speech on the Senate floor.

The Senate, certainly in the 1940s, was a parliamentary body built on tradition. There was a dignity and a sense of decorum which was insisted upon—largely by the southern Democrats who had run it more or less ever since the end of Reconstruction. Part of that tradition included the respect due the senior senators by their juniors. In 1949, Hubert Humphrey was not only "junior"—he was a freshman senator. Freshman senators, much like children, spoke only when spoken to. Furthermore, a personal attack by one senator on another was something that was simply not done. Coming from a freshman senator, it was unthinkable. Coming from a freshman like Humphrey, already blackballed by the "Club," and being levelled on one of the dons of that body, it was an unmitigated disaster.

As if it were possible, Humphrey in fact made the matter worse by rising to deliver his attack when Byrd was absent from the Senate chamber (although Amrine claims that Humphrey had at least observed the courtesy of notifying Byrd of his intentions beforehand). The reason for Byrd's absence: to visit his seriously ailing mother in Virginia.

Humphrey forever afterward acknowledged that it was the worst mistake of his Senate career. He was given little chance to make any other consideration. In the day following Humphrey's attack, one senator after another, Republican and Democrat alike, rose in a seemingly endless succession to denounce the junior senator from Minnesota, and to praise their good and trusted friend, the senior senator from Virginia. It was an utter humiliation which Humphrey was forced to endure for four and a half hours. His feeble attempts to speak on his own behalf were hammered down by the pounding gavel. Paul Douglas maintained a silent vigil throughout the ordeal, and Millard Tydings of Maryland rose to offer a consoling speech, but that was the extent of the sympathy that Humphrey was to receive that day, and for many more days to come. On his way out of the chamber, once there was "no one left to heap scorn on me,"[9] Humphrey ran into Byrd at the elevator. He extended his hand and said to the unsmiling Virginia patriarch, "Senator, I know when I've been licked."[10]

The Byrd incident was both a cruel and a crucial lesson for Humphrey. It was a terrible mistake, and one that made the "most miserable period of my life"[11] even more miserable. Yet, as has already been indicated, one of the ways that Humphrey was to prove his distinctiveness was by his ability to turn his contemporary losses into future gains. He was vital enough to learn from his mistakes and to, often enough, actually turn them into eventual assets.

The lesson that he was to learn from this particular mistake was twofold: always make sure you have your facts straight, and, even more importantly, recognize and acknowledge the political power of tact. He had received, in other words, a great lesson in protocol, in this case in the necessity of heeding tradition and rules of procedure, and most importantly, that "in the senate it is not as important what a man says as how he says it."[12] For the midwestern "twister," this was quite a lesson indeed. "Protocol" is hardly a radical "virtue," yet it is for any political figure who wishes, over the long haul, to get things *done*, not to mention be *liked*, as Humphrey very much wished on both counts. Thus, in one brief, yet extremely poignant incident, the "radical" had recognized the need to go from twister—something that is sensational and dramatic, yet short lived—to something more steady and lasting, not to say productive—like a trade wind.

In the aftermath of the Byrd debacle Humphrey's response was characteristic: "work became my escape. I set out to know more about more things than other senators. If I couldn't get their affection, I might get their respect."[13] In his isolation, not to say his misery, the idealist settled down to prove himself to his realist adversaries.

At first he had little luck. Congress stopped the Missouri Valley Authority project which Humphrey had argued for in his maiden Senate speech. Southern Democrats, including former Dixiecrat Strom Thurmond, voted down a ruling proposed by Vice President Barkley by which each newly convened Senate would be given the power to make its own rules. The target in this had been the infamous Senate Rule 22 – the so-called filibuster rule. In a Democratic caucus convened by Majority Leader Lucas, Humphrey rose to challenge the Southern opposition to the ruling. It was to no avail. The ruling was voted down forty-five to forty-one. After such a bright start, civil rights was dead in the waters of the 81st Congress.

Switching to other causes, Humphrey attempted to take on "Mr. Republican" himself, Robert Taft, in hearings held by the Labor and Welfare Committee on the Taft-Hartley bill. Humphrey had, in his Senate race, run on the promise to have the Taft-Hartley bill repealed. He saw the hearings as an opportunity to challenge the main force behind it. His inability to do so was demonstrated in Solberg's account of the encounter:

> It was Taft's style to draw from the parade of witnesses approving words for one specific proviso or another of his law, thereby building up a body of assent to a measure that none might have accepted individually. Humphrey, arriving late one day, broke in to cry foul. "That's not the right way to go at it," he said. To this, Taft retorted, "Do I understand that if you do seven just things, each one right in its field, then as a result all of them may not be just?" As pencils scribbled furiously at the press table, Humphrey spluttered: "Wait a minute. I don't think we should permit inferences such as this to be drawn." Then when Humphrey defended union practices that had been outlawed by Taft-Hartley, Taft caught him up on his facts. Stung, Humphrey began to ask why, if Taft-Hartley required union officials to sign affidavits that they were not Communists, corporation officers should not be asked to do the same. As reporters, startled at the notion of capitalists swearing they were not Communists, looked up from their notes, Humphrey exclaimed: "I don't want to make this look absurd" and, reddening, let his question drop.[14]

The March issue of *The Nation*, a magazine which had initially praised Humphrey upon his entrance into the Senate, now wrote that the Senator "who first loomed as a dominant figure in the civil rights group appeared after three weeks as a moderate-sized man with an unfortunately self-righteous style of speaking."[15]

One day Humphrey was at least given an opportunity to show the more sparkling – and not so self-righteous – side of his personality. The ADA, in a leaflet it had published at that time, was offering summer trips for young people to study the English form of government, then under Labour leadership. Conservatives saw this as an opportunity to expose the more radical side of the ADA itself and, in so doing, addle its then-current chairman, Hubert Humphrey. In a heated debate about the correctness of the ADA position, Styles Bridges of New Hampshire attacked the ADA by asking Humphrey repeatedly what was so unique about the British form of government that made it worth the ADA's study program. Bridges referred to free speech, free press, free assembly, and so on, regularly jabbing that "we have all these freedoms in this country, have we not?," to which Humphrey could only answer affirmatively. After a series of such taunts, Bridges moved in for the coup de grace by ending with the query of, "What have the British got that we haven't got?" Humphrey's unhesitating rejoinder was, "Westminster Abby."[16] The gallery broke into approving applause. Embarrassed smiles shot through the Senate chamber, the gavel pounded, and Bridges, clearly bettered, was forced to relent. The incident raised eyebrows on the opposition side.

Humphrey was determined not to rely simply on wit, however, to gain the respect of the Senate leadership. One day he delivered a four-hour, thoroughly researched speech in which he defended his proposed bill to repeal Taft-Hartley. Taft himself appeared impressed by it, but it was to no avail. It was defeated, as were the fifty-seven other proposals that he supported that year. Instead of being defeated himself, however, Humphrey became more determined than ever. He began looking for a new issue by which he could prove his mettle.

The 1951 tax bill had come to the Senate Finance Committee from the House. The committee was controlled by Eugene Milliken of Colorado and Walter George of Georgia, the latter acting as chairman. Both were experts on tax law, and George in particular was a highly esteemed member of the "Club." They expected no serious opposition to their bill despite its many loopholes and clear advantages for those favored by the conservative leadership.

In characteristic style, Humphrey decided to take up the challenge. He believed that there were simply too many loopholes, and that the bill, therefore, ought to be at least debated. To all involved it seemed like yet another hopeless and thankless uphill prospect. Paul Douglas and Humphrey—both freshmen senators—would have to go it alone against the formidable veteran leadership of

Milliken and George. The latter two had been in control of the Finance Committee for so long that no one seriously questioned their judgment any longer. Furthermore, while Paul Douglas was a trained economist, Humphrey had comparatively little economic expertise. Since Douglas had been badly wounded in the Second World War, however, he would not have the physical stamina necessary to support Humphrey day in and day out. Humphrey would be largely on his own. He was, given the circumstances, hardly the obvious choice for one likely to succeed in altering the U.S. tax code in 1950.

Nevertheless he went to work. He began to study the intricacies of the American tax system. He consulted with his friend Walter Heller,* formerly both a University of Minnesota professor and a Treasury aide. They gathered together a team of advisers, including Joseph Pechman and Al Oberdorfer, from the Treasury and Justice departments respectively. Study sessions went on to two and three in the morning every night. The sessions were intensive and the material difficult. Though skeptical at first, however, Humphrey's tutors were quickly amazed at how easily their pupil absorbed the arcana of tax law.

Once the debate was enjoined, it lasted nearly a week. Humphrey maintained a constant and painstaking hammering of every item on the proposed bill. Douglas would interrupt regularly to relieve and/or assist Humphrey. During one stage, Humphrey held the floor for most of two straight days. The entire senate watched. Despite Milliken and George's attempts either to trip him up, or simply to bait him, he maintained his sense of humor and dignity throughout. Together, Humphrey and Douglas made it clear that for once there were liberals who were to be reckoned with, and on the conservative's own home court.

By the end of the week only one of the twenty-seven proposed Humphrey-Douglas amendments had passed. Yet, once again, there was a significant victory to emerge from amongst the ashes. When it was finally over, both Milliken and George, to the astonishment of all, walked over and offered congratulations to their

*Later to become President Kennedy's chief economic adviser on Humphrey's recommendation.

liberal antagonists, complete with bear hugs. As Solberg said, "They chaffed and joked with him [Humphrey]. They admitted him to their friendship." Solberg's conclusion as a result was the following: "That performance *made* Humphrey in the Senate."[17]

It was quite true, as were Humphrey's following words: "In the single debate, I proved that I wasn't just talkative, just another emotional liberal, but rather, a student of government, willing to work, state my case, debate, call for a vote, and accept the decision."[18] He was from now on determined never to "enter a debate on any bill without being prepared to debate in detail."[19] It was a lesson that, within one week, had gained him the respect of the entire Senate, where only a week before he had been the outcast, taunted and targeted for nothing but derision. It marked a crucial, perhaps the most crucial turning point in his career. As Bill Moyers said, "Humphrey . . . learned that the Senate was an institution and not an arena."[20] The text of Humphrey's week-long challenge was printed in a booklet that ran to forty-eight pages. Unions bought and distributed 500,000 copies. Humphrey's senate career (including his career-long struggle against tax loopholes) had begun.

Beyond the lesson of never talking without actually having something to say, this period taught Humphrey another lesson as well:

> that as long as you treated other Senators as honest men, sincere in their convictions, that you could usually gain the tolerance, if not affection, of even those who disagreed strongly with you.
>
> That code of behavior makes sense. Where widely disparate positions confront one another, where opposing ideologies meet head on, rules that are designed to curb emotions and establish rational discussions are important. You do not question motives or attack the character of another or the state from which he comes. You keep your word. You do not embarrass a man through trickery or double cross. Sometimes, when the issue is important and you feel deeply about what you are doing, it is tough to abide by that code. Your opponent appears stupid or intellectually dishonest, your anger rises, and you want to flail out. Very likely, your opponent is not stupid, and believes what he is saying, too. It is imperative to understand that.[21]

To put it another way, Humphrey had learned that "success in the United States Senate comes most readily to those who are able to get along with people of different philosophies, from different walks of life."[22] In other words, Hubert Humphrey had become a parliamentarian—he had gained an appreciable degree of the kind of maturity expected, not just of a politician, but of a political leader. This was to come a very long way from simply proving that one could generate large and enthusiastic audiences, whether in front of a garage on Minneapolis's Plymouth Avenue, or even at the Democratic National Convention. More significantly, he had come to see that conviction alone, no matter how idealistic, will not guarantee worthwhile results. The prairie populist who was raised to believe in the importance of "not the creed, but the deed" had grown to the point where he could now in fact begin to accomplish such deeds, and not just where they affected the livelihood of the citizens of Minneapolis, but of the entire United States—and with that, perhaps the world at large. Thus, Humphrey was beginning to mature sufficiently as to begin to be able to effect those ideals which had been instilled in him in that drugstore on Main Street—to begin to "do his part," which was to put to effective political use the egalitarianism and the sense of fair play that he had gained while growing up in the midwest. He had traversed the 1,342 miles that separated Doland and Washington, not just in the physical sense, but now in the symbolic sense as well.

The full sign of this was encapsulated in as telling and as significant a sentence as any that he wrote in his autobiography: "Compromise is not a dirty word."[23] What he had come to see in those first few years of national political experience was that by simply relying on and appealing to those who agree with you entirely you will always lead a minority, but only to defeat. He saw that success in politics in a democracy consisted not only in having a particular well-defined ideological view, but at the same time in being able and willing to offer common objectives to others who might not necessarily share that view. (There are those who argue that such a lesson was one lost to the Democratic Party in the years following Humphrey's death.) In a nation like the United States, this is simply common sense. In a governing body such as the United States Senate, it is indispensable. For Humphrey, the key to being able to do that successfully was the ability and willingness to make the effort to foster courteous, if not actually warm relationships with your opponents. Ultimately, of course, this meant being willing to compromise, and thus the relevance of Humphrey's words. Humphrey believed in the rightness of compromise for the same twofold reason that he believed in the rightness of most things: it was decent, but it also worked. It was decent because, in a democratic society consisting of diverse groups, compromise was the only way that even a rough sort of equality of representation would ever be achieved. It was also decent in that "to make losing a habit in the name of moral principle or liberal convictions is to fail to govern and to demonstrate the incapacity to persuade and convince and to develop a majority."[24] That it was at the same time pragmatic, of course, was obvious. That it was therefore easy, however, was not.

There will be times in a legislative struggle when, by winning a battle, you may lose the possibility of winning a particular "war." Compromise, in addition, can oftentimes become a rationalization for either not being willing or simply not being able to see legislation through the entire cameral process successfully. It can also all too easily become the refuge for those who "believe in little or nothing," for "those who live solely by political expediency," or for those who "have arrived at a point of political power without any visible amount of political commitment."[25] Such people were, for Humphrey, as much of a threat to the democratic process as were the extremists of either side who were ideologically bound to their own point of view without being willing to consider, let alone be considerate of any opposing view. It is interesting, not to say ironic, to note that in the course of his political career, Humphrey would be accused of *both* failings: of both being an ideologue and of "selling out" his ideology.

In between such extremes, however, there is a more balanced position. It is the position that seeks the following legislative course. First,

> your goal must be clear, not fuzzy; you must prepare your arguments carefully, lining up the natural advocates as best you can both inside and outside the Senate. And then, after fighting as hard for it as you can—in the subcommittee, committee, on the floor, and in conference—you had better know precisely where you are willing to compromise. You can end up with nothing two ways: by being so rigid that the entire legislation is lost, or so flexible that your opponents gut the bill. But strong and sensible arguments, together with

a responsible compromise, prepare the way for a later effort. It is better to gain a foot than to stand still, even when you seek to gain a mile.[26]

Here, in a few choice sentences, was the Humphrey formula for success in legislation. It was, in other words, politics as "the art of compromise" according to HHH. It combined hard work and parliamentary prowess with personal conviction and a willingness to show genuine regard for others. It was, in many respects, a combination of common sense, experience, and a commitment to maintaining respect for one's opponents—all as a very realistic assessment of what was necessary to achieve idealistic goals.

Such an outlook not only allowed for compromise—it embraced it. As a result the worst criticism Humphrey felt he was forced to endure throughout his political career tended to come not from the right, but from the left. For Humphrey, "in a democratic society and in a parliamentary body in which the majorities are constantly fluctuating, it is literally impossible for any one senator or small group of senators to get exactly what they want to in exactly the form they want it."[27] This was not a partisan point of view. This was fact. It was certainly accepted—and asserted—by Humphrey to be so. Because he believed it to be so, and because he operated on the basis of it, he was regularly forced to experience "the wrath of the intellectual liberal who can see only utopia now, and is unwilling to create an approximation of utopia by slowly building it brick by brick." For Humphrey, such wrath was "something unbounded,"[28] as he would learn much more painfully later on. In fact it was precisely such "unbounded" attack by those whom he had regarded as his friends that hurt him the most in his life—more than any other personal affront he was forced to suffer in politics.

True to form, however, he nevertheless argued for a "necessary and vital place" for it. The "secular theologians," the "purists" who would "create the heavenly city on earth by fiat" were necessary because "without them demanding more than humankind can deliver, those of us who feel that pragmatism is the better method might slide into self-serving rationalizing."[29] Therefore, while "irritating," they remain nonetheless "indispensable" by "creating the tension and the goals that are necessary for any legislative achievements."[30] Such was the extent of Humphrey's belief in balance—in seriously and sincerely taking into account *both* sides—as a political mainstay.

Though initially a champion of "radical" causes, then, (civil rights was a radical cause in the thirties, forties, fifties, and sixties in America though Humphrey himself never believed that it ought to be) Hubert Humphrey was now considered to be a member of "the pragmatists." The radical caste of the 17 January 1949 *Time* cover had, in other words, become inappropriate. One explanation for this—the one that came from "the purists"—was that he "changed," by which was meant he failed to maintain his moral resolve. This was a real possibility, but before it is accepted as conclusive, an alternative consideration might also be made. That is that rather than Humphrey changing essentially or substantively in terms of the things he believed in, it was simply instead that one of the things that he *did* believe in was that reform is to be effected from *within* the system, not from without. To put it another way, it was that one of his principles was to be an *institutionalist*. Furthermore, he also recognized and accepted the fact that doing so meant that change would take time—would be achieved only in *increments*. Thus, in addition to being an institutionalist, he was also an *incrementalist*. For him this was precisely what ought to and did in fact demarcate liberalism, as he saw it, from radicalism.

It can certainly be said that Hubert Humphrey criticized the system and worked for its change. What Humphrey understood by "the system," however, was the societal structure built on America's foundational principles—the way in which those principles were *practiced*. It was never those principles themselves. In fact, it was often on the *basis* of those very principles, he argued, that his reforms were proposed. Social change, for Humphrey, essentially meant "reform"—but reform effected *within* the bounds and by the rules already established. A radical, in his view, did not accept the rules, and therefore refused to honor them. Humphrey had every intention of honoring them, even if he disagreed with a practice that they sometimes ensured.

Thus Humphrey could and would take a position on a particular issue that at the time might not have been popular. Yet over years of effort—effort which often enough included real sacrifice—he would gradually work to build a consensus behind it. Though it might take decades, the bill, often enough, would eventually come to be adopted.

The key was "consensus." It was the only way, Humphrey believed, that rightful, and therefore lasting political change could truly be effected in a democracy. The later Humphrey was criticized many times for changing—for "selling out" his views for the sake of political expediency. The question is, what is meant by "rightful change"? Was it "right" simply because the change itself was right, or did the means of effecting it also have to do with its "rightness"? For Humphrey, there was little question in this. In a democracy, democratic means should be used to accomplish democratic ends. That meant that in order for those ends to be achieved, there must be those who were masters at the means. Thus, for Humphrey, being a liberal and being a consummate politician at the same time was not only possible—it was the *ideal*. Once he became convinced of that he directed the force of his considerable abilities and convictions towards achieving it. As is made clear in the next chapter, his holding, and eventually achieving such an "ideal" was to have "real" effect.

Notes

1. Humphrey, *Education*, 122.
2. Ibid., 123.
3. Ibid., 53.
4. Ibid., 124.
5. Ibid.
6. Ibid., 125.
7. Harry Truman, as quoted in ibid.
8. Humphrey, ibid., 129.
9. Ibid., 130.
10. Ibid.
11. Humphrey, as quoted in Griffith, *Candid*, 196.
12. Ibid., 194.
13. Humphrey, *Education*, 147.
14. Solberg, *Humphrey*, 138.
15. Thomas Sancton, "The Great Debate," *The Nation* (26 March 1949): 351.
16. Humphrey, *Congressional Record*, 81st Cong., 1st sess., 1949. Vol. 95, 4048. Cohen provides another example of Humphrey's ability to use wit to turn potential political liabilities into political assets instead. It involves a story told by Robert Forsythe which goes as follows: "I remember one campaign where someone got the bright idea that they were going to charge Humphrey with being one of the founders of the ADA—the Americans for Democratic

Action. At that time the argument that it was wrong to be associated with it may have been considered somewhat persuasive. Well, the charge came out just prior to Turkey Day down at Worthington, and Humphrey was very big at Turkey Day. He got on the platform, and you know, he never tried to hide the charges against him. He just took that newspaper up on stage with him and he waved it around, and he said, 'Now look what they're charging me with. They say here that I am a member of and a founder of the ADA. I just want you good people to know that I am a founder of the ADA, and I am proud of my membership in the American Dairy Association.' Well, that was the last anyone heard of that charge." Robert Forsythe, as quoted in Cohen, *Undefeated*, 230.

17. Solberg, *Humphrey*, 147.
18. Humphrey, *Education*, 150.
19. Ibid.
20. Moyers interview.
21. Humphrey, *Education*, 150–51.
22. Ibid., 136.
23. Ibid.
24. Ibid., 137.
25. Ibid.
26. Ibid.
27. Ibid., 138.
28. Ibid.
29. Ibid.
30. Ibid.

5

Idealism Applied: The Civil Rights Act of 1964

In his thirty years of seeking his "dream" Hubert Humphrey did direct the force of his considerable abilities and convictions towards a myriad of causes. Centermost among all of them, however, was civil rights. It was the one thing above all else for which he wished to be remembered. As such it may well have been the greatest wish he ever had to come true.

What is certainly true is that amidst the many achievements in civil rights for which Humphrey is remembered, one similarly stands centermost: the Civil Rights Act of 1964. In his autobiography Humphrey declared it to be "the major legislative achievement of my Senate career."[1] Many considered it to be the major achievement of his entire lifetime. While there are many Humphrey achievements deserving of in-depth attention—achievements such as Food for Peace, the Arms Control and Disarmament Agency, the Peace Corps, the 1963 Test-Ban Treaty, Medicare—his role in passage of the Civil Rights Act of 1964 best exemplifies the qualities that Humphrey successfully combined to pass landmark legislation. The story of its passage is remarkable, not only for the complexity of effort that was required for its enactment, but for the drama, both individual and national, that it encompassed. It was to be Hubert Humphrey's finest hour.

In its 13 April 1964 issue, *Newsweek* described Humphrey as being "a sixteen-year-old senator who had outgrown his image to become his party's majority whip, a member of that mystical body called the Senate 'Club,' and one of the most influential men in the U.S. Congress."[2] That "image" was, of course, the one portrayed on the "whirlwind" *Time* cover of over fifteen years ago. Evidently the fact of his having matured into a parliamentarian—beyond simply being a polemicist—had become nationally acknowledged. The effect of his committing himself toward working for consensus had come to be fully felt by the national media. *Newsweek*, in the same April article, described Humphrey's "apostolic liberal fires" as being "banked though still burning," and discussed how his "New Deal rhetoric" was now threaded with "aphorisms about the courage to be a moderate" and "to be a half-loaf pragmatist instead of an all-or-nothing martyr." It noted that Humphrey had "discovered not only the means of power but the manners that Senate etiquette demands of those who use it."[3]

Such a discovery had evidently been rather widely noticed, as was denoted by *Business Week*'s 1 June 1963 article, "Firebrand Senator Cools Down." In that article, Humphrey was described as being "a changed man." The reason for this "change" was in part ascribed to his new responsibility as majority whip, but it was also in part ascribed to "a sharp change in approach, a new way of getting things done."[4] The process begun with the 1951 tax bill debate had clearly come to some appreciable degree of fruition.

Humphrey *had* grown a great deal. After the breakthrough of the 1951 tax bill, Russell Long, whom Humphrey had met back at LSU, began inviting Humphrey to an occasional lunch in the privacy of the "Senators Only" dining room. These were not simply courtesy calls—Humphrey was being invited to dine with the "Bourbon Circle"—he was being ushered into the Senate sanctum sanctorum, *The* Club within "The Club." As a result, Humphrey began to meet with the Senate's patriarchs, including John McClellan, James Eastland, John Stennis, Lister Hill, and most importantly, Richard Russell.[5] Lyndon Johnson would also be present on occasion.

These informal social gatherings provided the opportunities by which Humphrey was able to prove himself on a personal level to the Senate establishment. As a result of them, coupled with his success in the 1951 tax bill debate, the freeze on Humphrey gradually began to thaw.

One sure sign of this change of "season" was the friendship that developed between Humphrey and Walter George. They became close enough, for example, so as to engage in this brief but personal Senatorial postal exchange:

February 6, 1953

Dear Walter,

As you know, I was down with the flu and out of the city last week. Had I been here on the job, I surely would have wished you a Happy Birthday. Please accept this belated note of congratulations and good wishes.

I know you must have a great sense of satisfaction when you look back over the many years of service you have given to our country. As one of the younger members of the Senate, I just want you to know I am honored by your friendship and feel privileged to be able to serve with you.

My best wishes for your continued health, success and happiness.

Sincerely yours,

Hubert Humphrey[6]

February 9, 1953

Dear Hubert:

Thank you for your note of February 6. I am sorry that you have had the flu but am glad to see that you are up and looking equal to the job ahead.

I appreciate your statement regarding our service in the Senate. It isn't a question of agreeing on all problems: it's a question of being honest with one another and the striving toward a common end.

With best regards, I am

Sincerely yours,

Walter George[7]

Max Kampelman relates a humorous, yet telling story to this same effect:

I remember years and years ago I was working for him [Humphrey] and inadvertently I find myself in the Senate Democratic cloakroom which is behind the Senate—where phones are present and Senators can do their work. It was late at night—[and] Walter George . . . was talking in his deep voice. I wasn't paying much attention, but it grew on me as I was on the phone that they were talking about Hubert. And I remember George saying, "You know

> that guy Hubert (pronounced, "Hoobert")? That fellow Hubert, Hubert Humphrey? Well, he really *believes* this civil rights stuff!"
>
> Now these Southerners . . . couldn't believe that anybody would believe this. They thought it was political. They thought that the Northerners were doing this for political reasons . . .
>
> We tend to feel Southerners at that time [saw only the worst kind of motivation in Civil Rights legislation]. Today the situation has changed—and this is what Hubert conveyed. He conveyed genuineness—and this was only one of a number of instances where George helped Humphrey.[8]

Another was where George actually came to Minnesota to stump for Humphrey's reelection bid in 1954—a very far cry from the situation that had existed just a few years beforehand.

Humphrey had indeed gained the respect (and often enough the friendship) of many senators. If nothing else this was at least the result of his coming to be acknowledged as one of the most productive senators on the Hill. By 1960 alone he had sponsored 1,044 bills and joint resolutions. By the time of the debate on the '64 bill he had either authored or been principally responsible for the major legislative achievements already mentioned—Food for Peace, the 1963 Test-Ban Treaty, the Peace Corps, and the Arms Control and Disarmament Agency. Eleanor Roosevelt had described him as having "the spark of greatness." That greatness had resulted in Humphrey's being considered as a vice-presidential running mate by Adlai Stevenson in 1956, and in 1960 it saw him run, however unsuccessfully, for the presidential nomination against Jack Kennedy. He had met with Nikita Khruschev in a private and unprecedented eight and one-half hour personal interview, resulting in a front page photograph and lead article in *Life*. With Lyndon Johnson he had overseen the passage of the 1957 Civil Rights Bill, which, though weak, still represented the first civil rights legislation to pass Congress since 1875. He still clearly felt the tap of his father's finger when the latter had averred: "Activity!"

As part of his education of that time Humphrey had placed himself under the tutelage of such political sages as Carl Hayden, Sam Rayburn and Alben Barkley. In Hayden's case Humphrey had acted on a tip he had received from Harry Truman. When Humphrey had asked Truman for advice on how to conduct himself in the Senate, Truman's response had been, "The man to watch and the man to pattern your Senate career after is Carl Hayden."[9] Humphrey accepted the president's advice and made Hayden his mentor as a result. Humphrey thus began to learn about the power of the Appropriations Committee which Hayden headed. He also began to see the importance of striking a balance between the demands of regionalism and those of nationalism. Most important of all though, he began to learn how the Senate operated. He saw how Hayden, as head of the Appropriations Committee, "was in a position to permit funding of other senator's projects and to tacitly receive their support for votes he wanted. There was no crass quid pro quo, but a gentleman's agreement."[10] He came, in other words, to see the sense of Sam Rayburn's famous aphorism: "You have to go along to get along." In his own words,

> The sense of the "Club," which offended me in principle and whose rules I violated when I felt it necessary, nevertheless demanded forms of behavior that permitted the Senate to be a legislative body and not simply a debating society. The Senate was, after all, a body of people, not philosopher kings, and it had certain rules and traditions.[11]

Sam Rayburn, as another of Humphrey's tutors, showed Humphrey a congressional format that was not formally recognized, yet was as crucial to the passage of every piece of legislation as any other. After the day's session, Rayburn would host what he would call a "Board of Education" meeting in his office. Once the honored guests were gathered, Rayburn, with mock dignity, would announce, "It's time to strike a blow for liberty!" This was the signal to break out the bourbon.

Such a scene smacks of the image of the smoke-filled room. For Humphrey, however, there was nothing dubious involved:

> over a drink or two in a relaxed atmosphere, serious talk of national import took place. Many debates on the floor had less relevance than most of those afternoon sessions. It was there that strategy was planned, compromises worked out, decisions made.[12]

These "Board of Education" meetings were, for Humphrey, an important and even gracious way for political business to be done. Rayburn never let the ambience of such meetings slip into one of rancor, nor did he allow them to become occasions for petty partisan scheming. He consistently maintained a level of dignity that all respected. Humphrey would later observe Rayburn at White House breakfasts and note how he would never say much, "but when he did, everyone, including the president, listened."[13] It did not take long for Humphrey to recognize that Rayburn "knew Washington and what could be done so well that his every comment seemed on target, without superfluous or irrelevant padding. The sound of his own voice was of little interest to him."[14]

Then there was another relationship that had also helped to form "the new Hubert Humphrey," namely, the one that had grown between Humphrey and Lyndon Johnson.

As a result of Russell Long's luncheon invitations, Johnson gradually had been able to take a good look at Humphrey. Johnson began inviting him back to his own office as a result, frequently for a drink, and frequently to meet with one of Johnson's closest associates, Richard Russell. Though elected to the senate in the same year as Humphrey, Johnson, unlike his radically labelled colleagues from Minnesota, had been quickly accepted into the Senate's inner circles. He had, after all, already served in the House for three terms where he had become quite close to Sam Rayburn. He was also simply "a formidable figure" in his own right. In Humphrey's eyes, Johnson

> knew Washington, and he knew Congress as no other man in my experience. He understood the structure and pressure points of the government, and the process and problems of legislation. He understood the men of Congress, both the elected members and the appointed officials. He knew how to appeal to their vanity, to their needs, to their ambitions.[15]

That Johnson was a power to be reckoned with was simply acknowledged as fact early on by all. By 1950, one year after his swearing-in as senator, Johnson was already the minority whip, under Ernest McFarland of Arizona. In 1952 McFarland was defeated for reelection, and Johnson was thereby in a position to assume the minority leader role. Such a prospect dismayed the ADA contingent. Because it did it eventually involved Hubert Humphrey. Oddly enough the confrontation that ensued provided the occasion by which the relationship between Humphrey and Johnson would congeal.

There was no chance of a liberal upset over Johnson's bid for the minority leader's position. Yet, as Humphrey said, "at that stage of American liberalism, it seemed important to have a symbol, even if you lost with it."[16] In this case, that "symbol" was James Murray of Montana who was chosen by the liberals to be their preference for the minority leader spot.

As the consequent maneuvering began to take place, Johnson called Humphrey at his home to talk things over. Humphrey stated candidly to Johnson that he had already made a commitment and that he therefore could not support Johnson's bid for the position. Johnson responded by saying that he was sorry, in part because he had been considering Humphrey for the minority whip post. Humphrey responded in turn by saying that the liberals had other goals than attaining such positions—they wanted better committee assignments and more power on the steering and policy committees of the Senate Democratic caucuses.

Some time after this conversation took place Humphrey led a delegation of liberal senators to meet with Johnson. The delegation, in addition to Humphrey, consisted of Lester Hunt of Wyoming, Herbert Lehman of New York, and Paul Douglas. They wanted to make a deal. Johnson "listened to us briefly, then politely but curtly dismissed us by telling us that he had the votes he needed and that he wasn't in the mood to make concessions."[17] Humphrey provides an illuminating account of what happened afterward:

> I had just returned to my office from that awful meeting when Johnson called and said, "Come on down here alone. I want to talk to you." In his office I found him in a take-charge, no-nonsense mood I would see often after that. He said, "Now, look here. Let me tell you something, Hubert. You're depending on votes you don't have. How many votes do you think you have?"
>
> "Well, I think we have anywhere from thirteen to seventeen."
>
> He stared at me for a quiet moment and said, "First of all, you ought to be sure of your count. That's too much of a spread. But you don't have them anyway. *Who* do you think you have?" I went down the list of senators and checked some off. He shook his head on most of them. "You don't have those senators. I have personal commitments that they're going to vote for me. As a matter of fact, Senator Hunt, who was just in here with you, is going to vote for me. You ought to quit fooling around with people you can't depend on."

> His stern tone changed to a friendlier one. "Now look, I think you're honest about these matters. You turned me down when I called you and that was a foolish mistake, because I took Mike Mansfield instead of you. You could have been minority whip, and you'll regret your decision, but at least you told me straight. You didn't talk out of both sides of your mouth. When this election's over and I'm Leader, I want you to come back to me and we'll talk about what we're going to do. I want to work with you and only you from the bomb throwers."
>
> When the vote was taken, Senator Murray had his own vote and mine, plus three or four others. Everyone else had gone over to Johnson. Murray withdrew from the race, and Johnson was elected unanimously.
>
> After the meeting, I went back to his office and he said, "Now, what do you liberals really want?"
>
> The dialogue was brief and to the point. "The first thing we want is some representation on the policy committee."
>
> "All right, you'll have it. Who do you want?"
>
> "Well, I think it ought to be Jim Murray."
>
> "I don't think he's the right man, because he's older and he won't be effective, but if that's who you want, that'll be done. What else do you want?"
>
> I listed our other requests (formerly demands), which included representation on the steering committee and the major substantive committees of Finance, Judiciary, Commerce, and Appropriations. Johnson agreed and said, "Now you go back and tell your liberal friends that you're the one to talk to me and that if they'll talk through you as their leader we can get some things done."[18]

This is a true insider's account of politic's inner machinations. In 1968 Humphrey would lose much of the liberal vote because of his perceived association with this kind of "cronyism" in general and with Johnson in particular. He received a similar reaction from his liberal colleagues then as well: "They looked on it as tokenism, and since it flowed from Johnson, it was suspect."[19] Johnson was, in the standard liberal view of the day, too Southern and too closely allied with the conservative leadership in both style and outlook. To associate with him meant, in turn, making one's self correspondingly suspect as well.

Yet, as Humphrey went on to point out, this "suspect" figure, now the minority leader, and soon, in 1954, to become majority leader, "produced on his promises."[20] In fact, as Humphrey went on, "[he] ultimately went beyond our limited objectives."[21] Before 1954, freshmen Democrats were rarely if ever assigned to major committees in their first year. From that time on, however, Johnson made it a common practice. As a result the liberal leadership was able to begin to influence such committees as Appropriations, Finance, Foreign Relations and Judiciary—the very sanctums of southern senatorial sovereignty.* Liberalism was being allowed to assume an albeit limited, yet nonetheless assured position of power in the United States Senate as a direct result of Johnson's leadership. For Hubert Humphrey, it was Lyndon Johnson who had thereby made the liberal ascendancy of the 1960s possible. The irony, of course, is that with that ascendancy, the liberal leadership would then turn on Johnson and eventually be instrumental in his defeat.

For Humphrey himself his arrangement with Johnson was not something that he discussed very much. He "simply tried to make it work. From a position of weakness, we [the liberal faction] had accomplished what we had wanted. That was enough for me."[22] That satisfaction in meeting pragmatism's demands—in making progress even if it represented a compromise of sorts—by now had become characteristic of Humphrey. As an idealist, this never troubled him, however, for he fully believed that in the long run such a method of operation was to work in idealism's favor. The Civil Rights Act of 1964 may well stand as the best evidence in support of such a claim.

John Kennedy, despite appearances to the contrary, had been disappointingly perfunctory in regards to civil rights throughout the major part of his administration. His 28 February 1963 civil rights message to Congress, while forthright in language, was in fact weak in substance. It did not call for fulfillment of the Democratic platform promises of an FEPC law, authority for the Attorney General to file civil injunctions in civil rights cases[23] and immediate first-step school desegregation. All that the proposal called for instead was patchwork improvements in existing voting legislation, technical assistance for school districts voluntarily seeking to desegregate, and extension of the Civil Rights Commission. For civil rights advocates this was thin gruel indeed.

*Hubert Humphrey, for instance, was placed on the Rules Committee in 1952 and on the Foreign Relations Committee in 1953. Both places were granted by Johnson.

Unforeseen events, however, were to thicken things soon enough. In April of 1963, Martin Luther King, Jr. and his followers, against the advice of many, even those close to him, began to demonstrate in the streets of Birmingham, Alabama. "Bull" Connor was to make the confrontation a national issue—one much larger than the President could ignore. Neither could he ignore the fact that liberal Republican congressional figures were introducing civil rights legislation of their own that called for everything that his administration was proposing, yet added a public accommodations bill as well (and thus was reminiscent of the summer of the 1948 Democratic National Convention). This was all occurring when, for the first time, a private poll had shown that JFK's popular approval rating had slipped to below fifty percent. Civil rights groups, encouraged by the growing national awareness of and sympathy for their cause, began demanding a *full* public accommodations bill, an FEPC, immediate first-step school desegregation, federal registrars for voter registration, and the "Part III."

On June 19 Kennedy sent his civil rights bill to Congress. With the exception of an offer of support for pending FEPC legislation, it was unchanged from the earlier bill. It was, in effect, the administration's best estimate "of what could be enacted, rather than what was needed."[24] Even so, it stood as the most comprehensive civil rights program ever to be submitted to Congress.

That was small consolation to those who were looking for a truly substantial bill. In a White House meeting chaired by Vice President Johnson two days later, Joe Rauh asked, "what attitude the Administration would take if the civil rights groups sought to strengthen the bill by amendments, including an FEPC and Part III, and whether this would cause friction?"[25] As Rauh relates, "Mr. Johnson responded that there had to be 'flexibility' in a campaign of this kind and he saw no difficulty in the civil rights groups going beyond the Administration in their demands."[26] This agreement for "flexibility" in effect provided a green light for the civil rights advocates.[27]

After the meeting, Walter Reuther gathered a number of the participants together to discuss ways of mobilizing public support for the upcoming bill. Martin Luther King thought that a giant march on Washington would be the most effective thing. Roy

Wilkins mentioned that an expansion of the Leadership Conference on Civil Rights would also be instrumental. Both were subsequently to become crucial elements of the effort to pass the bill (not to mention significant parts of American history in their own right).

On July 2 approximately one hundred groups endorsing civil rights met in New York's Roosevelt Hotel. This represented a nearly fifty percent increase in participation in the Leadership Conference. Many of the groups included religious and political organizations which had hitherto not been directly involved in the civil rights efforts of the Conference, yet were willing and quite able to attract widespread public attention in favor of its causes. There was excitement about the possibility of passing a significant bill—an excitement that the Kennedy proposal had triggered, however watered down that proposal had actually been. Demand quickly arose, however, for a bill that would be more than just "significant"—that is, "significant" in the sense that the 1957 bill had been—namely, as a token gesture toward civil rights. A bill with teeth to it was now insisted on. That meant one which included provisions for an FEPC, Part III, and complete public accommodations. In looking for what difficulties lay in the path of such proposals, both the House Judiciary and Rules committees, along with the Senate filibuster, were all seen as the major obstacles that would have to be overcome.

Hubert Humphrey had no control over events on the House side. The Senate filibuster, however, was a phenomenon that did occur directly within his purview. As one of the major powers of the Senate, he had the potential to do something about it.

In an article published at the time on this potential, *The New Republic* lauded Humphrey's "passion for infinitely calibrated legislative maneuver."[28] "Humphrey," it said, "brings to the Senate floor a skill and a subtlety which has no parallel in the body except when we watch a Southerner exercising similar qualities in a committee."[29] This was extremely high praise indeed, yet the same article then went on to speak of a "main cloud on the future of the civil rights bill." That "cloud" was the fact "that the coalition has just fifty-nine votes and will need sixty-seven to invoke cloture against the filibuster."[30] Everett Dirksen was acknowledged to be the storm center of this cloud by his being described as "the last hope of the resistance."

This came conclusion was reached a week later by *Newsweek* when, after praising Humphrey as "a man of great ability" (and "almost no mystery or majesty")[31] it also projected that "in the end, the man with the key may well be mellifluous Everett Dirksen."[32] Passing the bill itself, in other words, was not the major difficulty—it would be gathering the votes necessary to invoke cloture that would present the real obstacle.

Cloture had been originally instituted in 1917. It stipulates that debate will be limited to one hour per senator by a vote of two-thirds of the Senate. Since its institution, eleven attempts had been made to invoke it by civil rights advocates. None had been successful.

Until 1959, the rule had been that two-thirds of the *entire* Senate was required to invoke cloture. Under the guidance of Majority Leader Johnson, however, this rule was modified to two-thirds of the senators *present* and *voting*. Nevertheless the best that the pro-civil rights forces had been able to achieve up until the 1960s had been approximately thirty votes for cloture. This accounted for the fact that no significant civil rights legislation had been passed for generations, and that the two bills that finally had been passed, the 1957 and the 1960 bills, were either so weak to begin with, or were so gutted by the time that they finally did pass, that they had no significant impact on the continuation of Jim Crow practice. The civil rights forces would need the votes of the key Republican swing votes involved in order to overcome the inevitable filibuster. Everett Dirksen was "the key" to all of this because he led that small but all-important bloc of swing votes.

As the bill began to move in Congress events at large began to move with it at an ever-accelerating pace. Hearings began in June before House Judiciary Subcommittee No. 5, the first hurdle in the legislative path. They would continue on through July and into August. Meanwhile, in the first of many more publicized events, Governor Wallace of Alabama attempted to block the admission of black students to the University of Alabama, forcing a showdown with the administration. President Kennedy went on television to rally national support to the civil rights side on June 10.

That same night Medgar Evers was shot and killed in Mississippi. Then on August 28 the historic march on Washington took place. Dr. King announced, "I have a dream," and it awakened the nation. Those who shared his dream became all the more committed to making it a reality. That commitment only hardened when, on September 17, news was reported of the church bombing in Birmingham in which four young schoolgirls died.

On September 25 Chairman Cellar of Judiciary Subcommittee No. 5 proudly announced in a press conference that his committee had approved a "very strong bill"—including FEPC, Part III, and full public accommodations. While representing a successful completion of the first hurdle, the bill now had to move on to the full House Judiciary Committee.

The administration was not pleased with the bill and made its displeasure known before the Committee. Attorney General Robert Kennedy, for example, argued on October 15 that Part III would bring the Attorney General "into disputes involving censorship, church-state relations, confiscatory rate-making, searches and seizures, and other matters totally unrelated to minority rights."[33]

Meanwhile on October 22 a motion to adopt the subcommittee bill over and against the wishes of the administration was made by Republican Congressman Moore of West Virginia. An ugly fight seemed to be in the making. The meeting was adjourned as a result, and one scheduled for the next day was cancelled.

On the night of the 23rd President Kennedy called Congressional leaders together to work out a compromise. The compromise included keeping the FEPC; retaining Part III, but limiting it to Attorney General intervention; and limiting the public accommodations. This compromise bill was accepted on October 29. While a compromise, the Leadership Conference was still pleased, since it represented a bill stronger than the one originally proposed and one that they could at least be content with for the time being.

Southerners on the committee stalled the bill until November 21. Congressman Cellar asked the Rules Committee that afternoon to send the bill to the House floor for action. Its chairman, Howard Smith, made clear his intention to bottle up the bill, and the matter rested for the time being. Twenty-four hours later word was received that President Kennedy lay dead in Dallas.

The Kennedy assassination unquestionably gave the Civil Rights Act of 1964 greatly added momentum. Though the president had initially balked at proposing a strong bill, he had, by the time he died, nevertheless come to associate himself with the cause of civil rights. In mourning his tragic death the country, too, came to associate civil rights with him. A sympathy vote thus developed in favor of the civil rights legislation proposed at the time. With his words, "Let us continue" President Johnson skillfully and wisely attached the full weight of his own administration onto that legislation. By so doing he harnessed the power of the sympathy vote to it as well. Suddenly, there was a groundswell in favor of a major civil rights bill.

Despite these impressive forces amassing behind it, however, the Civil Rights Act of 1964 in truth lived a very tenuous life.

True to his word, Chairman Smith continued to bottle up the bill successfully until the Christmas recess. Nevertheless, during the recess Congress began to feel the full effect of that public groundswell that had so recently formed. Repeated demands at home for some strong form of civil rights legislation began to be heard. By January 9, Chairman Smith made clear the effect that that kind of demand can ultimately have by announcing, "I know the facts of life around here." Majority Leader Albert announced that the bill would be reported out by the Rules Committee on January 30 and would move to the floor of the House the following day.

After a tremendous disciplined effort on the part of the civil rights forces*—an effort that included necessary gallery participation to watch and mentally record each "teller vote" cast for "Committee of the Whole" votes on proposed amendments[34]—House Bill 7152 finally was passed on February 10th by a count of 290 to 130—just in time for Lincoln Day speeches back home.

When the Senate returned from its Lincoln Day recess, the bill was waiting for it. Majority Leader Mike Mansfield announced that the bill would be placed directly on the Senate calendar. This

*See *The Longest Debate* by Charles and Barbara Whalen for a comprehensive study of this effort.

was a highly unusual procedure, though not one without precedent; such procedure had been used successfully by Senator Knowland during passage of the 1957 bill. Though unusual, it was a move necessitated by having to avoid having the bill referred to Senator Eastland's Judiciary Committee—a committee grimly known then as "the graveyard of Civil Rights legislation." On February 26 Mansfield moved that the bill in fact be placed on the calendar. Senator Russell acted for the Southern contingent by bitterly denouncing such a movement and by attempting to block it. He was overruled fifty-four to thirty-seven. On March 9 Mansfield moved to take the bill from the calendar. With that the struggle began in earnest.

The traditional tactic utilized by the filibustering minority in order to block undesirable legislation that had come to this point was simple. They would divide into three teams, each team allotted an eight-hour shift. One person would speak while four or five others would remain with him in the Senate chamber for support. With this kind of "teamwork" the advantage was on the filibustering side, for it was incumbent on the majority to consistently maintain enough present members so as to constitute a quorum. It was the quorum call, initiated with the words, "Mr. President, I suggest the absence of a quorum," that provided the filibusterers' with their most potent offensive weapon. It delayed senate proceedings, broke the tedium of the filibusterers' own drone, and, often enough, forced the Senate to adjournment, since a quorum oftentimes in fact did not exist. Time is on the filibusterers' side, since there will always be those in the majority who will be unwilling to undergo the rigors of all-night vigils in the Senate cloakrooms, not to mention see their own pet projects shunted aside for weeks and even months simply for the sake of one highly controversial issue. As long as the filibuster endured no other piece of legislation was allowed to come up for consideration.

These are the facts that in the past had conspired to either block all civil rights proposals, or to so weaken them that they remained more or less inconsequential. In 1964, however, there were a number of new factors at work. One was the determination of religious groups to take an active part in pushing for the bill's passage. Another was having a president who was equally committed to seeing the bill become law. A third was the everswelling tide of national opinion in favor of a strong civil rights bill. The televised accounts of the violent attacks on the determined yet intentionally nonviolent demonstrators had awakened America's long-dormant conscience in regards to the civil rights issue. The assassination of the young John Kennedy had aroused that conscience to a state of active determination to do *something*. In this case that "something" meant preventing "business as usual" from taking place. When Lyndon Johnson, on taking the presidency, asserted that "no memorial or eulogy could more eloquently honor President Kennedy than the earliest possible passage of the civil rights bill for which he fought so long" the nation took him at his word. As Humphrey said, "This time the country was watching and ready."[35] This time, too, the pro-civil rights forces were determined to maintain the requisite discipline. They were, in addition, now to be led by someone who was also "ready" to see to it that the discipline was enforced. That "someone" was Hubert Humphrey.

Normally the floor leader of an important bill is the chairman of the appropriate committee. In this case that committee was Judiciary. Its head, however, Mississippi's James Eastland, clearly was not an appropriate choice. Because this was so Majority Leader Mansfield was able to choose Humphrey to fill the job instead.

For Humphrey the choice represented both a responsibility and an opportunity. Humphrey had substantially based and built his political career on his advocacy of civil rights. In 1960, for example, he had campaigned for the presidential nomination as "The Civil Rights Candidate." All along he had stood as the kind of advocate who was determined to master and utilize the established procedures by which any such legislation would have to be passed. As floor leader for this bill he would ultimately bear the weight of responsibility for something to which he had fully committed himself. At the same time, however, it would also afford him the opportunity to demonstrate the skills and expertise that that commitment had forced him to acquire. The fact that Lyndon Johnson was looking for a running mate to be chosen in the coming summer only made such a position that much more of *both* a "responsibility" *and* an "opportunity."

In their first meeting Johnson told Humphrey outright that he did not think that the bill would pass. He simply did not have confidence in the Senate liberals whom Humphrey now led. In Humphrey's words, he "launched into one of his traditional speeches about liberals: 'You bombthrowers make good speeches, you have big hearts, you believe in what you say you stand for, but you're never on the job when you need to be there. You spread yourselves too thin making speeches to the faithful.'"[36]

He went on to point out that the opposition was headed by Richard Russell, someone who knew *all* the Senate rules, and who was the acknowledged master at utilizing them in the service of whatever cause he chose to champion. Johnson then talked about liberal ineptness when it came to dealing with such a test of parliamentary skill as this bill would present, and predicted that, as had in fact been traditionally true, the liberals would "fall apart in dissension, [and] be absent when quorum calls were made and when critical votes were being taken."[37]

Humphrey suffered this dressing-down mostly in silence. He did so because he knew fully well that Johnson was right. He only pledged that this time things would be different. As he left, Johnson shifted his tone and said, "Call me whenever there's trouble or anything you want me to do."[38] What Humphrey did was to go immediately to work to prove that this effort would represent a break from the rather ignominious past that Johnson had referred to.

The first important tactical decision in regards to the actual debate was one made by Mike Mansfield when he announced that there would be no round-the-clock sessions. Mansfield did this over and against the arguments of the pro-civil rights forces. The round-the-clock session was a tactic that was used specifically against older senators, which most of the civil rights opponents were, because it was a test of one's physical stamina, and one used blatantly as such. Humphrey supported Mansfield's decision because it marked a commitment to maintaining a level of dignity below which the pro-civil rights forces firmly intended not to sink, no matter what. This commitment proved to be one of the crucial factors in the eventual success of the struggle.

A second commitment that proved equally crucial was one simply to logistical rigor. There were many facets of this effort that required different kinds of discipline. In a sense the most important of all of them was meeting the simple physical, yet ever-present threat of the quorum call. In order to meet this threat Humphrey devised a plan for liberal "teamwork" as well. Staunchly insisting on bipartisan cooperation throughout all of the process, Humphrey worked out a "quorum watch" schedule with his Republican counterpart, Thomas Kuchel of California. It was meant to ensure that the requisite number of senators would be on hand at all times. A master chart, listing all out-of-town speaking engagements of pro-civil rights Democrats, was posted in the Democratic Policy Committee Room. Those Senators up for reelection in 1964 were given priority to fill these engagements. A similar chart was prepared by the Republicans. Certain senators, or their administrative assistants, were held responsible for calling the offices of colleagues designated to be on hand that day to make sure that a quorum was available at all times. In addition, a *Bipartisan Civil Rights Newsletter* was begun and was distributed to every Senator each morning so as to keep them abreast of the bill's progress. Individual senators were chosen as "captains" to be responsible for particular sections of the bill. Seven were chosen in all—one for nearly each of the eleven titles—and it was seen to it that there was a representative sampling of both Democrats and Republicans scattered among the choices. Regular meetings were scheduled for key senators, members of their staffs, and Leadership Conference representatives for every Monday and Thursday morning before the Senate convened. Clarence Mitchell, Washington bureau chief for the NAACP, maintained a constant vigil as chief liaison between the Leadership Conference and the Senate civil rights forces. Finally, the Majority Whip's office was made a headquarters for those combined forces, and it was from there that their efforts began to be principally directed.

The fact that such organization actually came into being was soon attested to by an article in the *New York Times*. The article read,

> Civil rights forces, not to be outdone by southern opponents, have thrown up their own well-manned command post in the Senate. "We, too, are ready to do battle," said Senator Hubert H. Humphrey. As militarily precise as the southerner's three-platoon system, the Humphrey forces are organized down to the last man.[39]

President Johnson played a key, though indirect role. He chose not to become directly involved in the struggle, largely so as to avoid antagonizing his southern colleagues. Indirectly, however, he was able to lift a great burden from the civil rights proponents by making it clear in a January 21 meeting that he did not care if all other legislation was ignored for months – he wanted a strong bill. In subsequently making this clear to Congress as well he put time – traditionally the filibusterers' greatest offensive asset – on the side of the pro-civil rights forces instead. In so doing, he seriously qualified the potency of the anti-civil rights forces' greatest weapon, the filibuster, and simultaneously gave the pro-civil rights forces an advantage of their own: the attention of the nation was now focused on this one bill. As a result, given the substantial national groundswell in favor of the bill, a majority of the Senate from early on supported it as it had been originally proposed. Those opposing it, including Everett Dirksen (who wanted a bill, but in modified form), were forced to be on the defensive from the beginning.

Dirksen's objections centered on the FEPC and the public accommodations sections. He favored the standard conservative approach of voluntary compliance with such statutes, opposing federal intervention both in principal and in practice.

Though a traditional conservative in terms of outlook, that is not to say that Dirksen was therefore not distinctive. If for nothing else, Everett Dirksen was at least known for his flair for the dramatic. In Humphrey's terms,

> he had a magnificent sense of drama, loved the center stage, enjoyed the sound of his mellifluous, some said unctuous voice filling the Senate chamber. He loved the legislative game, manipulating language, cadging a vote for an amendment. Laws to him were organic, growing, flowering like the marigolds on which he lavished such care and affection in his yard.[40]

Humphrey decided on a strategy of playing to these Dirksenesque characteristics. As he had done long ago with his friend, Bob Wishart, so now, rather than attempting to bludgeon Dirksen into submission, Humphrey would seek to cajole him into compliance instead. Humphrey met with him almost every day. In public Humphrey constantly appealed to Dirksen's higher sensibilities by predicting that Dirksen would look upon this issue "as a moral, not a partisan one,"[41] and by repeatedly asserting how Dirksen was "a responsible man." Privately he would regularly approach Dirksen with such flattering assurances as, "Now Everett, this is *your* bill" or, "Everett, we can't pass this bill without you." Humphrey sought to elevate Dirksen to a point where he would appear as "the statesman above partisanship, the thoughtful architect, the master builder of a legislative edifice that would last forever."[42] Such deference to a hardline conservative aroused liberal ire. Once again, liberals accused Humphrey of selling out to Dirksen and resented the lavish praise Humphrey poured out on him in a continual public display. Humphrey's justification for this was characteristically pragmatic: "I'm not in this to be a hero. If Everett Dirksen can walk out of this with the olive wreath in his wavy locks, that's fine with me—if it gets us a good bill."[43]

Yet another crucial factor in the process of passing the bill was the need to resist calling for a cloture vote too soon. The advocates believed that an early vote would likely fail and thus that pressure for a compromise would rise. By waiting until cloture was assured, a strong bill could be preserved. Patience—balanced with fairness—was to be a virtue, perhaps the key virtue in the eventual success of this endeavor. Recognizing this, Humphrey and Kuchel, at one of the first Monday/Thursday meetings, insisted on not calling for cloture until they were assured of the necessary votes. For Joe Rauth this was "*the* crucial decision."[44]

Meanwhile action continued on the floor. On the eve of the Easter recess a Mansfield motion to take up the bill was adopted by a vote of sixty-seven to seventeen. On this vote, at any rate, the magic "sixty-seven" had been reached. By March 30 the debate on the floor was fully enjoined, with Humphrey giving the introductory speech in favor of the bill.

Action was continuing elsewhere as well. After many weeks of debate and maneuvering, Dirksen finally came to Humphrey to negotiate. Many found his proposal shocking. It included literally dozens of differing amendments to the bill. Many of the civil rights backers were so exasperated that they called for attempting cloture without Dirksen. Humphrey called for patience instead. He argued that while it clearly was to be a long and laborious negotiation, at least Dirksen's proposal represented a step forward, and an important one.

Because of the laborious nature of the struggle, Humphrey began to depend heavily at this time on Attorney General Robert Kennedy and members of his staff, principally Nicholas Katzenbach, as well as on a young member of his own staff, John Stewart, for legwork, for ideas, and for new language. The language issue was critical because the bill's successful passage depended on mollifying Dirksen, yet at the same time on doing so in a way that would leave the substance of the bill essentially intact.

Humphrey met with Dirksen "on the floor, in the cloakroom, in the corridors and on the elevators."[45] The negotiations, themselves conducted largely by staff assistants and Department of Justice representatives, convened daily in Dirksen's minority leadership office. They quickly assumed the proportions of an ad hoc committee all their own. Mutterings about them were soon heard up and down the halls of the Senate. Resentment of the meetings was characterized by references to the "troika" of Humphrey, Dirksen, and Kennedy. Meanwhile the Leadership Conference representatives, principally Rauh and Mitchell, were beginning to become particularly worried about a "sell-out" to Dirksen.

Despite this rising tide of uneasiness and dissension, however, Humphrey remained determined to win by winning over his opponents with charm, grace, and good humor, as well as by impressing them with the strength of the civil rights proponents' determination—the same "means" that he had committed himself to a long time ago. As such it was a policy of "Talk softly, but carry a big list of votes"—a parliamentary adaptation of Teddy Roosevelt's diplomatic modus operandi. However controversial the issue might be, Humphrey remained steadfast in preventing it from becoming an embittered argument. There was to be no invective, no matter how provocative the opposition might become.

Humphrey knew fully well how provocative that opposition could be. He had taken the brunt of conservative assaults on civil rights proposals since his earliest days in the Senate. One good example of this is in a 1950 debate he had with Senator Holland of Florida over Humphrey's proposal for a national FEPC. A representative sample of that debate goes as follows:

MR. HUMPHREY: . . . Mr. President, today the Senator from Florida has stated to the Senate that this proposed legislation is Communist inspired, that the source of this legislation is the Communist Party.

However, to the contrary, I say that the source of this legislation is the Declaration of Independence, which says—

That all men are created equal.

And that—

Governments are instituted among men . . . to secure these rights . . . [of] life, liberty, and the pursuit of happiness.

. . . I mention first some of the great spiritual leaders who have testified in behalf of this legislation. I say it is sheer distortion and adulteration of the facts and the evidence to try to label this kind of legislation as Communist inspired.

I happen to have known, [for example], the late Msgr. John A. Ryan, one of the great Christian leaders of this Nation and of this century. He testified before the Senate committee in 1944—a great Catholic spiritual leader—in behalf of this legislation. He based his advocacy of this legislative proposal, not upon some political doctrine, but upon the moral doctrine of the Christian faith.[46]

Humphrey then went on to recite the names of other religious leaders and organizations that had openly supported FEPC legislation at that time. The argument was joined when Humphrey stated,

May I refer also to the Senator with a request for his comment [on] the remark of the Catholic bishop, the Most Reverend Bernard J. Shell, of Chicago, who said:

I conclude by stating that in Paul's letter to the Corinthians he said:

Ye are neither Jews nor Gentiles, neither bond nor free: Ye are all one in Jesus Christ our Lord."

I ask the Senator what does he really think is the source of FEPC in the face of the testimony of Bishop Haas, Bishop Shell, and the beloved and late lamented Monsignor Ryan, who said:

"The Christian precept of brotherly love is not satisfied by mere well-wishing, nor benevolent emotion nor sentimental yearning. It requires action."

I wish the Senator from Florida would give me his observations. Is FEPC equality of treatment a fundamental part of the Christian doctrine, or is it a Communist-inspired doctrine? I think an answer should be forthcoming.

MR. HOLLAND: The answer will be forthcoming, and at once. There is no doubt in the world that his proposal for the creation of a governmental agency to

> engraft upon our Government the principle that men have to be hired or fired, depending upon religion and religious beliefs, race and racial beliefs, or color, comes from Communist inspiration. There is not the slightest question of it. The Senator from Minnesota will find no ground for any other conclusion.

MR. HUMPHREY: Mr. President, will the Senator yield further?

MR. HOLLAND: I shall not yield at this time. I prefer to continue in my own way.[47]

This kind of adversity was all too familiar to Humphrey by 1964. He was determined nonetheless that a sense of fairness and courtesy be the hallmark of the effort to overcome it. In fact he was convinced that adopting such an approach was the only way to overcome it.[48] For Humphrey, pushing for passage of the Civil Rights Act of 1964 was meant to be a bipartisan, communal attempt to establish justice for everyone, pro *and* con alike. There was, however, to be strict discipline in maintaining maximum pressure on the opposition at all times as well. It was to be an effort made strictly in accordance with Humphrey's own credo of "disagreeing without being disagreeable." As such it represented a form of nonviolent coercion similar to that practiced by Martin Luther King, Jr. It balanced genuine regard for the opposition with a rigid determination to nevertheless prevail over them at the same time.

Humphrey relates one small story that illustrates this commitment to ensuring forever that the door be kept open to the opposition:

> One day, on the floor, Senator John Stennis of Mississippi inquired about this newsletter (the *Bipartisan Civil Rights Newsletter*). "I should like to ask," he said, "who writes these mysterious messages which come to senators before the *Congressional Record* reaches them, and . . . attempts to refute arguments made on the floor of the Senate."
>
> I was glad he asked. It gave me a chance to publicize our organization effort.
>
> "There is no doubt about it," I said. "The newsletter is a bipartisan civil rights newsletter . . . For the first time we are putting up a battle. Everything will be done to make us succeed . . . I wish also to announce that if anyone wishes to have equal time, there is space on the back of it for the opposition."[49]

Solberg offers another such story where he described how Willis Robertson [Pat Robertson's father] of Virginia walked up to Humphrey at his front row whip's desk and offered him a small flag for his lapel. It was the Stars and Bars. Humphrey gladly accepted it, compliments were exchanged, and the two retired to the whip's office for a refreshment.

This kind of commitment to *in*clude, not *ex*clude, the opposition was hardly new to Hubert Humphrey, nor exclusive to this particular legislative effort. As early as 1951, for example, in an article for *Progressive*, McNeil Lowry talked about "the unheralded achievements of the young Minnesota Democrat in these early days of the 82nd Congress"—achievements that "have involved detailed, behind-the-scenes activity which only separate articles could treat fairly"[50]—yet for which Humphrey received no recognition. Lowry cited as an instance a "Grain for India bill." He talked about how Humphrey first carried the bill alone, yet, "as bipartisan support grew and smothered the distaste of Foreign Relations Committee Chairman Tom Connolly for the project, Humphrey dropped back to being merely one of the cosponsors."[51] When asked why he had purposely stepped out of the limelight at the precise time at which he deserved to be stepping into it instead, Humphrey explained that he did what he did because "any other course might have jeopardized the support that was building up."[52] In a bill to support racial integration in the armed services which Humphrey had proposed, Lowry similarly described how Humphrey's GOP colleague, Edward Thye, also of Minnesota, "got the publicity." Humphrey's response to this decision not to publicize his efforts was: "I'm not looking for miracles, nor for the millennium. But I'm looking for at least inch-by-inch progress every month, and I'm getting the reports."[53] Such a pattern still clearly held true fourteen years and over a thousand legislative battles later.

As time passed the effectiveness of the public campaign mounted by the Leadership Conference, and in particular by the religious groups involved, began to become clear. The public was wearying of unending talk with no apparent progress being made. The ranks of the filibustering senators and their supporters were ever shrinking. Many of those originally hesitant about the bill began to join those who openly called for it. In an article in an April issue of *The New Republic*, Humphrey warned: "just wait until they start hearing from the church people,"[54] and "they" did. The initial majority of objections to the bill that Humphrey and others received in the mail gradually began to dwindle. As a result, conservatives like Mundt of South Dakota and Hruska of Nebraska, for example, voted to table a Morse motion to send the bill back to Judiciary—all the while muttering about pressure from ministers back home.

An early lapse in discipline did occur on Saturday, April 4, when only thirty-four senators responded to a quorum call. Angry about the slip, civil rights leaders saw to it that notices went out to the home states of those senators who were absent at the time of the call. No other "absence of a quorum" was to occur thereafter.

Again, religious groups had been key to maintaining this kind of necessary pressure. Clerics of all kinds formed a regular stream of visitors to senators. Humphrey met with them constantly, and he even brought some of them to the Senate floor during the closing days of the battle. Meanwhile seminarians outside the Lincoln Memorial maintained a silent but steady vigil day and night. There was to be no letting up.

In early May a Harris poll reported that seventy percent of the public supported the bill in its entirety. Much of this support was seen as the direct result of work done by religious groups. Of this work Richard Russell, in his closing speech on the final day of the debate, would say,

> I have observed with profound sorrow the role that many religious leaders have played in urging passage of the bill, because I cannot make their activities jibe with my concept of the proper place of religious leaders in our national life. During the course of the debate, we have seen cardinals, bishops, elders, stated clerks, common preachers, priests and rabbis come to Washington to press for the passage of this bill. They have sought to make its passage a great moral issue. But I am at a loss to understand why they are 200 years late in discovering that the right of dominion over private property is a great moral issue. If it is a great moral issue today, it was a great moral issue on the day of the ratification of the Constitution of the United States. Of course, this is not, and cannot be a moral question; however it may be considered, it is a political question.
>
> Day after day, men of the cloth have been standing on the Mall and urging a favorable vote on the bill. They have encouraged and prompted thousands of good citizens to sign petitions supporting the bill—but all without the knowledge of the effect of what they were demanding of the representatives in the Congress of the United States.

> This is the second time in my lifetime an effort has been made by the clergy to make a moral question of a political issue. The other was prohibition. We know something of the results of that.[55]

As Norman Sherman said, "the churches—religious groups—were the sine qua non of getting the civil rights acts passed in '64 and '65."[56] Their work, as well as that of the many other black, labor, and even business groups that formed the support for the Leadership Conference was proving to be one more indispensable factor in the passage of the bill. Things were looking up.

On May 13, after weeks of being locked in negotiation, a tentative agreement between Dirksen and Humphrey was reached. As Joe Rauh relates, "The next morning the Leadership Conference representatives received the still unpublished text of the tentative agreement. Reading the changes with trepidation, it soon became evident that Humphrey's patience, good humor, and courage had won the day."[57] On May 26 the Humphrey-Dirksen package was formally introduced by Senators Dirksen, Humphrey, Kuchel, and Mansfield as an alternative to the originally proposed bill. Some of the more significant sections where the House and the Senate versions differed are listed in Appendix C.

The issue between Dirksen and Humphrey had been mainly over delineating when and to what degree the federal government in general, and the Attorney General specifically, would be authorized to intervene. After ten days of protracted discussion, the suggestion of the phrase "pattern or practice of resistance," as seen, for example, in Title I, Sect. 3; and Title II, Sect. 5; by a member of Dirksen's staff finally broke the impasse. Title III, Sect. 4; Title VII, Sect. 3(i); and Title VII, Sect. 3(k) deal with the thorny issues of busing, sex discrimination and job quotas. Title VII, Sect. 16 stipulates that the bill be federally enforced when necessary, that is, in the South, but allowed for having it handled by state agencies where they already existed—as they did, for example, in Dirksen's Illinois. Overall, the modifications were meant to placate Dirksen's conservative objections. Evidently they failed to placate Richard Russell's. When the revised version of the bill was read on the Senate floor his response was: "It puts Charles Sumner, Thad Stevens, and Ben Wade to shame."[58]

On June 1, Majority Leader Mansfield announced that he

would file a cloture petition during the week and that the vote on cloture would be held on June 9. With Dirksen's promise of twenty-five votes for cloture all seemed assured.

This assurance soon wavered, however, when a new snag arose. Bourke Hickenlooper of Iowa had been constantly critical of the Dirksen-Humphrey proposal, largely out of jealousy of Dirksen's midwestern leadership. He had walked out of the negotiation meetings early on in the going and was not bound to their outcome. Now the Senator from Iowa had decided to make that point manifestly clear, though he would still not disclose how.

Then, only to add to the difficulties, on June 2 Everett Dirksen took sick. His leadership missing for a number of days, certain members of his bloc began to voice misgivings about their cloture commitment.

On Friday, June 5, Senator Hickenlooper decided to make his move. He rose to ask for unanimous consent that three amendments to be added to the Civil Rights Bill be acted upon before the cloture vote, just announced by Mansfield to be Tuesday the 9th. This posed a dilemma to the Humphrey-Dirksen contingent: if they refused the unanimous consent agreement, they would lose their votes for cloture. If they agreed to it, however, they risked having the amendments passed, which might result in a watered-down bill after all. Dirksen arose in a meeting of the civil rights forces to state bluntly that he simply would not have the votes for cloture if they opposed the unanimous consent agreement and the Hickenlooper contingent bolted from the bloc. Still undecided, the civil rights contingent deferred its final decision until Saturday.

On Saturday Mansfield filed his cloture petition and said that he would withdraw it for a day if the Hickenlooper agreement went through. The Humphrey-Dirksen forces decided not to object. This meant taking a risk, but it also meant putting the ball into the opponent's court. Senator Russell now had to decide whether or not to agree to the Hickenlooper request. If he did not it would mean that the bill itself might pass nearly intact. If he did he would have to risk Hickenlooper's revenge, which would unquestionably assure passage of the bill. Russell decided to forego objection.

After furiously working to line up support against the amendments over the weekend, the civil rights forces learned that most of the Hickenlooper group would vote for cloture whether these amendments passed or not—the amendments themselves had been proposed principally as a means of demonstrating that Senator Dirksen did not necessarily wield all Republican power that there was to be wielded in the United States Senate. By Monday it was clear that only one of the amendments, Senator Morton's amendment for jury trial in cases of criminal contempt, had a chance of passing. After promising to vote against the amendment, Senator Jackson ended up voting for it instead, and it carried fifty-one to forty-eight. The other two, however, were voted down decisively.

Because of the delay, the cloture vote itself was put off until Wednesday the 10th, seventy-five days after the debate on the bill had begun.

For Humphrey, the tension of the morning of the 10th

> was palpable. Confidence and enthusiasm were muted by a fear that, somehow, something had come unravelled. We were uneasy actors in a historical drama. And there gloriously was Dirksen, the sung hero, who intoned, "Stronger than all the armies is an idea whose time has come. The time has come for equality of opportunity in sharing in government, in education, and in employment."[59]

Johnson had phoned Humphrey the night before to ask about the prospects. "I think we have enough" had been Humphrey's reply. As could by now be predicted, LBJ exploded upon hearing this: "I don't want to know what you *think*. What's the vote going to be? How many do you have?" Humphrey answered, "66," one short of the necessary two-thirds majority. Later that night, however, Humphrey learned that Senator Hickenlooper, along with John Williams of Delaware, would indeed vote for cloture, and Humphrey happily conveyed the news to his chief.

At 11:10 A.M. buzzers sounded through the corridors and offices of Capitol Hill, calling the senators to their desks. Every senator presented himself. Senator Engle of California, dying of a brain tumor, had to be wheeled into the chamber just before the vote. The vote itself was taken in virtual silence. Hubert Humphrey and Richard Russell alike sat at their separate desks with pads and pencils, marking the tally. Humphrey had hoped for sixty-nine favorable votes—two beyond the necessary sixty-seven, even though he was unsure of his count. Once Senator Cannon of Nevada voted "aye," and Senator Hayden declined to answer to his name, the outcome appeared clear: civil rights were to become a reality. When Senator Williams provided the sixty-seventh vote, Humphrey raised his arms over his head in relief. The longest filibuster in Senate history was over. The final tally was seventy-one for, twenty-nine against, including Senator Engle's, who, because he could not speak, had to point to his eyes to record his "aye" vote. Humphrey turned to look at Paul Douglas, sitting in one of the back rows, and the two shared a moment of quiet satisfaction.[60]

Meanwhile, however, Richard Russell angrily insisted on using the remainder of his allotted hour under the cloture rule to complain of how he had been "confronted with the spirit of not only the mob, but of a lynch mob in the Senate of the United States."[61]

For Humphrey, the cloture vote "was the culmination of the full year's fight for the Civil Rights Act, of fifteen years' battle for civil rights in the United States Senate, and of a lifetime in politics in which equal opportunity had been *the* objective above all others."[62]

However much the cloture vote marked the culmination of what was, in essence, generations of struggle, "*the* objective" ultimately was not to invoke cloture but to pass a strong civil rights bill. That objective had still not been reached. Yet with the successful cloture vote over, the struggle for passage of a strong bill was now anticlimatic.

There was, however, a certain personal drama that would still remain.

Because the Dirksen forces stood loyally by the bill, the amendments proposed day after day by the Southerners went down to defeat, one after another. The Southerners acknowledged the hopelessness of their own position by only speaking for one minute out of the full hour allotted each of them. There were certain difficulties, but all were eventually overcome. Everything seemed headed for a successful conclusion when on June 17 Humphrey was called off the Senate floor in midafternoon by an urgent call from Muriel. One of their sons, Bob, had not been feeling well recently, and had entered a hospital to have a swelling in his neck checked. As Muriel tearfully related, the swelling was discovered to have been the result of a serious malignancy. Bob was to undergo an immediate and massive surgical procedure in which his lymphatic system would have to be removed.

Dazed, Humphrey simply had to say that he could not leave—not now when he was so near to accomplishing the thing that he had worked so long and so hard to achieve. After he hung up, Joe Rauh and Clarence Mitchell entered his office, jubilant with a recent success. Their joy quickly turned to gloom, however, once Humphrey conveyed the latest news. All three men were soon shedding bitter tears.

With the greatest of difficulty Humphrey reluctantly returned to the Senate floor to continue the fight. Two days later, on the 19th, one year after President Kennedy had sent the initial bill to Congress, the Civil Rights Act of 1964 passed the Senate. Once again all senators, including Senator Engle, were present. Instead of sharing the joy he richly deserved, however, Humphrey was in tears a second time upon hearing his son say over the phone, "Dad, I guess I've had it," following his operation. Humphrey caught the next available flight and was soon at his son's side at the Mayo Clinic.*

On July 2 the House voted to accept the Senate bill. Hours later, with television cameras trained on him, Lyndon Johnson signed it into law.

As indicated, and as ought certainly to be acknowledged, there were many actors responsible for the successful passage of the Civil Rights Act of 1964. One such actor already mentioned but not fully acknowledged was Clarence Mitchell. Humphrey and Mitchell were close friends as well as co-workers, and Humphrey sought in his autobiography to give Mitchell the credit that he thought he deserved by describing Mitchell's contribution this way: "While others drew headlines and the accolades, Clarence Mitchell did the day-to-day work, making every defeat, every compromise,

*Bob was eventually to enjoy a complete recovery.

every minor victory part of a forward movement."[63] Humphrey additionally talked of how, following the cloture vote, when everyone else had gathered for a celebration and for a chance to parade before the press, Mitchell instead had walked Richard Russell back to his Senate office and consoled him by insisting that he had done all he could in the struggle—an act typical of the quiet kind of dignity that Mitchell had steadily exemplified.*

Another person also mentioned, but not fully acknowledged, was Joe Rauh. Rauh, as one of the founders of the ADA, had worked with Humphrey on many liberal issues, as well as on Humphrey's 1960 campaign. He too had been a key behind-the-scenes factor in the bill's passage.

Another major player, and one also mentioned, yet deserving of additional attention, was Robert Kennedy, whose cruciality was obvious.

There were, of course, many others, yet Humphrey finished his own personal list by putting one person above all others: Lyndon Johnson. Humphrey gave credit to Johnson, not so much for his direct involvement in the bill's passage, which was comparatively small, but for his more indirect involvement of over ten years before H.R. 7152 ever came to the Senate floor. It was Johnson as majority leader who had gradually cracked the southern grip on Senate procedure; it was Johnson who had appointed liberals to important committees; it was Johnson who had gradually promoted the idea of federal intervention to his southern colleagues; and it was Johnson who had had rules changed and who had fought for civil rights himself, skillfully, diplomatically over the years—and did so as a Southerner over and against the opposition of his southern colleagues and friends. In Humphrey's view, therefore, it was Johnson who deserved credit for simply allowing the Civil Rights Act of 1964 to become a possibility. *This* was the Johnson

*Mitchell himself later related a story of equal significance. It was how, on this walk, Russell "was just singing Humphrey's praises, saying that because of the way Humphrey had conducted the operation, it was possible for a southern group to yield gracefully because they weren't beaten in a way that they were humiliated." From an interview with Jim Mann, as printed in *The Crisis* 91, 3 (March 1984): 40.

whom Humphrey considered to be "larger than life"—a liberal giant who was so often unacknowledged as such, especially by the very liberals who benefited the most from his efforts.

It was Johnson, too, who had years before written Humphrey such letters as the following:

> I was, of course, interested in the newspaper clipping [which Humphrey had sent him from the *St. Paul Pioneer Press* praising Johnson as majority leader]. But I am far more interested in the friendship of Hubert Humphrey—my strong right arm in the Senate.
>
> That friendship is worth more to me than any amount of newspaper space and I am very grateful to the Minnesota electorate who had the wisdom and the good sense to send you back to me and to the Senate.[64]

and,

> Your generous remarks on the Senate floor after passage of the housing bill meant as much to me as any tribute I have ever received in my life. But I would like to revise and correct your remarks in one respect—any man can be a strong leader when he has a strong right arm like Hubert Humphrey.[65]

The significance of Johnson's repeated reference to Humphrey as his "strong right arm" should not be missed, as it certainly would not be by any Southerner: in an earlier age, Robert E. Lee had comparably used precisely the same reference in regards to a young protégé of his: Stonewall Jackson.

As the cameras focused on this same Lyndon, now President Johnson, signing the Civil Rights Act of 1964 into law, he wrote (with Hubert Humphrey standing behind his right shoulder): "To Hubert, without whom it couldn't have happened."

After the bill had passed the Senate, Griffith tells of how Humphrey

> left his colleagues and a score of reporters and photographers and walked down the east front steps [of the Capitol] toward the crowd. The people recognized him and applauded. Many were negroes. Humphrey shook hands, gazed into their faces, and said, "Isn't this fine?" "You're happy, aren't you?" Some of the people shouted, "Freedom" as he walked among them. Others called, "God bless you." One woman whispered, "I hope you get picked to be vice president." An old man said, "I'm from Georgia, and I want you to know a lot of us are with you." A student said, "You gave us justice, Senator. Thank you." Others cried, "Good job . . . you did a good job."[66]

Humphrey had walked into the bright sunshine.

Notes

1. Humphrey, *Education*, 289.
2. Peter Goldman, "Cracking the Whip for Civil Rights," *Newsweek* (13 April 1964): 26.
3. Ibid., 29.
4. "Firebrand Senator Cools Down," *Business Week* (1 June 1963): 29–30.
5. Since there were separate rooms for Democrats and Republicans within the Senate Dining Room, the leaders Humphrey met during these luncheons were strictly Democratic.
6. Hubert H. Humphrey, letter to Walter George, 6 February 1953, Humphrey Collection.
7. Walter George, letter to Hubert Humphrey, 9 February 1953, Humphrey Collection.
8. Kampelman interview.
9. Humphrey, *Education*, 152.
10. Ibid., 153–54.
11. Ibid., 154.
12. Ibid., 155.
13. Ibid.
14. Ibid.
15. Ibid., 162.
16. Ibid., 163.
17. Ibid.
18. Ibid., 164–65.
19. Ibid., 165.
20. Ibid.
21. Ibid.
22. Ibid.
23. That is, the proposed "Part III" of the 1957 bill that was eventually deleted from that bill as the compromise needed in order to have it passed.
24. From a draft of an article prepared for *Progressive* by Joe Rauh.
25. Ibid.
26. Ibid.
27. This was to be the same meeting in which, after hearing a derogatory remark made about Bull Connor, JFK would quip, "Bull Connor has done more for civil rights than anybody in this room."
28. Murray Kempton, "The Senate/Mr. Humphrey's Conquering Hosts," *The New Republic* (4 April 1964): 6.
29. Ibid.
30. Ibid.
31. Peter Goldman, "The New Hubert Humphrey," *Newsweek* (13 April 1964): 27.
32. Ibid., 32.
33. Rauh, "draft."

34. Joe Rauh described this process in his draft on the passage of the 1964 civil rights bill: "Mobilizing for a battle on the floor of the House requires unusually detailed preparation. When the House takes up a bill, it goes into 'the Committee of the Whole' for the purpose of considering amendments. Writing in the galleries is not permitted. To keep a list of how Congressmen voted requires enough watchers to cover each Congressman and to remember whether and how each voted. Over 220 Congressmen had committed themselves to the bill without dilution, but these commitments were of little value unless the Congressmen were on the floor."

    That that commitment was honored as a result of the gallery "watch" was evidenced in the remarks made by Congressman Haley of Florida, who called the final bill "monstrous," and who stated that the bill would have never passed without the "vultures in the galleries."
35. Humphrey, *Education*, 273–74.
36. Lyndon Johnson, as quoted in ibid., 274.
37. Ibid., 274.
38. Ibid., 275.
39. Marjorie Hunter, "Rights Command Set Up in Senate," *The New York Times* (22 March 1964): 41.
40. Humphrey, *Education*, 276.
41. Ibid., 276–77.
42. Ibid., 277.
43. Humphrey, as quoted in Griffith, *Candid*, 282.
44. Rauh, "draft."
45. Humphrey, *Education*, 278.
46. Humphrey, *Congressional Record*, 81st Cong., 2nd sess., 1950. Vol. 96, 7102.
47. Ibid., 7097.
48. Griffith offers the one exception to this. It involved the protracted negotiations with Dirksen: "Before one negotiating session he [Humphrey] arranged for a liberal Senator to stage a political tantrum in the meeting. At a critical point in the conference when Dirksen was about to protest that Humphrey was not conceding enough, the liberal pointed a finger at Humphrey, shouted 'This is a goddamned sellout,' and stalked out of the room. Humphrey was then able to turn to Dirksen and say, 'See what pressures I'm up against? I can't concede any more on this point.'" From Griffith, *Candid*, 281–82.
49. Humphrey, *Education*, 278.
50. McNeil, Lowry, "The Education of a Senator," *Progressive* (May 1951): 22.
51. Ibid., 23.
52. Ibid.
53. Ibid., 22–23.
54. Humphrey, as quoted in Kempton's "Conquering Hosts," 8.
55. Richard Russell, *Congressional Record*, 88th Cong., 2nd sess., 1964. Vol. 110, 13309.
56. Sherman interview.
57. Rauh, "draft."
58. Richard Russell, *Congressional Record*, 88th Cong., 2nd sess., 1964. Vol. 110, 11943.

59. Humphrey, *Education*, 282.
60. The depth of that satisfaction would be indicated four years later amidst the chaos of the 1968 Democratic convention where, as Cohen tells: "as youthful anti-war activists changed 'Dump the Hump'—the late Senator Paul Douglas, then 76 years old, sat with the Illinois delegation. Suddenly he clutched his chest in agony. Turning to a friend, he gasped that he was having a heart attack. The friend told Douglas not to worry: he would be rushed immediately to a waiting ambulance. 'No,' Douglas answered. 'I'm not leaving until I vote for HH.'" From Cohen, *Undefeated*, 333.
61. Russell, *Congressional Record*, 88th Cong., 2nd sess., 1964. Vol. 110, 13320.
62. Humphrey, *Education*, 283.
63. Ibid.
64. Lyndon Johnson, letter to Hubert Humphrey, 17 June 1955, Humphrey Collection.
65. Lyndon Johnson, letter to Hubert Humphrey, 9 June 1955, Humphrey Collection.
66. Griffith, *Candid*, 284–85.

6

The Irony of Idealism Applied: Vietnam

As already indicated, the successful cloture vote of 10 June 1964, and the subsequent passage of the Civil Rights Act of 1964 represented the culmination of fifteen years of both personal and professional growth for Hubert Humphrey. In many ways, June of 1964 can be said to be the highwater mark of his career. The bill itself was very likely the most significant piece of liberal legislation to be passed in a generation. His role in the successful cloture vote that had made it possible marked Humphrey as one of the most powerful, and possibly as one of the most distinctive liberals of his age: he had established himself as one who matched the strength of his liberal convictions with an ability to *effect* them.[1] In working for cloture's, and therefore for the bill's passage, he had also demarcated a distinctively liberal *mode* of effecting the liberal ideals: instead of employing the traditional strong-arm tactics, as exemplified, for instance, by Lyndon Johnson, Humphrey had achieved success by overcoming his opponents with eminent good will. "Good ole' Hubert" just could not be turned down. Yes, the discipline was there, as it had to be. Yet it was by steadfastly appealing to his opponent's higher and more humane instincts—and by impressing upon them that they [such instincts] were *precisely* what were at stake, not to mention by refusing to call such attention to one's self—that proved to be the distinguishing and finally decisive factor in the successful outcome of the 1964 bill. Because the bill was not only based on principles embedded in the foundational documents of the land, but was passed via the procedures similarly established in those documents, it represented, for those convinced of its virtue, not just liberalism, but America at its best. It was indeed the guarantee of life, liberty, and therefore the pursuit of happiness being bestowed on all of America's equally created peoples. As such it represented the fulfillment of America's promise for mankind.

For Humphrey, it represented the fulfillment of his own promise that "the cause" was indeed "mankind," just as the title of his 1964 book had indicated it was. Humphrey had always been committed to that cause. Yet his ability to have the strength of that commitment *realized* was something which had been achieved only over time. He had proved to all that he had learned from his early, painful experiences, and that he had now grown into a truly potent force for the kind of good that he believed in—so potent, in fact, that the possibility of his eventually attaining the ultimate dream—the presidency—might now begin to assume more the look of "fact" than "dream." It must surely have been a time of tremendous personal satisfaction.

Nevertheless, it was also to be a time of tremendous irony as well. One of those ironies, on the pleasant side, was that much of the skill used to ensure the bill's passage was skill learned from the very group that had successfully opposed it for generations. The care for and mastery of parliamentary procedure that was crucial to passage of the bill was learned largely from those who had so carefully utilized that same mastery to effectively halt all civil rights legislation proposed since Reconstruction. This is, naturally, a reference to the southern Senate patriarchs. As such, they were, quite literally, beaten at their own game—and on the one issue that they had opposed more vehemently than any other.

Still another irony, however, and a much more bitter one for Humphrey, was that as a result of this *most* satisfactory experience for Hubert Humphrey, he was guaranteed the position that would in turn lead him into his *least* satisfactory experience. Once again, as with his "Bright Sunshine" speech leading to the bitterness of his first years in the Senate, so now his role in passage of the Civil Rights Act of 1964 would lead to an even more disastrous outcome. His role in that bill confirmed, indeed elevated his position as a leader in the front rank of liberalism in America. As liberalism was the dominant force of the time, he was one of the dominant figures of the time. Yet, ironically enough, it was that very "elevation" that would result in his fall. Within one year, rather than being one of the ultimate "insiders," he would be one of the most marked "*out*siders" to the Washington establishment. Within two years, the respect that he had gained with the Washington establishment would turn to ridicule. Within three years, the political force of liberalism that he had sought and eventually came to represent, would turn against him—to the point, in fact, that within four years, when he finally came within grasping distance of his ultimate goal, the presidency, it would not only *not* support him—it would actually work *against* him, and all over one issue. How could such a remarkable, not to say disastrous turn of events occur, and within such short order? By his becoming LBJ's vice president. And what was this one viciously destructive issue? Vietnam.

Albert Eisele and others have contended that had their positions been reversed in 1964, Hubert Humphrey and Gene McCarthy would have found themselves in similarly reversed positions in 1968. McCarthy was one of the most likely choices for Lyndon Johnson's vice-presidential running mate in 1964. He was a personal favorite of the Johnson's and a northern liberal, which provided a good balance to Johnson's more conservative southern appeal, just as Humphrey did. He was articulate and had a genuine flair. Even more important, though, he was a Catholic, and was so at a time when LBJ was under considerable pressure to justify his *not* choosing Bobby Kennedy as his running mate. Nevertheless, as the convention neared it became clear that McCarthy was no longer being seriously considered by Johnson. When he felt that he was simply being manipulated by the Johnson machine, McCarthy broke with it. Many have, consequently, seen McCarthy's run for the presidency in 1968 as nothing more than a grudge match in response to this. If McCarthy *had* been chosen as Johnson's running mate, Humphrey would have remained in the

Senate as the leading figure that he was. He thus would not have been forced by both personal and professional constraints into a position that many regard as his downfall, namely, of becoming the administration's leading spokesman for its involvement in Vietnam. Humphrey, as the theory continues, would have been free to be critical of the administration's policy in Vietnam, and McCarthy instead would have been faced with the extremely difficult position with which Humphrey actually ended up having to contend.

Dan Cohen goes even one step further than this by speculating that

> had John Kennedy lived, his brother would probably have remained in the Cabinet, and Humphrey in the Senate. It is not unlikely that their roles would have been reversed: Humphrey still leading his national constituency on the left as a critic of the war and [Bobby] Kennedy defending administration policy.[2]

Both are interesting theories, but the facts of history were to be otherwise. Nevertheless they do indicate yet another ironic aspect of Humphrey's vice-presidential experience.

In terms of this irony, however, *Look* magazine had the final say. Its 6 April 1965 edition is, in retrospect, an apparent product of divination. The issue was dedicated to "The Big Change in Washington" by which it meant the "Texanization of Washington." The mood was upbeat. There was talk of how "shrewd older men have come into power," and of how Lyndon B. Johnson could "proudly count off a swelling list of accomplishments."[3] The emphasis was on how Johnson got things done—on how he was a *doer*. The anticipation was that "his administration could become the success of the century,"[4] and light-hearted reference was made to the rush in sales of western-style clothing that was overtaking Washington at that time.

Not too many pages afterwards, however, the lead on another article reads, "Vietnam: Washington's biggest problem." The tone of this article was anything but lighthearted. References here were to the potential that this "dirty little war" had for becoming a major conflict; how "time has run out for our hope of victory-by-stalemate"; how "for all the pushing courage of 25,000 U.S. advisers, South Vietnam's anti-guerrilla war has largely failed."[5] There was discussion about the ever-strengthening VC, the militantism of the Buddhists, and of how "the democracy we are supposed to be protecting here" could not be found. A captured guerrilla is interviewed. He does not know what either Peking or Washington is. He denies that he is VC; "I am Vietminh," he asserts. He joined the guerrillas because "we have to fight foreigners who come here." The author discusses how "paradoxically, it has been our failure to provide the South Vietnamese with any effective, popular government that has driven the common people of all Vietnam closer to their ancient enemies, the Chinese."[6] The article concludes by refusing to end with a standard war joke. The reason given: "there isn't anything funny about Vietnam."[7]

On the very next page the lead then asks, "Can an optimist from Minnesota stay happy as Vice President?"[8]

No one could have stated a more ironic, let alone fateful juxtaposition. The image that many have of HHH regarding Vietnam is that his downfall was one that he deserved—that he had betrayed the very cause that he had purported to lead, namely, liberalism. The charges of "warmonger," and the classic taunt of the sixties: "'HHH, LBJ, how many kids did you kill today?" were, from this particular viewpoint, his just desert.

It is true that Humphrey did become the administration's "cheerleader" on Vietnam, and there are many and vivid images of his doing so. As a great "liberal," and particularly as one who had championed the cause of peace and nonviolence, not to mention embodied it in his own life, such images did *appear* to be the very picture of hypocrisy, for which he rightfully paid a political price. If that is so, then, as far as Humphrey provides a case study in religious-political ethics, the "case" would appear to be "closed." Such in fact is the "verdict" for many. A more involved study of this issue, however, might provide a different and hopefully more nuanced view.

Such a study begins at the time of Humphrey's own highwater mark—1964—but includes, as well, a period of Philippine history, and the involvement of a particular American in that history. In late October of 1964, just before the landslide election that would place Hubert Humphrey in the vice president's office, one of Humphrey's key and long-term staff members, William Connell, received a memo from a certain Rufus Phillips. Phillips had been recruited into the CIA after his graduation from Yale in the 1950s and had been stationed in Vietnam very nearly ever since. Phillips was part of a team headed by then Colonel, later Major General Edward Lansdale. The Lansdale team was a special unit assigned to carry out intelligence, civic action, and psychological warfare activities. Phillips and Connell were friends, and the tone of the memo reflected that. It also, however, reflected the desperateness of the situation in Vietnam at that time. Certain segments of the memo read as follows:

> Bert Fraleigh who has been back in Saigon for several months . . . gives Vietnam only from 30 to 60 days unless our personnel and policies are changed. As you know, Bert is not normally pessimistic . . .
>
> 1. In September, General Taylor ordered the one American close to the Vietnamese, Lt. Col. Lucien Conein, out of the country within 24 hours. This happened because General Khanh [then currently the ruler of South Vietnam] preferred to talk to Col. Conein, who understands him and was a friend, rather than to General Taylor, and Khanh made his preference known. Since then the U.S. has been operating totally blind.
>
> 2. The new USAID [United States Agency for International Development] Mission Director, James Killen, is in the process of completely destroying the USOM counterinsurgency effort. His motivation is difficult to assess but seems to be based on firmly held preconceived notions that Vietnam is no different from Korea (his previous post) and on a desire to build an impregnable position against possible Congressional criticism should Vietnam be lost.
>
> 3. On the Vietnamese side, temporary order has been restored among various contending factions but the leadership appointed to the job is not up to handling it, the division among the Vietnamese military remains deep and unresolved, and the U.S. is providing no meaningful backing or assistance to meet Vietnamese political needs because our representative does not have the skill or inclination.
>
> Bill, I can appreciate how tired you and the Vice President-elect are going to be after the campaign is over. Nevertheless, I urge you to prevail on him to turn his attention almost immediately to Vietnam. He is the only man I have spoken to about it (including the late President Kennedy) who grasped the essentials of that situation and what the U.S. needs to do. Because of this I most strongly urge the following action.
>
> The Vice President-elect should go to Vietnam, after the election, to make an on-the-spot assessment of the situation for President Johnson (after the inauguration would be too late). *He* must do this, *not* Secretary McNamara, if any meaningful changes are to be made out there before it is too late. And the hour is very late indeed.

> It is the unanimous opinion of those who know Vietnam and counterinsurgency well that revolutionary changes are required in the structure and thrust of our efforts there if we are to have even a slender chance of salvaging the U.S. position, not only in Vietnam, but in all of Asia. Those to whom President Johnson has so far assigned the responsibility have such a vested interest in past and present policy that they cannot be expected to generate the changes required. Thus the sole hope, as I see it, rests with you and your boss. I can only hope that you will respond.[9]

The memo is noteworthy for the sense of urgency with which Phillips portrayed the situation. It is also noteworthy for its consideration that Humphrey "is the only man" who grasped "the essentials of that situation" and that he is, therefore, "the sole hope."

Edward Lansdale, Rufus Phillips' chief, was an Air Force officer who worked for and was supported by the CIA. In his book, *In the Midst of Wars*, he told of how he joined the Air Force following World War II mainly because, as a new service, "there would be more elbow room for fresh ideas . . . than in the older military services."[10] Fresh ideas were to prove to be Lansdale's forte. Having served in intelligence in the western Pacific during World War II, he had been assigned, in September of 1950, to the Philippines in order to help suppress the insurrection that was occurring there at that time. The rebellion was known as the "Huk" Rebellion. The Huks were a communist insurgency group following the tactics of Maoist Asian communism. "Huk" was short for "Hukbong Bayan Laban sa Hapon," or "People's Anti-Japanese Army." They had formed during the war and were credited with the deaths of some 5,000 Japanese troops. At the same time, however, they were also credited with the deaths of over 20,000 Filipinos as well. They were, in other words, much more a "pro-Communist" than an "anti-Japanese" army.

When Lansdale first arrived in the Philippines he suspected that backward laws and flimsy governmental structures supporting the fledgling nation were the main cause for the discontent upon which the Huks thrived. On studying the Philippine constitution, the electoral code, and the laws on agrarian reform, however, he found them to be "models of enlightened social thinking."[11] On studying the situation further, Lansdale soon saw evidence that the trouble lay either in faulty execution of the laws, or simply in flat failure to execute them at all. This cause of injustice was, for

Lansdale, the obvious fuel for the Huk fire, yet he was surprised to see that in his briefings with both Philippine and American officials, political and social factors were rarely mentioned, if at all. Focus was almost exclusively on the military situation. In quickly seeing that he could expect little else from the regular military and political figures with whom he was in contact, Lansdale struck out on his own.

He befriended a number of Philippine people, yet no friendship was more important than the one he formed with Ramon Magsaysay. Magsaysay was at the time Secretary of National Defense. This was the same Magsaysay of whom Albert Gore would later rise in the Senate to say, "I regarded President Magsaysay as the greatest democratic statesman in the entire Asiatic theatre."[12] Lansdale's aim was to help him attain that position after playing a key role in successfully ending the Huk rebellion. The question is, how?

The Lansdale-Magsaysay approach, in essence, was quite simple. The communists use injustice as the leverage by which they pry their way into a society. Remove that leverage, and the society shuts them out. Have right, in other words, on your side, and the communist might will wither away. Such a theoretical understanding of "right" and "might," however, was not understood to simply be a matter of working for justice; it was also understood to mean using one's "might" effectively as well.

Hence, as an example, one of the most important reforms that Lansdale and Magsaysay effected was the BCT or Battalion Combat Team. A BCT was a unit more heavily manned and armed than its normal counterpart, to be stationed in every zone in every province. Yet the point was not to rely principally on its increased firepower, but rather on its mobility. It was to be a unit principally designed, in other words, to go on the offensive. This *was* innovative, for up until that time the strategy had been simply to use company-sized units to defend cities and highways—a strategy that had kept the government forces constantly on the defensive and thus vulnerable and demoralized. It had simultaneously allowed the guerrillas tremendous freedom of movement and action. The only offensive tactic used up until that time had been a highly colorful, yet ineffective "sweep" of a large area, followed by an intensive artillery barrage—something which the shadowy Huks easily eluded time and again. The parallel between such an arrangement and what was to be practiced later in Vietnam is clear.

The BCT strategy altered this arrangement. So did another reform, namely that of the Philippine Scout Rangers. The idea here was to

> set up small teams of volunteers, each made up of an officer and four men, who were to be given intense training in jungle warfare, scouting, and survival. After training, each team would be sent to a remote area to make contact with the enemy—either keeping the enemy under close observation until detailed information was gathered or eliminating him by ambush or surprise attack. The choice would be left to the team's on-the-spot decision.[13]

The contribution made by these units was to prove to their fellows that the jungle was not necessarily "owned," and thus that the enemy was not necessarily as fearsome as had been supposed. He was as human as were those opposing him. By stationing, in addition, the Rangers with the BCT troops, they proved to be a source of both confidence and challenge to their regular comrades.

Finally, on an individual level, Magsaysay himself mounted an "offensive" all his own. Acting against the desires of the General Staff, and on the advice of his American friend and adviser, Magsaysay began to make unannounced spot checks on the field, frequently by flying in on a small military liaison aircraft. Where he found officers being lax or derelict in their duty he would either criticize them or demote them on the spot. If, on the other hand, he found them to be performing well, the opposite would hold true—he would lavish praise—praise that would often include a promotion right then and there. Once word went out that the Defense Secretary himself was taking a direct and active interest in the affairs of even remote posts, morale shot up and responsible soldiers were encouraged.

While Magsaysay was conducting spot checks on the field, he and Lansdale instituted an innovative form of social gathering back at headquarters. It was called a "coffee klatsch," and was designed to provide a way that officers from both on and off the field could get together on an informal yet regular basis.

Lansdale described how the idea had come about:

> It began in so natural a fashion that I didn't realize at first that a pattern was being set that I was to follow thereafter. Philippine staff officers calling on Magsaysay at the house [of Gen. Lansdale]* were treated hospitably while they were waiting to see him, usually having coffee in the "sala." Often one of the people on my team would pass the time of day with these waiting officers and, of course, talk shop about the war. We discovered that some of them had been doing a lot of thinking on their own about the situation and in this informal atmosphere they would really express freely their views on what was going wrong and would suggest changes. Sometimes our own friends from combat units in the field would stop by to say hello, while in Manila, and would join in the conversations we were having with waiting staff officers. Usually they added details and ideas from their own current experiences to whatever topic was being discussed. The desk officers from the headquarters staff and the combat soldiers, encouraged by the warm interest and contributions of us Americans, would find themselves exploring all possible ideas. From time to time, Magsaysay would sit down and join us too.[14]

The Scout Ranger program was one such coffee klatsch notion. There were to be many others.

All told, the Lansdale-Magsaysay approach served to greatly boost military morale. For the first time the war was being taken to the enemy. The army was not simply hunkering down in a static defensive position but rather was actively engaging the enemy. This was true even for their own defense secretary, who, wearing "a vividly colored sport shirt and a farmer's straw hat" while visiting his troops, made it clear that he "was with them in the field."[15]

While restoring the army's faith both in itself and in its leadership was important, what was much more important, given the nature of the struggle, was restoring the *public*'s faith in its armed forces. The fundamental lesson of dealing with an Asian communist insurgency of this type was realizing the significance of Mao's dictum that "the people are the sea in which the guerrilla fish swim." The essence of the struggle was to render the guerrillas as fish out of such a "sea." This was "People's War," and as such was unlike any contest that America had ever entered into before, short of the revolution of its own nascency. The battleground of this was not the northern plain of Europe or the sands of Iwo Jima. It was instead the hearts and minds of the Filipino people.

*The two shared the same house at the time.

There were many ways that the Lansdale-Magsaysay team waged this war. At one coffee klatsch session the idea of a ten-centavo telegram to the secretary's office by which anyone could send in advice or offer their criticism came up. Magsaysay liked the idea and it was instituted. He made it clear that *all* criticism, pro *and* con, would be welcome, and he appointed a staff to process whatever amount of such mail would come into the office. When word went out that he actually acted on some of the advice, and that retribution was not waiting for those who did criticize the army, what had begun as a trickle soon became a flood. It was a simple but effective means of demonstrating that the government, and especially the military wing of the government, intended to be responsive to the people that it was meant to serve. When rewards were offered for knowledge of the whereabouts of Huk leaders, information on Huk movements and activities began to flow in.

Such a simple measure was all part of a larger strategy of what became known as "civic action." Lansdale had read Mao's Chinese Communist 8th Route Army's "three great disciplinary measures" and "eight noteworthy points." The measures are: "Act in accordance with orders; do not take anything from the people; do not allow self-interest to injure public interest." The points are: "Put back the door (after being used as a bed); tie up straws (after use as a mattress); talk pleasantly; buy and sell fairly; return everything borrowed; indemnify everything damaged; do not bathe in view of women; and do not rob personal belongings of captives." These rules, however simple, capture the essence of People's Warfare. If they are followed, and if the spirit that engenders them prevails, the support of the people is gained, and the course of the war is turned. As General Lansdale said, "Asian Communists understand this. Too few on our side do. People still get trampled under as our soldiers strive for the tactical goals given them. As long as this happens, we cannot win."[16] He wrote those words in 1972. Given much of the criticism of our involvement in Vietnam, history would seem to vindicate him.

Orders were issued that arrogance was to be replaced with courtesy. The theft of livestock was punished. Army engineers began to dig wells (dubbed "Liberty Wells") for communities needing water.

The idea of utilizing judge advocate lawyers to assist poor farmers in land disputes with larger landowners came out of another coffee klatsch session. A similar idea was to have civilian casualties of the war treated in military hospitals. The "EDCOR" or "Economic Development Corps," still another coffee klatsch brainstorm, began to offer land, along with agricultural and building supplies to captured Huks who were willing to reform. During the entire campaign against the Huks, 6,874 Huks were killed and 4,072 captured; 9,458 however, surrendered—many of them talking about EDCOR as they did.* At the same time they muttered about how they had been misled by the Huk leadership in regards to the nature of the Philippine government and the people who ran it.

Lansdale had promised that if local commanders carried out civic action programs like EDCOR, and did so with integrity, their "raw take" of tactical intelligence would increase 100 percent within a week. To their surprise, it was a promise that was made good again and again. The guerrilla "sea" was beginning to dry up.

That sea finally evaporated altogether with the election of 1953. Out of a total of 5,603,000 eligible voters, 2,912,992 cast their votes for Magsaysay, who had been convinced to run on the opposition ticket. The incumbent (and corrupt) president Quirino was only able, even with his armed thugs and strong-arm tactics, to garner 1,313,991 votes. The landslide Magsaysay victory signalled the end of not only the Quirino administration, but also of the communist insurgency that it had inadvertently nurtured. Within weeks, having no more cause to fight for (and few troops to fight with), the Huk leader surrendered (with a certain reporter present, Benigno Aquino). For the Lansdale-Magsaysay forces there could not have been a more satisfying victory.

Lansdale did not view the victory as simply one for Ramon Magsaysay, or for the tactics that Lansdale had himself inspired. This victory was one for democracy itself. American had championed democracy, but that was not to say that therefore democracy was simply another American "product." General Lansdale's credo included the belief that "men are created equal, that they are endowed by their Creator with certain inalienable rights," and

*See appendix D for a more complete story of EDCOR success.

"that the provisions of our Bill of Rights . . . make that great precept a reality among men."[17] He believed that this was true for all people everywhere—very much, and not coincidentally, like his political counterpart, Hubert Humphrey. This, for Lansdale, constituted an ideology—but an ideology which was not, nor should be represented as being singularly "American." Rather, it was an ideology in keeping with what St. Paul wrote when he said, "Where the spirit of the Lord is, there is liberty."[18] He believed, in other words, in both the universality and the inherent decency of democracy. He also believed in its power to attract all people to its cause, given the proper chance. In his view, "When we Americans give of our substance to the people of other countries, we should give as generously of our ideology as we do of our money, our guns, our cereal grains, and our machinery."[19] This would not be a matter of our imposing our view on others. Quite to the contrary, it would mean "making others strong enough to embrace and hold it [democracy] for their own." He fully believed that he had helped to do this in the Philippines.[20] The 1953 election was the culmination of just such an effort—an effort intended to help "the Philippine people fulfill the promise of their own laws and form of government, not in imposing something strange and different upon them."[21]

Lansdale's role in the 1953 election became something of a legend in the Far East. Among other things it would earn him the nickname of "Colonel Landslide." When he returned to Washington, however, he found that his fame had not quite reached the Potomac. He was greatly frustrated by the fact that no one was interested there in civic action or People's War—only the military aspect of the conflict. There was no one who wanted to hear about Mao's 8th Route Army rules. Ironically enough, by so behaving, the American military was missing yet another of Mao's points: "There are often military elements who care for only military affairs but not politics." Such "one-track-minded officers," for Lansdale, "ignoring the inter-connection between politics and military affairs, must be made to understand the correct relationship between the two. All military actions are means to achieve political objectives while military action itself is a manifested form of politics."[22] This *is* ironic because this outlook was one held not only by

Mao, but also by the figure generally regarded as being the West's greatest military theorist, Carl von Clausewitz.

Following his unsatisfactory debriefing experience in Washington, Lansdale was issued a new set of orders: "Proceed without delay by first available transportation" to—Saigon.[23] Lansdale was to go, after receiving these orders, to serve in Vietnam for several tours of duty. It was to be a frustrating experience, particularly after his success in the Philippines. He summarized his assessment of the situation, based on that experience, in an article in the October 1964 issue of *Foreign Affairs*.

He began by stating that "on December 20, 1960, the communists set up the political base with which they hoped to win Vietnam by revolutionary struggle. The base consisted of an idea and of an organization to start giving that idea reality."[24] The "idea" was "to gain control of the 14,000,000 people living in South Vietnam by destroying their faith in their own government and creating faith in the inevitability of a Communist takeover."[25] The organization created in order to implement that idea was "The National Liberation Front of South Vietnam," whose more derogatory nickname was to become "Viet Cong." General Lansdale argued that since the Communists "have let loose" this revolutionary idea, "it will not die by being ignored, bombed or smothered by us." This is so because "ideas do not die in such ways." While firmly believing that we were perfectly right to be in Vietnam, our *method* of offering assistance there was defective:

> The harsh fact, and one which has given pause to every thoughtful American, is that, despite the use of overwhelming amounts of men, money and materiel, despite the quantity of well-meant American advice and despite the impressive statistics of casualties inflicted on the VC, the Communist subversive insurgents have grown steadily stronger.[26]

As an alternative to our then current policy, he argued that we ought to follow the course that was successful in routing the communists in the Philippines, namely,

> to oppose the Communist idea with a better idea and to do so on the battleground itself in a way that would permit the people, who are the main feature of that battleground, to make their own choice. A political base would be

> established. The first step would be to state political goals, founded on principles cherished by free men, which the Vietnamese share; the second would be an aggressive commitment of organizations and resources to start the Vietnamese moving realistically toward those political goals. In essence, this is revolutionary warfare, the spirit of the British Magna Carta, the French "Liberte, Egalite, Fraternite," and our own Declaration of Independence.[27]

He cited the successful counterinsurgencies of the Philippines and of Malaya as teaching "the great lesson" that "there must be a heartfelt *cause* to which the legitimate government is pledged, a cause which makes a stronger appeal to the people than the communist cause, a cause which is used in a dedicated way by the legitimate government to polarize and guide all other actions—psychological, military, social, and economic—with participation by the people themselves, in order to bring victory."[28]

It was correctly identifying and using the right *cause*, then, that was the key to stopping the communists successfully. By doing so the fight was made a "pro-people fight, with the overwhelming majority of the people then starting to help what they recognized to be their own side."[29] Nurturing such a "pro-people fight" was crucial for it was only by so doing that one could rob the communists of the one thing that they needed to survive, namely, the support of the people whom they eventually sought to dominate, that is, Mao's "sea."

General Lansdale went on to argue that because this was true, the most urgent step to take is to "make it the No. 1 priority for the military to *protect* and *help* the people."[30] He cites an example of how this has not happened in Vietnam. When Tay Ninh province was overrun by two VC battalions, the government's response was to pour in artillery and air strikes—after the VC had slipped out—only to find afterwards that the people were hateful of the government and "grateful to the VC for making them dig foxholes." "American bounty," he wrote, "whether in the form of military-civic action or economic aid by U.S. civilians, cannot make up for such mistakes." "Nor," he added, "can it buy the friendship of the Vietnamese people." What America should do, then, is to teach the Vietnamese to "insist on an attitude of behavior, an extension of military courtesy, in which the soldier citizen becomes the brotherly protector of the civilian citizen."[31] This is part of the VC code—Part 9 of their "Military Oath of Honor," as adopted by General Giap from Mao's 8th Route Army code, and it had been crucial to the success they enjoyed.

The lessons from the Philippine experience that could be and needed to be taught in Vietnam could not be more apparent. The problem was finding those who would be willing to listen. Lansdale met with and attempted to convince many political figures on all levels in Washington of the wisdom of his approach. The only figure that Lansdale was able to find who was so convinced was the highly unmilitaristic, yet nonetheless politically astute Hubert Humphrey.

Hubert Humphrey and Edward Lansdale were first brought together sometime in the very busy spring of 1964. The meeting went well. The two found that they agreed enthusiastically on the kind of policy that had been outlined in Lansdale's *Foreign Affairs* article. It marked the beginning of a relationship in which Lansdale was to become the soon-to-become vice president's chief adviser on Vietnam. Lansdale described it as "a relationship where we could talk very openly to each other, and he [Humphrey] understood what I was talking about."[32] For Lansdale, "as I talked to him, he seemed to feel that that [the Lansdale approach] was the answer out there."[33]

Finding such a willing ear must have been gratifying, given Lansdale's experience up to that point. As he said,

> I had hoped to do more than I ever did—ever got a chance to do when I got out there. I got stopped pretty cold. Some of the things just took a lot of patience and I finally decided, "Well, I'll just outwait them all—outlast them and try to get my ideas across." I was trying to let the Vietnamese have much more say in their own affairs. This seemed to make a lot of sense. I would think, "Well, they've got to try things and do things and make mistakes and learn, and we have got to be big enough to understand that—to get our hands off of them, and get them pointed in the right way."[34]

In meeting Humphrey, Lansdale had for once found someone who was indeed "big enough" in this way.

Lansdale himself was a highly controversial character. His career was marked, whether intentionally or not, by challenging the status quo, as he did in Manila, Saigon, and Washington. He was known for his close friendships with colorful figures who opposed the ancien regime in whatever country he was assigned to. Many times he had been threatened with being "shipped home in a coffin"—his name had appeared on any number of assassination lists, both Filipino, French, and communist—yet he had always survived, sometimes narrowly. The case can be built, however, that the main reason why he gained such bitter enmity was his ability to engender the respect and devotion of the people that he had been sent to assist—an ability that aroused the jealousy of many who prided themselves on their ability as administrators, yet who forever lacked, or just simply denied the efficacy of such a humane (not to mention shrewd) touch. One of the more moving examples of this "ability" occurred in the midst of a civil war that had taken place in 1955 when the newly formed South Vietnam was still in its birth pangs. The fighting centered mostly in and around Saigon, and the city was largely in chaos. Amidst the chaos Lansdale learned that *both* the French *and* the rebel forces (whom the French were clandestinely aiding) were attempting to have Lansdale killed, blaming him in newspapers, leaflets, and radio broadcasts for all of the troubles then besetting Saigon. Lansdale's story continues from there:

> Early the next morning, April 29, I was awakened by a hubbub on the street in front of my house. I looked out. The block was filled with people along the sidewalks and curbs on both sides of the street, where pedicabs, taxis, and even an old truck were jammed into parking areas. There were several small fires laid against garden walls, where people were cooking breakfast. My first guess was that the people were refugees from the conflict and great fire in Cholon [the Chinese sector of Saigon], which I judged from the smudges in the sky must still be burning. The fighting was continuing, too, its sounds plain in the morning air. Yet the people didn't look like refugees. I could see no children, no bundles of possessions.
>
> My houseboy came in and told me that the people had started arriving before dawn. No, they were not refugees. They had come to where I lived *to protect me* because of the "papers." They were leaflets in various sizes, some from a printing press, others from mimeograph machines, my name displayed prominently in each. It seems that different groups had come up with the same idea at the same time of offering a large sum for my head. The leaflets had been distributed last night and earlier this morning. As for the radio broadcasts, they were a new hourly appeal on the Binh Xuyen [the name of the rebel forces] radio station, offering a large sum to anyone bringing me in *alive* to the Binh Xuyen. The broadcasts hastened to explain why I should be lugged in alive, in case a listener got the wrong notion that the gangster Binh Xuyen forces were

> turning effete. The radio audience was assured that I would be suitably tortured, until, finally, my stomach would be torn open, my guts stuffed with mud, and my body floated down the Canal de Derivation for all to see. Leaflets and broadcasts blamed me for all the current troubles in Saigon-Cholon.
>
> I went out on the street to meet the crowd before my house. They were some of the elected neighborhood officials from the days of the social action committee who had come from all over the city, along with taxicab and "cyclo" drivers who were friends of the Ocampo family, and even a group of well-dressed bureaucrats who explained to me that they were residents of a nearby apartment house. From their many remarks, I gathered that I represented something "good" to them and that it had become evident "the bad ones" were out to destroy me. They didn't want it to happen and were at my house to prevent it.
>
> It was a stunning way to start the day. I must have stood there amongst them for several minutes, unable to speak. It was one of the grandest moments of my life.[35]

This is not exactly "the ugly American" as is pictured by most of the world, including America itself. But then, that is the likely reason why William J. Lederer and Eugene Burdick, the authors of the book of that name, depicted Lansdale as they did in the form of the heroic Colonel Hillendale.

True to his controversial form, however, he was later to be negatively depicted by Graham Greene in *The Quiet American* (although, then again, Greene himself was later to compare Ho Chi Minh to Mr. Chips). By championing such a controversial character, Hubert Humphrey immersed himself in the same supposedly dark waters.[36]

There are a number of those, however, who by so doing not only believed that Humphrey was distinctive, but distinctly *right*. Bert Fraleigh, an economic adviser and expert in Far Eastern affairs for AID37 became a friend and adviser on the Far East to Humphrey after first meeting him in 1960. For Fraleigh, Humphrey was a uniquely approachable and discerning figure. Fraleigh describes how, in his first visit with Humphrey, he "expected a perfunctory handshake and a few minutes of pleasantries. Instead, he [Humphrey] was intensely interested in the poor people of Asia and how America could really reach them."[38] This was not in terms of military hardware and expertise, for "Hubert simply did not believe in military solutions." In Fraleigh's view "there was a lot of farmboy and common horse sense and human feel in him which gave him the vision that the American farm successes might hold the key to eliminating world hunger and strife."[39]

This "human feel" was also attested to by Rufus Phillips, who at one point had been Fraleigh's chief in Vietnam.* He spoke of how he had "found him [Humphrey] to have, you know, to have a real feel for . . . [an] understanding [of] what things were really like in Vietnam." This was opposed to the example of most people who thought in "pre-formed abstractions" about how "if we applied a lot of power that this [or that] would happen" yet lacked "any understanding of the dynamics, the political dynamics of Vietnam . . . why it was important . . . to establish a political base . . . for the Vietnamese to establish their own political base."[40] For Phillips, Humphrey could and did understand these "dynamics." In Phillips' view, Humphrey saw clearly "that our aid had political impact and [that] we should try to think about that and try to promote, not the form of U.S. democracy, but the substance of it, and to try to get assistance into the hands of groups to try to build pluralism and so forth." This was "very much a part of Humphrey's philosophy" and was, for Phillips, "what drew us to him and him to us."[41]

In more specific terms, Phillips discussed how the Lansdale team had attempted to build a "viable kind of village infrastructure where people had something—where development was going on—where villages were developing themselves." In the Lansdale view, of course, "this was really the best way to establish a stable and peaceful Vietnam over the long run, and it also would be successful in preventing the Communists from coming back in and doing what they did." Phillips asserts that this approach "was something that Hubert Humphrey kind of instinctively understood."[42]

For Phillips, Humphrey also appeared to have an instinctive understanding of the Vietnamese need to develop and propound *their own* nationalist identity—independently of any outside influence. When discussing this, Humphrey, in Phillips' words, "responded eagerly and enthusiastically."[43] Humphrey

*Fraleigh, for instance, is mentioned in Phillips' 29 October 1964 memorandum to William Connell.

> wasn't ashamed of believing in . . . what may seem like platitudes, but [which] can be translated into action out on the ground . . . the essential concept of American democracy which is basically that the government depends on the will of the governed . . . that the people really are sovereign. . . . He [Humphrey] understood that these ideas have . . . a lot of currency and popularity in *many* countries and that this is something that instinctively farmers and peasants out in the country understand. They understand the difference between a government that is arrogant—in which everything comes from the top down—and a government that comes out and tries to work with you. And they understand the difference in the attitudes and behavior of local officials as they reflect these attitudes. So he [Humphrey] understood the necessity of trying to get some kind of democratic philosophy imbued into the actions of the government in order to generate the support to make the country as a whole impervious to communism and fascism and whatever kinds of "ism" that anybody wants to impose.[44]

In Phillips' view, this "is in the Judeo-Christian ethic—certainly that is an essential part of that idea—and I think he [Humphrey] really believed in the brotherhood of man."[45]

When discussing the personal nature of the Lansdale approach—the emphasis on relating to those whom the American advisers were supposed to be helping as *friends*—Phillips again insisted "that Humphrey understood. He had this gift for communication—he would understand that there were Americans who would really do these kinds of things and that in their own way [were] a helluva lot more important than the generals sitting over in the Pentagon."[46]

When asked if there had been anyone else in Washington that he and others of the Lansdale view could talk to in this way, Phillips' response was: "No, I didn't find anybody. Frankly, I found a lot of people that would discuss tactics [a Marshall Plan, amphibious operations, etc.] . . . but they didn't understand how to work with developing countries."[47]

In Phillips' view, many Washington officials simply did not know how to work with new ideas, and the reason for this was largely egoistic. Phillips cites a story in this connection of how, in response to a proposal that Humphrey had made on Vietnam, Phillips had simply told him "that he was wrong." For Phillips, Humphrey's response was "astonishing" because, "he *took it*!" This was astonishing, given "the numbers of people that you run into at a national political level who can't understand anything that is contrary to what they already think." In Phillips' mind, being able to do just that was the sign of "a great man." By so doing, Humphrey showed that he had "enough humility to understand something . . . [a] kind of no-nonsense sort of personality" which Phillips likened to Harry Truman.

Phillips concluded by asserting his belief that Humphrey was distinctive because "he knew the right questions to ask . . . he wasn't blinded by all of the facts and figures and appearances of power." He was remarkable for perceiving that in dealing with a foreign country "you had to go in and understand what was happening there . . . who the political leaders were and what the problems and opinions were, in order to get anything done." Humphrey had "this wonderful faith in the power of people to move things and he believed in *people*—he didn't believe in programs and abstractions and numbers."[48]

This kind of testimony is not to be found solely among Americans. Bui Diem, who first came to Washington as a journalist in 1964, and then later as South Vietnam's ambassador to the United States,[49] similarly found Hubert Humphrey "very much willing to listen." This was so even in the early days of 1964 and 1965, before Vietnam had become the central topic of policy debate, and before Bui Diem himself was able to have doors as easily opened as he would later on once he became ambassador. While still a journalist Bui Diem had explained to the then Senator Humphrey the concept of "pacification"—not pacification in the military sense of the term, but "in terms of building up democratic attitudes, in helping the villages, in getting their rights and social reform and so forth." Diem found that this was something that "Humphrey was very very enthusiastic about."[50] After describing the group of Americans who "opposed the idea of military intervention," who "hesitated a lot in committing large numbers of troops," Diem asserted that Humphrey "belonged to this kind of group." When Diem later returned as ambassador and went to see this same man who had by then become vice president, he expected that "there [would be] no way for him to express . . . his reservation about the policy undertaken by his president." Yet in the conversations that he did have with both the vice president and with members of the vice presidential staff he was surprised to find that "he was much in favor of all the efforts to help [the] Vietnamese build up their society and the efforts to help the Vietnamese on the social field." "He talked rarely about military matters," and if he did, it was only out of "the necessity of the hour."[51]

Humphrey, in Diem's view, certainly did believe in the correctness of the *idea* of the American presence in Vietnam. In this Diem likened Humphrey to a "[Henry] Jackson Democrat"—one who is "very strongly anti-Communist abroad, but very liberal on domestic issues," yet at the same time Diem insisted that Humphrey specifically "advocated some special ways of dealing with this problem of anti-Communist war." For Diem this meant implementing "strong social reforms for the benefit of the Vietnamese people, in the sense that if the Vietnamese people can see the benefits of those reforms, they will turn away from Communism." In this, Humphrey "was among the rare persons, at that time" who advocated the prosecution of the war through People's War. "He understood the problem of Asian war through his own special lenses" and did so even when "all the people by that time didn't have much understanding about the problem." Humphrey, however, "was among the persons who were familiar with the problem of war . . . for [many] years already," and "took it for granted."[52]

Such testimony only further corroborates the evidence for the assertion that Humphrey was distinctive in his ability and willingness to consider the point of view of those whom we ostensibly wished to help, yet whom we in fact, often enough—and in Vietnam's case, tragically—hindered instead.

When asked what America should have done in Vietnam, Ambassador Diem's response was first that, "I did not think, and do not think that the Americans were wrong in helping the Vietnamese." At the same time, however, "I think that the Americans were wrong in trying to do everything by themselves. In trying to do everything by themselves they . . . took away the kind of legitimacy that the South Vietnamese . . . who fought against Communism had." This legitimacy is "not only military, but equally psychological . . . a total war I mean."[53] In Diem's view, Humphrey was one of the few who was willing to understand such "total war."

The significance, then, of Humphrey's evidently rare characteristic of showing a willingness to listen, to believe steadfastly in the cruciality of the principles of "People's War," and, perhaps most importantly, to be able to admit that he could be wrong, ought not be overlooked. It certainly was not for General Lansdale and those who believed in his approach to the Vietnam War. There is a small but telling story regarding this which General Lansdale himself related. The story has to do with a room in Lansdale's home in Saigon where he and his team would often meet to discuss the issues of the day. On a wall of that room hung a portrait of Hubert Humphrey. General Lansdale told of how, often enough, he would point to that portrait and state to the group present that "there is our patron saint."[54]

In his autobiography "the patron saint" himself stated that "instinct said Lansdale was right—at least more right than Taylor"[55] by whom he meant Maxwell Taylor. For Humphrey, Taylor "considered Vietnam a military problem amenable to military solution."[56] In Humphrey's view, however, Lansdale "urged a political approach, which was much different."[57] Humphrey was somewhat reluctant at first to lend support to Lansdale because of the limits of his own personal military knowledge, yet he nevertheless decided to make himself the conduit of Lansdale's ideas to Lyndon Johnson.

As early as June of 1964 Humphrey had begun sending memos on Vietnam to Johnson. In a 8 June 1964 memo from Humphrey to Johnson the Lansdale influence was already clearly present. Portions read as follows:

1. . . . military/political situation is no more hopeless than it was in 1954, but it is extremely critical . . .
2. . . . will take time . . .
3. . . . no one is convinced that we are there to stay . . .
4. . . . ARVN officers are not trusted . . . too often there is a master-servant relationship . . . real estrangement between people and the Army . . .
5. . . . No attention to winning the people—only . . . concentration on heavy weapons . . .
6. . . . people not so much against the government as indifferent . . .
7. . . . The Vietnamese must be skillfully and firmly guided, but it is they (not us) who must win the war . . .
8. The two most urgent fundamental needs in Vietnam are: stabilizing the Vietnamese leadership and giving some hope to which the Vietnamese people can rally . . . a political base is needed to support all other actions toward genuine victory. The winning of the people's minds and hearts is

imperative. No amount of additional military involvement can be successful without accomplishing this task.

9. . . . the government of Vietnam should announce a sweeping program of economic and social reform and progress, and the identity of its own role as care-taker. Looking toward more self government and democratic rule, a practical program for establishing a new Constitution, for eventual national elections, and a return to civilian government must be set forth . . .
10. The Vietnamese army must undergo a thorough and detailed indoctrination to change its attitude and practices toward the civilian population . . . to *protect* and *help* . . .
11. . . . training and combat in night fighting must be instituted and the concept of close infantry combat substituted for the present reliance upon heavy weapons, especially napalm, bombs and heavy artillery, except under specialized circumstances . . .
12. . . . the key would appear to be not to increase the number of U.S. personnel committed in Vietnam, but to restructure the command and control organization . . . [and to rely on] counter-guerrilla experts . . .
13. . . . Advisers must be motivated and convinced that the way to win in Southeast Asia is to win the minds and hearts of the people and they must want to do so . . . the present emphasis is on killing the VC and God help anything that stands in its way . . . [58]

In a 13 September 1964, article in the *New York Times*, Humphrey similarly argued that

while aiding the South Vietnamese we must make it clear that the primary responsibility for preserving the independence and achieving peace in Vietnam remains with the Vietnamese people and their Government.

We should not attempt to take over the war from the Vietnamese. The present struggle is a conflict between Vietnamese of various political beliefs: no lasting solution can be imposed by foreign armies. We must remember that the struggle in Vietnam is as much a political and social struggle as a military one. What has been needed is a government in which the people of Vietnam have a stake.[59]

Again, the Lansdale influence is unmistakable. Humphrey emphasizes the cruciality of considering the political side of the war to be *the* most important factor in deciding the ultimate outcome. He insists that the war finally must and can only be won by the Vietnamese themselves: "no lasting solution can be imposed by foreign armies"; that a "political base is needed to support all other actions toward genuine victory"; and that such heavy weapons as artillery and napalm would be ineffective. He concludes that focus must therefore be placed on building stable and representative political institutions while at the same time urging reforms in both military tactics and courtesy—precisely the measures which Lansdale had implemented so successfully against the communists in the Philippines.

Humphrey would continue to forward such advice to Lyndon Johnson throughout his four years as Johnson's vice president. There is, for instance, the 12 February 1965 memo entitled, "The Internal Problem—A Proposal." This memo included urging Johnson to "stop trying to force 'moral' institutional arrangements to fit the special situation inside South Vietnam," since it would be wrong to try to "make them handle a job they were not designed to do." It proposed "a New Deal for Vietnam" of "political, social and economic reform," all the while remembering how important it is that the "Vietnamese feel these programs to be their own." It included proposals for a G.I. bill of rights for the ARVN, land reform, a college loan program, and a WPA program. He suggested that village chiefs be returned "to their old positions of respect and power" since "they are the only echelon of government in direct contact with the people," and called for "a mechanism for analysis that effectively uses feedback from current experience to improve doctrine and policy." It also called for more "intimate, informal and continuous discussion" with America's Vietnamese counterparts so as to get "the Vietnamese to adopt and act on sound ideas of their own"[60]—to begin instituting, in other words, the coffee klatsch approach.

Other Lansdale themes were also mentioned—calling for an end to political corruption; calling for an end of abuse of the people by the ARVN; emphasizing that "local authority and leadership is essential"; emphasizing that "it is essential for Americans to stay long enough in the country to get to know it and their Vietnamese counterparts"; encouraging American advisers to live as close to the Vietnamese as possible as to avoid having the latter feel "surprised" when new proposals were formally made, and making sure to avoid giving the South Vietnamese "no time to prepare a position" of their own in regards to such proposals. By so doing we would avoid having them feel "keenly aware that the ideas are not theirs" when they are suggested to them by their American counterparts.

This was followed by a 10 May 1965 memo where Humphrey indicates his concern that the military "plan will go forward hell-bent-for-leather without being geared and meshed into a total political plan for the area."[61]

In a 16 March 1966 memo he expressed confidence that the conflict can eventually be successfully won, yet remained cautious, for "ahead lies a long and costly struggle"—a twofold struggle "which will test our patience and perseverance," a struggle which consists of (1) "the struggle of nations to chart their own destinies and maintain their national independence while threatened by Communist subversion and aggression"; and (2) "the struggle to bring about a social and economic revolution for the people."[62]

In a 7 November 1967 memo, Humphrey, following his second trip to Vietnam, stated that "I was encouraged by the evident progress since my last visit," yet still forewarned that "the South Vietnamese have a tremendous distance yet to go, notably in building responsive, strong political institutions and in integrating all Vietnamese into a truly national government," and that "the critical task in the immediate months ahead will be to help the Thieu-Ky government build a base of popular support throughout the country and follow through on the establishment of a constructive relationship with the new parliament."[63]

Finally, in a 1 April 1968 memo, Humphrey urged that "it is essential that we keep the politics consistent with the policy." In order to do so "we should avoid the impression of being men of closed minds. On occasion we should explicitly mention that we are conscious of past mistakes" and that we should "demand reform and . . . an end of corruption in Vietnam . . . continue de-Americanization . . . call up reserves . . . increase taxes, and college deferments, have dialogues, weekly press conferences . . . provide transcripts to members of Congress and governors"[64]—to work, in other words, to overcome what by then had become "the credibility gap."

Of all of these memos, however, the most cogent and the most compelling is the one of 15 February 1965, prepared for a National Security Council meeting on Vietnam. Its complete text is to be found in appendix E. It is the most significant of all because it clearly shows Humphrey's concern as well as political perceptiveness in deciphering the significance of the Vietnam issue for the Great Society.

He began by refusing to offer foreign policy advice per se—he would not be another armchair quarterback. He instead remained firmly in the area of his own expertise—politics. On that front he cautioned Johnson about escalating the war and by thereby following Goldwater's path—the very path that had been rejected in the resounding 1964 Democratic victory. He pointed out that the Democratic Party had "always stressed the political, economic and social dimensions." He mentioned that the opposition to the war would most likely be "more Democratic than Republican," and that "this may be even more true at the grassroots across the country." He warned against "creating the impression that we are the prisoners of events in Vietnam." In what is perhaps the most important, not to mention farsighted statement of all, he insisted that "American wars have to be politically understandable by the American public," and that "there has to be a cogent, convincing case if we are to enjoy sustained public support"—support which had clearly begun to waver in the last year of the war in Korea, and which was already wavering over the war in Vietnam.

In hindsight, the impressiveness of such an assessment must be admitted—particularly his prediction that "serious and direct effects," not only for the Great Society, but for the Democratic Party as a whole, will be incurred if some sort of resolution is not achieved soon. It is hard to think of more percipient advice that could have been given for this particular circumstance. The Great Society went on to founder precisely for the reasons which Humphrey here gave, almost point for point.

Apparently this memo was not meant to be delivered to Johnson. Humphrey evidently wished it to be used solely for his own purposes. Yet Bill Moyers admitted that after Humphrey gave him a copy of it, "I made the mistake of giving it to Johnson . . . [though] it wasn't intended for him. It was just a copy and Humphrey wanted me to have it."[65]

Its effect on Johnson once he did read it: "It angered him."[66] Following this LBJ would say to Humphrey, "We do not need all these memos . . . I don't think you should have them lying around your office."[67]

In light of the many liberal criticisms of the war that developed—criticisms that finally resulted in our failed resolution of that war—it could be argued that these memos were *exactly* what LBJ needed, and thus that Moyers had done precisely the right thing in passing it on. The stress on the political aspect of the struggle, the demands for reform within the South Vietnamese government, the insistence that the war be kept Vietnamese, the skepticism in regards to what can be achieved with heavy weaponry, particularly bombing, the fact that this was a totally different kind of war from any other that we have participated in before, and, perhaps most significantly, the counsel that "American wars have to be politically understandable by the American public" and all that that implies, namely, the political barrenness of the argument of "national interest" in regards to Vietnam, were all consistent with the great part of the criticism of the Vietnam war that developed. As such they may have, had they been heeded, saved the Great Society from that criticism—or at least deflected the great part of it and thus avoided the eventual calamity that it suffered at its hand.

The memos just cited are one part of the body of evidence by which the fact that Hubert Humphrey did attempt to argue the "hearts and minds" case to Lyndon Johnson as his vice president can be documented. Bill Moyers, in addition, remembers Humphrey as "often infiltrating the discussion with that rhetoric [of the hearts and minds]—that philosophy, that view . . . he would *always* argue for it [in White House discussions]."[68] One of Humphrey's military aides, then Colonel, later Lieutenant General Herbert Beckington USMC(Ret.) remembers Humphrey to have consistently taken this position as well. Johnson himself would often enough refer to "Hubert's War" or to "the Other War." There were a number of important instances that indicate why this would be so.

On 7 February 1965, communist guerrillas successfully mortared the American base at Pleiku, destroying fifteen aircraft and either killing or wounding over 100 American soldiers. This was the first direct and blatantly provocative attack on an American facility in Vietnam by the communist forces. McGeorge Bundy, Johnson's National Security Adviser, had been in Vietnam at the time. In a telephone conversation, and then in subsequent cables back to the White House, the normally placid Bundy appeared to some to be almost hysterical with rage. A response was demanded. The question was, what should it be? The majority opinion opted in favor of retributive bombing strikes by B-52s over North Vietnam. Humphrey had his own opinions on such bombing—opinions formed, at least in part, by advice he had received from Rufus Phillips in a 25 November 1964 memo entitled, "United States Policy Options in Vietnam: A Synopsis." In this memo Phillips first argued why bombing might seem feasible:

> It would employ our vaunted technical and material superiority against a corresponding weakness of the enemy; it would allow us full initiative in choice, time and place of attack; and it would vent our righteous indignation against the aggressor without experiencing ourselves the discomforts and casualties of ground warfare, and with little fear of retaliation in kind. . . . It is further pointed out that great target selectivity is possible; that militarily significant installations can be destroyed with minimal casualties to non-combatants.

Following this, however, he went on to offer reasons why, in the final run, bombing would be a bad idea. He began with the more obvious considerations of

> the strong incentive and excellent pretext which it would offer for the Communist powers to patch up their differences and reunite in a common front against a common foe; the international and domestic static from neutral and friendly powers which overt offensive action would inevitably generate; the certain increased toll in American lives; and the possibility of escalation to nuclear war.

In addition to these, he also suggested the following less apparent, yet still vitally important arguments for why bombing should be opposed:

> To Vietnamese, especially in the north, attacks on industrial and communications installations which the northern government says belong to the people, and which were certainly created by their labor, would give far greater weight to the Communist contention that the Americans are the enemies of the Vietnamese people. More, they would furnish invaluable grist to the Chinese Communist propaganda mills. The inevitable casualties, vastly exaggerated by their government, would go far to furnish the final proof needed to unite the presently apathetic people of the north behind that government, and might well make possible a Korea-style attack which could only be stemmed by the introduction of major U.S. troop units.

The final reason, though, that Phillips gave for not bombing was simply that

> it could not achieve victory for the proclaimed US purposes; could not establish a free, stable, South Vietnam. The French found bombardment could not stop the build-up of Viet Minh semi-conventional forces far more dependent on supplies than any Viet Cong forces which exist in South Vietnam today. Even in Korea we found bombardment unable to stop Chinese and North Korean supply columns in relatively open terrain. And since the Viet Cong are not dependent upon supply routes from the North for the majority of their personnel, supplies or equipment, interdiction of those routes or of the sources, even if feasible, is not likely to seriously weaken Viet Cong capabilities in the South. *At best*, we might achieve a conference agreement on a meaningless "neutrality"—but that we could have today. To gain more would necessitate the commitment of major US ground forces to an enterprise which could lead only to a conventional war—or the same old conference table.

His conclusion, then, was that

> the adoption of this course would be a confession that the United States, dedicated to freedom and the rule of right rather than might, finds itself incapable of defeating a vastly inferior enemy who appeals to ideals and fights only to achieve a political goal, by any means except the use of naked force.[69]

In one of the crucial meetings called immediately after the Pleiku incident (an incident which was followed shortly thereafter by another similar incident at the coastal base of Quinhon), Humphrey argued against bombing for many of the reasons just cited. He then went on to add that because Alexei Kosygin, the Soviet Premier, happened to be visiting in Hanoi at the time, bombing it would be unnecessarily, and perhaps even dangerously provocative.

Following this, Humphrey had his 15 February 1965 memo drawn up—the one which Johnson would inadvertently see. Then, in late March, Humphrey would personally argue the "hearts and minds" line at yet another National Security Council meeting. This in turn was followed by the whole host of succeeding memos already cited.

Views on the wisdom of Humphrey consistently arguing this way vary. The consensus on the net effect of his arguing this way, however, is unanimous: for the second time in his career in Washington, Humphrey was "frozen out."

Ted Van Dyk argued that the February NSC meeting was the crucial incident. For Van Dyk, "here went Humphrey in the presence of all these other people [McNamara, Bundy, Rusk, etc.]—spouted off, didn't have any data, [though he did have] a lot of common sense . . . he was right on substance, [but] . . . wrong on procedure. He should have more carefully marshalled his arguments and asked to meet with the president either before or after [the meeting]." In Van Dyk's view, to fail to do so was simply "his mistake . . . it was a stupid mistake."[70]

Solberg agrees. For Solberg, like Van Dyk, it was a matter of Humphrey "popping off" in the presence of others. Both Van Dyk and Solberg believe this was a matter of Humphrey breaking a pledge that Humphrey had made to Johnson on accepting Johnson's offer to be his vice-presidential running mate. This "pledge" had to do with Humphrey's assurance to Johnson that he would be loyal, as, for instance, he clearly stated in the second paragraph of his 15 February 1965 memo to Johnson. According to Humphrey, the conversation he and Johnson had at the time that Humphrey accepted the vice-presidential offer went something like this:

> (Johnson): "We're old friends and we get along well, but you have to understand that this is like a marriage with no chance of divorce. I need complete and unswerving loyalty. I know I don't need to impress this on you, but it's a fact that there are always temptations and there will be times when a Vice President can get out of step, out of line, causing the President difficulty and embarrassment.
>
> "I don't want this to happen. So I want us to have a very good understanding that we're going to work together. I want you to feel free to come to see me anytime. My office will be open to you. I want you to feel that you can confide in me and I want to be able to confide in you. That's what I want in a Vice President, Hubert. Do you think that you're that man?"
> I said, "I think I am. You can trust me, Mr. President." I went on to say that I understood what he was saying very well, that I was prepared to be the kind of Vice President he was describing, that I was prepared to be loyal, that I would try to confine my activities to consultation and discussion within the administration, that I surely wasn't going to be leading any kind of effort that might be embarrassing or contradicted administration policy.
>
> I said I could be helpful because I had wide contacts in the country and that my relationships with congress were good. He said he knew all of that and agreed, but he continued, "I think we make a great team. Yet, I know there will be some difficult days ahead and there may be times when you will wish that you never accepted this assignment."
>
> I told him I was prepared for that possibility, it was a great honor even to be considered for the office, and that if we were elected I would be prepared to do whatever was required to fulfill my obligations and responsibilities.

> Johnson, a powerful and confident President, looked at me and said, "If any man can do it, I think you can." Then he said privately what he was to say publicly—that he felt I was "the most capable of all the men (he knew) to take on the duties of the presidency if anything should happen."[71]

From there he and Johnson discussed how "seldom do a President and a Vice President get along," and how Johnson had remained loyal to Kennedy as his vice president despite all the grievous treatment he had received at the Kennedy brother's hands: "The news belongs to the President," Johnson said. "I never went around the country making speeches without the President knowing about it. Even when it came to Democratic party functions, we had a working agreement."[72]

It was precisely this kind of "working agreement" that both Van Dyk and Solberg believe was violated, at least in spirit, by Humphrey when he spoke out in that and other National Security Council meetings. In Van Dyk's words, it was "a private agreement before he [Humphrey] went on the ticket which was that he should feel free to disagree with Johnson on any point but it should be private and never in front of others."[73] By speaking out as he did, Humphrey "broke his word . . . stupidly."[74] Solberg goes on to argue that Humphrey did this because he had "erred in his judgment of the president and their changed relationship."[75] This "changed relationship" was that of going from Majority Leader/Strong Right Arm, to President/Unqualified Supporter. For Solberg, Humphrey never took this change into account.

Bill Moyers offered a somewhat different interpretation of this. For him, two considerations must be maintained. The first is that at the time that Humphrey agreed to become Lyndon Johnson's vice president, "there was no contemplation of a big war in Vietnam, and, in fact, that would have been considered by both men at the time [to be] ludicrous . . . that [with] the assumption of loyalty, no one had ever contemplated a war that no one understood." The second is that "when Johnson went around the table [at meetings at the White House] he seemed to want everybody to offer his unvarnished views . . . speaking individually, personally, confidentially, and intimately within that room. After the discussions he would go around and ask everybody, 'Do you support this decision?' and everybody would say, 'Yes.' . . . And so Johnson would have had the debate he thought he wanted and then . . . the unanimity that he considered [to be] the objective of the meeting." For Moyers there was, therefore, no "formal agreement broken by either man." In Moyers' view, the scenario by which the break between Humphrey and Johnson occurred was more like the following:

> Humphrey felt that the bombing was a mistake . . . posed it privately, told the president that he did . . . told the president that he did less ardently than he told others around the president, including other members of the cabinet, who then reflected it back—relayed it back to the president who thought that Humphrey was not only expressing his opinions to the president directly, but lobbying outside for that position, which Johnson didn't appreciate on the part of anyone.[76]

It was mostly as a result of this perceived semipublic criticism that Johnson became angry with Humphrey. It was *this* perception, and Johnson's "own internal schizophrenia over the policy he himself was conducting," that led, for Moyers, to Johnson's resentment over what he believed to be his vice president's "insufficient accountability."[77]

Clearly the issue was over the "private" clause of Humphrey's pledge to Johnson. Did the "private" of "it [Humphrey's criticism] should be private and never in front of others" really mean *all* "others" at *any* time, or did it simply mean the kind of political gathering from which leaks to the press would be likely? Moyers believes that a "working agreement" based on the former definition of "private" between two professional pols "wouldn't have been necessary" because they each "knew the game and how to play it."[78] The accounts of Van Dyk and Solberg obviously disagree with such an assessment. Which is more accurate is hard, and perhaps finally impossible to say.

In either case, the outcome was the same: Hubert Humphrey became anathema. Having such a decree originate from the leadership of the Senate at the beginning of one's senatorial career was bad enough. Having it originate from the president himself once one was fully established in the national limelight made it devastating. This time there would be no Harry Truman to call on at 1600 Pennsylvania Avenue.

The freeze lasted for about one year. Its effects were multifold. The vice president was by law guaranteed a place on the National Security Council. Johnson, as a means of circumventing it, therefore began to call NSC meetings only infrequently, and declined to carry on important business at the ones that he did call. The real business (of foreign policy) began to be carried on at what were to become the famous "Tuesday luncheon" meetings where the various key members of Congress, the Cabinet, and the White House staff—everyone, in other words, except Hubert Humphrey—would be invited. When Humphrey's name did come up on a list for a particular meeting, Johnson became "vehement," yelling: "I don't want him here . . . I told you that a hundred times!" and would take a black felt-tipped pen and draw a heavy line through the name 'Hubert H. Humphrey' or 'The Vice President' wherever it appeared."[79]

David Halberstam described how Washington is a "tough and gossipy town; everyone knows who is and who is not going to meetings, who is and who is not in on the inner-memo traffic." He described how, "when a man is moved outside the flow, it is fatal, everyone else avoids him, fearing the stigma may be contagious; what starts as a partial isolation soon becomes almost total." He then went on to provide instances of this as well as rather graphic illustrations of how Johnson would say he did not "want loyalty. I want *loyalty*! I want him to kiss my ass in Macy's window at high noon and tell me it smells like roses. I want his pecker in my pocket," and, "Boys, I've just reminded Hubert that I've got his balls in my pocket." Thus, Humphrey "was stained, and it was not a good stain; every one of the other principals, wanting to keep their effectiveness and credibility with this tempestuous president, knowing his vagaries, became wary of being seen with Humphrey; he had become a cripple and everyone else knew it."[80]

One glaring instance of this was the Dominican Republic incident. In April of 1965 a decision had to be made whether or not to send Marines into the Dominican Republic in order to prevent a communist takeover of that country. When Humphrey attempted to convey a message from the Venezuelan ambassador who had opposed hasty action, he was snubbed by Bundy who told him,

"We've [already] had a meeting this afternoon. The intervention is on."[81] Humphrey's advice clearly had not been sought.

Humphrey himself tells a story of how this "stain" could, in fact, taint anyone who was touched by it:

> the State Department had recommended strongly that Eugenie Anderson be made director of the Foreign Service Institute and it seemed certain that she would get the appointment. John Macy, who was in charge of personnel selection on the highest levels, mentioned that I had special interest in Eugenie's appointment. Johnson said, "She's not my choice. Take her name off the list."[82]

Naturally enough, this had a tremendous effect on Humphrey. After the hard-earned joy of the passage of the Civil Rights Act of 1964, and after the subsequently ebullient campaign of '64, culminating in the overwhelming victory in November of that year, this was a devastating development. As Majority Whip he had been at the peak of his powers, and the tremendous landslide victory of 1964 had confirmed the nation's endorsement of the policies he had stood for all of his life. Yet now he was rendered not only helpless, but humiliated by the same man whom he respected and believed had made much of it possible. It was a vexing position, to put it as politely as can be done, for a "strong right arm" to be placed in.

A break did not occur until nearly a year later when, in January of 1966, Johnson notified Humphrey that he wanted him to make a trip to Vietnam. The notification was done in typical LBJ style:

> In January 1966, Johnson met in Honolulu with Thieu and Ky and other Vietnamese chiefs. A few days before he left, he said he might want me to do some traveling after his meeting: "Keep your schedule loose."
>
> Once burned, I told no one, not even Muriel, that a trip might be coming. As a result, I was in Chicago when a call came to Washington from Honolulu to a staff member at eleven-thirty one night.
>
> The message was simple, if cryptic. Humphrey was to be ready to leave for a two-and-a-half-week trip to Asia the following day. I would meet Johnson in Los Angeles on my way out and his way back.
>
> The next morning was chaos. Members of my staff, for example, most of whom had never been out of the country, were suddenly required to get passports and a half-dozen medical shots. They went home to pack summer- and

> winter-weight clothes, say good-bye to husbands, wives, and children for several weeks, unable to tell them where they were going.
>
> So, after a year, more of isolation than participation, I was about to embark on a major trip in a delicate area, with no time for specific preparation, no briefing papers reviewed ahead of time, no time for study in depth.[83]

Barry Goldwater at the time sardonically quipped that the trip was "the most valiant rescue effort since the evacuation of Dunkirk."

Rescue effort or not the 1966 Vietnam trip marked the end of Humphrey's exile from the administration, though for a price, and hardly an inconsiderable one: Humphrey was to have a new role as vice president, namely, as "the Great Spokesman" for administration policy in Vietnam.[84] As such it was to be his most difficult hour. Most would claim that it was his darkest hour as well. It was a time during which he would make his controversial "fox in the chicken coop" remark in regards to Bobby Kennedy's suggestion of including the VC in the negotiations for a peaceful settlement in Vietnam. It was the same time when, during his second trip to that country he would announce: "This is our great adventure—and a wonderful one it is!"[85] Solberg describes how "when Columnist William Shannon, a longtime liberal Humphrey backer, published a piece in *Commonweal* defending the vice president against the charge that he had flipflopped," Humphrey responded in a letter by saying,

> There is a suggestion in your article that I may well have a different viewpoint on Vietnam from the President, but that I cannot express differences with the President because it would be highly irresponsible. I agree that it would be highly irresponsible, but I must tell you privately that I am thoroughly in agreement with the President.
>
> If somehow I should become President tomorrow, I would follow essentially the same pattern, I believe, on the basis of the evidence I now have.[86]

He had apparently not seen the evidence regarding the massacre at My Lai, for only one week before news of that massacre was to become public he asserted that "In Vietnam only the VC commit atrocities."[87]

This was also to be a time in which he would fail to honor the one virtue, in terms of foreign policy, for which he was unique. Ted Van Dyk recalls how

> one night we had a lot of area specialists in . . . what was then the Fairfax Hotel—and we had drinks and dinner and these people were all very sympathetic to him. They were knowledgeable . . . and it was a wonderful opportunity . . . to learn . . . about the anthropology, the cultural traditions, the political evolution of the whole Indo-Chinese area so he might have some basis for knowledge rather than just the selling line about the war.
>
> I was angered and humiliated because from the first moment he didn't let them talk and he kept saying, "How do I sell this war?" They were terribly disappointed in him. I remember riding home with him that night and literally chewing him out about how he had blown an opportunity to have learned something.[88]

As a consequence of such behavior this was to be a time in which he would not only lose the support of his former liberal allies—he would gain their enmity, along with that of the entire left. It would precipitate, for instance, a small but symbolic occurrence: at a dinner party held by the Rauhs as a hopeful attempt to cool the simmering differences between Humphrey and his old ADA colleagues—colleagues which included Arthur Schlesinger, John Kenneth Galbraith, and even Joe Rauh himself—a shouting match developed instead. With hope for peace marking its beginning, the evening ended instead with war, by those simmering differences boiling over into an even greater break—a break that would symbolize Humphrey's relationship with the left itself.

Deciding who, finally, was on the "right" side of such a "break" requires careful and considerable consideration. The attempt to provide it will constitute the next chapter.

Notes

1. Humphrey, for instance, was voted the second most effective senator—second only to Richard Russell himself—in a poll taken shortly after the passage of the 1964 bill.
2. Cohen, *Undefeated*, 282.
3. Henry Ehrlich, "Changing Washington," *Look* (6 April 1965): 21.
4. Ibid.
5. Sam Castan, "Vietnam: Washington's Biggest Problem," *Look* (6 April 1965): 72.

6. Ibid., 79.
7. Ibid.
8. Fletcher Knebel, "Hubert Humphrey: Advance Man for the Great Society," *Look* (6 April 1965): 80.
9. Rufus Phillips, memorandum to William Connell, 29 October 1964, Humphrey Collection, Vietnam materials.
10. Edward Lansdale, *In the Midst of Wars* (New York: Harper & Row, 1972), 5.
11. Ibid., 10.
12. Albert Gore, *Congressional Record*, 85th Cong., 1st sess., 1958. Vol. 103, 8386.
13. Lansdale, *Midst*, 49.
14. Ibid., 47.
15. Ibid., 39.
16. Ibid., 233.
17. Ibid., ix–x.
18. Ibid., 105.
19. Ibid.
20. Evidence of this is Lansdale's encouragement of and assistance in beginning NAMFREL, the Filipino election-monitoring grass roots organization that played a key role in Corazon Aquino's coming to power a generation later after Lansdale had served there.
21. Ibid., 106.
22. Ibid., 105.
23. Following the normal string of abbreviations and budget citations this same message ended with a startling "God bless you."
24. Edward Lansdale, "Vietnam: Do We Understand Revolution?" *Foreign Affairs* (October 1964): 76.
25. Ibid.
26. Ibid.
27. Ibid.
28. Ibid., 77.
29. Ibid., 84.
30. Ibid.
31. Ibid., 85.
32. Edward Lansdale, interview with author, no. 1, 3 February 1984.
33. Ibid.
34. Ibid.
35. Lansdale, *Midst*, 291–92.
36. Stanley Karnow, the author of the highly influential *Vietnam: A History*, also described Lansdale in highly disparaging terms: "A deceptively mild, self-effacing former advertising executive, Lansdale counted on 'Psychological Warfare' techniques that resembled advertising gimmicks. He also exuded a brand of artless goodwill that overlooked the deeper dynamics of revolutionary upheavals, and he seemed to be oblivious to the social and cultural complexities of Asia." From Karnow, *Vietnam: A History* (New York: The Viking Press, 1983), 220.
37. Fraleigh was described by General Lansdale to be "very free wheeling," yet also as "the most outstanding person they [AID] ever had—known for his fondness for North Carolina's Sugar Baby watermelon, seeds of which he

would take back from trips to the US to Vietnam and distribute to poor farmers who quickly discovered what a valuable and easy-to-grow crop they had . . . they are all over Asia now." From the Lansdale interview, no. 1.

38. Bert Fraleigh, letter to author, 5 May 1984.
39. Ibid.
40. Rufus Phillips, interview with author, 22 May 1984.
41. Ibid.
42. Ibid.
43. Ibid.
44. Ibid.
45. Ibid.
46. Ibid.
47. Ibid.
48. Ibid.
49. . . . and later to author *In the Jaws of History*.
50. Bui Diem, interview with author, 22 January 1985.
51. Ibid.
52. Ibid.
53. Ibid.
54. Lansdale interview, no. 2, 2 July 1984, McClean, Virginia.
55. Humphrey, *Education*, 317.
56. Ibid.
57. Ibid.
58. Hubert Humphrey, memorandum to Lyndon Johnson, 8 June 1964, Humphrey Collection.
59. Tad Szulc, "Humphrey Offers Policy Based on Spurring Red-Bloc Autonomy," the *New York Times* (13 September 1964): 1, 68.
60. Hubert Humphrey, memorandum to Lyndon Johnson, 12 February 1965, Humphrey Collection.
61. Hubert Humphrey, memorandum to Lyndon Johnson, 10 May 1965, Humphrey Collection.
62. Hubert Humphrey, memorandum to Lyndon Johnson, 16 March 1966, Humphrey Collection.
63. Hubert Humphrey, memorandum to Lyndon Johnson, 7 November 1967, Humphrey Collection.
64. Hubert Humphrey, memorandum to Lyndon Johnson, 1 April 1968, Humphrey Collection.
65. Moyers interview.
66. Ibid.
67. Lyndon Johnson, as quoted in Solberg, *Humphrey*, 274.
68. Moyers interview.
69. Rufus Phillips, memorandum to Hubert Humphrey, 25 November 1964, author's collection.
70. Van Dyk interview.
71. Humphrey, *Education*, 301–2.
72. Ibid., 303.
73. Van Dyk interview.
74. Ibid.
75. Solberg, *Humphrey*, 271.

76. Moyers interview.
77. Ibid.
78. Ibid.
79. Ibid.
80. David Halberstam, *The Best and the Brightest* (New York: Random House, 1969), 534.
81. As related in Solberg, *Humphrey*, 275.
82. Humphrey, *Education*, 325.
83. Ibid., 329–30.
84. Even though, as he said himself about the trip, "Nothing I saw or heard, however, destroyed my conviction that it was still a political war. Indeed, the experience in Saigon seemed to support the view that we were beginning to understand and wage that political war. I was for that approach, and continued to encourage emphasis on it. When we left Saigon, I was still troubled by our military rather than political emphasis, unsure that it could lead to 'victory.' But I was, in honesty, impressed and heartened by what I saw and heard." From Humphrey, *Education*, 332.
85. Humphrey, as quoted in Solberg, *Humphrey*, 312.
86. Humphrey, as quoted in ibid., 292.
87. Humphrey, as quoted in Solberg, *Humphrey*, 301. Edgar Berman provides a number of revealing remarks of Humphrey's from this time as well. For example: "I hope they know what they're doing. As of right now I'm damn sure we're not doing the Vietnamese or ourselves any good. We're murdering civilians by the thousands and our boys are dying in rotten jungles—for what? A corrupt, selfish government that has no feeling—no morality. I'm going to tell Johnson exactly what I think, and I just hope and pray he'll take it like I give it" (Berman, *Hubert*, 116).

    Van Dyk also claims that, on his second visit to Vietnam, "he wanted . . . [to] look at [examples] of AID redistribution and so called 'other war' [efforts]. . . . We had a furious argument over there with Westmoreland who abruptly, without consulting anyone, changed his schedule" (From the Van Dyk interview).

    In addition, *Time* in April of 1966 talked about how "it is 'the other war' as he calls it—the struggle for social and economic progress in Vietnam—that has most deeply stirred the Vice President's imagination and energies" (*Time*, under, "The Vice Presidency/The Bright Spirit," [1 April 1966]: 21).
88. Van Dyk interview.

7

HHH and Vietnam: A Retrospection

As already noted, Hubert Humphrey was a person who believed that "the man who wields power must live in the pit of reality," and that doing so meant being "ever reconciled to the limited and the partial." That 1968 was "the pit" is clear. Humphrey found himself squarely in the middle of the maelstrom that that year was to be. Of this examples abound. *The New Republic* provides one: in its 12 October 1968 edition a double page advertisement entitled "Is Hubert Humphrey Really a Lesser Evil?" ran, sponsored by a group named RESIST. Noam Chomsky, Harvey Cox, Bishop James Pike, and Benjamin Spock were among the more familiar names listed as supporters. Part of their message ran,

> In 1968 the electoral arena presents Americans with no pretense of a meaningful choice, only a tawdry Roman Circus.[1]

In the 19 October 1968 edition, Martin Peretz wrote, "we should participate in Humphrey's defeat. To do otherwise is simply to surrender all that we fought for, and simultaneously to betray the young who are and will be the ultimate source of our strength and much of our vitality."[2] Murray Kempton, who only four years earlier had praised Humphrey in *The New Republic* almost without qualification, now, writing in the same pages, asked, "is there anyone who can tell a voter that, if he votes for the vice president he will not again be ashamed?" and asserted that, "in honor, the Democratic Party deserves to lose."[3] Chants of "Dump the Hump" became common. When an antiwar mob attacked his car at Stanford University, yelling "War Criminal!" and "Murderer!" it only provided a symbol of what was to characterize the entire 1968 campaign.

In the midst of that campaign, Humphrey was not only insulted constantly, he was spat upon, had human excrement thrown at him, and his life and the lives of his family were repeatedly threatened. Attempts were made to prevent him from speaking at nearly every campaign stop that he made up until his Salt Lake City television address on September 30. Humphrey describes one moment in the campaign that typified the kind of frustration that he would have to endure throughout that time:

> One day at Kent State, a panel of students questioned me. A young, articulate black man named Robert Pickett challenged my credentials and commitment to civil rights, asking in effect what I had ever done for black people. I was shocked by his attack, and spoke with some feeling about my career. At the end of the meeting, he came over to me and asked if he could join my campaign staff.[4]

The student's offer of help was certainly appreciated, but, as with so much else in that campaign, it was too little too late, and after causing how much grief?

Edgar Berman recounts another incident that caused only grief:

> Even when we were not campaigning, the insult of protestors dogged us. I shall never forget one incident in particular—one that stunned Humphrey and depressed him more than most. Rudolf Serkin, the pianist, had invited Humphrey to his Marlboro Festival in Vermont. It was going to be our first day off in weeks. The outdoor setting was informal. A barnlike music hall, seating three hundred to four hundred listeners, was filled with mostly young music students and some professionals. We had had a pleasant lunch with the Serkins, and for an hour or two, Humphrey hadn't a care in the world. He talked with Serkin about taking piano lessons, joshed with Serkin's wife, and signed autographs for the kitchen help. We then walked over to the hall for a concert—performed by a quartet, with Serkin playing the piano. Humphrey was totally relaxed, oblivious for a moment to the noisy, hurried ambiance of campaigning: hotels, inedible banquets, and dinning rallies—enjoying the music, deep in the green woods of New England.

> After the concert he went onto the stage to congratulate Serkin and the rest of the artists. At the side entrance to the hall, a small crowd clustered, waiting for Humphrey to come out, many wanting to shake his hand. He came down from the stage. Serkin was leading the way, Humphrey was next, and I was behind them, with the Secret Service making a path on either side. As we approached the entrance, a woman, no more than twenty-five years of age, suddenly thrust her head out of the crowd—and spit directly in Humphrey's face. Shouting, "Warmonger!" she spit again, and brazenly stood there facing him, as he wiped his face with a handkerchief. Rudolf Serkin screamed at her, "Get out of here, you scum. He is my guest. You don't belong in a hall of music." She just faded back into the silent crowd; we walked on, with Hubert still wiping the spittle off his face and shirt. We were supposed to stay for dinner, but we left early.[5]

Perhaps the most graphic illustration of this, however, was the confrontation that took place in Seattle. As Albert Eisele relates, Humphrey was interrupted, while attempting to speak:

HUMPHREY: Thank you, ladies and gentlemen. Thank you, Senator Magnuson. . . . Now you'll have equal time. Shut up. Distinguished guests, Senator . . . Ladies and Gentlemen, there's a man that wants to make a speech. Let's listen to him. All right, go ahead. Make your speech.

BULLHORN: Mr. Humphrey, Mr. Humphrey, in Vietnam there is a scream that does not end.

HUMPHREY: Yes, yes I'm listening. [Loud booing from the audience.] One set of bad manners is enough. We'll keep quiet. We're going to let this fellow talk. Go ahead.

BULLHORN: In Vietnam, there is a scream that does not end. There is a wound that does not cease its bleeding. I'm talking about the scream of death and the wound of war. Why is the scream being heard in Vietnam by our soldiers and innocent Vietnamese people? Why is there this wound because of war—not a war for democracy but a war which supports a puppet government, a government where the now number-two man said his hero is Adolph Hitler? You have supported this man. You have supported Johnson. You have supported this war, this needless waste, this murder. We have not come to talk with you, Mr. Humphrey, we have come to arrest you.

HUMPHREY: Proceed. Be sure there's no police brutality, that's all. Proceed.

BULLHORN: What about democracy in Chicago?

HUMPHREY: This is Seattle. Shut up.

BULLHORN: Mr. Humphrey, you are being accused now of complicity in the deaths of tens of thousands of Americans and hundreds of thousands of Vietnamese. This is not a joke to us, it is not a ploy. This is serious.

We charge you with crimes against humanity. They did not escape. You shall not escape. Will you come to stand trial before the world, before the

United Nations? Do you dare to do that? Do you dare to stand forth before the nations of the world at the United Nations and let them try you?

HUMPHREY: Are you through, sir?

BULLHORN: I have only begun, but for the moment I'll be quiet.[6]

Not only was Humphrey thus required to experience such scorn and humiliation, but such humiliation, not to mention despair, only culminated in his losing the election to Richard Nixon by .6 percent of the vote, after clawing his way up from a nearly 30 percent deficit in August, and thus very nearly pulling it off in what came to be known as the "miracle of October" (Richard Nixon himself is reported to have said that had Humphrey had only two more days, the latter would have won). How he was to become "reconciled" to such a "limited" and "partial" outcome was another question. Evidence of his being able to do so, however, exists: years after his 1968 defeat he actually wrote that, "despite the immense miseries of the Vietnam years for our country, for the Johnson administration, and for me personally, I liked being Vice President."[7] In nearly every way, then, even despite his experience as vice president, he relished the political life.

To say, however, that Hubert Humphrey relished "the limited and the partial" is not to say that he therefore disdained the saint's "dream" or the philosopher's "ideal world." Humphrey was often accused of being an idealist, yet his view was not so much that a politician ought not or could not consider the ideal world,* as it was that the politician had the task of actualizing it, and that such a task, taking place as it does in that same "pit," will only be accomplished in a way that *is* limited and partial.

"Politics and ethics are closely related," he believed. "Every political decision is a moral decision" simply because "political decisions affect, for good or ill, the destiny and welfare of human beings."[8] For Humphrey, such decision making had not only a moral dimension but a religious one as well, the one that asserted that "the way you treat people is the way you treat God"—the one,

*Although, on the other hand, there is evidence that suggests that Humphrey may not have considered it very much, at least in his adult life. Norman Sherman stated that in the years from 1956 until he became vice president Humphrey had only read one book: *Seven Days in May*.

in other words, which he had inherited from the Social Gospel. His early commitment to civil rights as mayor, his response to the Byrd debacle of his early senate career, his working for and his manner of working for the passage of the Civil Rights Act of 1964, and even his belief that treating people decently, in the Lansdale manner, was the most effective way of halting totalitarian advances—are all significant examples of his belief in and commitment to effecting religious-moral principles in the world via the political process.

As already cited, however, his "effectiveness" in this regard is severely questioned by the left. After the election John Kenneth Galbraith had scornfully remarked that, "I'm proud I didn't vote for Hubert Humphrey." Given Galbraith's prominent position in the ADA—and thus long-term association with Humphrey—this was an especially bitter pill for Humphrey to have to swallow. It symbolized, perhaps better than any other single incident, the humiliating and venomous spite that Humphrey, whether fairly or not, had incited in the group that he had once been a champion of.

It was, furthermore, a spite whose venom was to last: Carl Solberg's biography, when published in 1984, was the most substantial Humphrey biography to date. For Solberg, however, "as vice president, [Humphrey] forfeited the liberal essence that was the source of his commanding autonomy."[9] This represents a severe, though quite typical indictment. It is justified, in Solberg's view, because of Humphrey's Vietnam stand, which is to say, because of his anti-communism. For Solberg, this aspect of Humphrey's character "revealed a flaw in his political character that would keep him eventually from becoming president of the United States."[10] He cites in this regard a story of George McGovern's about a former professor at the University of South Dakota, Herbert Schell, who said of Humphrey early in his senate career: "A leader who would play fast and loose with liberal standards, ignoring the Holmes doctrine that ideas, however odious, are dealt with in the competition of the marketplace and in no other way, would stumble on some other issue."[11] This was a reference to Humphrey's support, in 1954, for the Communist Control Act of that year, yet it is here used by Solberg to provide a final verdict on Humphrey's entire political lifework.

Such was the verdict from the very political force that Humphrey had drawn his support and his strength from all his life, yet which now denounced him outright . . . all because of his stand on one issue, albeit a momentous one.

Solberg also argued that "Hubert Humphrey, the pioneering progressive who had for three-quarters of his career been way ahead of public opinion, went down to defeat in 1968 because he had fallen behind American attitudes and American opinion."[12] He cites, as an example of this, Humphrey's denunciation of the use of arrant and prolonged profanity by the protestors at the Chicago convention in an interview with Roger Mudd:

> Goodness me, anybody that sees this sort of thing is sick at heart, and I was. But I think the blame ought to be put where it belongs. I think we ought to quit pretending that Mayor Daley did anything wrong. He didn't . . .
>
> I know what caused these demonstrations. They were planned, premeditated by certain people in this country that feel all they have to do is riot and they'll get their way. They don't want to work through the peaceful process. I have no time for them.[13]

After hearing this, the American public, in Solberg's view, no longer had time for Humphrey: "the man who had always been ahead of his time had been overtaken by changing attitudes and opinions."[14] (One might wonder, on hearing this, whether Solberg ever heard Jerry Rubin's statement made after the Chicago convention, namely, that "we were guilty as hell.")

After making this assertion, Solberg goes on to cite Woodrow Wilson and FDR—two of Humphrey's greatest heroes—as further examples of figures who were each, in the course of their otherwise "liberal" careers, to become "as good a warmonger as anybody."

It is true that Humphrey did not follow the liberal consensus as it developed in the sixties regarding the legitimacy of the war. He never seriously questioned the rightness of our *being* in Vietnam, as American liberalism had come to do by the late sixties. At the same time, however, he certainly never agreed with the standard conservative argument for massive and unrestricted use of force either. His personal view was somewhere in the middle. As such he was neither hawk nor dove. His strong anti-communism and belief in a vital American role to play in world affairs, which he inherited directly from the American liberal internationalist tradition that had prevailed up to that time, led him to the conviction that we were perfectly right to be in Vietnam. Our commitment to the government of South Vietnam was, for Humphrey, simply one more instance of letting "every nation know, whether it wish us well or ill, [that] we shall pay any price, bear any burden, meet any hardship, support any friend, oppose any foe, to assure the survival and the success of liberty." For Humphrey, that was not, on the other hand, to say that therefore our behavior there was to be unqualified or unrestrained by any parameters whatsoever—that we should "bomb them back to the Stone Age."

Humphrey rejected the options provided by both left and right as offering only failure either way. Though his own view was, in certain respects, a middle-of-the-road approach, it was also in another sense, highly unconventional. Though "highly unconventional," it was an approach that had apparently been quite natural to Hubert Humphrey. Many statements indicate that he instinctively sensed and believed in the Lansdale view long before he and Lansdale had ever met.

As early as 1949, for instance, he wondered "what kind of society it is that can do away with the menace of totalitarianism?" In his view, it is "in unemployment, in lack of opportunity, in discrimination, in prejudice, in an economic society that is disintegrating and degenerating that the Communist threat is really found."[15]

In 1951 he explained the nature of the conflict with communism to be "on both the military and [the] political fronts." He went on to argue, however, that

> it is on the political or in a more comprehensive sense, the ideological front that we are weakest. The conflict with Stalinism is not merely of a military character. Equally important, it is political or ideological in nature. Ideologically, as the great protagonists of democracy and freedom, we stand opposed to those doctrines which enslave and reduce men to mere machines. We believe in the inherent dignity and worthwhileness of man, that man is an end in himself, that only in a genuinely free society can man attain his true nature . . . yet while we may be winning the conflict in military terms, I believe . . . we are losing ground on the ideological front.[16]

In a 1959 article for the *International Journal of Religious Education*, Humphrey wrote that "the existence of a powerful and aggressive Communist bloc is the main threat to peace and security today," yet then went on to talk of how "the Communist challenge is a total challenge—military, political, economic, cultural, and above all, moral." For Humphrey, "to be politically effective and morally sound, the response of the free world must be many-sided. A one-sided strategy which emphasized military strength and overlooks the needs of underdeveloped countries is neither politically wise nor morally responsible." By the same token, however, Humphrey also felt that "a strategy which emphasizes economic aid and overlooks the requirements of security in the face of the Soviet threat is equally irresponsible." Yet the point overall remained that "we cannot win the battle for men's minds with machine guns and mortars. We can win it basically only with superior ideas."[17]

In a speech before the Harlem YMCA, also in that same year, he actually used the "hearts and minds" phraseology:

> As our example, and our fresh proof of our belief in the rights of man takes hold, democracy will be better strengthened, better defended, and more secure here and everywhere in the world. It will penetrate where no weapon or missile can go—into the minds and hearts of the very people who today are uncommitted and who will either believe democracy's promise of both bread and freedom or accept Communism's promise of bread now and a caricature of freedom later.[18]

Then, in a 1962 speech on American weapons research given on the Senate floor, Humphrey stated that "there is strong evidence that VC forces are finding increasing difficulty in maintaining or winning the support of the peasant population in many areas. This, I believe, is the most reassuring development of all."[19] Our failure to supply our troops there with appropriate equipment was the point of the speech, yet at the same time Humphrey expressed his wish to not "overstate this matter of weapons and devices." This was so because "victory in Vietnam will come when the Vietnamese people, themselves, want victory, and are prepared to fight and die for victory. It will come from the belief in themselves and in their cause and opposition to the Communist cause." "Morale," he continued, "of the indigenous population is the crucial ingredient." "The right weapons can help," he said, but meanwhile, "we have become overly educated, and we do not seem quite to understand this type of primitive struggle that we see going on in country after country around the world."[20] Therefore, "what is needed is the modernized training of special forces, and the training of such troops to fight the kind of battle that those countries must fight for their survival, just as our country had to fight this kind of battle for its own survival in the Revolutionary War."[21]

All of these statements provide evidence of the naturalness with which Humphrey found himself consonant with the Lansdale approach, even before he knew who Edward Lansdale was (although perhaps the most impressive of all such statements is one given in appendix F). They confirm the argument that Humphrey instinctively held this distinctive view of what American foreign policy in halting Communist advances ought to be. It only follows, therefore, that such a view could easily become the basis for his specific policy views regarding Vietnam once he became vice president. If this really *was* his view, and assuming that such a view is *not* that of a "warmonger" (not a necessary assumption), then the question becomes, Why did he not go on to champion this view in a more public fashion as vice president?

The obvious answer from the American left on this question is that he "sold out." He was believed to have so severely compromised his convictions and so utterly prostrated himself for the sheer sake of his ambition that he had made himself worthy of the contempt that it [the left] heaped on him without restraint. When Solberg accused Humphrey of having, as has already been cited, "forfeited the liberal essence that was the source of his commanding autonomy," he [Solberg] appeared to have assumed that the "liberal essence," at least in terms of foreign policy, was the opposite of the internationalist tradition already referred to, and did so without offering an argument to support his case. Solberg's dependence on a story provided by George McGovern to then offer what is propounded as the final and percipient summation of Humphrey's career in regards to this is telling. It is so because it reveals a particular viewpoint at work that is perhaps too typical of the criticism that has come from the left ever since Vietnam arose as a national issue.

As has also already been mentioned, Solberg had referred to Wilson and FDR as each having become "as good a warmonger as anybody." Certainly for Humphrey, such a statement would be historically incorrect at best, and disingenuous at worst. In Humphrey's mind, Wilson and FDR were never examples of leaders who, by committing America to war, had therefore capitulated to conservative pressure. They had acted as they did according to what they fully believed were *liberal* principles, principles that have been politically implemented in such things as Lend-Lease and NATO, and eventually, SEATO. The internationalism of such figures as Wilson and FDR, and, as in later years, the anti-communism of Truman and JFK, were examples, for Humphrey, of liberal *strength*, not weakness. They were hardly betrayals of the liberal essence. How else could one account for the relatively impressive influence that an organization like the ADA—founded as a liberal organization opposed to communism—was eventually able to wield by 1964, other than by its relying on such strength? If such an assertion appears farfetched, consideration ought to be given to the fact of the ADA's subsequent decline following its stand in 1968 against *any* American involvement in Vietnam. Raising *that* question, in turn, raises an even larger question regarding the decline of the Democratic Party itself in the entire post-Vietnam period. Is the humiliation of George McGovern's crushing 1972 defeat at the hands of Richard Nixon to be ascribed to the fact that McGovern, too, had "fallen behind American attitudes and American opinion"? Was it because he, too, at some point had "played fast and loose with liberal standards," as Solberg insinuated that Humphrey did? If the magnitude of McGovern's defeat in comparison with Humphrey's just four years earlier—and against the same opponent (60.7 percent Nixon/37.5 percent McGovern in 1972 vs. 43.4 percent Nixon/42.7 percent Humphrey in 1968)—is to be used as a measure, one would have to say by extrapolation that he, McGovern (and the Democratic Party with him), had not only fallen behind American attitudes and opinions, but had lost sight of them altogether. And what, then, was the "fatal flaw" in McGovern's character that reaped the kind of whirlwind that made Humphrey's ever-so-narrow defeat appear as a mere breeze in comparison?

To extrapolate in this way is, admittedly, to play with historical fact. It is done only to suggest that the kind of analysis that Solberg conducts in this regard represents a similar playing with fact. Solberg would appear to assume by the nature of his argument that the "authentic" liberal position regarding the two World Wars, Korea, and Vietnam was to oppose our involvement in all of these cases, just as he appears to assume that leaving an estate of over a half a million dollars, as Humphrey did, is also illiberal, not to mention ardently opposing communism. Such assertions are at least *arguable* in every case. Since they are arguable, it is therefore unfair to assume, let alone to judge Humphrey as having forsaken the liberal cause because of his stands on these various issues. Such assumptions, however, became only all too characteristic of the left wing of the Democratic Party in its Vietnam and post-Vietnam history.

Like Solberg, Albert Eisele argued that

> he [Humphrey] was too absorbed in the visions of the Great Society and in his own unfulfilled yearning for the presidency to recognize that the Vietnam war was a great moral evil that could destroy everything he dreamed of.
>
> The man who did recognize that evil and who stood up at a critical moment in American history to warn the nation of it was McCarthy.[22]

The issue is whether it was Humphrey who "failed to keep up with the times" in 1968, or was it rather liberalism in general—and the Democratic Party in particular—when it refused to support him in that year, and then again in 1972? The surprising rise and equally surprising endurance of Ronald Reagan in the post-Vietnam era is only fairly cited as further testimony in support of choosing the latter.

When Humphrey said, "I know what caused these demonstrations [at the 1968 Democratic National Convention in Chicago]. They were planned, premeditated by certain people in this country . . . I have no time for them," his words bespoke the character traits he had acquired in Doland, traits which he had utilized to secure, among other things, passage of the Civil Rights Act of 1964. Solberg agrees that "*that* was the authentic Humphrey speaking," yet, in Solberg's view, the matter of importance is that "to the young, he was both ridiculous, with his 'goodness me's' and 'good grief's' and infuriating with his 'the police had to take action.'" Because he was so to them, "he sounded out of date."[23] The question is, however, within three elections following the 1968 contest, *who* sounded out of date, and did so even to that *same* generation? Furthermore, is appealing to the young really to be the sole, or at least the most important criterion by which we are to judge political effectiveness?

Another consideration is the following: the most important lesson that Humphrey learned from his very first political race in 1943 was the value of loyalty. Finding someone who could be trusted, no matter what, was extremely rare in politics. It was also vital to a politician's success, not to mention simply his or her well-being. Humphrey had recognized this from early on, and therefore could understand its value to others as well.

Though clearly different in temperament and manner (and, often enough, in outlook) Hubert Humphrey and Lyndon Johnson had enjoyed a significant and highly productive working relationship—a relationship which had, in turn, resulted in a correspondingly deep personal relationship that covered many years. To an appreciable degree this relationship, and Johnson's Senate leadership, had enabled liberalism to gain a relative amount of strength throughout the otherwise conservative period of the fifties, and to then, in the sixties, flower into the predominant political outlook of the day. Not only had the Johnson-Humphrey ticket taken 61.1 percent of the popular vote in 1964, sweeping all but six states with it, it had ushered in a decisively like-minded Congress along with it, something that even the Reagan landslides of the 1980s failed to do. Liberalism was in its heyday, and Humphrey sincerely believed that the both conscious and able efforts of Lyndon Johnson had had a good deal to do with such a circumstance.

As vice president, Humphrey was not only involved with Johnson in an informal, personal relationship, but in a highly publicized (and therefore sharply scrutinized) formal relationship as well. For Humphrey, being elected to the second highest office in the land meant that he had earned the public trust to serve that office faithfully. "Faithfully serving" as vice president meant loyally serving the president no matter what.* Throughout the entire process of choosing the vice-presidential running mate, Humphrey

*Gene McCarthy, in 1964, for instance, said that he considered the responsibility of the vice president to be to "remain healthy and quiet."

had made it "crystal clear" that he understood the "loyalty requirement" perfectly. After a long conversation during that time with Jim Rowe (a longtime friend of both Johnson and Humphrey) about this requirement, Humphrey had told Johnson that he understood "your concern about relationships between the President and Vice President. You can rely on me. I will be loyal."[24] He had made that pledge before he was chosen to be vice president, and he fully intended to take it seriously once he had entered into that office.

There was another less noble, but equally weighty political consideration at work as well. Humphrey had come through the bruising 1960 primary contests with John Kennedy wary and somewhat forlorn at the prospect of ever having to face the Kennedy machine again. He felt that his greatest disadvantage regarding the Kennedys was his lack of money. The obvious public attention that he was able to command as vice president was critical, in his view, as a means of having any chance against a likely challenge from Bobby Kennedy. Humphrey wanted the presidency badly, as badly as any number of other prominent candidates of his day wanted it, liberal or not, and he firmly believed that becoming and remaining vice president was the only means by which he would ever have a real chance of attaining it.

As already suggested, until the mid-1960s, the internationalist side of liberalism had steadily prevailed through the efforts of Teddy Roosevelt, Woodrow Wilson, FDR, Harry Truman, and JFK. Humphrey utterly identified with these figures. As a child, Humphrey had memorized the Fourteen Points, just as all the Humphrey children had done. Humphrey's father had idolized Wilson. Humphrey's own idol had been FDR. In FDR Humphrey had seen America, under strong liberal leadership (and against the then-isolationist conservative opposition) stand up to fascist dictatorships around the world for the sake of democracy, and defeat them with the greatest show of armed industrial might and political will that the world had ever seen. To Humphrey, VE and VJ days represented as much a victory for liberal leadership as they did for America overall. Following those great victories, Humphrey had himself taken part in the subsequent liberal rebuilding of those same formerly fascist foes, and witnessed how they now had become some of our strongest democratic allies. Communist advances in Greece and Turkey in the late 1940s,[25] and then again in Korea in the early 1950s, had all been rebuffed by similarly liberal-led American shows of force. NATO was created under a liberal Democratic president. Furthermore, notable liberal figures, following this same line, had consistently supported our active presence in the defense of South Vietnam over the years. Although later critical of the war, Reinhold Niebuhr, for instance, in 1955 had written, "We are certainly more disinterested than the French in desiring only the health of a new nation, and their sufficient strength to ward off the Communist peril from the north."[26]

This was a profoundly powerful historical precedent not only to have lived through, but to, in some cases, have actually taken part in as well. The victories just mentioned were among America's greatest, moral and otherwise. They were at least in part responsible for America's paramount place in world affairs at that time. All of them had been wrought under liberal leadership, not conservative. To have regarded, in foresight, Vietnam as an entirely different situation which would demand an entirely different sort of strategy would, in turn, have required uncommon vision—the kind of vision normally provided almost entirely by hindsight alone. There were, after all, only two dissenting votes on the Gulf of Tonkin resolution, taken on 7 August 1964, out of a total of 516 cast by the entire Congress.[27]

The evidence already cited suggests that Humphrey did, at least to some degree, have such vision. Yet to hold to it unwaveringly during those most trying of days—days in which, as Bill Moyers said, "I don't think anybody held to anything consistently on Vietnam (except Dean Rusk)"[28]—would be to expect a very great deal indeed.

For Humphrey, too, there was the matter of the communist "menace." Korea was a much more vivid memory in the 1960s than it was in the post-Vietnam period. Furthermore, Humphrey had seen the tactics of the communists at work literally in his own front yard, and had been forced to deal with them for survival's sake. Communism was not, for Hubert Humphrey, an abstraction, a figure of speech, an image from a movie or book, or simply a political philosophy that one might study in a textbook. After struggling against and overcoming the communists in Minnesota, he continued the fight against them nationally by becoming a leader of what was itself to become one of the most powerful and articulate anti-communist organizations in America: the ADA (the irony being therefore all the more severe regarding the fact that it was Humphrey's ADA friends who later led the opposition to his 1968 campaign because of his stance vis-à-vis a war against communism). In his own mind Humphrey had very good reason to associate the cause of American liberalism with the cause of anti-communism, particularly so as to offset the constant charges of having "lost China" and of not having "taken back Cuba" hurled by the right at the liberal leadership. For Humphrey, then, to argue for the war in the way that he did did not represent having "suddenly" become a "hardliner." As he himself stated in a response to such a charge: "The purpose of the organized 'liberal' movement was to keep itself clear of the basic reaction, and I think consummate evil, of totalitarianism of any form and particularly Communism."[29] Thus, in June of 1966, for example, he would talk about how "we never see in the press the horrors of the VC—destroying schools, hospitals, murdering village chiefs," we do not see the positive effort being made by the U.S.—the "building of roads, schools," etc., nor do we hear from "the many Vietnamese who want us there," let alone hear the question asked of "when have the Communists ever won a free election?"[30]

There were additional factors involved in Humphrey's Vietnam stand as well. In the early 1960s, distinguishing between "Asian-style" communism and "Soviety-style" communism was not nearly as common a form of political analysis as has subsequently become the case. China was, in that period, a genuine cause for alarm, for it had shown consistently militaristic and aggressive tendencies for some time. Even in comparison to Russia, Humphrey believed that "the Soviet Union is a more responsible power," for "it recognizes the danger of confrontation and of war."[31] China, in other words, was reckless. In his 1961 State of the Union message, JFK had strongly argued that China was a real threat. Humphrey himself insisted that on his trips abroad, Asian leaders, particularly Indira Gandhi, again and again privately argued in strident terms for the need for a U.S. presence in Asia to deter the communists, even if publicly their statements were more neutralist in tone. Furthermore, Humphrey did not want the United States to "be put in a position of saying that we are able to keep our commitments to white people, [but] not to brown people or yellow people."[32]

There were also the consistently optimistic reports on the war from Saigon being filed by American military and diplomatic sources to the White House regularly—reports which only White House insiders were privileged to see.

Meanwhile, of course, there was the unforeseen impact of having the entire nation watch the war each night on its television sets in the first uncensored, let alone televised war in history.

Finally, there were the equally disquieting, not to mention repulsive reports of communist dominance by systematic murder of any aspiring opposition leadership, whether it be in the South or in the North. Murders and atrocities committed against village leaders, schoolteachers, priests, and others were steadily reported and documented by the thousands (50,000 was the rough figure that had been indicated to Humphrey), and as culminating in the massacre in Hue during the 1968 Tet offensive. In addition, we have now, in hindsight, considerable confirmation of North Vietnamese aggression and clear intention to simply use the NLF as a means to its own ends. Truong Nhu Tang, founder and subsequent Minister of Justice for the NLF, as an example, documents this eloquently and compellingly, as he does his harrowing escape by boat from the country he had dedicated his life to, yet which he found he had to flee under North Vietnamese rule.* The Lansdale approach that Humphrey had consistently argued for offered a comparatively humane option by which to counter this kind of terrorism—it was certainly more humane in relation to the policy that would order American troops to destroy Vietnamese villages "in order to save them." While the Lansdale approach was certainly controversial, at least it proposed a kind of warfare that was proportioned to the enemy's tactics, and therefore was ostensibly more just, at least according to traditional just war criteria. Whether or not it might have, in the final run, proved effective is now only one more matter for America to consider as it passes by its sobering memorial to that sobering experience.

*See Tang's *A Vietcong Memoir*.

Stanley Hauerwas argued that "Rules and principles appear to be sufficient because they are typically associated with rather common moral problems and situations. But our moral lives are not simply made up of the addition of our separate responses to particular situations. Rather we exhibit an orientation that gives our life a theme."[33] The "issue" of Vietnam was not "common," and to judge Humphrey's role in it by applying selected rules and principles to it, without giving full allowance to the overall "theme" of *his* understanding of liberalism, is to be injudicious. In passing judgment on Humphrey one must first weigh a great deal of contrary and counterbalancing testimony—testimony, quite literally, as "contrary" and "counterbalancing" as is the "testimony" on the war itself. For those who feel that they have "the answer" to the Vietnam War, i.e., that the U.S. was wrong, both morally and politically to be involved in any way, then their judgment of Hubert Humphrey's role in that war will likely be clear. For those, however, who are not so sure, and who tend to believe that making such moral judgments about an issue as extremely complex and difficult as the Vietnam War is a much more dubious and ambiguous exercise at best, then, perhaps, the judgment will not be so sure, or so swift. Furthermore there is also the argument that is key to the work in hand, namely that justice can and only will be attained after studying the entire *life* of the person in question, rather than selecting various highlights or specific cases as the basis for moral judgment about that or any person. Arguing *that* way, however, admittedly raises another and perhaps more disturbing question: How then can anyone ever arrive at a moral judgment that will *not* be "unfair and irresponsible"? When, in other words, is enough history enough, and who is to decide, and on what basis? How are we to avoid moral quietism, let alone moral relativism, if we are to hold the above advice? This is an extremely serious issue, and one to which no answer may be readily apparent. Perhaps one answer (and admittedly perhaps the safest) is that it is better to deal with *that* issue than with making peremptory judgments. Or, to put it another way, if doing so increases *humility*, even while it decreases *certainty*, then so be it.

Perhaps another and better response is to say that the ideal is maintaining a balance between moral preemptoriness, on the one hand, and moral timidity on the other. What is meant is that living according to such an ideal, while never guaranteeing moral correctness in any *specific* instance, might nonetheless offer the best assurance of such correctness in the long run. In other words, maintaining such a balance in "the long run," (that is in the course of a lifetime), might best engender *integrity*, something which is to be distinguished from and likely to be more beneficial for all concerned—the self, as well as all those that the self affects—than "perfection."

In addition, in this particular case recourse can still be taken to history itself by asking, did not Humphrey have other options?

The most obvious option that many argue he should have taken was simply to have resigned as vice president. By doing so, most likely early in 1968, he would have retained most of the advantages that the vice presidency conferred on him, yet could have made a clean break with Johnson and thereby freed himself from the stigma attached to being part of his administration. In a sense Humphrey had every moral, not to mention practical reason for doing so.

Stories of Johnson treating Humphrey atrociously are legion. During Humphrey's entire vice presidency, for instance, he was never once invited to Camp David. He had been forced to humiliatingly request permission for use of the vice presidential plane and even for the presidential yacht. Following the 1964 nomination, LBJ had forced Humphrey to dress in a ridiculous and ill-fitting Texas outfit for a cover shot for *Life* magazine. Humphrey himself relates another such demeaning experience at the LBJ ranch:

> In Texas, as Lyndon Johnson's guest, you did things his way. Early one morning the previous year [1963], we climbed into his Lincoln, and Johnson, guns at the ready, drove slam bang and lickety split across the countryside until we spotted one of the many deer that grazed on his ranch. He slammed on the brakes, and in his commanding voice said, "Hubert, there's one for you. Get it!"
>
> I am a good shot and have hunted duck and pheasant and quail fairly frequently throughout my life. It was an easy and natural thing on the South Dakota prairies and wetlands. But I never liked to shoot four-legged creatures, deer particularly. Nevertheless, I got slowly from the car, lifted my rifle, set myself for its kick, and brought down the deer. I turned to Johnson with a

mixture of satisfaction at having done so well what he wanted and revulsion at having killed the deer.
"Well," he said, "Bobby Kennedy got two of them. You're not going to let Bobby get the best of you, are you?" Before there was time for an answer, the car sped on its way again, until we sighted another deer. As he slammed on the brakes once again, Johnson said, "Now's your chance. Hit that one." I hit it, and the deer fell.

In the car once again, Johnson said, "That's enough. You've shot one more than McCarthy and the same number as Bobby. You're in good shape."[34]

General Lansdale tells of how

I was in Saigon when Humphrey came up for a visit. I was up in his bedroom and he wanted to talk to me and a call came through from LBJ and LBJ was bawling him out for some little thing and . . . [he used] the foulest language. I said, "Gee, do you take that from him? I wouldn't take that from anybody in the world." He said, "Oh well, that's the way he is. . . . " It was a dirty bawling out, really nasty—foul-mouthed and so on.[35]

Such tales only confirm a pattern that had begun at the time that Humphrey was in consideration to become Johnson's vice president. Things only got worse, however, when Humphrey made his own attempt for the presidency.

Following the 1968 convention, LBJ invited Humphrey down to the ranch for a brief and unheralded meeting. On the very next day, LBJ also invited Richard Nixon down to the ranch. This time the press was presented with a grandstand display. Six hundred thousand dollars of badly needed money (money which Humphrey had helped raise personally through many personal appearances as vice president) kept for campaign purposes in the President's Club was never made available for the Humphrey campaign. Neither was the money that LBJ had always relied on from his Texas oil friends. Berman tells an incident involving Texas as well. After meeting with LBJ, Humphrey, once back in his own office, exploded:

"That no good son of a bitch. The way I've treated him—I must be a goddamned fool." Humphrey was not one for cursing, but this time he couldn't hold himself in. . . . "Do you know what he had the nerve to say to me, after all the insults I've taken from him in the last four years? He said that if I didn't watch my p's and q's, he'd see to it personally that I lost Texas. And he intimated that he could hurt me even in some of my liberal states—that Daley still listened to him. He said he'd dry up every Democratic dollar from Maine to California—as if he hasn't already. Imagine, a Democratic president telling this to a Democratic nominee! I had trouble holding back, but I wasn't going to come to that bastard's level. I didn't even answer—not one word. I just turned around and walked out."[36]

Averell Harriman at one point offered Humphrey the equivalent of the vice president's salary if he would just resign. It was a magnanimous gesture, yet, as Berman related, Humphrey's position was, "I want to be loyal, and my guts, my heart won't let me do it any other way."[37]

Such a conviction was only confirmed in testimony given by others as well. Norman Sherman stated,

> The fact is that Humphrey never seriously considered resigning . . . never considered it for a moment . . . [He] felt—and he took this stuff seriously—[that] "The people of the United States have elected me to [the] second highest office in the land, and it is a contract that I have made with them. What if Lyndon Johnson were to die one day before he goes out of office? I am the Vice President . . . "
>
> Humphrey's sense of commitment, loyalty, was overwhelming, and even if there had been overwhelming political reason I don't think he would have done it. [It was] not out of loyalty to Johnson, I think in this case, but . . . loyalty to an abstraction—he had a commitment to the American people and that was it."[38]

Geri Joseph similarly said,

> I think also it was a part of this whole understanding of what he understood to be the American political system—that a person who has been elected with the president . . . worked in tandem with that president. If you had disagreements you told him in private . . . you worked with him as best you could, and I think he felt that very strongly. I never felt that [resigning] was a viable option [for him]. People who would say that to me—I just thought they were talking through their heads—they didn't know what they were talking about."[39]

In addition to that consideration, there is the thought that had he resigned, Humphrey also would have had to face the fully unmitigated wrath of Johnson and all the forces that he would have subsequently arrayed against him.

John Calhoun is the only vice president ever to have resigned the office of the vice presidency, and Humphrey clearly could not use the justification that Calhoun had for so doing (namely, to protest the efforts being made at the time to abolish, or at least contain slavery). He could have considered William Jennings Bryan's justification for resigning as Secretary of State (namely, as a protest over Woodrow Wilson's commitment to entering World War I), yet the circumstances were drastically different—Bryan was not, in this case, an elected official. As Bill Moyers said, "It is one thing . . . to resign as a special assistant to the President (made in reference to Moyers' own resignation from the White House Staff in 1967), and quite another to resign the office of the Vice President."[40] As Moyers also said, "What kind of principled act would it have been to resign when the going got tough, or to advance his own political ambitions?"[41] For Humphrey, there would have been little if any principle involved whatsoever.

There was, in addition, Humphrey's sense of forgiveness. Berman tells of how Humphrey once said: "As nasty as he's been I just can't quit Lyndon now. I have no doubt in the world he'd cut me up and out of the nomination if it was a matter of my spoiling his policy on the war. But that's not what holds me back. He's suffering like no other president I've seen before, and I just can't add to that."[42] Solberg recounts how Humphrey had told Berman a story of how LBJ could appear almost pathetic:

> He [once] said the saddest thing. He said "As much as I've tried to do for the Negroes and the poor, even they're against me. Now don't get me wrong. If I want that nomination, I can get it. There's no two ways about it. But the only way I can unite the nation is to do something about Vietnam now." And then he made the strangest statement: "Maybe the people just don't like my face."[43]

So Humphrey had seen other sides of LBJ as well—sides included not only in the above story, but also in the following letter:

> Mrs. Johnson and I are proud to go forward in that spirit with you, never forgetting the gifts of heart and mind that you have given so loyally and so generously for all our years together.[44]

Humphrey could not and would not forget all those "years together" either. He felt compelled by the complex that his history represented to follow the course that he did. As argued, there was compelling, though that is *not* to say by any means "absolute" reason for this. Just or not, such reason does not diminish the irony, let alone the tragedy of such a "course."

His dream was to effect his beliefs in the inherent goodness and moral worth of all people, which is to say, to bring the politics of joy to all. The most effective position from which one could do so was the presidency of the United States, and thus attaining that office was part of his dream as well. The dream came closest to realization in his role in passing the Civil Rights Act of 1964. Yet, to have the "dream" of seeing that role, and its consequent ascendance to the vice presidency—and thus with it the eventual possibility of the presidency itself—destroyed by the "fact" of Vietnam and all it represented, was, in both its irony and in its tragedy, the stuff of Shakespeare. His ability to play that role was based on his past: the religious-ethical virtues he attained in Doland, the political virtues he attained in his early years in the Senate, and his inheriting the liberal tradition as he understood it, culminating in the great victories of 1964. Yet those very same virtues, achieving their zenith in 1964 as they did, only resulted in his reaching his nadir in 1968, particularly in regards to the very different, not to say exasperatingly difficult issue that Vietnam represented. The change that occurred in that four-year period was among the most profound to have occurred in any period in American history. As a result, the remarkable achievement of going from Main Street to Pennsylvania Avenue, and indeed into the sanctum sanctorum of "The Club," hailed in 1964, was one that few recognized, let alone cared about by 1968. Furthermore—and here, perhaps, both the tragedy and the irony become especially poignant—his great strength that won the day in 1964, namely, in recognizing both the political cruciality and the moral correctness of building consensus as the key to political leadership in a democracy, failed him, or perhaps better, he failed it in 1968. If the latter is the case, then he should have known that reaching out to build an albeit new consensus during the '68 campaign, and even before it, was necessary, yet he did not. If nothing else, that, at least, was his clear failure with respect to Vietnam.

And yet, if only to maintain the kind of dialectical method that this work is committed to, if it is fair to judge Humphrey in the above respect, it would also seem fair to ask, given the nature of the times and of the "new consensus" of that most chaotic and least consensual of times, was bringing the order of consensus, even by a master, out of such chaos that 1968 was, truly possible, particularly in Humphrey's case where the contrast between his past and present—dream and fact—was so brutally extreme?

Whatever the answer, and thus with however much attendant guilt or innocence, Hubert Humphrey simply went on, as the country did with him, to his own particular and painful destiny determined by that small and faraway place called Vietnam.

Notes

1. *The New Republic* (12 October 1968): 50–51.
2. Martin Peretz, "What's To Be Done? Contra Confrontation," *The New Republic* (19 October 1968): 22.
3. Murray Kempton, "What's To Be Done? An Honorable Choice," *The New Republic* (2 November 1968): 13.
4. Humphrey, *Education*, 395.
5. Berman, *Hubert*, 203–4.
6. Eisele, *Almost*, 374–75.
7. Humphrey, *Education*, 407.
8. Hubert Humphrey, draft of an article entitled, "Christian Ethics and International Politics," prepared for *International Journal of Religious Education*, Humphrey Collection.
9. Solberg, *Humphrey*, 469.
10. Ibid., 328.
11. Herbert Schell, as quoted in ibid., 468.
12. Ibid., 407.
13. Humphrey, as quoted in ibid., 370.
14. Ibid.
15. Humphrey, *Congressional Record*, 81st Cong., 1st sess., 1949. Vol. 95, 4048.
16. Humphrey, *Congressional Record*, 82nd Cong., 1st sess., 1951. Vol. 97, 7018.
17. Hubert Humphrey, *International Journal*.
18. Ibid., 9938.
19. Ibid., 87th Cong., 2nd sess., 1962. Vol. 108, 22957.
20. Ibid., 22959. Humphrey went on from there to assert that "it may be in South America where tomorrow's proxy war will develop."
21. Ibid., 22960.
22. Eisele, *Almost*, 445.
23. Solberg, *Humphrey*, 370.
24. Humphrey, *Education*, 298.
25. *Time*, for instance, had noted in its 1 April 1966 edition that "liberals did not object to US support for Greece in the late '40s—despite the fact that its government then went through more gyrations than Saigon in the '60s."
26. Reinhold Niebuhr, as quoted in David Little's *American Foreign Policy & Moral Rhetoric* (New York: Council on Religion and International Affairs, 1969), 39.
27. Senators Wayne Morse of Oregon and Ernest Gruening of Alaska were the only "nays." Senators Anderson, Cannon, Clark, Edmondson, Johnston, Kennedy, Scott, Symington, Talmadge, and Yarborough were all absent yet had previously indicated their "aye" preference.
28. Moyers interview.
29. Hubert Humphrey, interview, *U.S. News & World Report* (14 March 1966): 75.

30. Humphrey, speech to the National Conference of Christians and Jews.
31. Humphrey, as quoted in, interview with Hubert Humphrey, "We Do Not Want a Group to Shoot Its Way Into Power," *U.S. News & World Report* (14 March 1966): 75.
32. Humphrey, as quoted in Solberg, *Humphrey*, 292.
33. Hauerwas, *Vision*, 74.
34. Humphrey, *Education*, 306–7.
35. Lansdale interview, no. 1.
36. Berman, *Hubert*, 210–11.
37. Ibid., 182.
38. Sherman interview.
39. Joseph interview.
40. Moyers, letter to author, 3 April 1985.
41. Ibid.
42. Berman, *Hubert*, 182.
43. Edgar Berman, as quoted in Solberg, *Humphrey*, 323.
44. Lyndon Johnson, letter to Hubert Humphrey, 31 August 1968, Humphrey Collection.

Part Three

Analysis

8

The Social Gospel Unleashed

No matter what the tragedy of the brutal contrast between Humphrey's past and present, dream and fact, that culminated in 1968, there was nevertheless much that was contained in such a paradoxical legacy. Humphrey's ability to legislate programs effecting his concern for all people is one part. Beyond that, however, was the mark he left on government overall. For Eric Severeid, "he became a kind of second Roosevelt, operating from the weaker end of the avenue. He showed more imagination and originality in the use of government on behalf of ordinary people than anyone to hit town since Roosevelt."[1] *The New Republic*'s TRB spoke of the lesson that Humphrey's life taught as showing "that it is possible to engage in the necessary compromises of political life and thirty years later to have adequately clean hands."[2]

For many, Humphrey's greatest lesson was not only that one could survive with "adequately clean hands" but that one could actually elevate the level of politics of an entire era. In Bill Moyers' view, for instance, Humphrey

> linked great principle and compassion to the . . . political processes of our society. He made it respectable for a whole generation of politicians to be in the system and yet committed to changing the system . . . Character, in my judgment, is everything in politics. However, character detached from the realities of politics is ineffectual. His virtue, I think, was being in and of and with the system, but [all the while] preserving that essential core of integrity and character.[3]

Max Kampelman saw the Humphrey legacy as being the "spirit of politics which he represented—the joy of politics that he represented—the fact that government in a democratic society was something—it was a great *blessing* that had to be enjoyed."[4]

Geri Joseph stated Humphrey's legacy to be that of making others realize "the importance of the political system and of having good people involved in it. He really attracted a lot of us because of what he believed, what he stood for, and because [of] this, this *devotion* he had to the American political system. A lot of people talk about it on the 4th of July, but that was another thing he really *lived*, and it was beautiful to see."[5]

For Adlai Stevenson III, "He made people realize that goodness in politics was possible."[6]

William Connell similarly spoke of

> this feeling, this welling—you could just feel it—tangible affection. Here were all these hard-boiled guys out there [in the House of Representatives at the time that Humphrey was invited to speak to them], 435 of them, and all of them, even the most conservative, had affection for him. He was irresistible, and they admired him and they loved him—literally loved the man. He had, by his example of love and giving, I think, just won everybody over, and he became an example . . . he was exemplary in that sense that people probably were changed by him. People . . . felt better about themselves for having joined in some enterprise of his . . . it gave them a purpose in a society which is always talking about being rootless and self-seeking and non-community oriented.
>
> You know, when you were involved with Humphrey it really made you feel good—you were caught up in something that made you feel good. And so he made people feel good about themselves and what they were doing, and that's—*that* was the source of his strength. He caught them up in his vision, and he made them see that you did not have to be a hater.[7]

Late in life Humphrey himself said,

> I feel . . . that not all of my life is in my own hands. There is a power beyond man—Divine Power, the will of God. It is a powerful source of strength if you can get in tune with it. Like everybody else's, my faith is sometimes rocked. When I'm feeling low, I draw strength from the prayer of St. Francis of Assisi. Part of it says, "Where there is doubt, let me sow faith; where there is despair, hope; where there is darkness, light; and where there is sadness, joy." I think it is the perfect prayer.[8]

For Humphrey it was indeed the perfect prayer. It *was* the prayer appropriate to a life of trying to bring hope where there was despair, joy where there was sadness—the prayer of the politics of joy.

For David Gartner, those politics would result in Humphrey being best remembered for "the sense of hope that he gave to the millions of people around the country and around the world who looked to him for doing those kinds of things that would help enrich their own lives."[9]

Calvin Didier remembered him for giving "us an access and an intimacy with a kind of a direct simple human reality that very few others are ever able [to do]. . . . He made politics intimate enough to make it believable."[10]

For Max Kampelman, "he tried to translate important issues into simple religious terms—feed the hungry, clothe the naked—this is what he would always say. He would say that this is our responsibility. He would not shy away from it."[11]

Humphrey did believe with all that was in him that religious principle and political practice were and ought to be *directly* related in a specific way. The focus of Humphrey's religion was on the democratic nature of God's providential regard: God loved all equally and therefore intended that all be equally able to receive the benefits of His care. For Humphrey, the significance of this was nearly entirely political in nature. Yet, at the same time—and by the same token—politics itself was inherently religious as well, at least in terms of its inspiration and its eventual goal. The focus of Humphrey's actual political life was strictly on what *worked*, to be sure, but on what worked for *all*. There was always that higher, broader vision that he kept with him, despite the daily blizzard of activity that was his normal routine. Ironically enough, it was that vision that also *prompted* the blizzard-like quality of his life; since he intended to see to it that *all* indeed have an equal opportunity to enjoy life's joy, he thus *had* to work as he did in order to achieve his end. "God did not ordain man to live a life of misery," he used to say. Humphrey felt ordained to see to it that God's ordinance was put into effect.

Humphrey was forced to maintain a consistent realism throughout his life—a realism forced on him by, among other things, bullet shots outside his home, by communist toughs denying him the right to speak, and by professional freezes imposing painful personal punishments on him for his having taken controversial stands. Yet his greater care remained preventing the necessity of that realism from becoming an excuse for moral cynicism, or worse—moral indifference. It was moral indifference that was the worst temptation for Humphrey, and therefore the worst of sins. His entire life was crafted to be one of fighting it. In that he identified with his nation as one engaged in the same battle. As Geri Joseph said, "I have heard Humphrey say a million times that you judge a country on the basis of what it does with the least of us. This was how he wished his own life to be judged as well."[12]

William Connell firmly believes that while Humphrey may have allowed his vision to become blurred by the feverishness of his daily regimen, Humphrey nevertheless consistently kept sight of that vision throughout his career, if only at a distance. As such it gave him a strength that was recognizable:

> When there is a crisis, people tend to scurry around in all directions—looking—"What do I do? What do I say? Where do I go?"—and there . . . are very few leaders that have the inner strength . . . and *vision* or world view—this, this *conviction* that persuades everybody else that *there* is someone . . . who really knows what is going on and who understands the ramifications of this event, and where we are going—*there* is someone that I can trust and rely on—and they rallied to him. And that is what was happening, I think, in the last few years—that ability to convert his basic ethical beliefs into a political framework—[it] was very unusual.[13]

As Humphrey was unusual, so, at least in his own eyes, was America unusual as well. When Humphrey asked, "What is it that really typifies our country?" he answered,

> not wealth; other countries have been rich, even though we surely have great wealth compared with other nations today. Not power; other countries have had power and have used it, and sometimes used it to their destruction. It is not size, because we are not the biggest country even today. So what is it that has exemplified and characterized what one calls an American? We Americans are not a unique breed of the human species. It is impossible to define an American from a point of view of anthropology or psychology. We are a conglomerate. So, what is it that identifies us? It is a sense of generosity, of compassion, of kindliness, of tolerance, of understanding.[14]

Humphrey certainly wanted America to be distinctive—distinctive in its dedication to the proposition that "all men are created equal." Humphrey saw his own life as simply one of increased devotion to that same cause.

As shown, his manner of applying such devotion took a twofold form. At home, he was an incrementalist—a manner he had had to learn the hard way by his early experiences in the Senate. Abroad he was an internationalist, as was exemplified in his stand against communism—a stand which would also lead him down a "hard way."

Instances of his referring to both such forms abound. Humphrey talked of how he felt fortunate, for instance, that "we live in a country where it is possible to institute change by democratic process."[15] As a liberal within that country Humphrey was proud that "the voice of the disinherited can be heard and social justice can be attained within the institutions of American society, within the framework of the rule of Law, of the Constitution, party rules, to each other."[16] In Frances Howard's eyes Humphrey "made [his] idealism come alive through his action and his teaching—he was quick to recognize that you could not win by forcing the issue, that you must have consensus . . . he was a consensus builder."[17]

His internationalism abroad was based on a similar commitment to the equal care and respect for others. Humphrey would proudly boast, for instance, that "no country has done more for the health of the human family than has the U.S.A. With high moral purpose we have gladly led the way in humanitarian effort in this as in so many other respects."[18] While critical of the policies of particular administrations, Humphrey was forever proud of America's record in acting for the international good.

The holding and expressing of patriotic pride is usually associated with the more conservative side of the political spectrum. Humphrey was extremely patriotic, yet he was so as a *liberal*. He took great pride in much of America's history and heritage, but for him that heritage was largely a *liberal* heritage. It was the kind of heritage that moved Humphrey to say,

> I want the people of Doland to know that America's greatness is not because it produces massive weapons, even though we do; that America's greatness is not

> because we put a man on the moon, even though we have; and America's greatness is not only because we have championed the cause of many nations, and been generous as a victor, even to the vanquished, because indeed all of that we have. American's greatness is because it cares about people.[19]

Associating the greatness of a superpower with its care for people represents the taking of a distinctive political tack. For Humphrey, it was the distinctly *liberal* political tack, one which defined America in a distinct way:

> America is another word for humanity. America—how do you define it? You define it by the words freedom and people. America is not a piece of geography between two oceans and two borders. American is an idea. It is an idea about God-given rights—that God Almighty gave to us in soul and in spirit of life, liberty and of the pursuit of happiness. These are the rights that belong to us because we are the children of God. They can't be taken away from us. And that is why in the Declaration of Independence it is written that governments are established among men to *insure* and *secure* and guarantee these rights.[20]

This distinctive kind of greatness was, for Humphrey, a *liberal* greatness. It was so because it made humanity—*humaneness*—the final goal and the final criterion by which all else was to be judged. Oftentimes Humphrey could indeed sound conservative. In some ways his foreign policy, so far as it has already been stated, could be construed to be conservative—certainly in contrast to what was generally regarded as the "liberal" foreign policy position of the Vietnam and post-Vietnam period. Domestically, he often voiced what could also be construed to be a conservative view on such things as the negative effects that big government can have on America's democratic society. His master's thesis has already been cited in this vein. There are other examples. In 1960, for instance, he called for a balanced budget (in times of prosperity) and argued that "expanded economic growth would broaden the tax burden enough so that increased taxes might not be necessary."[21] In 1964 he argued that "the ability to solve our problems does not lie exclusively within the executive agencies or Congress. State and local government, as well as labor and management, can participate in attacking the problems and in defining and meeting community and human needs."[22] "I do not think," he argued at the same time, that "we have many real grievances to be urged against bigness in business today. To the contrary, for the most part, big corporations are a source of strength and economic vitality," and even, "The most successful preventive to monopoly has been and continues to be growth of markets."[23] In a 1965 letter to *U.S. News & World Report* (his "favorite magazine"), he proudly took credit for being "an early advocate of a reduction in both corporate and personal income taxes." In that same article he stated his belief in "our private enterprise system" and "in an expanding and growing economy."[24] In 1967 he asserted that he didn't "believe that government has any monopoly on wisdom" and expressed pleasure that "in our war on poverty, for example, we haven't relied entirely on government. We've reached out to corporations to operate our job centers and our job core facilities."[25] In 1968 he presaged Ronald Reagan's "New Federalism" by calling for his own "Creative Federalism." This would be "a program not of handouts or of charity, but of opening new opportunities for self-help and dignity . . . a program not of the Federal government alone, but also of states and cities; not of government alone, but of the private sector and voluntary associations too, working together."[26] In his 1972 autobiography Humphrey agreed that "a certain amount of skepticism [of the private sector] is healthy," yet he at the same time cautioned that "democracy itself may die, the victim of patronizing indifference, if the mutual respect between the bureaucracy and the citizenry deteriorates further," and expressed concern that "a kind of elitism, a professional governmental snobbishness, has grown as bureaucracy has expanded and government programs increased."[27] In 1975 he declared that "unlike some of my liberal colleagues I am very concerned about capital formation."[28] Then, in 1976, on the eve of Jimmy Carter's inauguration, he wrote,

> Believe me, Governor, my years in Washington have taught me that there is an incredible lethargy in these huge departments of government. Whoever is President must first of all be in command and insist that they are the servants of the people. I really believe that the plush offices, those extra limousines, those additional personal staff aides have a tendency to build a wall between the realities of the country and the proper conduct of government.
>
> I simply wanted to have you know that as a so-called card-carrying bleeding heart liberal I believe in and support tough, effective, frugal administration.[29]

Upon being asked whether Hubert Humphrey was a typical "tax-and-spend" Democrat, Barry Goldwater responded, "I don't think Hubert was a tax-and-spend Democrat. He had a pretty good economic background having been mayor of his town and having worked in his own drug store, so I would put him down as a moderate."[30]

Being regarded as a "moderate" by Barry Goldwater, and urging "tough, effective, frugal administration" on Jimmy Carter could be used as examples for questioning whether Humphrey was a "cardcarrying bleeding heart liberal" at all. Such examples would only be further augmented by looking at a meeting Humphrey took part in with Carter's antithesis (and antagonist)—Ronald Reagan. In a 1975 forum entitled, "Government Regulation: What Kind of Reform?" sponsored by the conservative think tank The American Enterprise Institute, Reagan asked, "isn't the answer really that we have tried to centralize too much government at the national level; that you can't make a myriad of rules that will fit every corner of this country, across 3,000 miles; that we need more government control and management, particularly of these human problems, back at the local level?"[31]

Humphrey's response to this was, "I do agree that if we are going to have flexibility we've got to have the people living close to the problem enforcing the rules, and more and more authority has to be vested at the local level."[32] He also called for "periodic reviews of the rules and regulations from each department," advocating an "economic impact study or evaluation . . . of every rule and regulation and every piece of legislation that we pass."[33] Thus, Evron Kirkpatrick was quite fair in saying that had Humphrey become president, "we would have moved much more in the direction that Reagan has gone, and I say that because he was very much in that position before he died—[believing] that there has got to be some kind of deregulation . . . [and] that we have a vast bureaucracy, [that] small business enterprise ought to be encouraged."[34]

If this is true, however, it is not because Humphrey's political tastes were the same as Ronald Reagan's. The truth is closer to the fact that while the political palate that Humphrey developed in Doland *included* certain ingredients of the Reagan program, the overall *recipe* remained substantially different. When in 1926 he saw how hard-working, able, and decent people could be brought to their economic knees by forces beyond their control, he learned and from there on believed in the meaning of the concept "the deserving poor"—a concept not normally associated with the Reagan administration. It was precisely that concept that in turn formed the basis for this concept of the proper role of government. That role was, once again, and as Humphrey stated throughout his life, Lincoln's "legitimate object of government."

Thus, in that same AEI forum, Humphrey responded to Ronald Reagan's argument for replacing government intervention with "the magic of the marketplace," by retorting, "Governor, you're blowing bubbles," and went on to argue that

> We talk about everybody's having to pay his own way, but how would you like to be living out in Nevada, for example, if you couldn't have a federal highway system going through there? How are you going to develop the remote parts of the country? The postal system, the highway system, the transportation system, the rural electric system, the irrigation system. . . . Look, they tax us in Minnesota for irrigation projects out in the West. Why, that beautiful valley you have out there in California, Governor, gets a lot of water. If you don't believe it, ask the folks in Arizona who think you get too much. And a lot of that water comes out of federal appropriations for irrigation projects. I vote for those programs because I believe this is one country. I was brought up to believe that this is the United States of America. I believe that people may move from Worthington, Minnesota, to San Francisco, or from New York out into a small town like Mankato, Minnesota, and expect to find that there are basic minimum standards in this country for every human being.[35]

He had meant it when he said, as he often did, that "I learned more about economics in one dust storm than in any college course I ever took." That education included recognizing the problems associated with large government programs. Yet, when in the midst of the Depression, Humphrey witnessed firsthand how the WPA took people off the dole and gave them a chance to earn their income (and a measure of dignity along with it), no matter how minor the job, he had seen

> what government can mean to a society, how government can really affect the day-to-day lives of individuals—for the better. It taught me what government can mean in terms of improving the human condition . . . how government programs literally rebuilt the territory and again made life tolerable, filling the people with hope.[36]

For Humphrey,

> lives that seem hopeless and worthless can change and become productive. I've listened day after day, decade after decade, to political and theological arguments about cost per person, waste in government programs, and all the other cliches that come too easily to those who have. None of the arguments makes much sense to me when measured against the human gain—in dignity, sense of community, and even ultimate material benefit for society.[37]

And so, even while Humphrey could and did sound conservative on many occasions, at the same time he would also observe that

> conservatives say, as though it were their view alone, that "profits are the fuel that powers our economy. The only way a businessman can stay in business is to make a profit; the only way that government can collect taxes is when there is a profit." It is not illiberal to agree, and I do.
>
> But legitimate questions remain as to what kind of profits are reasonable—whether they arise from exploitation and deceit or from service fairly provided. It is clearly necessary for the government to "intrude" with some safeguards and standards to protect its citizens and to protect citizens from abuse.
>
> Big government is a necessary consequence of an urban, industrialized corporate nation. It is an institution whose power must be carefully used as a countervailing force to other institutions in the private sector, to prevent abuses.[38]

Thus, as is the case with his foreign policy, quite conservative sounding statements of Humphrey's on domestic policy can be readily found. Yet, to go on to claim that he was therefore a conservative can only be done by taking such statements out of context. While wary of bureaucratic sloth in big government, he was *also* wary of avariciousness in big business and of its threat to smaller concerns in the marketplace. Humphrey did believe in a free market, but in a *truly* free market—that is, one in which *everyone* had an equal opportunity to participate. This equal opportunity to participate was, for Humphrey, the essence of freedom. Any other kind of freedom was either meaningless or dangerous—a name, as already stated, "of noble sound and squalid results." In his book *Beyond Civil Rights*, for instance, he argued that "a program for equality must now become a program for *participation*,"[39] and stressed "the importance of the poor, the disinherited and the black acting for themselves."[40] This kind of participation—this ability to take part in the overall community—was what truly counted for Humphrey. Only when democracy worked in this way would there be genuine dignity and self-respect—the character traits necessary to ensure that real freedom flourished. According to the Humphrey outlook, rather than being a threat to this freedom, government's role was to act as guarantor of it. The free market does indeed have a very special role to play in seeing to it that freedom endures, but so does government:

> Well, I want to say that market forces are important, and they will take care of most things, to be sure. But the forces of the market do not take care of some things; and as I said to the Committee on Banking and Currency this morning, the Constitution of the United States doesn't mention "market forces." Nor does the Old, nor the New Testament, nor does the Declaration of Independence, which we celebrate this year in our Bicentennial.
>
> But it does mention "justice," and it does mention "life, liberty, and the pursuit of happiness"; and the Constitution does say that we, the people, come together for several purposes. And what were those purposes? They are very specific: To form a more perfect Union. To establish justice, that relates to welfare. To assure domestic tranquility, which surely relates to our inner cities. To provide for the common defense. Against what? Just against outside enemies? Maybe internal enemies, enemies of poverty and disruption, of violence. And to promote the general welfare and to secure the blessings of liberty for ourselves and our posterity.
>
> I think we have got to get our priorities straightened out. I think we have to know what we are talking about; I think we have to understand the difference between the Constitutional language and the corporate language. Once we begin to understand that we will maybe come to grips with what government is all about and what this society is all about. The definition of America is freedom and justice, not marketplace only. I am not unaware of the importance of the marketplace. I think it is tremendously important; but it is but a means to obtain justice. It is not an end in itself.[41]

For Humphrey, then, while the conservative "talks of the 'evil reaches of government power which curb our freedom' . . . he forgets that hunger curtails freedom in harsher, and more real ways than any imagined curbs produced by government planning. Poverty curtails individual freedom. So do illiteracy, prejudice, lack of education, [and the] inability to obtain the basic needs of life."[42] In Humphrey's view, "free enterprise—yes, individual private enterprise—cannot be based upon the philosophy of greed and selfishness or have as its rules the law of the jungle. Business enterprise has a responsibility not only to itself but to the rest of the community."[43] By opposing conservative jungle law, Humphrey believed—as did his father before him—that liberalism made itself the champion of freedom, that is, the right kind of freedom—the *American* kind:

> The American philosophy of liberty is not merely absence of restraint. More basically, it is the establishment of conditions of fair play and of equal opportunity that permits an orderly development of society and a development of individual ability for the benefit of the individual as well as the community.[44]

Thus, when he argued that "the first answer to poverty is full employment," he did not simply have "the magic of the marketplace" in mind. The idea of the Humphrey-Hawkins bill to provide for full employment, as proposed in 1977, was one already suggested by Humphrey's 1968 assertion that "a decent life, in this wealthy country, should now be considered a *right* for all men."[45] Government was to be responsible, at least in some substantial way, to see to it that that right was honored. This is what justice eventually meant for Humphrey—not the guaranteeing of welfare, but of opportunity—*equal* opportunity for *every* citizen:

> We should not want to provide charity but opportunity because you don't build character by just giving charity. You build charity by affording opportunity so that people can use their abilities, not to hide their talent under a bushel but to use their ability, and it's the duty of people in government and it's the duty of people in civic responsibility whether it's in business, professions, labor, education—whatever it is to so arrange the society of which we are a part so that men, all men and women of whatever capacity can utilize their abilities to the best of their capacity. In other words: to remove the handicap.[46]

Thus what Humphrey believed in, in the final run, was a "welfare program in which the government takes the responsibility—a responsibility that it alone can adequately fulfill—for seeing to it that a decent standard of living and of human dignity is assured to every American citizen"[47]—a responsibility, in other words, that the pursuit of happiness be a genuine possibility for all of America's citizens. In the Humphrey view, America ought to be corporately committed to the belief that life was forever not something simply to be endured, but enjoyed. While Humphrey agreed with

Reagan's assertion that "we have tried to centralize too much government at the national level" he simultaneously believed that "the standards of government in some counties make you wonder whether the local authority is really going to protect the public interest."[48] While he also agreed with Reagan about the benefits, under certain circumstances, of reducing taxes, he, again at the same time, argued that

> there is some equity and some equality of performance when taxes are paid. Not everybody can spend two weeks in the Caribbean on a yacht, but I'll guarantee you that you can spend a week on Lake Calhoun, in Minneapolis, if you want to, or you can spend some time in one of our public parks. In my opinion, many of the services that are provided out of tax funds—good roads, good schools, good public health offices, good parks and recreational facilities—are fringe benefits that go to a citizen that he would never get otherwise, unless he were well-to-do.[49]

According to the Humphrey view, then, we ought to "all pay for each other," for the issue finally is: "Do we want a country or don't we?"*

Humphrey did want a country. He believed in an America acting "like one big family"; of having "people very different" yet at the same time having "a sense of belonging, and a sense of caring." He believed in an America where *everyone* could have "the feeling that you were *wanted*"—an America, in other words, like Doland. As was so often the case, Humphrey was years before his time when in 1964 he called for "a sense of overriding national purpose which calls men to rise above their daily concerns with making a living, getting ahead of the competition, or expanding their sphere of influence"—a concept that emerged in the mid-eighties as a result of its successful application—economic as well as social—in Western Europe and Japan. While believing in competition (and in being extremely competitive himself,[50] Humphrey also believed in being decent—in showing due regard to our neighbor—that is, to *all* of our neighbors. This is so because "if it is right for individuals to be admonished to feed the hungry, to heal the sick, and to clothe

*For a more complete view of Humphrey's economic policy, see appendix h.

the naked, then is it not right for a government of the people, by the people, and for the people to undertake some of the same responsibilities as a moral duty?"[51]

Thus, by "country" Humphrey understood *community*—the kind of community that he considered himself—a "simple kid from the prairie"—fortunate enough to have grown up in, and therefore that everyone else should have an equal opportunity to grow up in as well. He sought, for example, full education

> for every child first of all because we affirm the worth of the child; we seek to overthrow the barriers of race not only to make our country stronger and richer—which it will—but because those barriers are unjust; we seek a society where human development comes first not only because our citizens are a "resource" like coal or oil, but because human development is what America is, or should be, all about—in Doland and in Harlem.[52]

In his "Meditation," delivered at Humphrey's funeral, Calvin Didier mentioned how, "early in the 1972 Presidential campaign, Hubert Humphrey said: 'What I want, if you'll let me, is to bring this country together as a family.'"[53] It was as good a summary of Hubert Humphrey's life as could be given in a single story.

Humphrey's vision of America was one of harmony—harmony between differing sectors of society and between differing sections of the country. For Humphrey, however, such a vision "is impossible and irrelevant without government acting positively."[54] Humphrey was therefore unquestionably (though that is not to say unqualifiedly) an advocate of big government. Despite the problems associated with it—problems which he himself consistently recognized—he nevertheless regarded government intervention as one of the crucial factors necessary for realizing the American dream.

Thus, for Humphrey, "the most important difference between the liberal and the conservative today is in their concepts of the role of government in our society and world."[55] "Historically," he wrote,

> the differences between the Democratic and Republican parties in this century have been the differences between satisfaction with the status quo and desire for change.

> Conservative thinkers assume that the world, in its present state, reflects the way things actually *ought* to be, and that the forces which shape our society, almost always work in the best interest of the people.
>
> Liberals are more skeptical of arbitrary society and economic forces. They have learned from history that too many of those forces result in inequality and lack of opportunity for enormous numbers of human beings, and they believe that these forces must be tempered by human agency if our society is to be truly just.
>
> Because the Republican Party in this century has been dominated by conservative spokesmen it has consistently supported the existing structure of privilege and economic reward. The Democrats, in contrast, have generally believed that our historical legacy of society power and economic rank keeps large numbers of Americans from fulfilling their full potential and living rewarding lives.
>
> The U.S. Constitution requires its keepers to "promote the general welfare and secure the blessings of liberty to ourselves and our posterity." History will judge which political philosophy has done the most to keep that promise.[56]

Again, the traditions, political and otherwise, that he inherited from Doland are manifest even here, at the end of his life.

The last time Bill Moyers saw Humphrey he was struck, in the long conversation he had with him, by "the attitude of a man whose life more or less embodied an old tradition which was part of the structure with which he grew up."[57] That "old tradition" was the one that Humphrey had described himself as having been learned in Doland, namely, that "one man was as good as another—that was what democracy was all about."[58] Hubert Humphrey's politics, then, were the assertion that "the duty of the government [was] to use its full power and resources to meet the social, economic and technological challenges of our time—to guarantee to the average person the right to his own political and economic life, to liberty and the pursuit of happiness—to provide government with a heart."[59] Humphrey himself sought to provide "government with a heart" for all of his days because with all of his own heart (and mind) he believed it best enabled us "to unfold and release the talents and abilities of every person so that they may be used fully and constructively in the pursuit of individual happiness and community well-being"[60]—the community well-being and the individual happiness that life in Doland had given him—and which he came to believe as the essence of the term "liberal."

And so, Humphrey should be considered as a liberal, in the final run, because he believed that remaining steadfast in one's commitment to humane values was what finally counted above all else. Insofar as both liberalism and America herself had done this, they both had achieved greatness, for that is what greatness consists of—provided that one of those "humane values" is a commitment to *effecting* those values. Defining greatness in this way is hardly, however, an act of secular inspiration. For Humphrey, the truth is that this is *precisely* what religion implied. As such, Humphrey represented a distinctive manner of relating religion and politics.

For Humphrey, religion described our belief that all people are of equal worth—that we all have rights that "belong to us because we are the children of God," whereas, politics was the means by which we acted as a nation on the basis of that belief. Religion was the institution by which we foster our belief in those rights; government was the institution by which we enacted it. The two always went hand in hand.

As we know, the dream, for Humphrey, came before the fact. The dream that preceded fact as Hubert Humphrey saw it was that all people achieve fullness in life—fullness and thereby the joy that they all deserve as the children of God. The means by which such a dream of the "politics of joy" was to be realized was the "creative federalism" that Humphrey represented at home, and the equally creative internationalism that he stood for abroad. "If we make up our minds," he said, "we can reaffirm what this country stands for. This country stands for the power of the people—the power of compassion, justice, social action, education, health. And this is made a reality when government and the people team up and work together."[61] His believing that this—his version of "the American dream"—came true when "government and the people team up and work together" is what distinguished the politics of joy as liberal. Of course it is understood that any such assignation involves considerable arbitrariness, given the clear arbitrariness of the terms "liberal" and "conservative" themselves. Milton Friedman, just to cite one well know example, claims to be the "authentic" liberal, yet he and Humphrey were at extreme odds over the issue of governmental intervention. So who, in that case, is the "real" liberal? and who is to decide? and on the basis of what criterion?

Nevertheless, within the liberalism that Humphrey represented it was understood that religion had to do with our making up our minds that the "power of the people" was indeed what our country was to stand for. Politics was a matter of getting people to work together within the framework that government provided so as to guarantee that we do in fact seek to find it.

Having people and government working together in this way was what Hubert Humphrey himself worked for throughout his life—it was his way of "trying somehow to arrive at heaven on earth." The familial model of a community working together that Doland had provided the young Humphrey was the same model that he in turn sought to provide for America in his maturity. Such provision, however, hardly ended there, for America itself was to be the Doland of the world at large. *This* was the America that Humphrey believed was worthy of our patriotic devotion. It was certainly the America that forever evoked such devotion from "that simple American kid from the prairie."

Jeane Kirkpatrick believed that "the popular response to Hubert Humphrey in the last months of his life was the kind of unplanned collective phenomenon through which nations and people express widely shared, deeply felt sentiments about their own purposes and identify as well as about the person honored."[62] For many, Hubert Humphrey (and often enough America with him) was simply too idealistic for what is an all-too-soberingly realistic world. Yet Humphrey believed that there is something human that forever yearns to believe in ideals—to believe that our highest aspirations are not simply delusions to be grimly avoided at all costs. That vision may very well have been what was being honored in those last few months—as well as the figure who had dedicated his life to such a vision with his own characteristically ever-increased devotion.

Whether this is so or not, the legitimate question can be raised of, Would Humphrey ever have gained the kind of affection that he did, let alone have achieved all that he did, had he lived by a more sober assessment of the American possibility?

In response to the assertion that "You're too happy . . . and this is not a happy world," Humphrey said,

> Well, maybe I can help make it a little more happy. Happiness is contagious just exactly like being miserable. Misery is contagious. I don't run around here

> like a buffoon or a pollyanna, with a pollyannish attitude. I realize and sense the realities of the world in which we live. I'm not at all happy about what I see with the nuclear arms race and the power, the machinations of the Soviets or the Chinese or what's going on in the Middle East, the misery that's in our cities, the pathetic problems that our country faces, individually and collectively . . . I'm aware of that. But I do not believe that people will respond to do better if they are constantly approached by a negative attitude. People have to believe that they can do better. They've got to know that there's somebody that's with them that wants to help and work with them, and somebody that hasn't tossed in the towel. I don't believe in defeat.[63]

Whether idealistic or not, Humphrey nevertheless was one of America's most productive political figures. The fact that Humphrey's bust sits with Clay's and others in the Capitol is no surprise to those who knew and worked with him. Neither is it to know that at the end of his life, all the while realising that he was seriously ill, and after failing to achieve his lifetime's ambition, he said,

> I have had more than most people ever had a chance to even dream of, and therefore I am a happy man. I am a fulfilled man. And at this time in my life I must say that I feel more of a sense of peace and yet more of a sense of fulfillment than at any time in my life.[64]

Here is, quite literally, the final portrait of "the Happy Warrior." It is also worth considering whether or not this is the end result of a life and career committed to the "politics of joy."

Humphrey was often described as a man who needed to be loved. Many times this was said disparagingly of him. Humphrey probably would have been puzzled by such a usage of the idea. In his view, everyone needed to be loved—this was simply a fundamental, perhaps *the* fundamental part of the human condition. This was not a weakness in certain people—it was a basic need that all shared. In a speech to the National Council of Churches Humphrey said,

> I have learned from my old friend Reinhold Niebuhr that a more equal justice is a sort of stand-in, a local representation in the area of politics, for the higher ideal of Christian love. There is another even farther-reaching implication of the ideal of love; the fact of our interdependence; the need for community.[65]

Needing to be loved, then, was a fact, a universal given for Humphrey. While working for justice in the political realm was the best that could be realistically hoped for according to Niebuhr, working for community and the happiness that accrues from its establishment was what was to be hoped for according to the politics of joy. Therein lies the distinction (as will be discussed in much more thorough detail in the next chapter).

Thus, for Humphrey,

> What is it that makes for security? Not just weapons, but love of country. When people love their country, when they feel they are a part of it, when they feel that their country gives them a chance, they then are true patriots. I have said it many times but I'll repeat it to my friends in Doland. A great English philosopher once said—John Stuart Mill his name—"Let a person have nothing to do for his country, and he shall have no love for it."
>
> America needs to be loved. And if it is going to be loved then it has to have people that feel they are a part of it, that they belong, that they are wanted, whether they are black or white, whether they are urban or rural, whether they are rich or poor—they have got to feel that this country cares about them, and that their government cares about them, and they have to feel that they care about their country.[66]

Caring for and being cared for is the essence of the kind of community built by the politics of joy. For Humphrey it was clear not only that this caring was a possibility for America, but also that it provided a particular kind of possibility for America:

> Dear friends, I find that there is a lot of that caring and feeling around America, and I am here to give you a report on the state of the nation. And the state of the nation is this: That our people are not satisfied with the yesterdays. That does not mean that they are bitter or embittered. It means that they know that they can do better; they know that America can set its own goals; that we can have our own standards; that we can have achievements that are meaningful to us. And there are people in America by the hundreds of thousands that are restless to get on with the job—not only of America being #1 in military power, but, dear friends, to be #1 in caring for each other; to be #1 in cleaning up our cities; to be #1 in health and health care; to be #1 in education for everyone—the handicapped, the normal, the child, the adult; to be #1 in the housing of our people; to be #1 in jobs for our people—these are the things that we ought to aspire to—and, dear friends, if we could be #1 in caring for each other, if we can be #1 in cleaning up the cities that are rotting from within, if we can be #1 in education for all of our people, and health care for all of our people—I'll tell you, we will be the strongest nation the world ever knew.[67]

The strength found in caring for others, and in having others care for you—the strength that religion refers to—is, for Humphrey, the greater strength—greater than any found simply in acting out of self-interest, crudely defined. In this way, according to the Humphrey view, the first shall indeed be last and the last first.

As with so many of his other views, there is evidence that Humphrey consistently held to this view as well. It was certainly evident in his foreign policy statements regarding the best way to oppose communism. Other statements include his 1945 speech to Emmanuel Lutheran Church, for instance, where he said, "But a republic without a set of principles is nothing. The thing that makes this country great is its creed, its philosophy of living, its philosophy of life."[68] In a 1949 commencement address to Bennington College he argued that "our security lies in the democratic philosophy, the democratic way of life and the democratic idea. That is our historical role; that is our historical mission."[69] In a 1956 article for *People Today* he wrote,

> What makes America strong? It is not the stock market; it is not our fabulous skyscrapers; it is not our mass production and high-pressure marketing techniques; it is not our shiny new automobiles and fancy kitchen gadgets. No, it is the people themselves—the spirit of our people. National strength depends on the capacity of government to see, feel, and act upon the needs of as many people as it possibly can—that is my concept.[70]

In a 1963 speech on the Alliance for Progress he said, "It is in the people that we have our strength. Governments come and go."[71] In his 1964 *The Cause Is Mankind* he said, "The real strength of this America, this free society, is the quality of its heritage and its people—people with a commitment to freedom and social justice."[72] Finally, in his 1976 speech at Doland he said, "The real strength of a nation is not in its machines, but in its people."[73]

Such a view, however, was made no clearer than in an article entitled "The Joy of Being 'Boppa.'" In that article Humphrey discussed what it had meant to have had a grandchild with Down's syndrome. Vicki had been born on the night of one of Humphrey's greatest senatorial victories—1960—where he won by a plurality of 240,000 votes. When the Humphreys discovered, however, that this, their first grandchild, was retarded, their initial reaction was natural enough—they were grief stricken. Yet, as Humphrey went on to say,

> She is, to me, the sweetest breath of life upon this earth. You will never know the meaning of love as it is described in the Scriptures until you know a child like Vicki. She is the greatest spiritual experience I have had, and because of her I know with certainty that the more you give, the more shall be given to you.*[74]

The kind of regard for others that characterized Hubert Humphrey's life was based precisely on this kind of outlook. Giving to the hungry, the sick, the unclothed, the handicapped *was* the love described in the Scriptures, according to the Humphrey hermeneutic. For Humphrey it *was* the greatest sort of religious experience. Bringing to bear the full power of mature legislative expertise on the issues involved in such giving was, in turn, the greatest sort of political experience—the politics of joy indeed. It was for this that one endured all the years of struggling through the difficult and decisive experiences that constitute a political career. Enduring such struggles for the sake of such a cause *was* great because in so doing we show the very best that humankind is capable of, namely, the decency of acting not for ourselves, but for others, just as we would have them do for ourselves.

For Humphrey, insofar as America did so act as a nation it truly lead the world. Believing in this, and basing a life on that belief, provides the fullest sense with which the "the Happy Warrior" is to be understood as one who spent his life seeking to "smite a pathway for the Almighty in human affairs."

As was noted at the beginning, the Social Gospel was characterized by the following features: (1) a sense of religious mission, namely, of instituting the Kingdom on earth; (2) an essentially nonreflective yet highly "enthusiastic" nature which sought to engender voluntary, individual effort; (3) a belief that religious values ought to be reflected in governmental practice; (4) an emphasis on *action*—specifically on active aid for the needy; (5) a

*The last rite performed in Humphrey's funeral was that of Vicki throwing flowers on the lowered coffin.

belief that democracy represents the closest thing in the political realm to the Kingdom yet attained; and (6) a belief that wealth, not government, represents the greatest threat to individual integrity, and consequently that government was the crucial institution by which this threat was to be thwarted.

Rauschenbusch provided an additional characteristic of the Social Gospel by talking about "the immense latent perfectibility in human nature,"[75] to which Ahlstrom added, "men must gain control of social forces. The 'bonds of evil' must be broken and finally—and here is the insistence that makes the Social Gospel a movement in the churches—religious faith and moral strength must be directed toward these last great social tasks."[76]

When John Stewart described Humphrey's religion as being "the Social Gospel unleashed,"[77] it would appear, given the above, that no more accurate or more apt depiction of Humphrey could be given. Reviewing the above list, and comparing it to the features of Humphrey's life, clear credence is provided for using this ascription. The enthusiasm with which Humphrey did unleash the Social Gospel—his "enthusiasm for humanity"—is what spawned "Hubert the Exuberant." His exuberance had much to do with his belief in the greatness of his country—greatness that he understood squarely in religious terms. The test of our success, for Humphrey, should always be measured in terms of what we have accomplished for, as he so often quoted himself, "the least of these." It was religion's role to provide that principle. It was, on the other hand, politic's role to provide the means to effect it. His chosen vehicle for so doing was the liberal-progressive tradition—a tradition that championed government's role in the nation's life, and a tradition that he never regarded as being "just politics," but rather as "morality, and in a very real sense, Christian morality." The liberal-progressive tradition, in his view, was a distinctly *American* political tradition, for it made people—humaneness—its priority, but it was a priority that could and was to be honored through the principles already inherent to the nation. Thus, America was the closest thing to "heaven on earth" that the earth had.

Holding such a view, which was a distinctly and unquestionably religious-political view, just as it was equally clearly one of "unreflective fervor," would fully appear to mean that Humphrey was indeed aptly characterized as being "the Social Gospel unleashed." Whether such an appellation is, in the final run, the most appropriate one, however, is the subject of the next chapter.

Notes

1. Eric Severeid, as quoted in Cohen, *Undefeated*, 45.
2. TRB (Richard Strout), "Before the Fact Is the Dream," *The New Republic* (28 January 1978): 8.
3. Moyers interview.
4. Kampelman interview.
5. Joseph interview.
6. Adlai Stevenson III, from *Sunshine*.
7. Connell interview.
8. Hubert Humphrey, "You Can't Quit Hubert Humphrey," *Reader's Digest* (August 1977): 59.
9. Gartner interview.
10. Didier interview.
11. Kampelman interview.
12. Joseph interview.
13. Connell interview.
14. Humphrey, *Congressional Record*, 85th Cong., 1st sess., 1957. Vol. 103, 14641.
15. Ibid., 82nd Cong., 1st sess., 1951. Vol. 97, 7020.
16. Frances Howard interview with author, no. 2, 2 February 1984.
17. Ibid. Bill Moyers tells a story to this effect: "In the 1964 campaign we ran a series of commercials that were very effective. The most controversial was the daisy commercial, of course, but the best—the effective one [had to do with] Barry Goldwater making the statement that we ought to just saw off the Eastern seaboard. [The ad, therefore,] showed a map of the U.S. floating in water and a saw came up as this voice quoting Goldwater [spoke] and sawed off the eastern seaboard, which just went floating out. . . . When I showed that to Hubert he laughed and laughed and said, 'You know, a lot of people wanted to do that to the south, including me, early on. But I realized we couldn't do what was right for negroes if at the same time we simply cut the south off—cut it loose and let it go. We had to have the Civil Rights movement, but we had to have the south emotionally and physically in the union [as well].' It was a very wise, mature observation from a . . . man who in his youth had been a firebrand." From the Moyers interview.
18. Hubert Humphrey, "Teamwork for Mankind's Well-Being," U.S. & World Health Organization Report (11 May 1959): 7.
19. Humphrey, Doland speech.
20. Ibid.
21. Hubert Humphrey, "The Campaign: The Liberal Flame," *Time* (1 February, 1960): 13–16.
22. Humphrey, *Cause*, 35.
23. Ibid., 53.
24. Humphrey, "Letter from the Vice President," *U.S. News & World Report* (25 October 1965): 53.

25. Humphrey, speech to International Newspaper Advertising Executives, 26 January 1967, Humphrey Collection.
26. Humphrey, *Beyond Civil Rights* (New York: Random House, 1968), 148.
27. Humphrey, *Education*, 47.
28. Humphrey, "Springboard," 70.
29. Hubert Humphrey, letter to Jimmy Carter, 3 November 1976, Humphrey Collection.
30. Barry Goldwater, letter to author, 14 November 1984.
31. Ronald Reagan, AEI forum, 36.
32. Humphrey, ibid.
33. Ibid., 30.
34. Kirkpatrick interview.
35. Humphrey, AEI forum, 49.
36. Humphrey, *Education*, 50.
37. Ibid., 71.
38. Ibid., 46–47.
39. Humphrey, *Beyond*, 148.
40. Ibid., 154.
41. Hubert Humphrey, speech to The National Leadership Conference on Welfare Reform, 25 May 1976, in a transcript provided by The Institute for Socioeconomic Studies.
42. Humphrey, *Cause*, 48.
43. Humphrey, as quoted in Sheldon E. Engelmayer, *Hubert Humphrey, The Man and His Dream* (New York: Methuen, 1978), 41.
44. Ibid., 42.
45. Humphrey, *Beyond*, 150.
46. Humphrey, Emmanuel Lutheran speech.
47. Humphrey, *Cause*, 16.
48. Humphrey, AEI forum, 36.
49. Ibid., 37–38.
50. David Gartner relates a story to this effect: "I remember one night when we were in Waverly and we had to get up really early the next morning . . . and Mrs. Humphrey had popped a big bowl of popcorn. We were sitting there playing [Monopoly]—and it got to be around 12:30 and he was way behind—I mean he had a couple of properties, but they were mortgaged or something—and I had a whole bunch. He said, "Ah, the hell with it, I'm going to bed." He was very competitive—extremely competitive. . . . So he got up and left the room and about five minutes later he was back in his pajamas and slippers sitting down and ready to whip my butt, and as a matter of fact got a lucky shake of the dice and would up winning the thing and ended up going to bed happy as hell." From the Gartner interview.
51. Humphrey, Griffith memorandum.
52. Humphrey, *Beyond*, 182–83.
53. Humphrey, as quoted in *Hubert H. Humphrey, Late a Senator from Minnesota/Memorial Addresses Delivered in Congress* (Washington: Government Printing Office, 1978), 280.
54. Humphrey, *Education*, 171.
55. Humphrey, *Think*, 7.

56. Hubert Humphrey, letter to Dr. J. C. Chapman, 11 August 1976, Austin, Texas, Humphrey Collection.
57. Moyers interview.
58. Humphrey, *Beyond*, 22.
59. Hubert Humphrey, statement for the *Fayatte Tribune and Montgomery Herald*, Humphrey Collection.
60. Hubert Humphrey, campaign keynote address, "Happiness and Community Well-Being," 5 October 1948, Bemidgi, Minnesota, Humphrey Collection.
61. Hubert Humphrey, speech to the National Municipal League's 77th Annual Conference, Humphrey Collection.
62. Kirkpatrick article.
63. From Bill Moyers' "A Conversation."
64. Humphrey, Doland speech.
65. Hubert Humphrey, speech to the National Council of Churches.
66. Humphrey, Doland speech.
67. Ibid.
68. Humphrey, Emmanuel Lutheran speech.
69. Humphrey, Bennington College commencement address, Bennington, Vermont, 1 July 1949, as given in Engelmayer, *Dream*, 35.
70. Hubert Humphrey, draft of an article entitled, "It is People Who Count," for *People Today*, Humphrey Collection, from the Senate years.
71. Hubert Humphrey, Alliance for Progress speech, 26.
72. Humphrey, *Cause*, 77.
73. Humphrey, Doland speech.
74. Hubert Humphrey, "The Joy of Being 'Boppa,'" *McCall's* (December 1967): 37.
75. Rauschenbusch, as quoted in Ahlstrom, *History*, 786.
76. Ahlstrom, ibid.
77. Stewart interview.

9

Dream and Fact Amalgamated: HHH as Nearly Christian Realist

In a crowded ballroom of the Shoreham Hotel, on 7 April 1968, Hubert Humphrey announced his candidacy for the presidency of the United States. He did so by calling for what he termed "the way politics ought to be," which was to say, "the politics of happiness, the politics of purpose and the politics of joy."[1] As with nearly everything else he said in that year, it was a remark that was to immediately generate controversy, not to say criticism. Perhaps the severest, certainly the most public, was to come from someone else who had announced a similar candidacy: Bobby Kennedy. Kennedy's point was simple and blunt: What did it mean to call for a "politics of joy" in this, one of America's most *un*joyous times? It was a point that registered.

The politics of joy were the kind of politics that could only be held by an optimist. Hubert Humphrey always thought of himself as an optimist, yet wanted, at the same time, to be regarded as a realist—to be included among the "pragmatists" as well—to be a member of what is suggested by Mario Cuomo's later label of the "progressive-pragmatist party." As such, it would appear fair to describe Humphrey's overall political outlook as "dialectical," if by "dialectical" what is meant in this case (and as is related to the understanding of the term utilized in this work) is refusing rigid adherence to the ideology of *either* side, including that of one's own background and upbringing, insisting instead that *both* sides be taken into account on an issue-by-issue basis. "Progressive-pragmatic party" and "dialectical," when defined in these ways, are strongly suggestive of a particular school of religious-political thought associated with its founder and principle proponent, Reinhold Niebuhr, certainly one of the most significant figures in religion and politics in American history. That "school" is Christian Realism.

Christian Realism was founded primarily by Niebuhr's critique of the Social Gospel and the kind of overly optimistic liberalism that was traditionally associated with it. While a product of both the Social Gospel and that liberalism, Humphrey at the same time was quite aware of and aspired to the kind of realism that Niebuhr proposed as an alternative. The suggestion of such a relationship might be further corroborated by the fact that not only had Humphrey been assisted by a number of people who knew Niebuhr personally (as well as understood his work thoroughly), but the fact that Humphrey and Niebuhr themselves had been directly associated through their mutual involvement in the ADA. Christian Realism, then, ought to be at least considered as a potential framework for analysis for Humphrey's career in addition to the Social Gospel.

Humphrey and Niebuhr first met in the formative days of the ADA, around 1947. The ADA was then the phoenix rising out of the ashes of Niebuhr's UDA (Union for Democratic Action) which had existed during the Second World War. Humphrey had been attracted to the ADA from the moment he first heard of it. Both he and Niebuhr were instrumental in its formation and development—Niebuhr was its most prominent speaker, whereas Humphrey was himself to eventually be national chairman. Though their relationship was apparently not a consistently intimate one, there was friendship between them, as well as professional respect. This kind of relationship appeared to have lasted for the rest of both men's lives.

Such a relationship, in a sense, had begun for Humphrey before they had ever met. Evron Kirkpatrick had had Humphrey read such early Niebuhr classics as *Moral Man and Immoral Society* and *The Children of Light and the Children of Darkness* in his classes at the University of Minnesota.[2] Frances Howard recalls Humphrey as having been influenced by Niebuhr's *An Interpretation of Christian Ethics* at the time that it was published. Thus it is likely that Humphrey knew very well who Niebuhr was before they ever met. Once they did meet, however, their relationship blossomed into one of mutual respect.

This is best evidenced in the fact that Humphrey was asked to give the main address at the dinner celebrating *Christianity & Crisis*'s twenty-fifth anniversary. That anniversary fell in May of 1966, and so Humphrey had to do so amidst the clamor of protestors both inside and outside of Riverside Church were the dinner was being held. He did so, nevertheless, praising Niebuhr for "taming the cynics and pulling utopians back to earth," and for making a greater "contribution to political wisdom and moral responsibility" than any other American figure. He compared Niebuhr to Twain and Lincoln—all coming "out of that great middle western river valley." Niebuhr, like Twain and Lincoln, "brought a mixture of profundity and practicality." He, like Lincoln, "showed how to combine decisive action with a sensitive knowledge of the complexity of life, including politics." To the East he brought "his realism, his humor, his energy and a brooding thoughtfulness." To his countrymen he pressed "urgent demands of social justice," and taught them that "life just wasn't simple." "In scores of books and hundreds of articles," Humphrey said, "Reinie has hammered away at this basic theme: 'Man's capacity for justice makes democracy possible, but man's inclination to injustice makes democracy necessary.'" For Humphrey this was Niebuhr asserting "his belief in the upper reaches of human nature; in what he called 'original righteousness': man is made in the image of God, and at his best, is capable of justice," yet "we all know that all men, including good men, have a tendency to pursue their private ambitions and interests, often to the detriment of the rights and interests of their fellow man."[3]

For Humphrey, Niebuhr's conclusion was that "the case for democracy must rest on its realism: democracy takes into account the full range of human nature, not the perfect man, not the imperfect man, but man." Only a government which takes *this* "man" into account can "recognize and respect the legitimate claims of all conflicting interests." By so arguing, "our friend Dr. Niebuhr helped many of us understand our obligation to work for social justice without falling into soft utopian nonsense."[4]

In summation, Humphrey concluded that "Reinhold Niebuhr has contributed to American life and thought because he has been a realist without despair, an idealist without illusions."[5]

Despite his clear Social Gospel background, Humphrey himself can, in light of certain considerations, be favorably proposed as a "realist without despair, an idealist without illusions." The whirlwind idealist had, after all, worked hard to no longer be "just another emotional liberal, but, rather, a student of government," a liberal who denied that "compromise is a dirty word." He had voted consistently for nearly every military appropriation that ever came before him, year after year,[6] even if he had at the same time consistently argued for options other than sole reliance on military force. At the same time, however, he had championed the great liberal causes of his generation: civil rights, Medicare, nuclear disarmament, and so on. On the face of it, he could appear to qualify as a realistic child of light. Many of his positions certainly mirrored Niebuhr's own.

On the domestic side, for instance, Humphrey would agree with Niebuhr when he argued against both "a conservative class which makes 'free enterprise' the final good of the community," and "a radical class which mistakes some proximate solution of the economic problem for the ultimate solution of every issue of life."[7] Both Humphrey and Niebuhr rejected these two extremes because, as Niebuhr had asserted, each "failed to recognize the corruption of particular interest in ostensibly universal social ideals."[8]

Humphrey had after all defended the New Deal for its opposition to American conservatism once "the objective of business was no longer the seeking of legitimate economic expansion," but instead had become more a matter of "exploitation by stock market manipulation and monopoly price maintenance."[9] At the same time, however, Humphrey had heartily concurred with FDR when the latter said, "No one in the U.S. believes more firmly than I in the system of private business, private property, and private profit." For Humphrey, all that liberals seek, as FDR had said, is "balance in our economic system"[10] such that the "operations of that system are to be hedged in the interest of the security of the working man, the farmer, and the small investor."[11]

Niebuhr asserted that "it is clear that absolute economic freedom fails to establish sufficient justice to make it morally viable,"[12] and criticized American conservatism as "an anachronistic espousal of physiocratic theories which promote justice through the emancipation of economic life from every kind of political and moral control."[13] Humphrey in turn endorsed American liberalism for having "proved capable of coping with the problems of the new industrial society" by recognizing "the danger that they [the new concentrations of wealth and power that emerged from the industrial revolution] would be used to control and cripple government, destroy competition, and increase the maldistribution of wealth."[14]

Yet, on the other hand, where Niebuhr would argue as well that "it has become apparent that the measures which it may take to establish a minimum of justice in the community are in danger of destroying the freedom and spontaneity which its economic life requires,"[15] Humphrey showed similar concern by talking about "the deadening influence" of government on "individual initiative and personal integrity," and that "bureaucracy may find a firm foothold in our governmental system and cease to be responsive to the will of the people."[16]

As someone who consistently received 100 percent approval ratings from organized labor, Humphrey certainly agreed with Niebuhr that "its [labor's] organization of the power of the workers was necessary to produce the counterweight to the great concentrations of economic power which justice requires."[17] And, when Humphrey called for economic planning he could have quoted Niebuhr in support: "The second weakness in the American political and economic situation is that the lip service which the whole culture pays to the principles of *laissez-faire* makes for tardiness in dealing with the instability of a free economy, when the perils of inflation and deflation arise."[18]

In terms of support for these and other ideas, Niebuhr and Humphrey each looked to similar sources as well. Niebuhr argued that "Madison feared the political tyranny of government as much as Jefferson, but he understood the necessity of government much more,"[19] and Humphrey regularly cited Madison's famous dictum that, "If men were angels, no government would be necessary." In fact, Humphrey at one point actually cited Niebuhr utilizing Madison: "Niebuhr called us to reconsider some of the basic insights of persons like James Madison who knew the necessity of checking power with power."[20] Niebuhr believed that "the necessity of strong government was recognized"[21] by our founding fathers, and Humphrey wrote nearly an entire chapter on that theme in his master's thesis, citing time and again the opening words to the Preamble to the Constitution: "We the people . . . in order to form a more perfect union."

Both believed that America *had* formed a more perfect union. Both, in fact, believed that "its success in establishing justice and insuring domestic tranquility has exceeded the characteristic insights of a bourgeois culture,"[22] and that America has done so with "enough virtue and honesty to disprove the Marxist indictment that government is merely the instrument of privileged classes."[23]

They at the same time believed, however, that "we failed catastrophically only in one point—in our relationship to the Negro race."[24]

On the international scene there is similar agreement as well. Niebuhr argued that there are "two ways of denying our responsibility to our fellow man. The one is the way of imperialism, expressed in seeking to dominate them by our power. The other is the way of isolationism, expressed in seeking to withdraw from our responsibilities to them."[25] On the issue of imperialism, Humphrey could have been speaking for both when he asserted that "we have responded maturely to the role thrust upon us after World War II." "Maturity" meant, "that a nation has used its energies and resources outwardly, for the sharing of freedom and the good life, and not wholly inwardly for self-protection and self-satisfaction."[26] America has thus

> taken seriously those great words of . . . the Bible: feed ye the hungry, heal ye the sick. We have taken those words to heart as a matter of national policy, and I can think of no program ever launched by any country that has done more good for more people who were in desperate need of help than the overseas food program of the American government and of the American nation—our Food for Peace program. It's been religion at work.[27]

But this is all in the context of having taken the initiative to stop fascism by the greatest outpouring of force that the world has ever seen.

Niebuhr similarly spoke of how "no powerful nation in history has ever been more reluctant to acknowledge the position it has achieved in the world than we,"[28] and of how "our lack of the lust for power makes the fulminations of our foes against us singularly inept," although he was at the same time careful to point out that, "relative innocency or inexperience in wielding power is not a guarantee of virtue. It is on the contrary a hazard to the attainment of virtue."[29] He believed firmly that "we must find a way of placing the power of America behind the task of world order," that "we must overcome the impulse toward domination toward which we are tempted by our power and the impulse toward irresponsibility to which we are tempted by our youth and comparative security."[30] In Niebuhr's view, then, "the world problem cannot be solved if America does not accept its full share of responsibility in solving it,"[31]—a view shared by Humphrey, who similarly "repudiated the false doctrine of isolationism in international politics."[32]

While Niebuhr fully believed that virtue could only be attained by assuming the responsibilities that come with the position of being a first-rate power, at the same time he recognized that "it is known that they cannot be fulfilled without some egoistic corruption."[33] Still, such corruption should be risked, given the major problem facing the free world following World War II—the widespread existence of totalitarianism. If America was to "repudiate the false doctrine of isolationism," and to indeed "accept its full share of responsibility," it must, both Niebuhr and Humphrey believed, deal with Communism directly.

Thus, for Humphrey, "most American liberals stand in the ranks of those who believe that the forces of totalitarianism must be met with the forces of free men."[34] "In a world of imperfect men and imperfect nations," he continued, "individuals and nations must be prepared to defend themselves."[35] This is so because "force is present in the world." Therefore, "the only tenable position of a liberal is that despite reluctance to use it unless all other sources are exhausted, one must still be prepared and willing to use force."[36]

This is in accord with Niebuhr's own view that "we must exercise our power," and do so "in global terms."[37] Such an exercise, furthermore, would, for both, be fully appropriate in *liberal* terms. In Niebuhr's lexionary, this is to say that the children of light "must be armed with the wisdom of the children of darkness."[38] Humphrey expresses his recognition of this same reality in different but nevertheless compatible terms: "There is nothing contradictory about striving for peace and at the same time being determined to defend our nation and our national interests." "Indeed," as he continues, "while some liberals are pacifists, liberalism is not pacifism." "Liberalism," he argues, "recognizes the fundamental object of government to [be to] maintain order and to provide for the common defense."[39] In fact, "liberal groups in America for the past twenty-five years [written in 1964] have conspicuously and consistently supported the building up, the maintenance, and the use, when necessary, of enormous military forces in the face of threats from fascism and Communism."[40]

In this, Niebuhr similarly applauded liberalism's achievements insofar as "whatever the weakness of American liberalism in the understanding of foreign policy, it has nevertheless produced a Wilson and a Roosevelt—the two great architects of responsible foreign policy, and has guided our nation in assuming responsibilities proportional to its power in the world community."[41]

Joe Rauh has no doubt that for Niebuhr part of that responsibility was to challenge communism, and that this was a challenge that Humphrey accepted, perhaps from Niebuhr directly. Rauh tells of how he [Rauh] "heard Niebuhr give his anti-Communist speech, oh, I bet ten times. He would say it a little bit differently each time, and it was fascinating each time because he would talk about Communism being more dangerous than fascism . . . and it *is* because it has that idealistic lure."[42] Rauh was sure

> that Hubert had heard it because it was impossible to be at ADA meetings [and not hear the speech since] we always had Niebuhr giving it. . . . There were certain circles of liberalism . . . that didn't agree that you exclude Communists from your operations, but Niebuhr, with his brilliant speeches—I always worried a little: "Is there an anti-civil liberties aspect from excluding Communists?" So I'd get worried about that and then I'd listen to Niebuhr and I'd get reinforced again—that it was OK.[43]

And so, in terms of both domestic and foreign policy, Humphrey and Niebuhr were quite compatible on many issues. In fact, judging by the evidence offered, the remark could be ventured that Humphrey was a veritable political "incarnation" of Niebuhr's "word." Such a remark must be ventured against, if nothing else, the fact that Niebuhr did come to be a critic of the war in Vietnam by the late 1960s, and that it was a criticism that he made clear to Humphrey. Yet that this represented a complete break, whether personal or philosophical, must be weighed against the fact that Humphrey was still nevertheless invited to be the main speaker at the *Christianity & Crisis* anniversary dinner.

No matter what the resolution of this issue, Humphrey and Niebuhr both did distinguish American liberalism from its conservative counterpart on the issue of the use of military force. They did this on the basis of the latter's "tendency to measure our power too purely in terms of military strength."[44] While the children of light "must be armed with the wisdom of the children of darkness," they must also "remain free from the [Children of Darkness's] malice." They must, in other words, "know the power of self-interest," yet must do so "without giving it moral justification."[45]

For Humphrey, this meant that while American liberals *have* stood "in the ranks of those who believe that the forces of totalitarianism must be met with the forces of free men," they have "also stressed that the nations' security does not depend solely upon the size of the armed services, the number of thermonuclear delivery systems, or the dollar amount of the Department of Defense budget."[46] "We must not," Humphrey argued, "let our fixation on security through more and bigger armaments lead to a stage where arms alone would control our policy, for this would invite our ultimate destruction,"[47] and furthermore, "we do no honor to our own character or image by aping the Kremlin."[48] Free men, in other words, have the forces of right at their disposal beyond those of might alone, and they ought to use them.

Thus, for Niebuhr, "in order to prevail against our Communist foes we must continue to engage in vast collective ventures, subject ourselves to far-reaching national and international disciplines and we must moderate the extravagance of our theory by the soberness of our practice."[49] For this reason he argued *against* "the hysteria of American conservatism," which "is making it almost impossible to analyze the attractive power of Communism, not only in Asia but in such nations as France and Italy, and equally difficult to state the political and economic programs which will eliminate the social conditions and resentments that are exploited by Communism."[50] He asserted that "we must exercise our leadership of the free world in the light of tremendous complications in our contest with Communism because the Asian and African continents are in ferment."[51] Yet what was crucial to doing so was not to rely simply on military potential alone, but rather to "develop a realism without cynicism which knows how to come to terms with the Communist menace on every level where it is a danger to the world." This is so because "Communism faces us as a military power and as a political force which uses every form of resentment and discontent as grist for its revolutionary mills. A realistic defense against Communism must not be indifferent to the military threat, but must also avoid a too-great emphasis on military power alone."[52] Such a defense is crucial, for only in adopting it will we be able to perceive "the illusions [that] enable Communists to pose as the liberators of every class or nation which they intend to enslave; and to exploit every moral and political weakness of the civilized world as if they had the conscience of civilization in their keeping."[53] For Niebuhr, the key to such a defense was provided by the French experience in Vietnam: "military power . . . [was] ineffective in Vietnam . . . [because] it [Vietnam] lacked the cohesion and morale to avail itself of the proferred aid"—lacked the wisdom, that is, to see that "military power is, in short, ineffective when it lacks a moral and political base."[54]

These last assertions are very near representations of Humphrey's own anti-communist strategy, particularly as he sought to have it applied in Vietnam. As already indicated, Humphrey believed that we have taken a simplistic approach to facing our Communist adversaries. By attempting to match them weapon for weapon—by "aping" them, in other words—we have, to a serious degree, unwittingly played into their hands, at least insofar as our policy has represented a matter of playing according to their game plan and not ours. In order to regain the offensive we "must demonstrate that Americans genuinely and unselfishly are interested in helping to alleviate deprivation and suffering of hundreds of millions in the underdeveloped nations of the world"[55]—to offer, in other words, a genuine and worthwhile alternative to the communist option. Because this is so we should therefore make our final goal to search "within our own experience to learn how we can maintain the military strength necessary in an uncertain world, and at the same time strengthen the democratic institutions that the mobilization is designed to protect and defend."[56] "Beyond that," Humphrey concluded, "I believe that any policy, foreign or domestic, based solely on anti-Communism is an edifice built on sand"[57]—the view, that is, of Major General Edward Geary Lansdale.

For both Humphrey and Niebuhr, such a view was not only politically expedient, it was what religion commanded as well. For Niebuhr, "the Christian ethic demands that we turn and face the world."[58] He did not believe "that the Incarnation is 'redemption' from history as conflict,"[59] but rather, asserted that it is "the business of a Christian to preserve some relative decency and justice in society against the tyranny and injustice into which society may fall."[60] In this he is quite compatible with the Hubert Humphrey who believed that "religion was more than a Sunday experience," and that, even after Vietnam, "the lesson which our religious communities must never let us forget—is that we cannot, in the face of all these complex challenges and seeming frustrations, retreat from our global responsibilities."[61] They both believed, in other words, in a Christianity that was fully active in *this* world.

The correspondence between Humphrey and Niebuhr went beyond such practical applications, to a more theoretical level as well. In addition to all the above, they also shared views in terms of the value of democracy itself. For Niebuhr, the challenge for society "was establishing harmony without destroying the richness and variety of life."[62] This was a serious challenge, insofar as man's essence, for Niebuhr, was his potential for free self-determination, and thus required freedom in order to be fulfilled. Man's government, then, must be compatible with such freedom, yet at the same time must see to it that basic standards for *community* are also met. Humphrey similarly talked about how "freedom is essential for the full realization of the individual personality,"[63] and how government in a democracy aids "in satisfying and harmonizing the aspirations and needs of the different and overlapping groups within . . . society."[64] Yet man could and often enough did abuse his freedom. Thus a system for checking his freedom was also necessary. Democracy best serves man because it balances the demands of his freedom with the need for such a system of "just confinement." Democracy, in other words, best provides for the distinctive kind of freedom that mankind experiences, as suggested by Niebuhr's assertion that, "Man is most free in the discovery that he is not free." Democracy allows him freedom, yet restrains that freedom at the same time. By so doing it allows for the irony that such a "restrained freedom" is, in fact, the freest state that man can achieve. This kind of freedom is the kind denoted by the Pauline concept of freedom consisting of bondage to Christ. As such it represents the greatest possible liberation, in political terms, from the condition of "The sin that I would not do, I do; yet the good that I would do, I do not."

Thus religion, when properly applied, fosters a genuine virtue, and therefore the greatest of political strengths. It teaches us what the good is, but also that the greatest threat to our achievement of it is our own undue confidence in our ability to attain it. "If we should perish," wrote Niebuhr,

> the ruthlessness of the foe would be only the secondary cause of the disaster. The primary cause would be that the strength of a giant nation was directed by eyes too blind to see all the hazards of the struggle; and the blindness would be induced not by some accident of nature or history but by hatred and vainglory.[65]

which is to say, of self-righteousness. It was religion's role, then, quite literally to keep our eyes open. That entailed keeping a healthy, that is, balanced perspective on ourselves.

A contribution of religious themes in this way to both Niebuhr's and Humphrey's political outlook is not incidental. They were both explicit in their reliance on religious justification for their political points of view. To say *that*, however, is not to say that therefore their justifications were identical.

Niebuhr himself defined Christian Realism as a school based on the conviction "that a realist conception of human nature should be made the servant of an ethic of progressive justice."[66] The question can be fairly raised: is there anyone who, in a political career, stood *more* for making "a realist conception of human nature" the "servant of an ethic of progressive justice" than Hubert Humphrey? It was precisely by making realism the servant of his progressive outlook that Humphrey became one of the Senate's greatest powers—powerful enough to overcome the prejudice *and* power of his more "realist" and therefore ostensibly more formidable opponents. The parallels, then, between Niebuhr's definition of Christian Realism and Humphrey's own career are clear.

While those parallels *are* clear, however, there is at least one crucial difference. As noted, for Niebuhr, the Christian contribution to a social ethic was to be in "strengthening both the inclination to seek the neighbor's good and the contrite awareness that we are not inclined to do this."[67] It was, in other words, to be that of providing both a positive *and* a negative critique of our culture. As such it was to be a balancing mechanism for society at large. Whether or to what degree Hubert Humphrey shared this same concept is open to serious question.

Though it is unlikely that Humphrey ever would have paused long enough to consider it, the truth is that Humphrey's view of the theological justification for democracy was always a positive one. "Real [moral] leadership," he wrote, "means that you point the way; you harness the resources; you help direct the energy; you inspire, you arouse, you get people to do what they ought to do anyway."[68] For Humphrey,

> the churches ought to speak up on such subjects as integration, immigration, civil rights, slum clearance and better housing, and the conservation of both human and national resources—the churches ought to lead in the struggle for education and health and for wholesome recreation and cultural activities for the young in particular and indeed the churches ought to speak up for the needy, those who through no fault of their own are the victims of personal disaster or unfortunate circumstances.[69]

While this was compatible with Niebuhr's view that "the very heart of the problem of Christian politics" was "the readiness to use power and interest in the service of an end dictated by love," it was hardly in keeping with Niebuhr's view that it was equally and concurrently the refusal to condone "an absence of complacency about the evil inherent in them."[70]

For Humphrey, religion's counsel was rarely so sober a one. Religion's contribution, for Humphrey, was more a matter of providing the impetus to act for the good *despite* "the fact of the persistence of self-love." An example of this is provided by the fact that Humphrey's scriptural choices for support for his programs focus nearly exclusively on man having been created in God's image, rather than, for instance, on Niebuhr's use of Paul when the latter insisted that "all have sinned and fall short of the glory of God."[71] In John Stewart's words, "Sin was not anything that Humphrey spent a lot of time thinking about. In fact, if Humphrey were around he would say [that] original sin was kind of unchristian."[72] Humphrey's religious-political theory, in other words, was hardly redemptionist or "negative" in the sense that Niebuhr's Reformed tradition implied. His was, to the contrary, more a "creationist" or "positive" outlook. For Humphrey we were all created in God's image, and created *equally* in that image. *Therefore* we were to work for equal opportunity in housing, in employment, in education, and so forth. Beyond faith, religion was, for Humphrey,

> also the courageous expression of human values. Religion is strength. Religion is boldness. Religion is using the talents you have to the fullest. Religion is the holding of deep convictions; it is commitment; it is confidence; it is individual achievement. It is cooperation, it is trust. All these, to me, are the good in man.[73]

Religion's role, in other words, was to identify this good and to foster our regard for it. Its contribution was not so much to elicit "the contrite awareness that we are not inclined" to seek our neighbor's good, but rather, simply to urge that we feed the hungry and heal the sick, basing such an appeal on our sense that that was their due, given that we were all the children of God. It was to work for the good out of the belief that goodness resides in all, and that all, therefore, were worthy of such an effort. In his article for the *International Journal of Religious Education*, Humphrey asked, "What is the main contribution of Christianity to the dilemmas of political life?" His response was, "In his recent book, *The Protestant and Politics*, William Lee Miller suggests an answer which appeals to me. He says that Christianity provides 'direction, understanding, commitment' rather than 'precise blueprints for dealing with day-to-day political problems.'"[74] He then again cited Niebuhr's famous dictum that "man's capacity for justice makes democracy possible; but man's inclination to injustice makes democracy necessary." Yet his interpretation of the meaning of that dictum was that

> I believe with Dr. Niebuhr that men and nations have the capacity to achieve greater democracy, peace and security that we now have, and I will continue to work for politics toward that end. I also believe with him that, in view of man's history of inhumanity to man, it is all the more imperative for morally concerned citizens to improve the instruments of democracy and international cooperation.[75]

This was not the realism that Niebuhr proposed. While Niebuhr may have agreed, at least in part, with Miller's sense of religious "direction," it is not at all clear that Niebuhr believed that "men and nations have the capacity to achieve greater democracy, peace and security than we now have." The truth was at *best*, for Niebuhr, that, at least for all modern liberal democratic states, nealy everything in the category of "greater democracy, peace and security" that could be achieved, had been. They had, in other words, "equilibrated power." It is not clear, then, that in stating that "man's inclination to injustice makes democracy necessary" Niebuhr intended to inspire "morally concerned citizens to improve the instruments of democracy and international cooperation." Rather, he was intending to point out the *limits* of such efforts, hoping that by so doing "American idealism [will come] to terms with the limits of all human striving, the fragmentariness of all human wisdom, the precariousness of all historic configurations of power, and the mixture of good and evil in all human nature."[76] It was true that Niebuhr did believe that part of the problem for a Christian social ethic was "to preserve a sense of responsibility for achieving the highest measure of order, freedom and justice despite the hazards of man's collective life."[77] At the same time, however, it was also to "derive from the Gospel a clear view of the realities with which we must deal in our common or social life."[78] For Niebuhr one of those realities, perhaps the most important of them, was that idealists were "too certain that there is a straight path toward the goal of human happiness."[79]

Humphrey was so certain. Indeed, how else is one to account for "the politics of joy"? Time and again he would refer to the "Traditional enemies of mankind—poverty, hunger, disease and ignorance"—as enemies that not only ought to be fought, but that *could be overcome*. We have the poor with us always only because we have not tried hard enough and creatively enough to eliminate the conditions that render them poor, hungry, diseased. In the midst of his first trip to Vietnam he stated that "two wars can be won—the war to defeat the aggressor and the war to defeat the ancient and persistent enemies, disease, poverty, ignorance and despair."[80] In the forward to *The Cause is Mankind* he similarly spoke of the struggle for "the triumph of the American spirit, humane and democratic, and the triumph of mankind over" these "traditional enemies," and finished by stating that "with an informed, common sense, and compassionate approach—the liberal approach, if you will—the American future will be wonderful to behold."[81] While this statement could be taken as all too typical of political rhetoric—*any* political rhetoric—the truth is that Humphrey really *did* believe this—that if we could *just* eliminate *those* problems, then "the future will be wonderful to behold" indeed. For Humphrey, such language was *not* just rhetoric. He was very much a latter day Carrie Nation, embodying the zeal that firmly believed, for instance, that passage of the "eighteenth amendment could reduce poverty, nearly wipe out prostitution and crime, improve labor organization, and increase national resources by freeing vast, suppressed human potential,"[82]—a zeal that believed, in other words, precisely in a "straight path toward the goal of human happiness." Humphrey believed with everything that was in him that America had the capacity and therefore the mission to follow that path. "That's why," for Bill Moyers,

> he was an essentially religious man. He was a man of faith—not faith as defined by the fundamentalists or evangelicals, but faith in the potential of human beings to make this [America] work—to recover Eden in a sense. I am being dramatic there, but there was . . . an almost utopian sense about Humphrey—that Humphrey had about the American possibility."[83]

While Niebuhr believed that there were indeed many wonderful things to behold within American democracy, he did not therefore predict that its future would necessarily follow along the lines that Humphrey envisioned. For Niebuhr there were as many causes for concern as there were for confidence.

In a 1950 article appearing in *Christianity and Society*, Niebuhr wrote,

> American Christianity tends to be irrelevant to the problems of justice because it persists in presenting the law of love as a simple solution for every communal problem. It is significant that the "social gospel" which sought to overcome the excessive individualism of the Christian faith in America, never escaped this sentimentality and irrelevance because it also preached the same ethic that it pretended to criticize. It insisted that Christians should practice the law of love not only in personal relations, but in the collective relations of mankind. In these relations love as an ecstatic impulse of self-giving is practically impossible.[84]

For Humphrey, on the contrary, not only were they possible, they were to be desired and worked for above all else. The thought of achieving them, in fact, was precisely the kind of thing that brought happiness to "The Happy Warrior." When Ahlstrom characterized neo-orthodoxy (a twentieth-century intellectual movement with which Niebuhr has been historically associated) by the "special vehemence" with which it attacked [American religious] liberalisms' optimistic doctrine of man, and with it, "its doctrine of historical progress."[85] Humphrey looms as an all-too-obvious target.

Humphrey did believe that America was in a position "to spearhead an international drive to feed the hungry, clothe the naked, heal the sick and teach the illiterate," and that we were religiously called to do so. For Humphrey, the challenge of our religious institutions in this was ever "to call our people to a renewed dedication to the many unfinished tasks which are before us—to demand that we press on toward the goal of assuring 'liberty and justice for all' precisely because we are 'one nation, under God'"[86]—to provide, in other words, Miller's "direction, understanding [and] commitment."[87] As indicated, his religion was that we were all created in the image of God and *therefore* we should act on that basis. That "therefore" is the keystone for Hubert Humphrey's entire social ethic.

The problem is, at least from the Niebuhrian viewpoint, that while all of this may be *heartfelt*, there still is no serious doctrine of the Fall incorporated into this view. Humphrey talked about "Christian Realism" as "led by my good friend and teacher of us all, Reinhold Niebuhr." Yet when Niebuhr "saw that we were not facing up to hard realities," for Humphrey this meant that we were not facing up to such things as that there is a "growing and dangerous gap between enormous wealth and pervasive poverty in this country and throughout the world."[88] It did *not* mean that "the excessively optimistic estimates of human nature and of human history with which the democratic credo has been historically associated" have become "a source of peril to democratic society."[89] *This* was the reason that Niebuhr had argued for Christian Realism—for "a more realistic philosophical and religious basis" for our liberal-democratic culture. Humphrey's realism, however, was more simply that of recognizing that problems do exist in our world that idealists need to overcome. Religious realism, in this view, did *not* have to do with the need for the idealists *themselves* to assess their idealism for its failure to account for its own limitations—for, acknowledging, as Niebuhr said, that "the 'dignity' of man must be accompanied in Christian thought by a recognition that this precious individual is also a sinner; that his lusts and ambitions are a danger to the community; and that his rational processes are tainted by the taint of his own interests."[90]

While Humphrey certainly did not believe that America was

without faults, neither did he believe that being realistic about facing them was a matter of criticizing America's mission. Rather, it came simply by enthusiastically affirming it. The Happy Warrior's apologia for, and religious justification of his country's outlook and activity remained a forever positive one. He was very much a product of the kind of religious liberalism that, as Ahlstrom described, was "fervently optimistic about the destiny of the human race," because of its "revised estimate of man's nature" and because of its "tendency to interpret the entire evolutionary process ultimately for mankind's benefit."[91] Humphrey could refer to the fact that "we are all sinners," that, "we all make mistakes," and even that, "we make a lot of them." But for "Hubert the Exuberant," such a sobering evaluation of American life and culture as Niebuhr proposed was never substantially incorporated into his religious-political theory. His view remained forever optimistic as he himself remained optimistic until the day he died. His religious story, to use another religious and specifically Christian analogy, was Christmas, not Good Friday.

One of the ironies of this interpretation of Humphrey is that there were two major experiences which had, in fact, an extremely sobering effect on him, an effect which never left him. The first was his struggle with the Communist Party for control of the DFL in postwar Minnesota. The second was his misinformed and misexecuted attack on Harry Byrd on the Senate floor in 1949. Both taught him critically important lessons for directing national policy. As a result he was quite realistic in perceiving what was at stake in facing the opposition both from within and from abroad along these lines. In *this* regard he *did* qualify as a Christian Realist.

His military aide, for instance, Herbert Beckington, once described him as "a tough guy." When asked to explain, General Beckington's response was

> I think [that there are] probably a lot of people who think of the vice president as being someone who did not believe in a strong American defense establishment. In fact I think he did. He was very strong . . . for our alliance with NATO. He was not someone who was at all comfortable with the idea of the U.S. being pushed around the world. He was a very strong anti-Communist. He had a healthy respect for the Soviet Union and at the same time I think he thought that they could not be trusted. It was up to us to be alert to the fact and to sort of keep our powder dry if you will.[92]

When pressed as to the Right's charge of Humphrey being a dove, General Beckington answered,

> You see, from my observation of him I would say the Right is very wrong. He was not a dove. He was a great believer in peace. He was a great yearner for peace. He was always . . . trying to construct something . . . put something together that would advance the prospect of peace, that would give a stronger base for reaching for peace, and so on. But he was the absolute antithesis, in my experience with him, of the popular picture of a dove, and I guess that is where I get my continuing impression that the guy had a backbone of steel.[93]

Humphrey knew the perils that our enemies posed to us, and had the resolve to face them. As Barry Goldwater said, "Hubert would never have sold us down the river to anybody."[94] Humphrey understood *that* part, at least, of the gravity of the situation in which we had found ourselves.

The question, however, is whether he was sufficiently realistic in terms of assessing America's potential for overcoming all the sources of such gravity. General Beckington also said that "he [Humphrey] was really a great believer in this country . . . proud of this country . . . proud of everything that we had done, of everything we had become . . . of the potential that he obviously thought we had."[95] Niebuhr would have taken no issue with Humphrey on any of those points except perhaps the last one. Niebuhr was also proud of the potential that America had for acting for the good, yet he matched his pride with concern about our naiveté regarding the hazards that imperil any such action, *particularly* the hazard of excessive optimism—the kind of optimism exemplified in one of the greatest of heroes in the Humphrey pantheon—William Jennings Bryan. Bryan once stated that "[the] Christian civilization is the greatest that the world has ever known because it rests on a conception of life that makes life one unending progress toward higher things."[96] From the Niebuhrian standpoint, this is precisely the kind of optimism that is at best childishly naive, and at worst, dangerously delusive—both for the nation that indulges in such a view, and for the world community of which such a nation is part. According to the Niebuhrian critique, however, Humphrey was all too prone to precisely this kind of optimism. This was made no more clear than when it came to the question of international cooperation—the U.N., for example. Where Niebuhr was wary at best about what could be achieved in and by the U.N., Humphrey was characteristically exuberant. Humphrey enthusiastically supported treaties of all kinds, whereas Niebuhr remained considerably more pessimistic about what could be expected from such "moral" agreements between "immoral" societies.

Humphrey may have applauded "our friend Dr. Niebuhr" for his having "helped many of us understand our obligation to work for social justice without falling into soft utopian nonsense." Yet in his heart, the real help that religion was to provide—for both Hubert Humphrey personally, and for America at large—was the kind reflected in Humphrey's simple assertion-posed-as-question: "God so loved the world—can we do anything less?"[97]

While Niebuhr certainly believed that, because of the effect of sin, we could indeed do something "less," that is not to say, on the other hand, that religion's contribution is only a matter of providing such sobering counsel. Despite the distinction between Humphrey and Niebuhr just delineated, the latter would write, for instance, that

> it was a dictum of George Washington that a nation was not to be trusted beyond its own interests; and on the whole this realistic advice has been the guide of all political science. But a mere consideration of the power of concern for the national interest easily obscures another side of the equation, namely, that self-concern can be as self-defeating in collective as in individual behavior. Nations as well as individuals stand under the law: "Whosoever seeketh to gain his life will lose it."[98]

Because "we are bound up in a web of mutual interests with other nations," just as we are each individually bound up in a similar web of relations with others, we must show regard for others, for "the national interest when conceived only from the standpoint of the self-interest of the nation is bound to be defined too narrowly and therefore to be self-defeating."[99] For Niebuhr, therefore, "we must draw on the profounder sources in our religious tradition and of our secular disciplines to solve this problem."[100] Such a tradition, coupled with such disciplines, ought to lead us "beyond prudence," for "the sense of justice must prevent prudence from becoming too prudential in defining interest." It ought to urge that "the citizens of a nation must have loyalties and responsibilities to a wider system of values than that of the national interest—to a civilization, for instance, to a system of justice, and to a community of free nations."[101] For Niebuhr, in addition, "such a combination of 'idealism' and 'realism' is given in the great historic faiths."[102]

Such a combination was suggested in Humphrey's faith. Humphrey was not simply a naive Social Gospeler. No matter how optimistic his view of America, and of religion's proper role in it, he believed at the same time in the place of prudence as well. He did so, however, in a distinctive way: being prudent, in the *long run*, dictated that we be charitable. Yes, we must stop the communists, but how? By providing the kind of assistance that will foster a sense of dignity within the people whom we seek to help. Only then will they find the kind of strength they will need in order to stop the communists. We must, in other words, act out of regard for who the recipients of our aid are in themselves. For Humphrey, what went wrong with our involvement in Vietnam was that "we were a world power with a half-world knowledge . . . we couldn't even spell their names or pronounce their names. Knowledge is power, as we used to say, but we didn't believe that. We began to believe that power was knowledge. We got it, you know, upside down."[103]

Such a view is not foreign or contrary to Niebuhr's. In Niebuhr's view, "ideally the presuppositions of biblical faith insist on both the moral imperative of the love commandment and the fact of the persistence of self-love in actual history. There is in these faiths therefore a safeguard against both sentimentality and moral cynicism."[104] Biblical faith, in other words, implies a balance between the two extremes of sentimentality and moral cynicism. Humphrey's "Judeo-Christian" faith has been cited as an actual political example of defending against the latter, whereas Niebuhr's faith tends to be cited as a defense against the former. George Will, for instance, talks about "realism" which is "sometimes called conservatism"—a view that purportedly exists in those politicians who have the strength of character to admit "seeing social imperfections that are as immune to governmental remedy as they are undeserved. These politicians preach governmental Niebuhrism—

acceptance of human finitude, the tragic sense of life, the politics of contracting expectations."[105] While the above are representative of *part* of "governmental Niebuhrism" the point is that they are not representative of *all* of it. While Niebuhr *would* argue for the above, he would also argue that we must "live by a religious faith which affirms that 'a man's life consisteth not in the abundance of the things which he possesseth.'"[106] Niebuhr was not just concerned about our naiveté, contrary to what many neoconservative figures have pictured. He was also concerned, for instance, that we have "lost that essential religious reservation about the *goals* of life which prevent[s] a too great preoccupation with the *goods* of life."[107] Though he did not expect a reversal in our materialist tendency, he did express hope that "the wealth so acquired will be dedicated to the task of giving strength to the free community of nations."[108] While we should be wary of excessive optimism in regards to what success is possible vis-à-vis our foreign aid programs, that is *not* to say that we should therefore do away with them—either for our own sake or for those who we seek to help.

Such was the kind of outlook that inspired such legislative efforts as the Food For Peace program and the Peace Corps—an outlook based on the belief that

> you will find that when people show a spirit of generosity, of openness, of kindliness, for some peculiar reason the country itself is in a better economic, political, and social state of health. This is why I feel the way I do about politics, and that is why I feel the way I do about these great programs.[109]

Humphrey recognized the importance of Niebuhr's remonstrance to "draw upon every resource in our several faiths, in our tradition, and in our immediate vitalities so that we shall not meanly lose but nobly save the last best hope on earth."[110] In his own way, Humphrey sought to make his life a matter of so doing. To this extent, at any rate, Niebuhr and Humphrey were agreed on the proper function of idealism in the formation of public policy.

It can be said, then, that for both Niebuhr and Humphrey, "the art of statecraft is to find the point of concurrence between the parochial and the general interest, between the national and the international common good."[111] Each agreed, in other words, that there was to be a balance between the dictates of prudence, strictly defined, and the aspirations of charity.

Thus, while certainly not impervious to the Niebuhrian critique of the Social Gospel, Humphrey at the same time is not wholly devastated by it either. While clearly a child of the Social Gospel, he nonetheless eventually matured beyond some of its "parental" influence. If Niebuhr's position does indeed represent a balance between the "dictates of prudence, strictly defined, and the aspirations of charity," then so, in its own way, does Humphrey's. While Humphrey did remain, in a substantial way, a naive child of light throughout his life—as represented in his nearly unqualified optimism regarding America—that is not to say that he did not, through the course of that same life, gain an appreciable amount of the wisdom that Niebuhr argued only the children of darkness tended to have, and yet which the children of light needed badly—as is represented by his consistent and lifelong anti-communism. Though Humphrey did gain an appreciable amount of this wisdom, it nevertheless remained less than the Niebuhrian critique stipulates. Such a difference is summarized in and by their separate view of the proper role of religion vis-à-vis society at large. For Humphrey, that role was simply to inspire idealism, whereas for Niebuhr it was that, but not that simply: its was at the same time to warn us of the perils of such idealism, which is to say of the power of self-interestedness in *all* of us—something that Humphrey acknowledged, but never took as seriously as his academic counterpart.

If the politics of joy were not simply, then, a product of the Social Gospel, yet at the same time did not quite qualify as "Christian Realist," the question remains of, How exactly are they to be distinguished and what answers does the study of them provide the student of religion and politics? Addressing those questions provides the content for the following and concluding chapter.

Notes

1. As quoted from Warren Weaver, "Humphrey Joins Presidency Race; Calls for Unity," *The New York Times* (8 April 1968): 66.
2. Dr. Kirkpatrick said that Humphrey had also taken courses from him on ancient and medieval political theory, and thus had had exposure to the ancients, as well as to Augustine and Aquinas.

3. Hubert Humphrey, "A Tribute to Reinhold Niebuhr," *Christianity & Crisis* (30 May 1966): 120–22.
4. Ibid., 121.
5. Ibid.
6. Max Kampelman tells about the one exception to this: "I remember [when] he voted against a merchant marine appropriation . . . bothered the hell out of him for days. He did it for political reasons. You know everybody called him a spendthrift and it bothered him. He worried about it . . . and so he was sick and tired of it . . . so he voted against the increase and later felt guilty about it because it had merit in it and he shouldn't have voted against it." From the Kampelman interview.
7. Reinhold Niebuhr, *The Children of Light and the Children of Darkness* (New York: Charles Scribner's Sons, 1946), 148–49.
8. Ibid.
9. Humphrey *New Deal*, 9.
10. Ibid., 11.
11. Ibid., 12.
12. Niebuhr, "The Christian Faith and the Economic Life of Liberal Society," *Faith and Politics*, ed. Ronald H. Stone (New York: George Braziller, 1968), 143.
13. Niebuhr, "Theology and Political Thought," ibid., 57.
14. Humphrey, *Cause*, 12.
15. Niebuhr, "Theology and Political Thought," 57.
16. Humphrey, *New Deal*, 77.
17. Niebuhr, *The Irony of American History* (New York: Charles Scribner's Sons, 1954), 31.
18. Ibid., 105.
19. Ibid., 97.
20. Humphrey, "Baptist," 7865.
21. Niebuhr, *Irony*, 97.
22. Ibid., 89.
23. Ibid., 100.
24. Niebuhr, "Liberty and Equality," *Faith and Politics*, 197.
25. Niebuhr, *Irony*, 37.
26. Humphrey, *Cause*, 107.
27. Hubert Humphrey, speech to Annual Convention of Mid-Continent Farmers Association, 8 August 1966, Humphrey Collection.
28. Niebuhr, *Irony*, 27.
29. Niebuhr, *Children*, 186.
30. Niebuhr, "American Power and World Responsibility," *Love and Justice*, ed. D. B. Robertson (Gloucester, Massachusetts: Peter Smith, 1976), 205–6.
31. Niebuhr, "The Possibility of a Durable Peace," ibid., 200.
32. Humphrey, "I Am an American Day," literature from the mayor's office, 15 May 1946, Humphrey Collection, from the mayoralty years.
33. Niebuhr, *Children*, 186.
34. Humphrey, *Cause*, 142.
35. Ibid., 140.
36. Humphrey, "I Am An American Day."
37. Niebuhr, *Irony*, 5.
38. Niebuhr, *Children*, 41.

39. Humphrey, *Cause*, 142.
40. Ibid., 143.
41. Niebuhr, "American Conservatism and the World Crisis: A Study in Vacillation," *Yale Review* (March 1951): 387.
42. Niebuhr confirms this himself: "The important point is that the ruthless power [of communism] operates behind a screen of pretended ideal ends, a situation which is both more dangerous and more evil than pure cynical defiance of moral ends [as with fascism].
43. Rauh interview.
44. Niebuhr, "American Conservatism," 389.
45. Niebuhr, *Children*, 41.
46. Humphrey, *Cause*, 142–43.
47. Humphrey, *Congressional Record*, 85th Cong., 2nd sess., 1958. Vol. 104, 1610.
48. Ibid., 1620.
49. Niebuhr, *Irony*, 10.
50. Niebuhr, "American Conservatism," 388.
51. Niebuhr, "America's Moral and Spiritual Resources," *The World Crisis and American Responsibility*, ed. Ernest W. LeFever (New York: Association Press, 1958), 29.
52. Niebuhr, "Why Is Communism So Evil?" ibid., 33.
53. Niebuhr, "The American Nationalism," ibid., 54.
54. Niebuhr, "The Limits of Military Power," ibid., 116.
55. Ibid., 16199.
56. Humphrey, *Cause*, 159.
57. Ibid., 141.
58. Niebuhr, "Repeal the Neutrality Act," *Love and Justice*, 179.
59. Niebuhr, ibid., 268.
60. Ibid., 270.
61. Humphrey, "Baptist," 7865.
62. Niebuhr, *Children*, 124.
63. Humphrey, *Cause*, 7.
64. Humphrey, "The Relation of Morals to Law," *Journal of Public Law* 1, 2 (Fall 1952): 307.
65. Niebuhr, *Irony*, 174.
66. Niebuhr, Introduction to *Love and Justice*, 9.
67. Niebuhr, "The Christian Faith and the Economic Life of Liberal Society," 147.
68. Humphrey, speech to the International Newspaper Advertising Executives.
69. Ibid.
70. Niebuhr, "Christian Faith and Social Action," *Faith and Politics*, 136.
71. *Romans* 3:23.
72. Stewart interview.
73. Hubert Humphrey, press release on Apollo 8, Humphrey Collection.
74. Humphrey, *International Journal*.
75. Ibid.
76. Niebuhr, *Irony*, 133.
77. Niebuhr, "Christian Faith and Social Action," 131.
78. Ibid.

79. Niebuhr, *Irony*, 133.
80. Humphrey, as quoted in Eisele, *Almost*, 242.
81. Humphrey, *Cause*, ix.
82. Carrie Nation, as quoted in Robert T. Handy, *A Christian America*, 2nd Edition (New York: Oxford University Press, 1984), 130.
83. Moyers interview.
84. Niebuhr, "The Spirit of Justice," *Love and Justice*, 25.
85. Ahlstrom, *History*, 944.
86. Humphrey, "Baptist," 7864.
87. Even though the specific "direction, understanding and commitment" that Humphrey had in mind may well have differed from Miller's.
88. Ibid., 7865.
89. Niebuhr, *Children*, x.
90. Niebuhr, "Theology and Political Thought," 61.
91. Ahlstrom, *History*, 780.
92. Lt. Gen. Herbert L. Beckington, USMC(Ret.), interview with author, 11 September 1984.
93. Ibid.
94. Goldwater letter.
95. Beckington interview.
96. William Jennings Bryan, as quoted in Handy, *America*, 114.
97. Humphrey, "Baptist," 7866.
98. Niebuhr, "America's Moral and Spiritual Resources," 38.
99. Ibid., 40.
100. Ibid., 40–41.
101. Ibid., 42.
102. Ibid., 42–43.
103. From a transcript of *Bill Moyers' Journal*, "Hubert Horatio Humphrey: A Conversation," 11 April 1976, author's collection.
104. Niebuhr, "America's Moral and Spiritual Resources," 43.
105. George Will, "Cool Hand Jerry Brown," *The Pursuit of Happiness and Other Sobering Thoughts* (New York: Harper and Row Publishers, 1978), 7.
106. Niebuhr, "America's Moral and Spiritual Resources," 46.
107. Ibid.
108. Ibid.
109. Humphrey, *Congressional Record*, 85th Cong., 1st sess., 1957. Vol. 103, 14642.
110. Niebuhr, "America's Moral and Spiritual Resources," 47.
111. Ibid., 41.

10

The Politics of Joy

In beginning to summarize the religious-political significance of an entire life, perhaps the best place to start is with the observation with which this work began, namely, as is often and ironically the case, the source of our strength is also the source of our weakness. As this work has attempted to point out the considerable place irony can have in a political life, it might thus be appropriate to begin its conclusion with this same observation.

Humphrey was often derided for his folksiness. The "homey" appeal that life in Doland had given him also provided him with great pain in the form of votes lost, certainly in the sixties, and especially when up against the more glamorous likes of a Jack Kennedy. When criticized for not having sufficient mystique for a presidential candidate, however, Humphrey's response was, "Harry Truman was a great President, but I never noticed his mystique. I did observe he had a lot of character. What is important are your convictions, character and commitments."[1] Humphrey similarly noted that Lincoln had been the homeliest of our presidents, while Harding had been our handsomest. Glamour was not everything in politics, yet, as the record has so often shown, it nevertheless counts for a great deal—especially in the race that really matters, namely, for the presidency of the United States. Then again, however, as Lincoln and as Truman demonstrated, glamour is not all that counts once one has actually attained that office.

Like Lincoln, Humphrey was in many ways homely. In his fond reminiscence of Humphrey, Edgar Berman talked of how, "when the double knits and zippered boots came out, he was among the first to sport them,"[2] and mentioned Humphrey's "adolescent habit of flooding his food with ketchup."[3] Berman also would tell of how Humphrey "craved the worst of tv. He was an avid fan of Kojak, the Fonz, and the Gong Show."[4] His "By Golly's" and "Gee Whiz's" remained standard fare for his ever prolix speeches. These characteristics, all of them part of his past, are hardly the characteristics commonly associated with the urbane.

In addition, Humphrey, like everyone, had his "warts." His probably most obvious such "blemish" had to do with his speaking style. Humphrey was a great speaker. There are certainly those who considered him to be the greatest orator of his generation, perhaps of the twentieth century.* Nevertheless, when the name "Hubert Humphrey" is mentioned, loquaciousness is the image that first comes to most people's minds. There are many accounts of how, after spellbinding his audience in the first thirty or forty minutes of a speech, he would then disillusion them in turn by going on for yet another thirty or forty minutes, largely repeating what he had already said, and thus lose that fineness with which he had first thrilled his listeners.

Hubert's rhetorical excess was the cause for many jokes both inside and outside the Humphrey household. Muriel's famous quip was that "a speech to be immortal, dear, need not be eternal." Henry Kissinger used to tell the story of how when Humphrey began speaking at the dedication of a wood named in his honor in Israel the trees were only knee-high. By the time he finished, however, he was speaking in the shade. The problem was that after initially appearing as someone who could not only persuasively *articulate* the great issues of the day, but offer a vision by which to *lead* people through them, he would end by appearing finally as a goofy sort who simply could not be taken seriously. Defenders of his tendency toward oratorical overkill would cite how he came out of a great midwestern political tradition that not only looked for

*See, for instance, Mel Elfin's, "That Was Hubert," *Newsweek* (23 January 1978): 24.

long speeches embellished with rhetorical flourish, but *insisted* on them. That may well be, yet an obvious response to that is that Lincoln represented another great midwestern political tradition, yet hardly one known for its loquaciousness, and which has had the greater impact on American history?

While a political liability, this was hardly a moral shortcoming. A more serious fault, and one on which his friends were nearly universal in their agreement, was his tendency to be undisciplined—undisciplined in direction, in properly apportioning his time, and in maintaining rigorousness in his thinking. Humphrey simply spread himself too thin over too many issues.

For Calvin Didier, for instance, "at times he stretched to be all things to all people. He tried to do politically too many things for too many people" and did so to the point that it "almost became a liability."[5]

Geri Joseph regarded this same tendency as reflecting "a certain lack of discipline" and believed it to be significant enough as to make "you often wonder what more would he have done had he focused better," since "there were a lot of people that took advantage of him as a result."[6]

Arthur Naftalin asserted that "his weakness was that he was just drawn to too much and to too many people and tried . . . to be too many things at the same time."[7]

For Bill Moyers, Humphrey's character included "a certain lack of self-discipline . . . he didn't know when to stop preaching, and in his heart never learned when to stop lobbying . . . he never got his calendar together . . . [never disciplined himself] to ration his time sufficiently, or [to] ever channel it."[8]

For John Stewart, "his greatest weakness was . . . his great difficulty that he had saying no to people . . . being tough-minded about that . . . he was too good a guy."[9]

Such images of Humphrey were reflected by a number of his biographers as well. Griffith, for instance, said, "In obeying his will to work he does not often allow himself enough time to take stock of himself and his efforts."[10] Eisele, in his biography, quotes Bradley Morrison of the *Minnesota Times* as saying, "Humphrey . . . scatters his energies over too wide an area."[11]

This tendency to overdo yet underreflect was indeed a political liability, but again, it was not a moral fault. Even so, Arthur Naftalin, after criticizing Humphrey for this same fault, felt compelled to say,

> even as I say it—you know very few people focused their energies as well as Hubert did. It is just that you always demanded more of him . . . he would make promises that were impossible for him to keep, [yet] he *would* [keep] most of them. I was always surprised—if I saw Hubert at a busy meeting, and he'd come out here [to Minnesota] . . . as vice president, and I mentioned something to him and he wouldn't remember—well gosh, the next morning, or two or three days [later]—my desk was covered with stuff that he remembered to send—even with fairly long memos on how good it was to see me and how he misses me and how he wishes I was in Washington with him—you know—buttering me up like that. And what's more, I would *believe* it! That was the wonder of it . . . it was just great—it was the old Hubert.[12]

Thus, even as a political liability, Humphrey had ways of making amends for his lack of intellectual rigor.[13]

There were, however, other faults for which he could not so easily make amends. One was that which Frances Howard pointed out: "That he had little time to spend with his family, and he felt guilty about this all the time—felt guilty about not spending more time with me—mostly guilty about not spending more time with his own children."[14] Humphrey had recognized this problem early on. In a 1946 letter to Franklin D. Roosevelt, Jr. he wrote, "I have found being in politics really consumes one's time and energy. I wish I were old enough to give somebody advice, and when that time comes, I am going to warn my younger friends that if they really want any family life, or enjoy just being a 'good fellow,' they better stay out of this game."[15] The tears he shed in June 1964 at hearing of his son's life-threatening cancer, all the while knowing full well that he would miss the imminent operation nonetheless were bitter tears indeed.

Another issue, equally bitter, was that of Humphrey's draft record. Humphrey never served in the armed forces. He claimed that he was consistently rejected for induction despite his many attempts to enlist during World War II. His WPA work and his courses at Macalester for the Air Force College Training Detachment program had provided him with deferments for different periods throughout the early part of the war. Then, in July of

1943, he was classified 1A-limited. He was not drafted, however, because the Army decided "it was too expensive to draft and support men with dependents."[16] In the midst of the Battle of the Bulge in December of 1944, when draft calls went up again, he tried to enlist once more but was again rejected for physical reasons.

Griffith offers the following account of the complete record:

> In 1940 he had first been classified 3-A and exempted from the draft because of his status as a father. Later, while teaching Air Force officers at Macalester College, he was classified 2-A and rated as an "essential civilian." In the spring of 1944 he requested and was granted a release from that classification, and applied for a Navy commission. The Navy disqualified him for a commission on physical grounds. He tried for a regular enlistment with the Navy, which would have made him an apprentice seaman, but the Navy was not then accepting volunteers. Growing more frustrated as he watched his friends and young political associates march off to war, he battled with the draft board. On September 6, 1944, he was finally classified 1-A. In midwinter he got as far as the Army induction center at Fort Snelling. With several news photographers present—he was then a political celebrity in Minneapolis—he was issued an uniform. Then, in February 1945 he was told that he had failed to satisfy the Army's physical standards: Army induction center physicians found that he had a double hernia, lung calcification (probably from his childhood case of pneumonia) and color blindness.[17]

Ryskind, however, challenges that record. To begin with he argued that "Barry Goldwater, suffering from an astigmatism and badly battered knees, was older than Humphrey and had three small children under six years of age when the war broke out. But by 1942 Goldwater was flying P-47 single engine fighter planes across the North Atlantic—a hazardous journey even under peaceful conditions . . . [and] Paul Douglas, father of two children, was fifty when the war broke out . . . [yet he] promptly joined the Marines."[18] Of Humphrey's 2-A deferment he quotes Theodore Mitau, a professor at Macalester during the war, as saying that only one course taught by Humphrey, his "Survey of Social Sciences," fell within "the framework of the Air Force College Training Detachment Program."[19] Ryskind also questions why Humphrey waited to have the hernia repaired until after the war was over.

These are all serious questions, despite the insistence of the

Navy's recruiter in Minneapolis that Humphrey "made every reasonable effort to join the Navy that he could," and the claim of Clinton Norton, the Hennepin County Draft Board's clerk, that "at no time did Humphrey fail to comply with the requests of the board. It is unfair to imply that he tried to dodge the draft."[20] Questions, on the other hand, about Ryskind's own fairness can themselves be raised. His book is a transparent campaign piece (published in 1968) designed clearly to discredit Humphrey in a year in which the latter was running against Richard Nixon—a man later to resign the presidency as a result of his campaign of dirty tricks. The validity of Ryskind's assertions can thus be brought into question themselves, though they nevertheless remain troubling.

Suffice it to say, the issue of Humphrey's draft record remains something of a question mark. It was questionable enough to be used against him during the 1960 presidential primaries. In the midst of the West Virginia campaign, Bobby Kennedy prompted FDR, Jr., Humphrey's longtime ADA friend and political associate, to charge Humphrey with having been a draft dodger. Afterward FDR, Jr. denied the truth of the allegation, offered his apologies, and admitted that Kennedy had put him up to it, but the damage had been done. Whether or not there was truth to the charge, it remained a political albatross, given the obvious moral opprobrium attached to it (though it is also questionable how serious an issue it actually remained after 1960).

Another such albatross was the one George McGovern's story as cited by Solberg referred to, namely, Humphrey's sponsorship of the ill-fated Communist Control Act of 1954.

1954 was the last year of influence for Senator Joseph McCarthy of Wisconsin. It was the year that saw Robert Oppenheimer nationally disgraced after being denied a security clearance, and witnessed Wyoming's Senator Lester Hunt commit suicide as a result of McCarthy's innuendoes. It was also the year in which the still-young Hubert Humphrey would have to make his first reelection bid for the Senate.

Humphrey's anti-communist record, begun in his early days in Minnesota, had continued on into the Senate. In 1952, for instance, Humphrey had chaired the Labor-Management Relations subcommittee – a subcommittee responsible for investigating communist infiltration of the labor movement. In the summer of 1954 Senator John Butler of Maryland introduced a bill that called for empowerment of the attorney general to call any organization deemed "communist-infiltrated" before the Subversive Activities Control Board. That board would have the right to deny that organization any right to collective bargaining. The bill frightened labor and its supporters, and greatly angered Humphrey. Ever since the ascent of McCarthy, the Democrats had been steadily charged with being "pro-Red" or "soft on communism." Humphrey considered himself as much an anti-communist as he was a Democrat and was determined to prove it. He was also concerned about securing his reelection in a time of consistently successful use of Red Scare tactics. As a result, on August 12 he rose on the Senate floor to shout, "I am tired of having people play the Communist issue. I want to come to grips with the Communist issue. I want senators to stand up and to answer whether they are for the Communist Party or against it."[21] He then proposed a substitution amendment that was designed to take the wind out of the Republican sails. It would do so by calling for an outright ban on the Communist Party itself.

Humphrey's behaving this way could be called a case of what he had himself once described: "We who become disturbed and shout and holler, we do not show our greatness, we show our emotion."[22] Nevertheless, Democrats opted for showing just that by jumping on the bandwagon, glad to parade their anti-communist glee. Wayne Morse, for instance, one of two people out of the entire Congress to later vote *against* the Gulf of Tonkin resolution, agreed to cosponsor the bill. The Republicans could not oppose such a measure without appearing hypocritical, let alone upstaged, so they leaped onto the wagon as well. As a result, it, and the bill to which it was attached, passed 85–0. When the Eisenhower administration heard of it the next day, however, it was shocked by the extremity of the measure and registered its concern with Congress. As a result it was considerably softened in both tone and substance. In that modified form it became the Communist Control Act of 1954.

Humphrey defended his involvement in the measure by insisting that it helped the Democratic Party bolster its image in that very conservative period (the Democratic Party would, in fact, go on to gain enough seats in the 1954 elections to recapture control of both the House and the Senate), and stung the Republican Party by dealing it some of its own medicine. He also argued that constitutionally speaking, "the Communist Party isn't really a political party, it's an international conspiracy." The additional argument is also made that what eventually passed as Humphrey's amendment bore little resemblance to the kind of legislation that Humphrey had originally conceived.

Despite such arguments, however, he nevertheless admitted later that "it's not one of the things I'm proudest of."[23] Its dubious constitutionality and slipshod wording was recognized most poignantly in the fact that it was never enforced.

What he should have been even less proud of is that despite his liberal record, he did little, in the years in which it was called for, to oppose the tactics of Joseph McCarthy. Of this he similarly said later, "I think I could have been a little braver during that time."[24] Once again, bravery was an issue.

Though never seriously tainted with scandal himself, over the years a number of Humphrey's staff and closest associates were themselves caught up in political imbroglios. In 1967 Herbert Waters, Humphrey's administrative aide and campaign manager, had to resign his position as assistant administrator for AID. The charges had been that he had accepted gratuities, including sexual favors, for a European firm that held an AID contract. In 1967 Max Kampelman was forced to withdraw from the race for chairman of the District of Columbia city council after involving himself in a dubious foreign aid transaction. Jack Chestnut, Humphrey's campaign manager in 1972, was convicted in 1974 and sentenced to four months imprisonment for his role in obtaining illegal corporate contributions to Humphrey's 1972 campaign. Norman Sherman was fined $500 for his involvement in the same incident. Evidence was even uncovered that Humphrey's niece had had some sort of connection with Tongsun Park—Park had sent $10,000 to Humphrey's 1972 campaign in order to fly her out to the West Coast in the midst of the California primary.

While these are all, comparatively speaking, minor political scandals, and they did not involve Humphrey himself, he was nevertheless accused to the end of his days of being remiss in carefully monitoring his friends and staff.

There were other accusations as well. In letters printed on stationery stolen from the Muskie campaign headquarters during the 1972 primary, Humphrey was accused of having been stopped for drunk driving in Washington while seated in a big convertible, call girl at his side. The truth of such charges was revealed in the following letter:

October 11, 1973

Dear Sen. Humphrey,

I wish to personally apologize to you, your family, and your staff for my activities during the 1972 presidential campaign.

You are a man of stature and integrity, and I deeply regret any harm that may have come to you. In part, I regret my involvement in a letter on Sen. Muskie's campaign letterhead alleging you were involved in certain indiscretions. Such allegations were false. I hope my public statements and guilty plea have made that point clearly evident to the public.

I trust others will not get involved in such activities in the future. They have no place in the American political system.

Sincerely,

Donald H. Segretti[25]

Another kind of charge that people in political life must reckon with constantly, yet which is rarely considered by that public, is revealed in the following letter:

May 29, 1974

I know that you and Mao Mondale are doing all in your power to help the Jews in their plight and for that reason I refer to both of you as shabbez-goi merchants. You know what happens to shabbez-goi when the chips are down? They can take a shower bath with the Jews until the gas ends their efforts.

. . . for my white race and my nation[26]

In addition to this kind of threat, of which Humphrey received thousands, the Secret Service reported that Humphrey had received three times more death threats in the four years that he was vice president than Eisenhower had received in his eight years as president. That, too, must be figured into the bravery equation.

Perhaps the most obvious charge hurled against Humphrey was

that he lusted after the presidency. In the 1956 convention he was badly embarrassed when Adlai Stevenson threw the nomination for vice president to the floor after Humphrey had proclaimed that Stevenson had promised it to him. In 1960 he was beaten decisively in Wisconsin by Jack Kennedy, yet went on, against much good advice, to West Virginia, where he was then soundly trounced. As vice president there was much talk of how he truckled up to big business for their support. The record in 1968 is clear enough. In 1972 he was stymied in his quest for the Democratic nomination after allegedly employing dubious tactics in his efforts to obtain it. He had come very close to running again in 1976, deciding against doing so only at the last minute. With such a record one could be viewed as dominated by ambition.

There are, however, a number of stories that can be used to refute such an ascription. Joe Rauh tells one such story having to do with the 1964 campaign. It involved LBJ who, for Rauh,

> makes Machiavelli look like Santa Claus. Here's what he did: He found out I . . . was lawyer for the Mississippi Freedom Democratic Party. He [LBJ] wanted to get me by the balls, so he used Hubert, who was my political love, [and] Walter Reuther, who was my employer—I was general counsel for the . . . UAW at the time—and . . . at the [1964 Democratic National] Convention Johnson had [Jim] Rowe and [Max] Kampelman all tell me that I was costing Hubert the vice presidency, and if I didn't stop Hubert wouldn't be vice president. Every night . . . before I'd go to bed I'd go and see Hubert—it would be sometime between 3:00 and 5:00 . . . and I would talk to him alone. Never once did Hubert say, "Won't you take this last compromise so I can be vice president?" Never once. Now all those shits were saying to me around him [to give into Humphrey]—but I don't believe he was putting them up to it. I mean, it would have been so normal for a politician to say: "Just take this last [compromise]. I know it's not perfect, but it's alright—and I can be the vice president—I may even be president, Joe" . . . I'll help *you* sometime . . . —never was there a trace of that in that whole thing. And that's why I made that statement [that Humphrey represented the highest ethical standards that Rauh had witnessed in his life], and that's why I believe it today.[27]

Any number of times during the 1968 campaign Humphrey similarly refused to compromise himself for the sake of electoral gain. In a meeting with oil millionaires in Waverly, Humphrey denied himself desperately needed funds, in this case millions, by refusing to back off from his oil depletion allowance stand. As a result, as

Humphrey said, "I kept my honor. They kept their money."[28] In a similar vein, Humphrey denied himself other potential millions by refusing to embrace Gene McCarthy's view on Vietnam when liberal monied interests made that the price for their support.

On a small scale, yet still indicative, there is the story of Humphrey's refusal to take advantage of the phone system made available to him by the Secret Service when it was so badly needed amidst the chaos of the Chicago convention where all (Humphrey and Gene McCarthy were both staying in the same hotel) had to go through the beleaguered Hilton Hotel switchboard. (In fairness, though, it ought to be said that this may have been done out of sensitivity to similar charges that had been raised against him when he had been mayor of Minneapolis.)

Finally, on a much larger scale there is the story of Humphrey's refusal to take advantage of the Anna Chennault incident.

Lyndon Johnson claimed that he had declined to run for a second term as president purely in the interest of peace. From the date of his April announcement not to run up until the end of his administration he did indeed seek peace. These efforts came to a head in October of the campaign. In the middle of October the North Vietnamese had agreed to a date—November 6—as the day to begin peace talks in Paris. In return the U.S. had agreed to halt its bombing of North Vietnam. This was the break that Johnson had been looking for. Clearly it was the kind of break that Hubert Humphrey was looking for as well. If the announcement of peace talks could be disclosed before the election, the issue that had dogged Humphrey throughout that campaign—his identification with an administration of war—might finally be sloughed aside. The Johnson administration would become instead the administration of peace, which is precisely what the American public wanted—and which Hubert Humphrey obviously wanted along with them. It would mean that Hubert Humphrey—already closing in fast on Nixon in the "Miracle of October"—may very likely become the next president of the United States.

It was not to be. After various suspicious messages had been intercepted between Anna Chennault and the South Vietnamese embassy, LBJ ordered an FBI wiretap of that embassy, as well as surveillance of Anna Chennault. Through those means Johnson learned of her efforts to have the South Vietnamese government intentionally delay its entrance into the talks as a means of assisting her "good friend," Richard Nixon, in his election bid.

This was the tactic that the China Lobby had attempted once before—in the 1948 election—when they felt that the Republicans would offer them greater support than the Democrats in the struggle then raging in China. Now they were trying the same tactics again. They were evidently successful: on the day after Johnson announced his October 31 bombing halt, the South Vietnamese proclaimed that they would not enter the talks. Through Jim Rowe, Johnson informed the Humphrey campaign why this was so.

There were those who demanded, even pleaded that Humphrey make the news public. He refused to do so. He claimed that he did not have first-hand evidence that Nixon in fact knew of the details of the affair. He argued that it could backfire—the American public may view it as a cheap ruse to win what was now a race too close to call. He simply would not do it. Of this, Theodore White wrote,

> What could have been made of an open charge that the Nixon leaders were saboteurs of the peace one cannot guess; how quickly it might, if aired, have brought the last 48 hours of the American campaign to squalor is a matter of speculation. But the good instinct of that small-town boy Hubert Humphrey prevailed. Fully informed of the sabotage of the negotiations and the recalcitrance of the Saigon government, Humphrey might have won the Presidency of the United States by making it the prime story of the last four days of the campaign. He was urged by several members of his staff to do so. And I know of no more essentially decent story in American politics than Humphrey's refusal to do so; his instinct was that Richard Nixon, personally, had no knowledge of Mrs. Chennault's activities; had no hand in them; and would have forbidden them had he known. Humphrey would not air the story.[29]

Unlike his opponent in that campaign, Humphrey would not go to *any* length to win the prize that he desired more than anything else in the world.

One of the great ironies to come out of that fact is that Richard Nixon's first public act, following his disgrace for being so willing, was to come to Humphrey's funeral. He had asked Muriel about coming, to which she had responded, "Of course!" When he entered the Capital Rotunda where Humphrey's body lay in state, an audible gasp raced through the chamber.

Dismissed as a loser, derided for being "all heart and no balls," laughed off as a gabby politico who would say anything to anyone just for a vote, spat upon and denounced as a swine, Hubert Humphrey, in the end, prevailed. For someone who, after all, did *not* become president, the nation exhibited a remarkable outpouring of affection that seemed to well up from within itself at the time of his death. His courageous fight against cancer, witnessed by the nation over the year that ended in his death, provided a final consideration for the bravery issue.

There were many summations made and many fine tributes given. In the Senate nearly everyone rose to pay him homage (in some cases after rising to denounce him nearly thirty years earlier). Strom Thurmond stated how

> I cannot pretend that Hubert Humphrey and I did not disagree profoundly on many matters of public policy. Political disagreement, though, was no barrier to an appreciation of the virtues of this man. The philosopher, Bertrand Russell, once wrote about the philosopher, Socrates, whose philosophical views he, for the most part, rejected. "The ideas of Socrates," he maintained, "were noble but flawed." In order to be perfected, they would have to go to "a kind of logical purgatory." Socrates the man, however, he could only regard as one of "the company of saints." That is the way I feel about Hubert Humphrey.[30]

Bob Dole said, "His consuming passion has been to make America a little better, to make the world a little better, to make life itself a little better—and, reaching out for those goals, he overshot his nation's highest office and became instead one of the great world leaders—one of the major moral forces of our time or of any time."[31] Dole then introduced S. 2219 by which the south portal building of the Department of Health, Education and Welfare was named in Humphrey's honor—an honor rarely, if ever, bestowed on one who was still able to attend the ceremony. Barry Goldwater, with tears streaming down his cheeks, talked of how he had known

> Hubert for over twenty-five years. I served with him in the Senate, I ran against him in campaigns, I debated with him, I argued with him. But I don't think I have ever enjoyed a friendship as much as the one that existed between the two of us. I know it may sound strange to people who see in Hubert a liberal and who see in me a conservative, that the two of us could ever get together; but I enjoyed more good laughs, more good advice, more sound

> counsel from him than I have from most anyone I have been associated with in this business of trying to be a senator.[32]

In the House, Jim Wright said, "When the annals of our time are written, I believe the name of Hubert Humphrey will stand for all that was best in American society. Throughout this remarkable American's career his clear calls to the national conscience have been a comfort to the afflicted and, occasionally, an affliction to the comfortable."[33] The House itself had honored him by having him become the first member from the opposite chamber to address them from their own well. President Jimmy Carter publicly apologized for his "harsh words" uttered in the 1976 primary. Walter Mondale delivered his moving eulogy in which he said, "He achieved something much more rare and valuable than the Nation's highest office. He became his country's conscience," and, "He taught us all how to hope and how to love, how to win and how to lose, he taught us how to live, and, finally, he taught us how to die."[34]

Perhaps the most moving of all of the tributes made was that of a young man who wrote Humphrey the following note during those last few months:

> You don't know me and I am certain you do not remember my rude and inconsiderate behavior during 1968 in the city of Boston. You came to speak and I, along with a large crowd of unfair individuals, would not allow you to voice your opinions. I certainly want to ask your forgiveness for my actions on that day. I know you are very ill now, but I also want you to know that the prayers of my family are with you on a daily basis.[35]

For a full week his death and funeral were the national news. Three presidents stood by his casket. Foreign dignitaries from around the globe attended the services. Front covers of magazines, including *Newsweek* and *The New Republic* carried the story. Hundreds of editorials and reminiscences were printed. State legislatures drafted resolutions in his honor. Television networks hosted interviews with people who had known Humphrey well and televised all of the week's proceedings. President Carter, in one of many solemn tributes, provided Air Force 1 as transport for Humphrey's casket when it was carried from Washington to Minnesota, going so far as to have seats torn out of the cabin so that Humphrey's remains would not be denigrated by otherwise having to be stowed in the baggage compartment.

Finally, and perhaps most significantly of all, there were the tens of thousands of mourners who braved Minnesota's January weather for hours, just to have their own final glimpse.

The question that arises amidst all of this is, Why? Was it, as Jeane Kirkpatrick asked, "simply gratitude and guilt that motivated the solemn tributes?" For her, "certainly there were ample grounds for both."[36]

Perhaps the answer lies in a second irony in the adulation that Humphrey received at the end of his life. After being viciously abused by Lyndon Johnson for not having the kind of manly force of will required to be president, Humphrey, after *not* becoming president, clearly received a kind and degree of heartfelt affection that Johnson had always craved yet had never received on his own, neither in life nor in death. The difference in the receptions to the news of their separate deaths is the most compelling evidence of this. Humphrey was remembered as much for the warmth of his humanity as he was for his ability to legislate. Johnson was remembered only for the latter. The irony of the distinctiveness between their separate legacies peaked in the fact that in the last week of his life Humphrey was voted the most effective senator of the last fifty years in a poll taken among congressional aides on the Hill. Lyndon Johnson was ranked second. The humanity responsible for this distinctiveness was revealed in Humphrey's response to hearing this news while on his deathbed: "I guess when I see Lyndon he'll give me holy hell about that, too."[37] There were other ways that this humanity had also been revealed.

Humphrey was noted in the political community for his *not* holding a grudge—something entirely out of character for that community. In 1960, after being threatened with political annihilation by the Kennedys for not supporting them at the Democratic convention, Humphrey forgave Jack and Bobby and went on to earn at least their respect, if not their friendship. By 1962, for example, Humphrey was being described as JFK's "most valuable ally on Capitol Hill,"[38] and Bobby himself later admitted, "Humphrey as majority whip was the most consistently substantive and provocative thinker at the leadership breakfasts and the one senator on whom JFK depended."[39] In 1966 he proved his forgiveness for FDR, Jr. for his behavior in the 1960 West Virginia primary (described by the *Washington Star* as a "new low in dirty politics") by saving his job in the Johnson administration when it was threatened. He forgave Gene McCarthy who, after being Humphrey's protégé, friend and colleague, had not only refused to support Humphrey when he desperately needed him (McCarthy did finally give Humphrey his endorsement, half-heartedly, on October 31 of a campaign that was to end on November 5), but who actually said that, "It's no use being bitter about Hubert. He's too dumb to understand bitterness."[40] Joe Rauh, who had supported McCarthy in the '68 campaign instead of Humphrey, was moved to say, "He [Humphrey] was very—when we talk about traits—he was a very forgiving man."[41] Humphrey forgave Jimmy Carter for calling him a "has-been" and for sneeringly taunting him to run in 1976 so that he [Carter] could beat him. In fact Humphrey's manner of forgiveness was the same for Jimmy Carter as it had been for Jack Kennedy sixteen years earlier—he went on to become his greatest senatorial asset (an asset which Carter eventually and at too late a date came to recognize that he needed badly). Finally, and most significantly, Humphrey forgave his "good friend Lyndon," or, as Norman Sherman said: "He [Humphrey] was burdened with an irascibly paranoid president who said awful things about Humphrey. He treated him badly. [Yet] I never once with one exception ever heard him say while he was vice president anything harsh about Lyndon Johnson, or to Lyndon Johnson. He suffered quietly and within him."[42]

Thus, as Harold Hughes said, "He [Humphrey] had the greatest capacity for forgiveness in the political wars that he fought of any man I've ever met. For this reason alone he commanded the admiration of many who were his colleagues and co-workers in the body of politics for many years."[43]

There were, however, those close to Humphrey who argued to the contrary that this tendency to forever forgive was a political liability. They argued with him that it made him appear weak and that it sent out a signal that he could be taken advantage of. Humphrey simply shrugged it off.

Geri Joseph provides a story depicting Humphrey's commitment of forgetting the past and moving on. It involves the incident with Bobby Kennedy at the 1960 Democratic convention:

> I was in the suite, and Bobby Kennedy was in there with him . . . and I guess Bobby berated him something fierce, telling him they'd take care of him because Humphrey had gone for Adlai instead of John Kennedy. And you know, afterward, Humphrey was very somber, and I asked him what was the matter, and he said, "Well, Geri, my career is all over with—you should have heard Bobby Kennedy . . . "
>
> He was really pretty hurt, and he was standing, looking out the window, and he stood there for a few minutes more, and all of a sudden he squared his shoulders and he said, "You know, it really doesn't matter—I'm going to go back to Washington and I'm going to support Jack Kennedy just as hard as I possibly can . . . " That was it! And he did! He was one of the very few people—never mind politicians—one of the very few people I've ever known, who genuinely never held a grudge.
>
> I asked him about that once, because it was so amazing to see . . . [since] most political people, and maybe most of the rest of us always keep book, and he said, "Geri, you know, if I spent my time and my energy seeking revenge, I wouldn't have time to do all those other things that I care about. So I just shrug my shoulders and get on with the next thing. . . . " And that is just exactly what he did . . .

to which she then added,

> Talking to you about him really . . . [makes me] think. All of us who worked closely with him miss him a great deal . . . not every minute, and not every day, but just, just *there*. He was really . . . unique, he was unique.[44]

Perhaps Daniel Patrick Moynihan summed it up best when, after voting against Humphrey for majority leader in return for a seat on the finance committee—and doing so after pledging "anything" to Humphrey—he said, "Hubert's superior fight was his forgiveness to those of us who had not understood. By that act we knew we were in the presence of grace."[45]

In talking with his closest friends there is almost unanimous consent as to what might be referred to as the greatest sign of this grace. For Max Kampelman it was

> human brotherhood and whatever was associated with it . . . first municipal FEPC in the history of the country—it wasn't even good politics. I am convinced that this was the dominant characteristic—wheat for India, foreign aid, Food for Peace program to take care of the hungry. . . . Everything he did was

> dominated by the concept, I think, of human brotherhood . . . and that's the way he [even] treated his enemies . . . with human dignity, with respect as human beings.[46]

For his old high school friends from Doland, Humphrey's greatest virtue was "looking out for the little guy" and not "bowing to the pressure of large interests."[47]

For Calvin Didier it was "loyalty to the truly human thing. That is, he really believed . . . that it came to the question of whatever was the most truly and deeply human thing. It was one human family and he was loyal, whatever the condition that applied."[48]

Geri Joseph said that "I don't know that I ever recall him saying something specifically in just those terms [of virtue] but I would say from the way he acted—a commitment to people really was the sort of undergirding of his whole life. What he did and the way he did it [reflected] a commitment and a concern, particularly for people who were—who had problems in life—the poor, the sick, the elderly."[49]

For David Gartner, "In terms of virtues he would be best described as decent—he really truly did want people to have the best that we had to offer and wanted to do what he could to insure that that was possible. I don't think that you can say that there is any one virtue unless it is just defined in that general observation."[50]

For William Connell,

> kindness as a person [was] . . . probably the most important characteristic. You have to, to a *degree* . . . separate the public man from the private man, but nevertheless, what you saw was what you got. What he was in public was the real Hubert Humphrey. It is not with other people. What you see is not what is there—what you see is a facade, it's an elaborately constructed image that people figure out how they want to be projected—they really do it very coldly and with the help of a lot of professionals. It is a little bit like the magician in the *Wizard of Oz*, you know—there is a little guy back there pulling the stuff.
>
> Well, that wasn't Hubert Humphrey, because what you saw was what you got. . . . He never tried to . . . establish these facades. He never tried to establish anything, never tried to erect any facade. He never changed in public from what he was in private or back and forth. There was a very basic integrity there, which was unusual in public life—not that it cannot be found on occasions—there are people like him—but it is unusual, very unusual for a major figure. . . . He just had a charitable outlook towards everyone. Chari-

table is a better word than kindness because . . . it tends to move you into a little more activist role."[51]

For Joe Rauh,

he certainly loved his fellow man. . . . He was very loyal to the people in our wing [namely the *left* wing] of the Humphrey camp. I remember once . . . at the Press Club [where he was] speaking, and he . . . [was asked a] question . . . from some right-wing son of a bitch: "Is your connection to the ADA and your friendship with Joe Rauh going to hurt you in the campaign?" Well, Hubert gave him two minutes of the goddamndest speech—I almost get teary-eyed thinking about [it].[52]

For Arthur Naftalin, Humphrey's greatest virtue was "that great capacity to relate one to one with whomever he was with."[53]

Ted Van Dyk talked of how "most people at high levels seeking high national office look at the people who worked with them and around them as manipulative objects on the way to fame and fortune and they use you up and discard you and couldn't care less—you are interchangeable parts. Humphrey, on the other hand, had a genuine concern with those around him . . . and cared about people as individuals rather than as objects."[54]

Frances Howard spoke of how he "identified, whether it was with his family . . . or whether it was a black family out in the inner city. He had this remarkable quality of really entering in empathetically, sympathetically."[55]

John Stewart described his greatest virtue to be "his caring about people and their problems, individually and collectively, without any artifice about that at all. . . . It was that concern for others that I think really motivated him in really everything he did—it was the thing that was evident all through his life."[56]

For Evron Kirkpatrick, finally, it was a "capacity for friendship and compassion, and an ability to put himself in others' shoes . . . his sense of empathy, concern, interest, *regard* for others."[57]

While these accounts vary somewhat, their overall thrust is unmistakably the same—it was as Evron Kirkpatrick said it was—Humphrey had genuine *regard* for others. He did not, as Van Dyk asserted, view people as means to his own ends. He could and did, as Arthur Naftalin stated, "relate one to one with whomever he was with," and that "whomever," as Joe Rauh indicated, covered the entire spectrum of foes and friends alike. It especially related, however, as Geri Joseph said, to those "who had problems in life." Each of these accounts, in other words, testifies to the same overall characteristic.

If, as the *Oxford English Dictionary* defines it, charity is "a disposition to judge leniently and hopefully of the character, aims, and destinies of others, to make allowance for their apparent faults and shortcomings; large-heartedness; fairness; equity; benevolence to one's neighbors, especially to the poor; the practical beneficences in which this manifests itself," then this is the proper definition of Hubert Humphrey's chief characteristic.

There remains, however, the question of, What "answers" does a life characterized this way finally provide for someone interested in applying religious principle to political practice? The one that this work attempts to make obvious is that the political life is such that an attempt at such application involves a great deal more irony, and indeed tragedy, then one might realize without actually "plunging" into the "pit" that political reality represents. A second that follows immediately is that that is *not*, therefore, reason to *not* make the attempt. The lesson is simply that, while noble, not to say necessary (necessary in the sense that if such an attempt is not made, what sort of political order will we be left with?), such an attempt will at the same time incur considerably more struggle, and in fact suffering, than would likely be anticipated. It can, though, also bring genuine and indeed profound satisfaction—satisfaction derived in no small part from bringing positive results to many. In all of the above, Hubert Humphrey's life was distinctive.

The true distinctiveness, however, of that life is embodied in the following question: while a number of people in politics might be characterized as "charitable," in the sense provided above, the question remains, how many have been able to combine *such* charitableness with *such* political effectiveness *at the same time*? The list of major legislative triumphs ascribed, whether wholly or in part to Humphrey's name is impressively long (see appendix H for an extended list). A much more abbreviated, but no less poignant portrayal of this is the fact that in a 1986 survey taken among

American historians as to who, in all of America's history, its greatest senator was, Clay was ranked first and Humphrey second, ahead of Webster.* It was that combination of "charity" or decency with political effectiveness, idealism with realism, optimism with pragmatism—of ability to *so* turn dream to fact that does distinguish Hubert Humphrey.

Alasdair MacIntyre has argued that, "there is no way to give us an understanding of any society . . . except through the stock of stories which constitute its initial dramatic resources."[58] The story herein given is that of a "simple kid from the prairie," quite literally brimming with small-town American ideals, journeying from the site of those ideals—Doland, South Dakota—to the very heights of power 1,342 miles away, in Washington, D.C. Such a journey, however, was hardly only geographic. Once establishing himself in the seat of political power, he saw his ideals nearly realized in 1964, only to have them founder in 1968, just as America's own ideals foundered at that same time and on the same hard rock called Vietnam. Such a story constitutes "dramatic resources" sufficient to provide America with considerable and indeed perhaps critical self-understanding. It is a story, then, that America might do well to consider.

Criticism of it from the left generally comes in the form of moral judgment based on the belief that compromise *is* a "dirty word"—which is to say that Humphrey compromised himself as far as his principles went, especially and most blatantly, of course, in his "selling out" on Vietnam. Put another way, it would be, for the left, to say that he leaned too far to the side of realism. From the right, the criticism is just the opposite—that he leaned too far to the side of idealism—that he was the quintessential "tax and spend Democrat"—not to mention that he would have "sold us out" to our foes, if he were to be given the chance. Juxtaposed, then, the two say that either his adherence to his principles was too weak, or that it was his principles themselves that lacked strength.

Clearly both sides cannot be right, or at least fully right. Is it possible, then, that this apparent contradiction illustrates quite

*Need the irony be here pointed out that none of America's three greatest senators was to become president, even though all three aspired to that position?

poignantly the ambiguity of making ethical judgments about political life, never mind the moral ambiguity of that life itself? More to the point, would, and indeed should Humphrey be vexed by such contradictory criticisms, given his lifelong commitment to the belief that at *best*, the results that a political figure can achieve are "limited" and "partial," that politics is to a considerable degree a matter of simply dealing with one dilemma after another as best as one can? Such dilemmas clearly did abound in Humphrey's own life, as has been already illustrated: deciding to give the "Bright Sunshine" speech to the 1948 convention, even though it went against every prudential consideration, including that of the safety of his own political future; deciding between remaining loyal to LBJ, which the history of their relationship insisted, or making a break from that history, and thus give him a real chance to become president, and so on. In addition, not only do dilemmas "abound," but so do the ironies that are attached to one's attempts to solve them, as, for example, the irony of having the triumph of '48 lead to the misery of '49, not to mention of having the even greater victory of '64 lead to the even more difficult and dismal defeat of '68.

Whether the above would have vexed Humphrey is not nearly so much to the point as is the question of whether or not it should vex *us*, which is to say, should we, regarding politics, be satisfied with the "limited" and the "partial"—with compromise or not? Should we, in other words, be realists or idealists? If "realists," then Humphrey's life poses the question of whether there is anyone who was so willing to compromise, as realists insist we must, yet who nevertheless did so so consistently for the sake of *idealism* as HHH? If "idealists," he poses the opposite question: if Humphrey did *not* maintain idealism's purity, as idealists insist we should, how many nevertheless achieved more in the way of concrete results for its sake?

Another somewhat related question might also be the one already implied. There is profound reason, historical and otherwise, for arguing that Hubert Humphrey was overly optimistic about America, no doubt for some, ridiculously so. Yet, if one *is* to argue that way, then the question is posed of: Would he have achieved as much as he did for the sake of the good *without* such optimism?

Such a question might in turn prompt the following: for Thomas Aquinas, "in the order of perfection, charity precedes faith and hope, because both faith and hope are quickened by charity," and thus, "charity is the mother and the root of all the virtues."[59] In that he was loosely paraphrasing St. Paul's, "So faith, hope, love abide, these three; but the greatest of these is love."[60] The correspondence between Humphrey being remembered primarily for his characteristic of charity (or love), and Christianity's traditional regard for charity as being the chief virtue may not be a coincidence. Geri Joseph stated that

> he [Humphrey] was my ideal of a truly religious person. He really lived what he believed, and you just don't find that very often. He genuinely loved people. He really did. I was active in politics for something like sixteen years and I do not recall ever having encountered anybody at all in that time—and I knew a lot of political people—who cared as much about just, you know—everybody—as Humphrey did.[61]

Evidently, then, there are those who believe that Humphrey had been a man of his word when he said,

> My religion and the teachings of the churches I have attended have brought me into a rich political philosophy and one that I hold very dear and one that is not subject to change on the matter of basic principle. There is no expediency in that philosophy. It is a way of life for me.

While Humphrey may indeed have genuinely embodied charity as a *religious* virtue, and given the extremely impressive list of his *acting* on the basis of such a virtue, the question remains—and his memory poses the challenge of: can charity, perhaps the supreme *religious* virtue, be effectively embodied as a *political* virtue as well?

And so, it is by providing such "answers" that analysis of the politics of joy concludes. Ending such a work with what are in fact more questions than answers may seem quixotic, if not dubious. It is done, however, for the sake of a general principle as well as for a more specific reason that follows as a consequence. The principle is Socrates': the unexamined life is not worth living. The consequent reason is to force precisely such an examination. At this point, then, a pertinent question arises: what exactly is to be meant by or expected from the "study" of religion and politics? That is, is the "study" of religion and politics meant to be a study of a particular "answer" as to how religious principles are to be applied to particular political questions? Or is it instead better conceived as more the reflection on the fact that when it comes to politics, applying principle to practice, rarely if ever straightforward in life, is particularly problematic in politics, given the profound ambiguities and ironies that a life committed to both inevitably entails, and that it is only by studying political life that this will be fully appreciated?

This work has opted for the latter view. Such a choice is based on the argument that to be in politics *is* to be in "the pit of reality," and thus the application of religious-ethical principles to political practice can *only* be "limited" and "partial" at best *if* a genuine balance between the integrity of one's principles is to be maintained, on the one hand, and yet, on the other hand, if those principles are to genuinely have *effect*. Such a balance is to be regarded as the ideal if "integrity" is to be understood as having to do at least partially with successfully and consistently *integrating* the multifold aspects of existence into a complete human life—in this case ideal and real, dream and fact. In other words, Is not maintaining a consistent balance between the ideal and the real, dream and fact, over the course of an entire lifetime of being immersed in "the pit of reality," and yet nonetheless emerging with *both* "adequately clean hands," *and* as one of the most effective political figures in one's nation's history, perhaps the most and fullest "integrity" that can be fairly expected in reference to religion and politics? Furthermore, must not such an "integrated" view involve looking at an entire *life*, with all its complexities of history that come and should be brought to bear as part of responsible reflection on as sensitive a topic as religion and politics (and hence the reason for the old convention of *not* speaking about either in "polite" company)?

It is understood that such an "answer" as the above implies is not as striking, and perhaps not nearly as immediately satisfying as a clearer "do *this*" or "believe in *that*." The summary argument, however, that follows from such an observation is one that is also to be posed as a (in this case compounded) question: is that which is "immediately satisfying" the same as that which is satisfying in the longer run?, and, to which, the former or the latter, is it finally better for us to devote our greatest energy?

If those questions are worth posing as possible keys to achieving the best meaning of "study" with regard to religion and politics, then, given Hubert Humphrey's commitment to *both* principle *and* practice, and given the particularly challenging times in which he attempted to honor such a commitment, the politics of joy are indeed well worth such "study."

Notes

1. Hubert Humphrey, *Time* (1 April 1966): 25.
2. Berman, *Hubert*, 31.
3. Ibid., 33.
4. Ibid., 38.
5. Didier interview.
6. Joseph interview.
7. Naftalin interview.
8. Moyers interview.
9. Stewart interview.
10. Griffith, *Candid*, 87.
11. Bradley Morrison, as quoted in Eisele, *Almost*, 59.
12. Naftalin interview.
13. Perhaps he did not have a need for more focus. Frances Howard told a story of how, at the time that he took his final exam for his pharmaceutical degree, "he had a very peculiar thing happen to him and he told me, 'you know, never quote this in a speech or tell my political friends, but,' he said, 'I was so exhausted . . . going up to [take the] exam—I passed out on the steps and I just didn't think that I was going to be able to manage it, I was so fatigued . . . just, just gone.' And when he wakened there was like a strength—his mind was clear, he said he couldn't remember how long—was it a half an hour? forty minutes?—but it was like, it was almost like a miracle, and he said from that day on he had direction." From the Howard interview, no. 2.
14. Ibid.
15. Hubert Humphrey, letter to Franklin Delano Roosevelt, Jr., 13 May 1946, Humphrey Collection.
16. Humphrey, *Education*, 86.
17. Griffith, *Candid*, 112–13.
18. Ryskind, *Unauthorized*, 256.
19. Theodore Mitau, as quoted in ibid., 257.
20. Clinton Norton, as quoted in Eisele, *Almost*, 57.
21. Humphrey, *Congressional Record*, 83rd Cong., 2nd sess., 1954. Vol. 100, 14210.
22. Humphrey, Emmanuel Lutheran speech.
23. Humphrey, as quoted in Solberg, *Humphrey*, 159.

24. Humphrey, as quoted in Eisele, *Almost*, 100.
25. Donald Segretti, letter to Hubert Humphrey, 11 October 1973, Humphrey Collection.
26. Letter to Hubert Humphrey, 29 May 1974, Humphrey Collection.
27. Rauh interview.
28. Humphrey, *Education*, 400.
29. Theodore White, *The Making of the President, 1968* (New York: Atheneum Publishers, 1969), 444–45. Afterward, evidence was revealed showing that Agnew did know of her activities, and thus, by implication, it is likely that Nixon must have known as well. See Solberg, *Humphrey*, 390–402.
30. Strom Thurmond, as quoted in *Memorial*, 11.
31. Robert Dole, as quoted in Engelmayer, 9.
32. Barry Goldwater, as quoted in Cohen, *Undefeated*, 257.
33. Jim Wright, as quoted in ibid., 245–46.
34. Walter Mondale, as quoted in *Memorial*, 146.
35. Letter from a Connecticut man, October, 1977, as quoted in Cohen, *Undefeated*, 369.
36. Kirkpatrick article.
37. As related in Berman, *Hubert*, 23.
38. As stated in Cohen, *Undefeated*, 234.
39. Robert Kennedy, as quoted in Berman, *Hubert*, 63. Humphrey also spoke fondly of the Kennedys: "His [JFK's] greatness in the presidency was not so much what he did as how he did it—he just made you feel good." from *Sunshine*; and, "I read from time to time how the Kennedys and the Humphreys are at odds. I can only say to you once again what I said while visiting you in the back of the Senate a little over a year ago. My great respect and admiration for President Kennedy, Bobby, you, and indeed your entire family is sincere and abiding. I truly cherish your friendship and respect your great abilities. I have said to many, as I have said to you personally, that some day you will be president of these United States and I hope I am around to help make that possible. In the meantime, I want nothing to interfere with our mutual respect and friendship. Your achievements and successes bring joy to me and rich rewards to our country." From a letter from Hubert Humphrey to Edward Kennedy, 22 September 1965, Humphrey Collection.
40. Gene McCarthy, as quoted in Eisele, *Almost*, 358.
41. Rauh interview.
42. Sherman interview.
43. Harold Hughes, as quoted in Cohen, *Undefeated*, 237.
44. Joseph interview.
45. Daniel Patrick Moynihan, as quoted in Berman, *Hubert*, 266.
46. Kampelman interview.
47. Dinner with Mr. & Mrs. Earl Hansen, Mr. & Mrs. Deschler Welsh, Mr. & Mrs. William Jones, Mr. & Mrs. Gordon Twill, Mr. & Mrs. Homer Krentz, Mr. & Mrs. Alvin Hahn, and Mr. & Mrs. Leslie Coats (almost all of whom were classmates of HHH's in Doland High), Doland, South Dakota, 13 September 1983.
48. Didier interview.
49. Joseph interview.
50. Gartner interview.

51. Connell interview.
52. Rauh interview.
53. Naftalin interview.
54. Van Dyk interview.
55. Howard interview, no. 2.
56. Stewart interview.
57. Kirkpatrick interview.
58. Alasdair MacIntyre, *After Virtue* (Notre Dame, Indiana: University of Notre Dame Press, 1984), 216.
59. St. Thomas Aquinas, *Summa Theologica*, II-II, Q. 62, Art. 4, from *Introduction to St. Thomas Aquinas*, edited and with an introduction by Anton C. Pegis (New York: Modern Library, 1948), 596.
60. *I Corinthians* 13:13.
61. Joseph interview.

Appendices

Appendix A: The "Active" Humphrey

Humphrey's prodigiousness in work is testified to by all who knew him, certainly by an ever-weary staff who were constantly exhausted from just trying to keep up with him. For anyone who saw him there, Humphrey was always bounding up and down the halls of Congress.

He was constantly "bounding" on the floor of the Senate as well—in this case from one issue to another. 5 June 1957 represents a typical day. On that day Humphrey first had an article containing a resolution of the National Executive Committee of Jewish War Veterans placed in the *Congressional Record*. He then similarly had an article on a resolution of the Cloquet Central Labor Union of Cloquet, Minnesota, placed in the *Record* as well. Following that he introduced a bill to amend the Federal Property and Administration Services Act of 1949. He then offered a letter supporting that amendment. He offered an address entitled, "The Human Approach to Foreign Relations," that he had given to the American Pharmaceutical Advertising Club Luncheon. Along with Senator Kennedy of Massachusetts and Senator Cotton of New Hampshire he supported Lyndon Johnson on consideration of S.B. 434—a bill to improve the methods of stating budget estimates and estimates for deficiency and supplemental appropriations (on which he had worked as chairman of a subcommittee on reorganization, as part of the Committee on Government Operations). He argued for the indemnification of owners of brucellosis reactors in Minnesota. He submitted an editorial from *The New York Times* on Louis Rabinowitz and discussed, along with Jacob Javits, his life and career as a way of honoring him. He argued for a nuclear test-ban treaty and debated the merits of it with Senators Neuberger of Oregon, Cooper of Kentucky, and Monroney of Oklahoma. He called for consideration of a bill for the U.S. to quit its claim of interest in certain lands in Indiana for the benefit of Vincennes University. Finally, he gave notice of hearings for the Agricultural Trade Development Act, then before the Committee on Agriculture and Forestry, and debated its merits with Mike Mansfield.

Such was a typical day—a typical day on the floor, that is. *Fortune* provides an insight into what the rest of a "typical" Humphrey day (in this case, as vice president) tended to look like in its "A 75 Percent Day":

> The Vice President's job is not the second most important in Washington, and much of it is downright trivial, but it's hard work just the same. . .
>
> Humphrey awoke at seven-thirty, read the New York *Times* and Washington *Post*, had a big breakfast, and studied the overnight cables and late reports pertaining to national security. (These are delivered to his Chevy Chase home every morning around eight.) From 9:15 until 10:00 he was dictating in his office in the Executive Office Building. By 10:25 he was at the Sheraton Park Hotel, telling some 300 members of the Amalgamated Meat Cutters and Butcher Workmen of North America that he was for the voting-rights bill, repeal of Section 14B of the Taft-Hartley Act, the poverty program, U.S. foreign policy, and his new job. ("I like it. Why not? The working conditions are good. The pay is better . . . ") Faulty air conditioning in the meeting room failed to dampen the butchers' response or Humphrey's humor; however, it got the better of his shirt, which he changed during a fast unscheduled stop at his office. . . . Meanwhile an aide hastily summoned North American Aviation executive Ralph J. Watson from his office a few blocks away. Watson, who had been waiting a month for an appointment, hustled over and presented to Humphrey (who heads the National Aeronautics and Space Council) a book of lunar photographs.
>
> By 11:40, Humphrey had been chauffeured to his other office, in the Capitol, and was telling reporters about a recent gift: the baritone horn he had played in the Doland (South Dakota) High School band. Then he posed on the Capitol steps with the family of Robert Short, a Minneapolis businessman who heads the President's new Discover America Committee.

> At 1:35, after some time on the Senate floor and several brief conferences in his office, Humphrey spent thirty minutes with the winners of a Minnesota world-affairs contest. He told them a story—one of his favorites—about the chandelier. Its tinkling sound, he said, kept Teddy Roosevelt awake and resulted in its removal from the White House. Said T. R. (according to Humphrey): "Send it to the Vice President. He has nothing to do; maybe this will keep him awake."
>
> At 2:15, Humphrey dashed to the Senate dining room, gulped down a glass of milk and some coffee with the Shorts and Senator Eugene McCarthy, and managed also to work in some table-hopping. By 3:00 he was back in his office for a discussion of voting rights and immigration legislation with Emanuel Celler, chairman of the House Judiciary Committee. . . . Forty minutes later, he sandwiched in a half hour of dictation before holding a conference . . . with Attorney General Nicholas Katzenbach, former Governor David Lawrence, and others about discrimination in housing. The meeting lasted until 5:45, but was interrupted by a picture-taking session . . . in which Humphrey, Senators Everett Dirksen and Paul Douglas, and two D.C. commissioners plugged a baseball game benefiting Washington's Children's Hospital.
>
> At 6:15, the Vice President went off to socialize with some Democratic Congressmen at a reception in the office of Carl Albert, House majority leader. Later he made an unscheduled visit to a party honoring retiring Budget Director Kermit Gordon, held in the glittering eighth-floor reception room at the State Department. He made a lighthearted off-the-cuff speech, then circulated among the guests. At 9:00 he was on the telephone in his car discussing some late business with an assistant, while being driven to a dinner engagement at the Willard Hotel. Had it been a tough day? Humphrey rated it only "about 75 percent busy."[1]

Such was the regular regimen of Hubert Humphrey's life. As a result he would receive the following kind of letter:

> May 26, 1962
>
> Dear Hubert,
>
> Happy Birthday to my good friend HHH, Democrat-Farm-Laborite, Senior Senator from Minnesota, Bachelor of Arts, Doctor of Pharmacy, Doctor of Laws, Doctor of Humane Letters, Phi Beta Kappa, Master of Arts, Master Politician, Father of Four—How have you done all this in only 51 years?
>
> Appreciate your assurance that the first 45 years were the hardest.
>
> JFK[2]

As Calvin Didier said, "I think he was one of the few people I've ever seen in political life who didn't count the cost."[3]

Notes

1. William Bowen, " A 75 Percent Busy Day," included within Bowen's "What's New About the New Hubert Humphrey," *Fortune* (August 1965): 144.
2. John F. Kennedy, letter to Hubert Humphrey, 26 May 1962, Humphrey Collection.
3. Didier interview.

Appendix B: The Humane Humphrey

It appears that anyone who knew Hubert Humphrey has a story to tell regarding this "power." Ted Van Dyk tells a number of such stories:

> I remember back in '64 [when] we were trying to make him vice president. We had a quiet campaign to get endorsements from major politicians and so on. Johnson gave us clearance—he didn't really want Humphrey to have it . . . [unless] we could prove that he could do it and if he could fix this thing in Atlantic City (the Mississippi Freedom Democratic Party issue). Pat Brown at that time was governor of California and had been rumored also as a possible vice presidential nominee. A fellow named Gene Wyman was on the national committee from California and I had the assignment and I called Gene Wyman and I said, "We have got a hunting license from Johnson to collect endorsements from other national figures"—we had a bunch of them—and I said, "if Pat Brown really does want Hubert Humphrey to be vice president an endorsement would not be frowned on by the president. It would be an enormous help to us. In fact, California would really put it over. . . . " I remember—very important—it was on a Saturday night that I called Humphrey, and I got the number to call Pat Brown in Sacramento, and I called Humphrey up and I said, "Senator, Pat Brown will endorse you if you call him at this number and ask him, and that will really do it—you will have the nomination . . . " and he said, "OK, I'll call him right now and I'll call you back to let you know what happens."
>
> Didn't call, and didn't call . . . so finally I called him and I said, "What happened?" He said, "Well, let me tell you. I called Pat and he's a good guy. Pat said, 'Sure, I'll endorse you if you want me to.' He said, 'On the other hand, *Life* magazine is coming out next week and it has got my picture in it as

somebody that might be a potential nominee,' and he said, 'frankly, this would kind of take the edge off that story, and I like it.'" He [Humphrey] said, "Well, heck Pat, just let it go . . . it's alright." And I said, "What?" He said, "I told him it was alright – not to worry about it" and I said, "OK. . . . "

He had no sense of, you know, no sense of the jugular. He had a great sense of the capillaries, but he could never close.[1]

Another was

when I got into a terrible argument with him. We had a good relationship where we argued all the time . . . I had the privilege, I mean, he gave me that . . .

I can't remember what it was about but it seemed very important at the time . . . we had this fierce argument about something, whereupon I got mad and went back to my office down the hall and typed out my letter of resignation and put it in the IN box and went home, fully thinking I had quit. . . . This must have been '66 or something . . .

I left and got home and it must have been about midnight at least, maybe even later, and the phone rang – it was Herb Beckington who was his military aide who had also been there at the office, and I said, "What is it Herb?" And he said, "Did Humphrey ever get in touch with you?" I said, "What do you mean?" He said, "Well, he opened a note from you, and I was in his office with him, and he said – he called his driver and with the Secret Service tried to find out where you parked your car. We drove for about 30 minutes around the Mall trying to find your car, and trying to find you in the EOB or in the . . . " and he made me feel so ashamed – that the Vice President of the United States was forced to go out and drive around in an automobile looking for some aide who had . . . I never mentioned it. I went back to work the next morning as if nothing changed, and neither one of us ever said a word about it [again]."[2]

And,

I went to Columbia as vice president, after we lost the election [in 1968], and it was really tough because I left my family here [in Washington] and I only did it for a year – but I remember one night about ten o'clock at night – on a Saturday night – and I was at home, and this had been a year since I had worked for him – phone rang and it was him and he said, "I don't know what I am calling about . . . Muriel and I were just sitting here and wondered what on earth you were doing and thinking where you had been . . . " and we must have talked for an hour on the phone. Well I can tell you that's really the exception – for people to pay that personal attention to people that worked for them. Most of them – if they are no longer at work they are dismissed from memory . . . he was really a caring person and I don't know anybody that ever did work for him who actually disliked him.[3]

Bill Moyers tell of how

when I was nominated by Kennedy to be deputy director of the Peace Corps, Frank Rouch attacked me on the floor of the Senate—opposing my nomination [for being] too young and inexperienced. Humphrey was a sick man [but] he took himself out of his sickbed and onto the floor of the Senate to defend me, although I hardly knew him. It was 1963—January of that year and I had been in the Peace Corps [and had] worked on the campaign in '60 [and thus had] seen him, but I wasn't a protege of his—I didn't share an intimate relationship, and yet he rose out of his sickbed and went to the floor and defended a 26½ year old youngster. To me, that was the essence of his decency.[4]

and Norman Sherman recounts how

when I went to work for Humphrey. He was so cheap—he's thought of as a big spender but the fact is that Humphrey was cheaper than hell—including not only his own money, but federal money.

He refused to put in an intercom system in our office—we had buzzers [instead]. So he had a little tier of buttons on his desk and he would push it and it would buzz at the appropriate desk which meant that the senator wanted to see you.

I was always insecure about working for Humphrey—I didn't know if I could cut it though I was not a youngster and I had been around a long time. But the pressure was different from anything I had done before, and so, when the buzzer buzzed I always figured maybe he was going to fire me or something. One day my buzzer . . . buzzed and I ran to his office—came in virtually breathless, because you're dodging around other people and desks and everything—and he said, "Norman, here's a letter I got and I want you to take care of it. You knew everybody in Minnesota . . . "—I had come just recently from Minnesota the year before—and I said, "Yes sir," and I took this letter . . .

It was written on this Irish linen that you get in a drugstore with lines on it. And it was written in a not illiterate, but not very polished [hand]. . . . It was from a woman named Mrs. Al B____, and the letter read that when her husband Al had been convicted of a felony and was at Leavenworth prison she had written to Senator Humphrey—"written to you Senator . . . and you had gotten him transferred to Sandstone, Minnesota, so that he could be close to his family and so that we could visit. . . . " She then recounts when Al got out of Sandstone—a convicted felon—he couldn't get a job. So they had written to Humphrey again.

Humphrey had never met the person. You can't talk about it—it has no political gain because you don't talk about helping convicted felons—and the guy can't vote for you—probably his family isn't registered—they wrote and said Al needed a job.

> [Humphrey] had gotten Al a job at Howard Lake, Minnesota, in a slaughter house—a little tiny family slaughter house, and this had gone on for some years. Al had been in there clobbering cows and butchering them. This letter came because the slaughter house [closed], as many of those little slaughter houses at the time had done—and Al was unemployed. He was now a convicted felon that knew how to kill cattle and he needed work.
>
> And so Humphrey called me and he said, "Get this guy a job." Well, I put the letter on my desk after reading it, and about three days later—I hadn't done anything about it—my buzzer buzzed and I ran up and Humphrey said to me, "What have you done for Al B____?" And I said, "Who?" And he said, " . . . in that letter I gave you?" I said, "Oh yes." And I can remember . . . even now whining about how busy I was. . . Here's Hubert Humphrey who is busier than I am by far, worrying about what I've done in three days for this guy, and I am whining about how busy . . . I go back and I call the governor's office in Minnesota and say, "Humphrey wants this guy to have a job. Can you get him on the highway department?"—figuring, you know, what the hell does it take to drive a truck? Well, they put him on the highway department, and I report with great pride to Humphrey about this. Subsequently it turns out that he had to take a test of some sort—a most elementary test—and he *flunked* it! And I went back to Humphrey and said, "Listen, this guy flunked the test"—my reaction being that we have done our duty to him—we forget him. . . . Humphrey says, "Get him another test." I said, "What?"—"Get him another test. . . . " So we got him another test and got the guy the job. So he drove a plow during the winter and a truck during the summer, and *that's* the kind of decency that Humphrey was capable of.[5]

Humphrey showed that he was capable of this same kind of decency, but in a more personal way, in another and quite humorous story that Sherman also told:

> I was about to get married, and Humphrey said to me one day, "I understand you are going to get married—that's wonderful . . . better get your date . . . on my calendar. You know how busy it gets."
>
> I was about to marry a Republican whose mother said she would not come to the wedding ceremony if Hubert Humphrey came . . .
>
> Humphrey a week later said to me, "Hey Norman, you don't have your marriage date on my calendar." And I said, "Mr. Vice President, you are not invited," and he laughed, thinking that I was making a joke, as I often did . . . I went on thinking that I had come through unscathed . . .
>
> About a week later he stopped me again because his weekly calendar came and he said, "Your marriage date is not on my calendar." And I said, "Listen, you may think I am kidding—you are not invited." "Oh, my God!" he said. "*Really*? Oh, I'm sorry I embarrassed you!" I said, "You embarrass me? You didn't embarrass me—I just . . ."

Anyway, we went through this. Well, I [was to get] married on a Friday afternoon, and on Wednesday morning [before the wedding] my mother-in-law-to-be, having reconciled herself to the marriage, called her daughter and said it would be alright if Hubert Humphrey were to come . . .

He is then the sitting Vice President of the United States. He is a very busy man. On Thursday, as soon as I can get to him, I go in to see him, and I said, "Mr. Vice President, if you want to come, and it would mean a great deal to me, my mother-in-law-to-be has changed her mind." He said, "Cancel my activities for the afternoon. Tell Vi where you are going to be married" and he showed up. He not only showed up, but he had great peripheral vision—he spotted the mother-in-law-to-be and moved in on her. I tell people I could hear the elastic in her pants snap because Humphrey had a way of looking in your eyes and holding your hand and just pouring out this. . . . And he said, "Boy, your daughter is so wonderful!" and so on and on and on.

After that, when we got within 200 miles of Portsmouth, New Hampshire, where she lived, she'd show up and say, "I'm Norman Sherman's mother-in-law. . . . " But the fact is that that was important enough for him to change a whole afternoon schedule after being insulted. I mean, what a humiliating sort of thing to say—"I want to come to your wedding," and I say, "You're not invited. . . . " He was capable of that kind of act.[6]

Notes

1. Van Dyk interview.
2. Ibid.
3. Ibid.
4. Moyers interview.
5. Sherman interview.
6. Ibid.

Appendix C: Significant Sections of the Civil Rights Act of 1964

Some of the more significant distinctions between the House and Senate versions of the Civil Rights Act of 1964 include the following:

Title I—Voting Rights, Sect. 3

(House): In a voting rights suit, the Attorney General or any defendant in the proceeding is authorized to request that a three-judge district court be convened to hear the suit.

(Senate): In a voting rights suit, where the Attorney General requests a finding of a pattern or practice of discrimination, the Attorney General or any defendant in the proceeding is authorized to request that a three-judge district court be convened to hear the suit.

Title II—Public Accommodations, Sect. 5

(House): A Civil action to enjoin a violation of this title may be instituted by a party aggrieved or by the Attorney General.

(Senate): A civil action to enjoin a violation of this title may be instituted (1) by a party aggrieved or (2) by the Attorney General if he has reasonable cause to believe that any person or group of persons is engaged in a pattern or practice of resistance to any of the rights secured by this title, and that the pattern or practice is of such a nature and is intended to deny the full exercise of the rights secured by the title . . .

Title III – Desegregation of Public Facilities, Sect. 4

(House): No such provision.

(Senate): Nothing in this title shall empower any official or court of the United States to issue any order seeking to achieve a racial balance in any school by requiring the transportation of students from one school to another or from one school district to another in order to achieve such racial balance, or otherwise enlarge the existing power of a court to insure compliance with constitutional standards.

Title VI – Nondiscrimination in Federally Assisted Programs, Sect. 10

(House): No such provision.

(Senate): Nothing contained in this title shall be construed to authorize action under this title by any department or agency with respect to any employment practice of any employer, employment agency, or labor organization except where a primary objective of the Federal financial assistance is to provide employment.

Title VII – Equal Employment Opportunity, Sect. 1

(House): Employers having 25 or more employees, labor organizations having 25 or more members, and commercial employment agencies are prohibited from discriminating against any individual in any phase of employment or union membership (including advertisement for employment) on the ground of race, color, religion, sex or national origin . . .

(Senate): Same except that an employer will only be covered if he has 25 or more employees for each working day in each of 20 or more calendar weeks in a current or preceding calendar year. In addition, a labor organization is covered if it operates a hiring hall while Indian tribes are excluded from coverage. But, it is provided that it shall be the policy of the United States to insure equal employment opportunities for Federal employees without discrimination because of race, color, religion, sex or national origin and the President shall utilize his existing authority to effectuate this policy.

and Sect. 3 (g)

(House): No such provision.

(Senate): It shall not be an unlawful employment practice for an employer to apply different standards of compensation, or different terms, conditions or privileges of employment, pursuant to a bona fide seniority or merits system, to employees who work in different locations, provided that such differences are not the result of an intention to discriminate because of race, color, religions, sex, or national origin.

and (i)

(House): No such provision.

(Senate): It shall not be an unlawful employment practice for an employer to differentiate upon the basis of sex in determining the amount of wages or compensation paid to or to be paid to employees of the employer if the differentiation is authorized by the provisions of the Fair Labor Standards Act.

and (k)

(House): No such provision.

(Senate): The title shall not be interpreted to require any employer, employment agency, labor organization, or joint labor-management committee to grant preferential treatment to any individual or to any group because of race, color, religion, sex, or national origin on account of an imbalance which may exist with respect to the total number or percentage of persons of any race, color, religion, sex, or national origin employed by an employer, referred or classified for employment by an employment agency or labor organization, or admitted to or employed in any apprenticeship or other training program, in comparison with the total number or percentage of persons of such race, color, religion, sex, or national origin in any community, State, section, or other area, or in the available work force in any community, State, section or other area.

and Sect. 16

(House): Every employer, employment agency, labor organization, and joint labor-management committee, subject to this title, shall make and keep such records and make such reports as the commission may prescribe by regulation, after a public hearing. If any such requirement might result in undue hardship, the party affected may apply to the Commission such notations on records which these parties are required to keep (under the State or local law) as are necessary because of differences in coverage or methods of enforcement between the State or local law and the provisions of this title. Moreover, where an employer is required to file reports relating to his employment practices with any Federal agency or committee pursuant to Executive Order 10925 or other Executive orders, prescribing fair employment practices for Government contractors and subcontractors, the Commission shall not require the employer to file additional reports.[1]

(Senate): Same, except that the provisions shall not apply with respect to matters occurring in any State or political subdivision thereof which has a fair employment law, to which the employer, employment agency, labor organization, or joint labor-management committee is subject, except that the Commission may require or bring an action in a U.S. district court for an exemption or other appropriate relief.

Note

1. *Congressional Record*, 88th Cong., 2nd sess., 1964. Vol. 110, 15999–16004.

Appendix D: EDCOR in Detail

The following story gives a greater flavor of the nature and success of the EDCOR (Economic Development Corps) program implemented by Edward Lansdale and Ramon Magsaysay in their campaign against the communist Huks in the Philippines:

> EDCOR was formally established on December 15, 1950, as a responsibility of the Department of National Defense, with Mirasol in charge. On February 22, 1951, the first EDCOR farm was established on sixteen hundred hectares (nearly four thousand acres) of land at Kapatagan, Lanao, on the island of Mindanao, far south of Manila and the Luzon battlegrounds. Magsaysay, Mirasol, a detachment of troops, surveyors, and I went to Mindanao and looked over the area. It was lush, virgin jungle several kilometers inland from the sea, reached by an abominable muddy track of a road. A few small farms lay along this road, with rich-looking soil and reportedly abundant crops. While troops were clearing a campsite and putting up tents, I listened to Magsaysay and Mirasol envisioning the future. They pointed out where the town site and a sawmill would be located and talked about milling boards from the trees as the jungle was cleared and building a community hall to shelter the first settlers. They spoke of building a chapel, a school, a dispensary, a mess hall, and a town hall which would be used as EDCOR headquarters. Listening to this amid the thick growth of the jungle, with the huge trees towering over us, I thought blackly that by the time the place was readied for the first settlers, the war would be over and with it the pressing need for the army to engage in a pioneering effort such as this. How wrong I was!

By that May, the site at Kapatagan was ready for its first settlers, with the road in shape, a hundred or so hectares cleared, the sawmill operating and the community hall and a dozen rude houses built. Retired military personnel, their families, EDCOR technicians and their families, and fifty-six Huk surrenderers, some with their families, along with household goods, cattle, and supplies, were loaded aboard an LST in Manila. This modern Noah's ark began its long voyage down the chain of thousands of islands to the big southern island of Mindanao. Magsaysay flew south and boarded the LST on its final day at sea, taking some of his staff and me along. Sailing those last hours with the settlers, I became involved in an incident which came to illustrate in a very human way just what EDCOR meant to the combatants in the Huk campaign.

Aboard the LST, I saw a young settler glare at me and then quickly turn his head away. This was strange. My curiosity aroused, I kept a discreet eye on him during the voyage. He moved around from group to group, singling out individuals for earnest conferences. I mentioned this to one of the EDCOR technicians. "Oh, yes, I know about him," the technician replied casually. "He's a nut, one of the Huk prisoners. He thinks he can get the others to join him in starting a Huk group where we're going. I don't think he's having much luck." His offhand revelation hit me hard. It would be savage irony if the whole bright EDCOR dream and all the hard work being done to make it a reality turned out to be simply a clandestine opportunity for the Huks to expand their movement into Mindanao. I told Magsaysay about the Huk and his recruitment attempts, adding that it looked as though the security screening of Huk settlers was somewhat lacking in thoroughness. Magsaysay went over to the Huk and had a long talk with him. Then he rejoined me at the rail, and we looked out over the sea and discussed the Huk. Magsaysay admitted that the man had used all the Communist cliches about social injustice and corruption in government, had disputed Magsaysay's glowing account of farming in Mindanao, and clearly felt that he and other Huks were just going to a new type of jail. The Huk had noted bitterly that he was the last remaining male in a family, consisting only of his mother and sister. His father had died not long ago, worn out by the inequities of tenant farming, leaving debts that the young Huk could barely pay the interest on, let alone pay off the principal. A rotten system! Magsaysay had concluded that the Huk, despite his youth, had sounded as though he were beyond rehabilitation. Sadly, Magsaysay had told the Huk that he would be returned to the prisoner stockade in Manila.

When the LST nosed ashore at the Kapatagan landing, a hundred people were grouped at the landing waiting to greet the new arrivals. There were engineer troops in fatigues, who had been working on the EDCOR project, and farm families from the area who were curious about their new neighbors. It was a small party which seemed even smaller against the backdrop of tall jungle trees. They waved, jumped up and down excitedly, yelled, and waved crude signs lettered with greetings to the new settlers. A three-piece band of drum, bugle, and tuba played lustily off-key. As we came ashore and the welcomers moved forward to greet us, dogs scampered around the edge of the crowd and barked at us. Amidst the clamor of music, shouts, and barking dogs, the faces of the welcomers were alight with pleasure at seeing the newcomers. It struck me suddenly that they must have felt lonely in what they believed to be a spot at the end of the world. The scene was touching. Later, as the new arrivals climbed into trucks and looked about at the lush growth, our renegade Huk settler ran up to Magsaysay and pleaded that he be allowed to stay. He said that it was all different than he had thought it would be, and that Magsaysay and the army really seemed to be sincere. He had never imagined that papayas could grow as big as those he saw there. Please, he implored, he wanted to stay. I watched the Huk and Magsaysay, wondering if the Huk had really caught the contagion of the welcomers' enthusiasm. Magsaysay frowningly explained that EDCOR was only for those who honestly wanted a fresh start in life, not for those who wanted to bring their old troubles to a new scene. The Huk pleaded harder. If he earned the title to a farm at EDCOR, he would be the first man in the whole history of his family ever to own his land. If Magsaysay would give him a second chance, he would like to bring his mother and sister down from Luzon, make a new home for the family. Please! At this, Magsaysay relented. He agreed that the Huk could stay provided he proved his sincerity. In a couple of weeks, Magsaysay would visit here again. If the EDCOR officer reported that the Huk was doing his share of the work and was behaving himself, then Magsaysay would take him back to his home town in central Luzon. There, he could tell the people about EDCOR, as well as help his mother and sister prepare for the move to Mindanao. There were tears in the eyes of the young man as we left.

Two weeks later, Magsaysay visited EDCOR and heard good reports about the Huk, and flew him back to central Luzon. The young man offered to speak about EDCOR not only to the people of his home town but in other towns where the Huks had been active. Magsaysay agreed and the Huk spent the next days in a dozen towns of "Huklandia,' sounding like a combination evangelist and president of the chamber of commerce. He admitted openly that he had been a Huk but now felt that being a Huk was wrong. He would stretch his hands, fish-story style, to show how gigantic the fruits and vegetables grew in Mindanao. He boasted that he was getting a house and would soon be the owner of an eight-hectare farm. When his speaking tour was finished, the Huk and his family, with their meager possessions, went to Mindanao and their new life at EDCOR.

A month later, Hank Lieberman, who was then covering the Far East for the *New York Times*, flew over from Hong Kong to report on the Huk campaign in the Philippines. I was at Kapatagan, marveling over the vast clearing that had been done, the streets of new homes and the classes of children in the rough schoolhouse, when Lieberman arrived. He questioned everyone in sight, then came over to me. He was disappointed. The people he had interviewed seemed to be happy, full of their daily accomplishments. None of them seemed ever to have been the enemy, he said, looking at the way they got along with one other in evident friendship. Was there actually any single person at EDCOR who had been a real Huk, who had fired a shot in anger at government troops?

I pointed out the former Huk renegade to Lieberman, explaining that I knew with certainty he had been a hard core Huk. Lieberman talked to him for a half hour or so. "You s.o.b.," he said to me bitterly, when he returned. He drank a mug of coffee with his back turned to me. I asked him what was wrong. Lieberman explained in deliberate tones that he was a professional journalist, which meant he was an honest and responsible reporter who was not about to be taken in by one of my propaganda agents. When I told him the whole story, he remained skeptical. The Huk had been too enthusiastic about his new farm and the possibilities for the future for anyone who hadn't known the man before to believe that he once had been an enemy.

At about this time, Huks were showing up at BCT camps and offering to surrender. As they did so, they would ask how soon they could get a farm at EDCOR! EDCOR, which at the time had settled only fifty-six Huk surrenderers, had become a favorite topic in the Huk camps despite countermeasures taken by the Communist political cadre to stop the talk. The EDCOR dream was too appealing to be erased by dialectics.

News of EDCOR spread.[1]

Note

1. Lansdale, *Midst*, 52–57.

Appendix E:
The Complete 15 February 1965 Memo

The following is the complete text of the all-important 15 February 1965 memo from HHH to LBJ:

> I have been in Georgia over the weekend, and for the first time since Inauguration, have had time to read and think about the fateful decisions which you have just been required to make, and will continue to be making, on Vietnam. I have been reading the Vietnam cables and intelligence estimates of the last two weeks. Because these may be the most fateful decisions of your Administration, I wanted to give you my personal views. You know that I have nothing but sympathy for you and complete understanding for the burden and the anguish which surrounds such decisions. There is obviously no quick or easy solution, and no clear course of right or wrong. Whatever you decide, we will be taking big historic gambles, and we won't know for sure whether they were right until months or perhaps years afterwards. The moral dilemmas are inescapable.
>
> I want to put my comments in the most useful framework. In asking me to be your Vice President, you made it clear that you expected my loyalty, help, and support. I am determined to give it. I don't intend to second-guess your decisions, or kibbitz after the fact. You do not need me to analyze or interpret our information from Vietnam. You have a whole intelligence community for that purpose. You do not need me for foreign policy advice. You have a wise Secretary of State and whole staffs and departments to do that. I am not a military expert. Plenty of others are.
>
> But because I have been privileged to share with you many years of political life in the Senate, because we have recently come through a successful national

election together, because I think your respect for me and my value to you significantly consists of my ability to relate politics and policies, and because I believe strongly that the sustainability of the Vietnam policies now being decided are likely to profoundly affect the success of your Administration, I want to summarize my views on what I call the politics of Vietnam.

1. In the recent campaign, Goldwater and Nixon stressed the Vietnam issue, advocated escalation, and stood for a military "solution." The country was frightened by the trigger-happy bomber image which came through from the Goldwater campaign. By contrast we stressed steadiness, staying the course, not enlarging the war, taking on the longer and more difficult task of finding political-military solutions in the South where the war will be won or lost. Already, because of recent decisions on retaliatory bombing,[1] both Goldwater and the Kremlin are now alleging that we have bought the Goldwater position of "going North."

2. In the public mind the Republicans have traditionally been associated with extreme accusations against Democratic administrations, whether for "losing China," or for failing to win the Korean War, or for failing to invade Cuba during the missile crisis. By contrast we have had to live with responsibility. Some things are beyond our power to prevent. Always we have sought the best possible settlements short of World War III, combinations of firmness and restraint, leaving opponents some options for credit and face-saving, as in Cuba. We have never stood for military solutions alone, or for victory through air power. We have always stressed the political, economic and social dimensions.

3. This Administration has a heavy investment in policies which can be jeopardized by an escalation in Vietnam: the President's image and the American image, the development of the Sino-Soviet rift, progress on detente and arms control, summit meetings with Kosygin, reordering relations with our European allies, progress at the United Nations, stabilizing defense expenditures, drafting reservists.

4. American wars have to be politically understandable by the American public. There has to be a cogent, convincing case if we are to enjoy sustained public support. In World Wars I and II we had this. In Korea we were moving under United Nations auspices to defend South Korea against dramatic, across-the-border, conventional aggression. Yet even with those advantages, we could not sustain American political support for fighting Chinese in Korea in 1952.

5. If we go north, people will find it increasingly hard to understand why we risk World War III by enlarging a war under terms we found unacceptable 12 years ago in Korea. Politically people think of North Vietnam and North Korea as similar. They recall all the "lessons" of 1950–53: the limitations of air power, the Chinese intervention, the "Never Again Club" against GI's fighting a land war against Asians in Asia, the frank recognition of all these factors in the Eisenhower Administration's compromise of 1953.

If a war with China was ruled out by the Truman and Eisenhower administrations alike in 1952–53, at a time when we alone had nuclear weapons, people will find it hard to contemplate such a war with China now. No one really believes that the Soviet Union would allow us to destroy Communist China with nuclear weapons.

6. People can't understand why we would run grave risks to support a country which is totally unable to put its own house in order. The chronic instability in Saigon directly undermines American political support for our policy.

7. It is hard to justify dramatic 150 plane U.S. air bombardments across a border as a response to camouflaged, often non-sensational, elusive, small scale terror which has been going on for ten years in what looks largely like a Civil War in the South.

8. Politically in Washington, beneath the surface, the opposition is more Democratic than Republican. This may be even more true at the grassroots across the country.

9. It is always hard to cut losses. But the Johnson Administration is in a stronger position to do so now than any Administration in this century. 1965 is the year of minimum political risk for the Johnson Administration. Indeed it is the first year when we can face the Vietnam problem without being preoccupied with the political repercussions from the Republican right. As indicated earlier, our political problems are likely to come from new and different sources (Democratic liberals, independents, labor) if we pursue an enlarged military policy very long.

10. We now risk creating the impression that we are the prisoner of events in Vietnam. This blurs the Administration's leadership role and has spillover effects across the board. It also helps erode confidence and credibility in our policies.

11. President Johnson is personally identified with, and greatly admired for, political ingenuity. He will be expected to put all his great political sense to work now for international political solutions. People will be counting upon him to use on the world scene his unrivaled talents as a politician. They will be watching to see how he makes this transition from the domestic to the world stage.

The best possible outcome a year from now would be a Vietnam settlement which turns out to be better than was in the cards because LBJ's political talents for the first time came to grips with a fateful world crisis and did so successfully. It goes without saying that the subsequent domestic political benefits of such an outcome, and such a new dimension for the President, would be enormous.

12. If, on the other hand, we find ourselves leading from frustration to escalation and end up short of a war with China but embroiled deeper in fighting in Vietnam over the next few months, political opposition will steadily mount. It will underwrite all the negativism and disillusionment which we already have about foreign involvement generally—with serious and direct effects for all the Democratic internationalist programs to which the Johnson Administration remains committed: AID, United Nations, arms control, and socially humane and constructive policies generally.

For all these reasons, the decisions now being made on Vietnam will affect the future of this Administration fundamentally. I intend to support the Administration whatever the President's decisions. But these are my views.[2]

Notes

1. As a result of the Communist bombing of our air base at Pleiku on February 7, 1965, we had begun retaliatory B-52 raids on North Vietnam.
2. As given in *Education*, 320–24.

Appendix F: Humphrey and Mansfield on Vietnam

An exchange between Hubert Humphrey and Mike Mansfield took place on the Senate floor amidst the Dien Bien Phu crisis of 1954. Humphrey thoroughly agreed at that time that "the loss of Indochina would be a tragedy for the free world," that in fact the "loss of Indochina would be worse than the loss of Korea" for it would mean "the loss of Asia and probably all of the subcontinent."[1] Yet, after so arguing he nevertheless questioned the *manner* of French (and with it American) policy there. The following dialogue between Humphrey and Mansfield revealed more fully what Humphrey (and Mansfield with him) was driving at:

MR. HUMPHREY. Is it not true that the forces of the Associated States and the French Union in the Indochina area are far superior in manpower to the Communist forces of the Viet Minh, as the Senator has noted in his address?

MR. MANSFIELD. They are superior, not only in manpower, but in war materiel as well.

I would be willing to make the assertion that no general in all the history of France has had at his disposal the amount of materiel which General Navarre has at his disposal today.

MR. HUMPHREY. The point I wished to have the Senator from Montana develop was that there is not only a ratio of about 5 to 3 in manpower: namely, more than 500,000 men in the forces of the Associated States and French Union, as compared with 300,000 for the Communist Viet Minh forces; but also that the Associated States and French Union forces have much better equipment, and in larger quantities, by far, than do the Communist forces.

MR. MANSFIELD. The Senator from Minnesota is correct. As I understand, 5,000 tons of supplies a month are coming from China over the border into Indochina, to assist the Communist-led Viet Minh. I understand that the total amount of supplies, including American aid, being shipped to the forces of the Associated States Union is in the vicinity of 50,000 tons a month, indicating, in contrast to the 5-to-3 proportion, so far as combat effectives are concerned, a ratio of 10 to 1 so far as war materiel is concerned.

MR. HUMPHREY. Is it now true that the Communist forces are without naval power?

MR. MANSFIELD. They have none at all.

MR. HUMPHREY. They have little or no air power?

MR. MANSFIELD. They have none.

MR. HUMPHREY. And the French have a substantial fleet, or at least naval forces in the area, and a very substantial air force, have they not?

MR. MANSFIELD. That is correct.

MR. HUMPHREY. The purpose of my questions is to point out that, as I see it, there is a great deal of manpower in the area, organized into combat or operational units. In other words, there are significant numbers of organized manpower; secondly, there is an organized navy and air force on the part of the Associated States and French Union. I ask these questions only to detail further the documentation of the remarks of the Senator from Montana. The central problem the Senator has mentioned and touched and elaborated on is the political problem or the psychological problem, is it not?

MR. MANSFIELD. That is correct.

MR. HUMPHREY. Does the Senator recall listening to Adm. Radford and other officials of our government pointing out the effective parts of the Navarre plan as it pertains to military operations?

MR. MANSFIELD. I do.

MR. HUMPHREY. Without going into any of the details, which were explained to us in executive session, does the Senator really believe that the Navarre plan can be successful as a military plan unless the political considerations the Senator from Montana has outlined in his address are fulfilled?

MR. MANSFIELD. Neither the Navarre plan nor the Dulles plan, nor any other plan is going to be fulfilled unless two conditions are met in Vietnam principally, but throughout the Associated States as well. First, there must be competent, respected leadership. The second is what I call, from my Marine Corps experience, an espirit de corps among the Vietnamese Army and Vietnamese population. It is essential that those people believe in themselves and in their own liberty and independence. If they do, with the right kind of leadership they will without any troops or any other help being sent. They are fighting their brothers, but their brothers fight with some determination, and the Vietnamese lack such determination. There is no reason why, given independence, given the right to decide their own leadership, they could not win, because once that is assured, it will be found that a great proportion of the Vietnamese population will get off the fence and on the right side.[2]

Notes

1. Hubert Humphrey, *Congressional Record*, 83rd Cong., 2nd sess., 1954. Vol. 100, 4210.
2. Ibid., 5116–17.

Appendix G: The Economic Humphrey

One of the most popular and consistent conservative charges thrown against Humphrey was that he was the epitome of the "tax-and-spend Democrat." The response to this begins by asserting that, if nothing else, Hubert Humphrey was a believer in the free enterprise system. "I believe in our private enterprise system," he used to say, arguing that "basic to our domestic well-being is a strong and flourishing economy." Hubert Humphrey was a liberal who fully recognized the dependence of the welfare programs he championed on the state of the economy: "LBJ's vision of what he calls the Great Society only has meaning in the context of an expanding economy."[1] While advocating free market principles, however, Humphrey simultaneously argued that "to me fair trade means a fair trade body of rules and regulations that preserves the competitive-entrepreneurial system but removes competition from the realm of unprincipled and vicious practices either by government or by business enterprise,"[2] (we should not, in other words, "let the market make the key decisions of public policy."[3]) Yet that, in turn, is not to say that Humphrey therefore favored an adversarial relationship between business and government. What Humphrey actually advocated was a partnership relationship instead: "What is needed is a partnership in which our public and private institutions, working together, can meet public and private need without any one institution becoming a dominant monolith."[4] He sought "not a monolith but a mosaic in which every part is distinct but each part adds to a beautiful pattern. Not a structure in which there is a dominating force but [one] in which there are cooperating elements."[5] Thus he called for what he termed a "balanced economy." It was a concept born out of concern that "for too long business and government have entrenched themselves on opposite sides of an imaginary line;"[6] that "it is high time that the traditional hostility between the intellectuals on the one hand and management on the other was ended."[7] "Politics," he said, "have to be handled by the combined resources of the individual, the economy, and the government . . . partnership is what we ought to be talking about, not sterile words like federalism but pooling our resources, commitments to planning."[8]

Thus Humphrey called for a cooperative effort between all segments of society—an effort that would join profits and morality in "wedlock." Such a "balanced and orderly free society," he urged, "requires not only competition but cooperation between the individuals and segments of that society."[9] In such a society, free enterprise is to be viewed as "a constructive force," having "a social object as well as a profit motive."[10] For Humphrey, maintaining the former in the long run will provide for the latter:

> Business expansion is not only dependent upon the establishment of new industries and business facilities. Prosperous and stable economic enterprise is possible only in a community where educational facilities are the best, where parks and playgrounds are modern and extensive, where homes and housing facilities are adequate and where people have a civic pride. Programs of community development must have the support of the merchant on the street. This is particularly true in a great wholesale and retail center such as Minneapolis. Community leadership is the responsibility of every merchant. It is not enough for a business man to think only in terms of his own enterprise. His success or failure is in part dependent upon the general conditions prevailing in the community.[11]

Humphrey was a great believer in the value of tax cuts as the means to stimulate the economy. "Tax cuts," for Humphrey, "result immediately in business investments in plants and equipment."[12] Such an increase in investment is crucial for it "will in turn bring more employment, more spendable income and consumer demands and greater revenue to the government."[13] This is so because "an increased rate of spending means that the national income subject to taxation will also rise. Tax revenue will increase as the economic health of the country improves."[14]

Humphrey not only argued for tax cuts—he argued for cuts "large enough to increase consumption to such an extent that new investment in plants and equipment will be induced."[15] By such tax cuts, however, he meant tax cuts largely for the great mass of consumers—the lower and middle classes: "If the tax reduction doesn't go to the lower and middle income groups in the main, then you lose the stimulus, because these are the purchasers."[16] His was, in other words, a percolator-up, not a trickle-down economic outlook, for, as he said, "the best economics I know of for private industry are jobs for the workers."[17]

Timing was also crucial—tax cuts should occur "before and not after a recession."[18] He urged and worked for tax cuts in 1954, 1958, 1964, and 1974. At the same time, however, he also urged that the tax system remain equitable, which for him meant progressive: he was concerned that "the present tax structure places a heavier burden on small concerns that on giant corporations,"[19] and called for the "closing [of] loopholes through which billions of dollars escape," especially "the mineral depletion allowances" and taxes on "dividends and interest."

For Humphrey, "unemployment is not and never will be an acceptable consequence of its [inflation's] control. We can never afford to forget people because our money is threatened."[20] For Humphrey, "that kind of economics went out with bleeding."[21] Humphrey believed fully that "every person has a right to have a job in which his or her talents can be utilized, a job that can result in meaningful work. I think this is an absolute basic right in this country that has to be established by law. It is the new civil right."[22] He believed that government spending on programs designed to take people off the dole and back to work was not only good economics in the long run, but the decent thing to do as well—it represented that "wedlock" between profits and morality. In this he would assert that "I'm not for spending. I'm for investing," for spending on job programs was, ultimately, a matter of not only providing an opportunity for greater dignity in the populace, but also for building a stronger economy as well. It represented the nation honoring its own pledge to "promote the general welfare." In order to facilitate this, government should also act to provide credit for those who need it.

Thus we have the Humphrey formula, which is to say the Keynesian formula, for achieving and maintaining economic well-being. Once prosperity is achieved, the temporary job programs can be cut back and taxes raised to balance the budget. Throughout, the tax system is key, for it "provides the balance wheel in our economy—restraining it when inflation threatens and stimulating it in depression,"[23] precisely as Keynes had asserted.

Another key to economic, and with it national health is small business: "I repeat—the heart and core of the American economic system is individual enterprise—the small independent businessman."[24] For Humphrey, "the real contribution of independent, small business will be seen as lying in its ability to make our economy truly free and competitive and, thus, dynamic, efficient, and profitable."[25] He worried that "inflation has extracted a heavy toll from small business" and that "looming large as a handicap for small firms has been the constantly climbing costs of doing business."[26]

In order to avoid such problems, he argued for such things as economic planning, an increase in exports, an economic climate that would foster new, small-scale industry, and, even as early as 1964, for the urgent need to promote research and development as the key to competing in the world marketplace, not to mention providing a healthy economic and social climate at home. His advocacy of government planning, along with Jacob Javits, is one key way by which he distinguished himself from Keynesian theory.

Humphrey was often accused of being a statist, of fostering the welfare state. David Gartner responded to such a charge by saying,

> I don't think he ever envisioned the welfare system. He obviously wanted to in fact help those who couldn't help themselves—the handicapped and people who were genuinely unable to help themselves . . . he wanted to give [those who *could* help themselves] a nudge so that they could get out on their

> own . . . and I think that he genuinely felt that that kind of thing ultimately would pay off for the government because ultimately those people would become tax paying, productive citizens. He realized the costs of these programs . . . but he never really looked at the deficit except in relation to the gross national product and the percentage of the GNP.[27]

Therefore, as Humphrey himself said, "While I have been called radical, socialist, sometimes Communist, accused of holding wild-eyed economic views, I have really never been anything other than an advocate of a pragmatic free enterprise."[28]

Whether his represents the most pragmatically feasible economics or not, it at least earned him the respect of more conservative-minded opponents. After his speech to the ultra-conservative Union League in Philadelphia, for instance, *Fortune* observed that Humphrey "was most heartily applauded."[29] During a 1965 meeting with the country's mayors, Mayor James DiPrete of Cranston, Rhode Island, was moved to rise and say: "Mr. Vice President, I'm a Republican. I thought you would breeze in and out of here. Here you've been with us for five hours talking bread and butter problems, and I want to say I'm impressed."[30] As chairman of the Joint Economic Committee Humphrey frequently was placed in an adversarial role in relation to Arthur Burns, then head of the Federal Reserve Board. Despite that relationship, however, Burns stated, "I find it more pleasant and more instructive to appear before your committee than any other in the Congress," and, "on economic issues, Humphrey is among the most perceptive people in Congress."[31] The charge that Humphrey was just another tax-and-spend Democrat does not stick.

Notes

1. Humphrey, *Fortune* (August 1965): 142.
2. Humphrey, as quoted in Engelmayer, *Dream*, 40.
3. Humphrey, *Progressive* (March 1960): 18.
4. Humphrey, speech to the National Council of Churches.
5. Humphrey, speech to the International Newspaper Advertising Executives.
6. Ibid.
7. Humphrey, *Cause*, 51.
8. Humphrey, speech to National Municipal League.
9. Humphrey, as quoted in Engelmayer, *Dream*, 135.

10. Humphrey, as quoted in ibid., 135.
11. Humphrey, remarks to the Central Business and Civic Association, Minneapolis, Minnesota, 20 November 1945, Humphrey Collection.
12. Humphrey, press release, "Action on Tax Cut Needed Now," Humphrey Collection.
13. Ibid.
14. Ibid.
15. Ibid.
16. Ibid.
17. Humphrey, from *Sunshine*.
18. Humphrey, "Action."
19. Humphrey, "The Role of Small Business in Preserving a Strong and Free America," speech to the National Association of Retail Druggists, 20 October 1958, Humphrey Collection.
20. Humphrey, "The Business of Business . . . ," statement on business policy, Humphrey Collection.
21. Humphrey, "Planning Economic Policy," *Challenge* (March/April 1975): 126.
22. Ibid.
23. Humphrey, draft of an article entitled, "Faith of a Liberal," for *Progressive*, Humphrey Collection.
24. Humphrey, N.A.R.D. speech.
25. Ibid.
26. Ibid.
27. Gartner interview.
28. Humphrey, *Education*, 46.
29. Humphrey, as quoted in Bowen, "What's New . . . ," 142.
30. James DiPrete, as quoted in "Humphrey: a Strong No. 2," *Business Week* (13 November 1965): 180.
31. Arthur Burns, as quoted in *Business Week* (15 December 1975): 70.

Appendix H: The Effective Humphrey

Among the prominent legislative achievements Hubert Humphrey associated with in his life, he is credited with the following (as included in *Memorial*):

- Medicare
- Aging—expanded benefits under Social Security; restriction on discrimination in employment on the basis of age; creation of the National Commission on Aging.
- Commission on Civil Rights
- Civil Rights policies, including the outlawing of lynching; elimination of the poll tax as a voting requirement; desegregation of public transportation; equal employment opportunity.
- Civil Rights Act of 1964
- Creation of Senate Subcommittee on Disarmament
- Establishment of the Arms Control and Disarmament Agency
- Senate approval of the Limited Nuclear Test Ban Treaty of 1963
- Establishment of the Peace Corps
- Creation of the Food-For-Peace program
- Immigration reform
- Continuation and major reforms of foreign economic assistance programs
- International Security Assistance and Arms Export Control Act of 1977
- Establishment of the Department of Housing and Urban Development
- Basic housing and urban assistance laws of 1961 and 1964

- Promotion of national policies and studies focused on balanced growth and development
- Revenue sharing
- Emphasis on developing effective intergovernmental relations
- Creation of Job Corps
- Migrant Worker assistance
- Jobs For Youth
- Establishment of Headstart
- First federal programs of aid to elementary and secondary education
- Federal scholarship program
- Washington seminar programs for high school youth
- Support for the creation of the Woodrow Wilson International Center for Scholars
- The Food Stamp program
- Nutrition programs for mothers, infants, and children
- Veterans and dependents assistance
- Creation of the National Council of the Arts, and the National Foundation on the Arts and Humanities
- The Wilderness Preservation Act of 1964
- The Forest and Rangeland Renewable Resources Planning Act of 1974
- The National Forest Management Act of 1976
- The Consolidated Farm and Rural Development Act of 1972
- Key improvements in federal programs to strengthen American agriculture and to assist farmers
- The Commodities Futures Trading Commission Act
- Policies addressed to combating world hunger
- Statutory law providing for the humane slaughter of livestock and poultry
- Major legislation in support of labor, including minimum wage, major emphasis upon formulating a comprehensive employment policy for the 1970s.
- Early and continuous efforts on achieving reforms in election laws, campaign financing, code of conduct for Federal officials.
- Humphrey-Durham Drug Act of 1951
- Programs for handicapped persons, including The Community Mental Health Centers Act of 1962 and other related bills
- Early and continuous emphasis on consumer protection
- The Solar Energy Research Act of 1974
- Promotion of scientific research, including Chairman of the National Aeronautics and Space Council
- Area Redevelopment Act of 1961
- Juvenile Delinquency and Youth Offenses Control Acts of 1961 and 1964
- Manpower Development and Training Acts of 1962 and 1963

- Trade Expansion Act of 1962
- Public Works Acceleration Act of 1962
- Vocational Education Act of 1963
- Nurse Training Act of 1964
- Urban Mass Transportation Act of 1964
- Library Services and Construction Act of 1964
- Land and Water Conservation Act of 1964
- Economic Opportunity Act of 1964
- Revenue Act of 1964

As stated, these include only the more prominent legislative efforts with which Humphrey is associated. In addition there are the many appointments and offices held as well, not to mention the hundreds, and perhaps even thousands of more minor legislative efforts.

Bibliography

"ABC's of More Government Planning: Is It Any Answer?" *U.S. News & World Report* (14 June 1976): 49–51.

Agnew, Spiro. Letter to Hubert Humphrey. 5 June 1969. Humphrey Collection.

Ahlstrom, Sidney. *A Religious History of the American People*. New Haven and London: Yale University Press, 1972.

"America Gathers Under a Sign of Peace." Interview of Hubert Humphrey in *Life* (24 October 1969): 37.

Amrine, Michael. "Hubert Horatio Humphrey." *Progressive* (April 1960): 9–15.

______. *This Is Humphrey*. Garden City, New York: Doubleday & Company, 1960.

"A Preference for Nixon." Editorial. *Life* (25 October 1968): 42A.

Aquinas, St. Thomas. *Introduction to St. Thomas Aquinas*. Edited by Anton C. Pegis. Modern Library College Editions. New York: Random House, 1948.

Beckington, Lt. Gen. USMC(Ret.), Herbert L. Interview with author. Washington, D.C. 11 September 1984.

Bennett, John. Letter to the author. 9 June 1983.

______. *The Radical Imperative*. Philadelphia: The Westminster Press, 1975.

Berman, Edgar. *Hubert*. New York: G. P. Putnam's Sons, 1979.

Berman, Harold J. "The Religious Foundations of Law in the West: An Historical Perspective." *Journal of Law and Religion* 1, 1 (Summer 1983): 3–44.

Bowen, William. "What's New About the New Hubert Humphrey." *Fortune* (August 1965): 142–47, 238–41.

Broder, David. "Triple H Brand on Vice Presidency." *The New York Times Magazine* (6 December 1964): 30–31.
Burnham, J. "A Coming ADA Government?" *National Review* (3 November 1964): 954–59.
Burns, Arthur. *The Wall Street Journal* (23 May 1975): 6.
Carroll, Gen. A. Memorandum to Hubert Humphrey. 22 February 1965. Humphrey Collection.
Carpenter, Liz. "Another Side of LBJ." *Parade* (5 June 1983): 4–6.
Carter, Jimmy. Letter to Hubert Humphrey, 16 February 1977. Humphrey Collection.
______. Letter to Hubert Humphrey. 3 August 1977. Humphrey Collection.
______. Letter to Hubert Humphrey. 23 October 1977. Humphrey Collection.
______. Letter to Hubert Humphrey. 9 November 1977. Humphrey Collection.
Castan, Sam. "Vietnam/Washington's Biggest Problem." *Look* (6 April 1965): 72–79.
Cater, Douglas. Interview with author. Chestertown, Maryland. 29 May 1984.
Central Intelligence Agency. Secret Study: "The Situation in South Vietnam." Humphrey Collection.
Chamberlain, John. "Humphrey: Dust-Bowl Economist." *National Review* (7 May 1960): 293–94, 297.
______. "The Wonderful World of Hubert H. Humphrey." *National Review* (8 September 1964): 767–69.
Chapin, Dwight. Letter to Hubert Humphrey. 20 May 1974. Humphrey Collection.
"Choose If You Can." *The New Republic* (19 October 1968): 2–3.
"Civil Rights Bill Passed By House in 290–130 vote; Hard Senate Fight Seen." *The New York Times* (17 February 1964): 1, 33.
"Cloture Planned To Act Rights Bill Before Senators." *The New York Times* (18 March 1964): 1, 22.
Coats, Roslea. Notes, newspaper clippings, and miscellaneous information. Author's Collection.
Coats, Roslea and Lester. Interview with author. Doland, South Dakota. 13 September 1983.
Cohen, Dan. *Undefeated*. Minneapolis: Lerner Publications Company, 1978.
Congressional Record. 91st Cong., 1st sess., 1969. Vol. 115, 18350–361, 18369–370, 18398–430.
Connell, William. Interview with author. Bethesda, Maryland. 27 October 1983.
______. Letter to author. 24 May 1984. Author's Collection.

Cooper, Chester. "Humphrey's Turning Point." *The New Republic* (28 January 1978): 11–12.
Cousins, Norman. "Vietnam. The Spurned Peace." *Saturday Review* (26 July 1969): 12–16, 58–61.
______. "Journeys with Humphrey—Memoir of a Peace Mission That Failed." *Saturday Review* (4 March 1978): 10–18.
Cowan, Wayne. Letter to author. 2 April 1985. Author's Collection.
"Cracking the Whip for Civil Rights." *Newsweek* (13 April 1964): 26–32.
"Debate on Civil Rights: Senator Humphrey vs. Senator Thurmond." *U.S. News & World Report* (30 March 1964): 102–10.
Didier, Calvin. Interview with author. St. Paul, Minnesota. 15 September 1983.
Diem, Bui. Interview with author. Washington, D.C. 22 January 1985.
Dombrowski, James. *The Early Days of Christian Socialism in America.* Morningside Heights, New York: Columbia University Press, 1936.
"Education of a Senator." *Time* (17 January 1949): 13–16.
Ehrlich, Henry. "Changing Washington." *Look* (6 April 1965): 21–29.
Eisele, Albert. *Almost to the Presidency*. Blue Earth, Minnesota: The Piper Company, 1972.
Eisenhower, Dwight. Letter to Hubert Humphrey. 21 October 1966. Humphrey Collection.
Elfin, Mel. "That Was Hubert." *Newsweek* (23 January 1978): 24.
Engelmayer, Sheldon D. and Wagman, Robert J. *Hubert Humphrey: The Man and His Dream*. New York: Metheun, 1978.
Farrer, Austin. *Reflective Faith*. Edited by Charles C. Conti. Grand Rapids, Michigan: William B. Eerdmans Publishing Company, 1972.
Ferguson, Ernest, B. Interview with Clarence Mitchell. *Crisis*, March 1984, reprinted from 1977 *Baltimore Sun* article, 44–49.
"Fighting Communism in Unions/Interview with Senator Humphrey." *U.S. News & World Report* (28 December 1951): 20–26.
Fine, Sidney. *Laissez Faire and the General-Welfare State*. Ann Arbor, Michigan: The University of Michigan Press, 1978.
"Firebrand Senator Cools Down." *Business Week* (1 June 1963): 29–30.
Fleishman, Joel L. and Bruce L. Payne. "Ethical Dilemmas and the Education of Policymakers," from *The Teaching of Ethics*, VIII, The Hastings Center, New York, 1980.
Ford, Gerald. Letter to Hubert Humphrey. 22 December 1975. Humphrey Collection.
______. Telegram to Hubert Humphrey. 17 March 1977. Humphrey Collection.
Forell, George W. *Christian Social Teachings*. Minneapolis, Minnesota: Augsburg Publishing House, 1971.
Fraleigh, Bert. Letter to author. 5 May 1984. Author's Collection.
Freeman, Orville. Letter to author. 31 May 1983. Author's Collection.

Frost, David. *The Presidential Debate*. New York: Stein and Day, 1964.
Gannon, James P. "Hubert Humphrey: Free At Last." *The Wall Street Journal* (2 February 1977): 16.
Gartner, David. Interview with author. Washington, D.C. 26 October 1983.
"Gene and Hubert come down the stretch." *Life* (23 August 1968): 24–26.
George, Walter. Letter to Hubert Humphrey. 9 February 1953. Humphrey Collection.
Goldish, Sydney. "We Are Less Hateful Now." *The American Jewish World* (12 September 1947). Humphrey Collection.
Goldman, Peter, "The New Hubert Humphrey." *Newsweek* (13 April 1964): 26–32.
Goldwater, Barry. Letter to author. 14 November 1984. Author's Collection.
Gore, Albert. *Congressional Record*. 85th Cong., 1st sess., 1957. Vol. 103, 8386.
Gorey, Hays. "I'm a Born Optimist." *American Heritage* (December 1977): 60–68.
Griffith, Winthrop. *Humphrey: A Candid Biography*. New York: William Morrow & Company, 1965.
Graham, Billy. Letter to Hubert Humphrey. 24 February 1959. Humphrey Collection.
Halberstam, David. *The Best and the Brightest*. New York: Random House, 1972.
Hamill, Pete. "Politics Is My Life." *The Saturday Evening Post* (10 October 1964): 82–85.
Handy, Robert T. *A Christian America*. 2nd ed. revised and enlarged. New York: Oxford University Press, 1984.
Hartt, Julian. "Hubert Humphrey and the Pieties of the Prairie." *Dialog* (Summer 1984): 23, 174–82.
______. Interview with author. Charlottesville, Virginia. 23 March 1983.
______. Letter to Hubert Humphrey. 7 March 1973. Humphrey Collection.
______. *Restless Quest*. Philadelphia: United Church Press, 1975.
Hauerwas, Stanley. *Vision and Virtue*. Notre Dame, Indiana: University of Notre Dame Press, 1981.
Hopkins, Charles. *The Rise of the Social Gospel in American Protestantism: 1865–1915*. New Haven, Connecticut: Yale University Press, 1940.
Howard, Frances Humphrey. Interview with author. Bethesda, Maryland. 27 October 1983.
______. Interview with author. Bethesda, Maryland. 2 February 1984.
______. "Hubert Humphrey's Springboard for '76." *Business Week* (15 December 1975): 68–70.

Hubert H. Humphrey, Late A Senator From Minnesota: Memorial Addresses Delivered in Congress. Washington, D.C.: U.S. Government Printing Office, 1978.

"Hubert Humphrey Takes Time Off." *Look* (19 April 1966): 47–52.

Hughes, Emmet John. "Humphrey: The Man With One Arrow." *Newsweek* (4 April 1966): 28–29.

"Humphrey—A Strong No. 2." *Business Week* (13 November 1965): 175–80.

"Humphrey Assails Contempt Rulings." *The New York Times* (22 February 1970): col. 1, 42.

"Humphrey—Happy Warrior." Editorial. *The Globe Times*. Bethlehem, Pennsylvania (16 January 1978): 6.

Humphrey. Photos by Marty Nordstrum, words by the Senator. Washington, D.C.: Robert B. Luce, Inc., 1964.

Humphrey, Hubert H. Jr. Note on rear of Macalester College program entitled, "Conference on Careers in National Service in Politics." 15 March 1945. Humphrey Collection.

———. Remarks to Central Business and Civic Association. 20 November 1945. Humphrey Collection.

———. Speech to Emmanuel Lutheran Church. St. Paul, Minnesota. 9 November 1945. Humphrey Collection.

———. Memorandum entitled, "This Town of Ours." 13 January 1946. Humphrey Collection.

———. Letter to Franklin Delano Roosevelt, Jr. 13 May 1946. Humphrey Collection.

———. Letter to Reinhold Niebuhr. 12 November 1946. Humphrey Collection.

———. Unpublished draft of article entitled, "The Christian Student in Politics." Prepared for YM/YWCA publication in 1946. Humphrey Collection.

———. Letter to Glenn MacLea. 16 January 1947. Humphrey Collection.

———. Bulletin written for "I Am An American Day." 19 May 1947. Humphrey Collection.

———. Letter to Arthur Schlesinger, Jr. 24 September 1947. Humphrey Collection.

———. Notes written on pamphlet for First Congregational Church Social Action Program for 1947. Humphrey Collection.

———. "Graduating Into the Community." Literature from the Mayor's office. 5 January 1948. Humphrey Collection.

———. Letter to D. H. Brown. 29 March 1948. Humphrey Collection.

———. Draft of an article entitled, "What's Wrong With the Democrats?" for *Progressive*. Humphrey Collection.

———. ADA cable. 28 May 1948. Humphrey Collection.

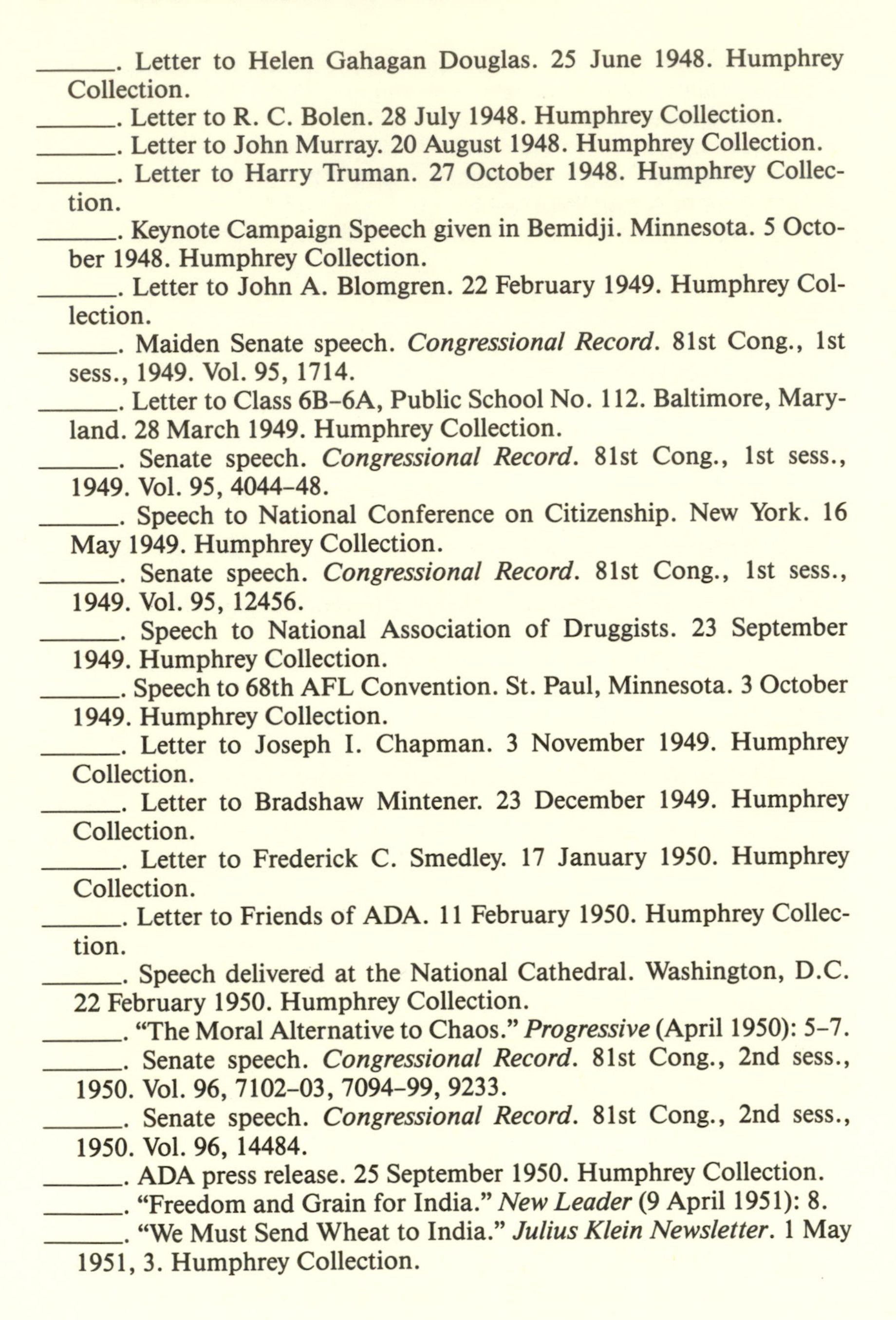

______. Letter to Helen Gahagan Douglas. 25 June 1948. Humphrey Collection.
______. Letter to R. C. Bolen. 28 July 1948. Humphrey Collection.
______. Letter to John Murray. 20 August 1948. Humphrey Collection.
______. Letter to Harry Truman. 27 October 1948. Humphrey Collection.
______. Keynote Campaign Speech given in Bemidji. Minnesota. 5 October 1948. Humphrey Collection.
______. Letter to John A. Blomgren. 22 February 1949. Humphrey Collection.
______. Maiden Senate speech. *Congressional Record*. 81st Cong., 1st sess., 1949. Vol. 95, 1714.
______. Letter to Class 6B–6A, Public School No. 112. Baltimore, Maryland. 28 March 1949. Humphrey Collection.
______. Senate speech. *Congressional Record*. 81st Cong., 1st sess., 1949. Vol. 95, 4044–48.
______. Speech to National Conference on Citizenship. New York. 16 May 1949. Humphrey Collection.
______. Senate speech. *Congressional Record*. 81st Cong., 1st sess., 1949. Vol. 95, 12456.
______. Speech to National Association of Druggists. 23 September 1949. Humphrey Collection.
______. Speech to 68th AFL Convention. St. Paul, Minnesota. 3 October 1949. Humphrey Collection.
______. Letter to Joseph I. Chapman. 3 November 1949. Humphrey Collection.
______. Letter to Bradshaw Mintener. 23 December 1949. Humphrey Collection.
______. Letter to Frederick C. Smedley. 17 January 1950. Humphrey Collection.
______. Letter to Friends of ADA. 11 February 1950. Humphrey Collection.
______. Speech delivered at the National Cathedral. Washington, D.C. 22 February 1950. Humphrey Collection.
______. "The Moral Alternative to Chaos." *Progressive* (April 1950): 5–7.
______. Senate speech. *Congressional Record*. 81st Cong., 2nd sess., 1950. Vol. 96, 7102–03, 7094–99, 9233.
______. Senate speech. *Congressional Record*. 81st Cong., 2nd sess., 1950. Vol. 96, 14484.
______. ADA press release. 25 September 1950. Humphrey Collection.
______. "Freedom and Grain for India." *New Leader* (9 April 1951): 8.
______. "We Must Send Wheat to India." *Julius Klein Newsletter*. 1 May 1951, 3. Humphrey Collection.

______. Senate speech. *Congressional Record*. 82nd Cong., 1st sess., 1951. Vol. 97, 7018–19.
______. Senatorial Symposium with McNeil Lowry. *Progressive* (July 1951): 13–16.
______. Senate speech. *Congressional Record*. 82nd Cong., 1st sess., 1951. Vol. 97, 11705–746.
______. "Ethical Standards in American Legislative Chambers." *Annals of American Academy* (March 1952): 51–59.
______. Senate speech. *Congressional Record*. 82nd Cong., 2nd sess., 1952. Vol. 98, 3825.
______. Senate speech. *Congressional Record*. 82nd Cong., 2nd sess., 1952. Vol. 98, 4378.
______. Senate speech. *Congressional Record*. 82nd Cong., 2nd sess., 1952. Vol. 98, 7096–97.
______. Roundtable: "What Shall Be the Relation of Morals to Law?" *Journal of Public Law* 1, 2 (Fall 1952): 306–11.
______. Letter to Walter George. 6 February 1953. Humphrey Collection.
______. Letter to Jack Kennedy. 17 March 1953. Humphrey Collection.
______. Letter to Gene McCarthy. 17 March 1953. Humphrey Collection.
______. "The Stranger At Our Gate: America's Immigration Policy." Public Affairs Committee, Public Affairs Pamphlet No. 202. January 1954.
______. Senate speech. *Congressional Record*. 83rd Cong., 2nd sess., 1954. Vol. 100, 4210, 5116–17.
______. Senate speech. *Congressional Record*. 83rd Cong., 2nd sess., 1954. Vol. 100, 25292.
______. Senate speech. *Congressional Record*. 83rd Cong., 2nd sess., 1954. Vol. 100, 14209–10.
______. Statement on Farm Proposals. 21 December 1954. Humphrey Collection.
______. Statement for Public Affairs Institute's Labor Press Service. 21 December 1954. Humphrey Collection.
______. "Family Farmer's Bill of Rights." Draft of an article for *Minnesota Farmer*. 26 January 1955. Humphrey Collection.
______. Senate speech. *Congressional Record*. 84th Cong., 1st sess., 1955. Vol. 101, 6103–04.
______. Memorandum to staff. October 1955. Humphrey Collection.
______. "Liberalism." *American Scholar* 4 (Autumn 1955): 419–33.
______. Letter to Paul Hayes. 9 November 1955. Humphrey Collection.
______. Speech to 60th Congress of American Industry. 7 December 1955. Humphrey Collection.
______. Letter to Lyndon Johnson. 9 December 1955. Humphrey Collection.

______. Letter to Albert Hartt. 19 December 1955. Humphrey Collection.
______. "It Is People Who Count." Draft of an article for *People Today*. 28 May 1956. Humphrey Collection.
______. Copy of "This Is the Real America." *Family Weekly* July 1956, written over as hate mail and mailed to Hubert Humphrey. Humphrey Collection.
______. Senate speech. *Congressional Record*. 85th Cong., 1st sess., 1957. Vol. 103, 8431.
______. Speech to the American Pharmaceutical Advertising Club. 3 June 1957. Humphrey Collection.
______. Speech to the Directors of CARE. 24 July 1957. As given in *Congressional Record*. 85th Cong., 1st sess., 1957. Vol. 103, 14641–14644.
______. "The World's Needy." *The National Lutheran* (Nov./Dec. 1957): 17–30.
______. Senate speech. *Congressional Record*. 85th Cong., 2nd sess., 1958. Vol. 104, 1607–20.
______. Statement submitted to *Newsweek*. 26 February 1958. Humphrey Collection.
______. Senate speech. *Congressional Record*. 85th Cong., 2nd sess., 1958. Vol. 104, 16198–99.
______. "The Role of Government in Maintaining a Stable Economy." Interview with Senator Ralph Flanders and Hubert Humphrey. *Social Action* (5 September 1958): 14–15, 20–25.
______. "The Role of Small Business in Preserving a Strong and Free America." *National Association of Retail Druggists Journal* 80, 20 (20 October 1958): 22, 23, 44, 49, 54–61.
______. "What Liberalism Means to Me." Draft of article for *The New York Times*. 26 January 1959. Humphrey Collection.
______. Letter to Billy Graham. 24 February 1959. Humphrey Collection.
______. Speech to Democratic Party brunch. Casper, Wyoming. 26 April 1959. Humphrey Collection.
______. Senate speech. *Congressional Record*. 86th Cong., 1st sess., 1959. Vol. 105, 4834–35.
______. Senate speech. *Congressional Record*. 86th Cong., 1st sess., 1959. Vol. 105, 8388, 14641–44.
______. Speech to 8th Annual Century Club Dinner of Harlem YMCA. New York. 25 May 1959. Humphrey Collection.
______. Statement submitted to subcommittee on Fair Trade. 16 June 1959. Humphrey Collection.
______. Statement on Fair Trade Bill. 16 June 1959. Humphrey Collection.

______. Senate speech. *Congressional Record*. 86th Cong., 1st sess., 1959. Vol. 105, 11780–83.
______. Letter to David Dressler. 30 June 1959. Humphrey Collection.
______. Senate speech. *Congressional Record*. 86th Cong., 1st sess., 1959. Vol. 105, 13864.
______. "Christian Ethics and International Politics." Draft of an article for *International Journal of Religious Education*. 31 July 1959. Humphrey Collection.
______. Speech to 50th Anniversary NAACP Dinner. New York. 15 July 1959. As given in *Congressional Record*. 86th Cong., 1st sess., 1959. Vol. 105, 13396.
______. Senate speech. *Congressional Record*. 86th Cong., 1st sess., 1959. Vol. 105, 16135–144.
______. "Works of Peace." *Progressive* (October 1959): 32–34.
______. Letter to William Benton. 30 October 1959. Humphrey Collection.
______. "Faith of a Liberal." Draft of article for *Progressive*. March 1960. Humphrey Collection.
______. Interview with Drew Pearson. 22 April 1960. Humphrey Collection.
______. "What is a Liberal?" *Think* (October 1960): 5–8.
______. Senate speech. *Congressional Record*. 87th Cong., 2nd sess., 1961. Vol. 108, 9137.
______. News Release. 16 May 1961. Humphrey Collection.
______. Senate speech. *Congressional Record*. 87th Cong., 2nd sess., 1961. Vol. 108, 9137.
______. Senate speech. *Congressional Record*. 87th Cong., 2nd sess., 1961. Vol. 108, 9288.
______. Senate speech. *Congressional Record*. 87th Cong., 2nd sess., 1962. Vol. 108, 22957–63, 23173.
______. "Big Business: Is It Too Big?" *Look* (22 May 1962): 102–107.
______. "Alliance for Progress: A Firsthand Report from Latin America." Speech given to the University of Minnesota. Minneapolis, Minnesota. 3 January 1963.
______. Draft for article on liberalism. 15 June 1962. Humphrey Collection.
______. Senate speech. *Congressional Record*. 88th Cong., 1st sess., 1963. Vol. 109, 17204.
______. Draft of note sent to Jacqueline Kennedy. November, 1963. Humphrey Collection.
______. Speech to Catholic Inter-American Cooperation Program. Chicago, Illinois. 20 January 1964. Humphrey Collection.
______. "What America Means to Me." *Pageant* (28 February 1964): 10–11.

______. Senate speech. *Congressional Record*. 88th Cong., 2nd sess., 1964. Vol. 110, 4597, 4681, 5159.
______. Senate speech. *Congressional Record*. 88th Cong., 2nd sess., 1964. Vol. 110, 5042–47, 6529, 7152.
______. Senate speech. *Congressional Record*. 88th Cong., 2nd sess., 1964. Vol. 110, 6529, 7152.
______. Memorandum to Lyndon Johnson. 8 June 1964. Humphrey Collection.
______. Senate speech. *Congressional Record*. 88th Cong., 2nd sess., 1964. Vol. 110, 12857, 13308–29.
______. Interview of Hubert Humphrey and General Omar Bradley. Spring 1964. Humphrey Collection.
______. Senate speech. *Congressional Record*. 88th Cong., 2nd sess., 1964. Vol. 110, 15999–16004.
______. "Spiritual Quest." *Library Journal* (15 September 1964).
______. Speech to Democratic State Convention. Little Rock, Arkansas. 18 September 1964. Humphrey Collection.
______. Speech on government and business. Houston, Texas. 18 September 1964. Humphrey Collection.
______. Memorandum to Winthrop Griffith. 1964. Humphrey Collection.
______. *The Cause Is Mankind*. New York: Frederick A. Praeger, Publishers, 1964.
______. *War On Poverty*. New York: McGraw-Hill Book Company, 1964.
______. *Integration vs. Segregation*. Edited by Hubert Humphrey. New York: Thomas Y. Crowell Company, 1964.
______. Speech to Plans for Progress Conference. 26 January 1965. Humphrey Collection.
______. Speech to National Conference on Civil Rights. 28 January 1965. Humphrey Collection.
______. Memorandum to Lyndon Johnson. 12 February 1965. Humphrey Collection.
______. Memorandum to Lyndon Johnson. 17 February 1965. Humphrey Collection.
______. Speech to Pacem in Terris Conference. New York City. 17 February 1965. Humphrey Collection.
______. Speech to Jewish Theological Seminary. New York City. 21 February 1965. Humphrey Collection.
______. Letter to James Weschler. 5 April 1965. Humphrey Collection.
______. Speech to AFL/CIO Equal Employment Opportunity Conference. Washington, D.C. 13 April 1965. Humphrey Collection.
______. Speech to National Conference of Christians and Jews. Omaha, Nebraska. 2 May 1965. Humphrey Collection.

______. Memorandum to Lyndon Johnson. 4 May 1965. Humphrey Collection.
______. Memorandum to Lyndon Johnson. 10 May 1965. Humphrey Collection.
______. Speech to National Conference on Social Welfare. Atlantic City, New Jersey. 28 May 1965. Humphrey Collection.
______. Speech to the National War College. 1 June 1965. Humphrey Collection.
______. Speech to Syracuse University. Syracuse, New York. 6 June 1965. Humphrey Collection.
______. "Letter From the Vice President/On Free Enterprise." *U.S. News & World Report* (25 October 1965): 53.
______. Speech to Washington University. St. Louis, Missouri. 28 October 1965. Humphrey Collection.
______. Speech delivered at Arlington Memorial Cemetery. Arlington, Virginia. 11 November 1965. Humphrey Collection.
______. Speech to Weizmann Institute Dinner. New York City. 6 December 1965. Humphrey Collection.
______. Speech at Rockefeller Public Service Awards. Washington, D.C. 8 December 1965. Humphrey Collection.
______. Speech to University of Chicago. Chicago, Illinois. 14 January 1966. Humphrey Collection.
______. Memorandum to Lyndon Johnson. 16 March 1966. Humphrey Collection.
______. Speech to 19th Annual Convention Banquet of ADA. 23 April 1966. Humphrey Collection.
______. "The Responsibilities of World Leadership," advance copy of a speech given to the Associated Press. New York City. 25 April 1966, as printed in *Department of State Bulletin* (16 May 1966): 769–72.
______. Speech to National Fellowship Awards Dinner. Philadelphia, Pennsylvania. 23 May 1966. Humphrey Collection.
______. "A Tribute to Reinhold Niebuhr." *Christianity & Crisis* (30 May 1966): 120–23.
______. Speech to Michigan State University. East Lansing, Michigan. 12 June 1966. Humphrey Collection.
______. Speech to American Agricultural Editors Association. Washington, D.C. 22 June 1966. Humphrey Collection.
______. Speech to National Conference of Christians and Jews. New York City. 28 June 1966. Humphrey Collection.
______. Speech to U.S. Junior Chamber of Commerce. Detroit, Michigan. 30 June 1966. Humphrey Collection.
______. Speech to NAACP National Convention. Los Angeles, California. 6 July 1966. Los Angeles, California. Humphrey Collection.

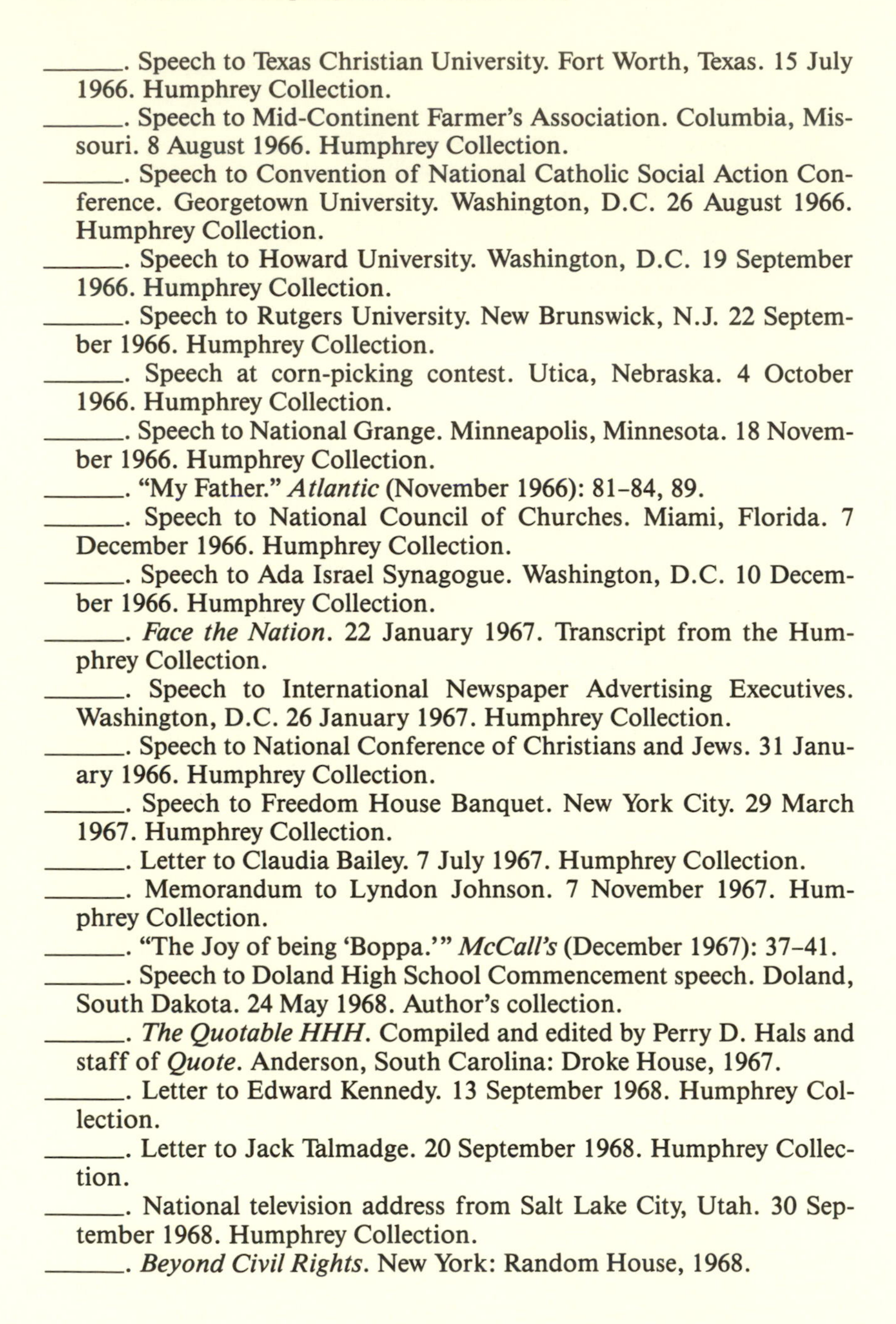

______. Speech to Texas Christian University. Fort Worth, Texas. 15 July 1966. Humphrey Collection.

______. Speech to Mid-Continent Farmer's Association. Columbia, Missouri. 8 August 1966. Humphrey Collection.

______. Speech to Convention of National Catholic Social Action Conference. Georgetown University. Washington, D.C. 26 August 1966. Humphrey Collection.

______. Speech to Howard University. Washington, D.C. 19 September 1966. Humphrey Collection.

______. Speech to Rutgers University. New Brunswick, N.J. 22 September 1966. Humphrey Collection.

______. Speech at corn-picking contest. Utica, Nebraska. 4 October 1966. Humphrey Collection.

______. Speech to National Grange. Minneapolis, Minnesota. 18 November 1966. Humphrey Collection.

______. "My Father." *Atlantic* (November 1966): 81–84, 89.

______. Speech to National Council of Churches. Miami, Florida. 7 December 1966. Humphrey Collection.

______. Speech to Ada Israel Synagogue. Washington, D.C. 10 December 1966. Humphrey Collection.

______. *Face the Nation*. 22 January 1967. Transcript from the Humphrey Collection.

______. Speech to International Newspaper Advertising Executives. Washington, D.C. 26 January 1967. Humphrey Collection.

______. Speech to National Conference of Christians and Jews. 31 January 1966. Humphrey Collection.

______. Speech to Freedom House Banquet. New York City. 29 March 1967. Humphrey Collection.

______. Letter to Claudia Bailey. 7 July 1967. Humphrey Collection.

______. Memorandum to Lyndon Johnson. 7 November 1967. Humphrey Collection.

______. "The Joy of being 'Boppa.'" *McCall's* (December 1967): 37–41.

______. Speech to Doland High School Commencement speech. Doland, South Dakota. 24 May 1968. Author's collection.

______. *The Quotable HHH*. Compiled and edited by Perry D. Hals and staff of *Quote*. Anderson, South Carolina: Droke House, 1967.

______. Letter to Edward Kennedy. 13 September 1968. Humphrey Collection.

______. Letter to Jack Talmadge. 20 September 1968. Humphrey Collection.

______. National television address from Salt Lake City, Utah. 30 September 1968. Humphrey Collection.

______. *Beyond Civil Rights*. New York: Random House, 1968.

______. Letter to Luci Pat Nugent. 5 January 1969. Humphrey Collection.
______. *The Political Philosophy of the New Deal.* Baton Rouge, Louisiana: Louisiana State University Press, 1970.
______. Speech to National Municipal League's 77th Annual Convention. 15 November 1971. Humphrey Collection.
______. "Perfectionism Is a Pitfall of Politics." *Progressive* (December 1971): 37–38.
______. "Young America in the 'New' World." *The Charles C. Moskowitz Lectures*, No. XII. New York: New York University Press, 1971.
______. "Toward Balanced National Growth." *National Civic Review.* (January 1972): 7–10.
______. Letter to John Tyler. 14 October 1972. Humphrey Collection.
______. Speech to 50th Anniversary United Methodist Church. Doland, South Dakota. 4 February 1973. Author's Collection.
______. Letter to Julian Hartt. 12 March 1973. Humphrey Collection.
______. Speech to Minneapolis Ministerial Association Breakfast. Minneapolis, Minnesota. 13 May 1974. Humphrey Collection.
______. Interview with Caspar Nannes in *The Link* (November 1974), Humphrey Collection.
______. *Meet the Press.* 16 February 1975. Transcript from the Humphrey Collection.
______. "Guaranteed Jobs for Human Rights." *Annals of the American Academy* (March 1975): 17–25.
______. "Planning Economic Policy." *Challenge* (March/April 1975): 21–27.
______. Quoted in *Time. Time* (12 May 1975): 20.
______. Letter to Henry Kissinger. 23 July 1975. Humphrey Collection.
______. Roundtable. "Government Regulation: What Kind of Reform?" American Enterprise Institute. 11 September 1975.
______. "Constructive Economic Interdependence." *Labor Law Journal* (2 October 1975): 615–23.
______. Roundtable. "Japanese-American Relations." American Enterprise Institute, 1975.
______. Speech to Southern Baptist Convention, as found in *Congressional Record.* 94th Cong., 2nd sess., 1976. Vol. 122, 7864.
______. Statement on Church-State Relations. 13 April 1976. Humphrey Collection.
______. "The Pragmatic Administration of Food Policies, Domestic and International." *Public Administration Review* (March/April 1976): 131–37.
______. "A Strategy for Putting America Back to Work." *The Washington Post* (14 May 1976): A27.

______. Speech to National Leadership Conference on Welfare Reform. 25 May 1976. Transcript provided by The Institute for Socioeconomic Studies.
______. Speech to All-Alumni Reunion for Doland High School. Doland, South Dakota. 12 June 1976. Author's Collection.
______. Letter to J. C. Chapman. 11 August 1976. Humphrey Collection.
______. "Reply to Milton Friedman." *Newsweek* (11 October 1976): 7–8.
______. Letter to Jimmy Carter. 3 November 1976. Humphrey Collection.
______. "Christmas Memories." Draft of an article for *Redbook*. 8 November 1976. Humphrey Collection.
______. *The Education of a Public Man*. Edited by Norman Sherman. Garden City, New York: Doubleday & Company, Inc., 1976.
______. Letter to Guy Cook. 10 February 1977. Humphrey Collection.
______. Letter to Gerald Ford. 31 October 1977. Humphrey Collection.
______. Letter to Theodore K. Pitt. 18 November 1977. Humphrey Collection.
______. *The Wit and Wisdom of Hubert H. Humphrey*. Ed. Jane C. Thompson. Minneapolis, Minnesota: Partner's Press Ltd., 1984.

Miscellaneous and/or Undated Humphrey Materials

______. "Annual Sermon." Humphrey Collection.
______. Copy of "Self-Survey." Circa 1946. Humphrey Collection.
______. Draft of article entitled, "What Liberalism Means to Me." Humphrey Collection.
______. Draft of article for *Baltimore Sun*. Circa 1975. Humphrey Collection.
______. Draft of article entitled, "Food for Peace," for *The Non-Partisan League Leader*. Humphrey Collection.
______. "How to Win in Vietnam." Report on situation in Vietnam in 1965. Humphrey Collection.
______. Interview with Caspar Nannes. 1975. Transcript from the Humphrey Collection.
______. "My Childhood." Interview of Hubert Humphrey and James Baldwin. Circa 1963. Transcript from the Humphrey Collection.
______. Interview with Norman Sherman for *The Education of a Public Man*. Transcript from the Humphrey Collection.
______. Interview with Theodore White. Circa 1975. Transcript from the Humphrey Collection.
______. Letter from Mayor's office to all new citizens of Minneapolis. Circa 1946. Humphrey Collection.
______. Memorandum to Lyndon Johnson. 1968. Humphrey Collection.

______. Memorandum to Lyndon Johnson. Circa 1966. Humphrey Collection.
______. Minutes of ADA meetings, 1947–1964. Humphrey Collection.
______. Newspaper clippings regarding Humphrey's choice for Civil Service Commission. Circa 1947. Humphrey Collection.
______. Newspaper clippings regarding "Kid Cann" incident. 7 February 1947. Humphrey Collection.
______. Newspaper clippings regarding 1947 telephone strike. Humphrey Collection.
______. Notes for a speech entitled, "A Time for Greatness." Circa 1947. Humphrey Collection.
______. Note. Circa 1946. Humphrey Collection.
______. Notes jotted in 1964. Humphrey Collection.
______. Notes on "Self-Survey" program. Circa 1947. Humphrey Collection.
______. Notes regarding Vietnam. Circa 1967. Humphrey Collection.
______. Notes written on Mayflower Hotel stationery. Circa 1945. Humphrey Collection.
______. "Ordeal by Hunger." *Cooperative Grain Quarterly*. Humphrey Collection.
______. Statement entitled, "Action on Tax Cut Needed Now." Humphrey Collection.
______. Statement entitled, "What's Right with American Labor." Humphrey Collection.
______. Statement for *Fayette Tribune and Montgomery Herald*. Humphrey Collection.
______. Statement of Purpose of Mayor's Council on Human Relations. Circa 1946. Humphrey Collection.
______. Statement of recession proposals. Humphrey Collection.
______. Statement on Apollo 8. Circa 1968. Humphrey Collection.
______. Statement on Public Education. Humphrey Collection.
______. Text entitled, "The Business of Business." Humphrey Collection.
______. Text on American schools. Humphrey Collection.
______. Text on nuclear disarmament. Humphrey Collection.
______. YM/YWCA National Intercollegiate Christian Council 1944 platform. Humphrey Collection.
"Humphrey in Minnesota." *The New Republic* (18 October 1948): 8.
"Humphrey for Vice President." *The New Republic* (27 June 1960): 4.
"Humphrey Looks at His Future." *U.S. News & World Report* (27 May 1968): 54–60.
"Humphrey, McGovern Clashing in California/Emphasizing One Theme." *The Wall Street Journal* (30 May 1972): 6, 24.
"Humphrey On What's Wrong." *Time* (25 October 1968): 27.
"Humphrey Themes Applauded: Four Freedoms Begin At Home." *Hartford Courant* (24 May 1947). Humphrey Collection.

"Humphrey Urges a Vote on Rights." *The New York Times* (19 March 1964): 20.

Hunter, Marjorie. "Rights Command Set Up in Senate." *The New York Times* (22 March 1964): 41.

Hyneman, Charles. Letter to Hubert Humphrey. 4 April 1949. Humphrey Collection.

Into the Bright Sunshine. Film documentary on the life of Hubert Humphrey. Directed by William Connell. Produced by Concept Associates, 1982.

"Issues: Defense, Prosperity—At Stake: Control of Congress." *U.S. News & World Report* (31 January 1958): 88–91.

Johnson, Lyndon. Letter to Hubert Humphrey. 28 January 1953. Humphrey Collection.

______. Letter to Hubert Humphrey. 9 June 1955. Humphrey Collection.

______. Letter to Hubert Humphrey. 17 June 1955. Humphrey Collection.

______. Letter to Hubert Humphrey. 30 June 1955. Humphrey Collection.

______. Letter to Hubert Humphrey. 18 September 1956. Humphrey Collection.

______. Letter to Hubert Humphrey. 31 August 1968. Humphrey Collection.

______. Letter to Hubert Humphrey. 7 January 1969. Humphrey Collection.

"Johnson-Humphrey." *The New Republic* (8 August 1964): 3–4.

Joseph, Geraldine. Interview with author. Minneapolis, Minnesota. 16 September 1983.

Letter to Rufus Phillips. 6 April 1971. Humphrey Collection.

Kampelman, Max. Interview with author. Washington, D.C. 27 July 1983.

______. "Hubert Humphrey: Political Scientist," reprinted from *PS*, the news journal of the American Political Science Association 11, 2 (Spring 1978).

Karnow, Stanley. *Vietnam. A History*. New York: The Viking Press, 1983.

Kempton, Murray. "Mr. Humphrey's Conquering Hosts." *The New Republic* (4 April 1964): 6–8.

______. "What's to Be Done?—An Honorable Choice." *The New Republic* (2 November 1968): 12–13.

Kennedy, Edward. Letter to Hubert Humphrey. 12 December 1963. Humphrey Collection.

______. Letter to Hubert Humphrey. 22 September 1965. Humphrey Collection.

Kennedy, John. Letter to Hubert Humphrey. 26 May 1962. Humphrey Collection.

Kennedy, Robert. Letter to Hubert Humphrey. 26 December 1963. Humphrey Collection.
Kenworthy, E. W. "Churches Termed Key to Rights Bill." *The New York Times* (21 March 1964): 14.
Kirkpatrick, Evron. Interview with author. Washington, D.C. 5 July 1984.
Kirkpatrick, Jeane. Draft of an article entitled, "The Celebration of Hubert Humphrey." Author's Collection.
Kissinger, Henry. Letter to Hubert Humphrey. 17 January 1970. Humphrey Collection.
______. Letter to Hubert Humphrey. 17 January 1977. Humphrey Collection.
Kitagawa, Daisuke. Letter to Hubert Humphrey. 22 July 1947. Humphrey Collection.
Knebel, Fletcher. "Hubert Humphrey/Advance Man for the Great Society." *Look* (6 April 1965): 80–88.
Koplan, J. M. Letter to Hubert Humphrey. 22 July 1947. Humphrey Collection.
Kozelka, Richard. Interview with author. St. Paul, Minnesota. 15 September 1983.
Kraft, Joseph. "Keeper of the Conscience." *The Washington Post* (30 October 1977): C7.
Kristol, Irving. "Why I Am for Hubert Humphrey." *The New Republic* (8 June 1968): 21–23.
"Landmark II: equal rights." Editorial. *Life* (26 June 1964): 4.
Lange, Arlen J. "Senator Humphrey Is Back and All of Washington Is Aware of the Fact." *The Wall Street Journal* (12 April 1971): 3, 20.
Lansdale, Edward, USAF(Ret.) Maj. Gen. "Vietnam: Do We Understand Revolution?" *Foreign Affairs* (October 1964): 75–86.
______. "Still the Search for Goals." *Foreign Affairs* (October 1968): 92–98.
______. *In the Midst of Wars*. New York: Harper and Row, 1972.
______. Interview with author. McClean, Virginia. 3 February 1984.
______. Interview with author. McClean, Virginia. 2 July 1984.
Latham, Aaron. "The Immortality of HHH." *Esquire* (October 1977): 84–86, 182–84.
"LBJ vs. HHH on Vietnam." *U.S. News & World Report* (23 September 1968): 42–43.
Lee, Oscar. Letter to Hubert Humphrey. Humphrey Collection.
LeFever, Ernest W. Letter to Hubert Humphrey. 21 April 1968. Humphrey Collection.
______. Interview with author. Washington, D.C. 23 May 1984.
Letter of complaint. 21 September 1951. Humphrey Collection.
Letter of complaint. 14 April 1955. Humphrey Collection.
Letter of complaint. 29 May 1974. Humphrey Collection.

Little, David. *American Foreign Policy & Moral Rhetoric*. New York: The Council on Religion and International Affairs, 1969.

______. "Francis Greenwood Peabody.' *Harvard Library Bulletin* 15, 3 (July 1967).

______. "Humphrey for President." *Christianity & Crisis* (10 June 1968): 127–29.

Lowry, McNeil W. "The Education of a Senator." *Progressive* (May 1951): 21–23.

Long, Russell. Interview with author. Washington, D.C. 8 December 1986.

MacIntrye, Alasdair. *After Virtue*. Notre Dame, Indiana: University of Notre Dame Press, 1984.

Manfred, Frederick. "Hubert Horatio Humphrey: A Memoir." *Minnesota History* (Fall 1978): 87–102.

Margolis, Richard J. "The Dreams of Hubert Humphrey." *New Leader* (13 February 1978): 15–16.

Martin, Ralph G. *A Man for All People: Hubert Humphrey*. New York: Grosset & Dunlap, 1968.

McNamara, Robert. Letter to Hubert Humphrey. 20 June 1968. Humphrey Collection.

Miller, Norman C. "Promises, Promises/Now the Front Runner, Senator Humphrey Pledges Something for Everyone." *The Wall Street Journal* (28 March 1972): 29.

Moley, Raymond. "Hubert Humphrey, Complete Statist." *Newsweek* (14 September 1964): 96.

Mondale, Walter. Letter to author. 21 June 1983. Author's Collection.

"Morals and Money." *Newsweek* (20 April 1959): 35–39.

Moyers, William. Interview with author. New York City. 18 January 1984.

______. Letter to author. 3 April 1985. Author's Collection.

______. "Hubert Horatio Humphrey: A Conversation." Transcript of an interview with Hubert Humphrey for *Bill Moyers' Journal*. 11 April 1976. Author's collection.

Nacy, Richard. Letter to Hubert Humphrey. 21 February 1946. Humphrey Collection.

Naftalin, Arthur. Interview with author. Minneapolis, Minnesota. 8 November 1984.

______. "I Remember Hubert." *Greater Minneapolis* (March/April 1982): 32–36.

Newman, Cecil E. Letter to Hubert Humphrey. 29 March 1946. Humphrey Collection.

Niebuhr, Reinhold. *The Children of Light and the Children of Darkness*. New York: Charles Scribner's Sons, 1946.

______. *The Irony of American History*. New York: Charles Scribner's Sons, 1954.

______. *The World Crisis and American Responsibility*. Edited by Ernest W. LeFever. New York: Association Press, 1958.

______. "The Long Ordeal of Coexistence." *The New Republic* (30 March 1959): 10–12.

______. *Faith and Politics*. Edited by Ronald H. Stone. New York: George Beziller, 1968.

______. *Faith and Justice*. Edited by D. B. Robertson. Gloucester, Massachusetts: Peter Smith, 1976.

Nixon, Richard. Letter to Hubert Humphrey. Humphrey Collection.

"Now It's a Humphrey Boom." *U.S. News & World Report* (26 April 1976): 19–21.

Osgood, Endicott Robert. *Ideals and Self-interest in American Foreign Policy*. Chicago: University of Chicago Press, 1953.

Peretz, Martin. "What's To Be Done? Contra Confrontation." *The New Republic* (19 October 1968): 22–23.

Phillips, Rufus. Letter to William Connell. 29 October 1964. Humphrey Collection.

______. "U.S. Policy Options/A Synopsis." Report to Hubert Humphrey. 25 November 1964. Author's Collection.

______. Memorandum to William Connell. 10 May 1968. Author's Collection.

______. Memorandum to William Connell. 14 May 1968. Author's Collection.

______. Memorandum to Hubert Humphrey. June 1968. Author's Collection.

______. Letter to Hubert Humphrey. 25 September 1969. Author's Collection.

______. Interview with author. Arlington, Virginia. 22 May 1984.

Pianin, Eric. "Meet the Master of (Risk) Free Enterprise." *Washington Monthly* 13 (April 1981): 31–38.

Polsby, Nelson. "What Hubert Humphrey Wrought." *Commentary* (November 1984): 47–50.

"Politics Without Joy—On the Road with Humphrey." *U.S. News & World Report* (12 August 1968): 30–31.

Ramsey, Paul. *The Just War*. New York: Charles Scribner's Sons, 1968.

Rauh, Joseph. Draft of an article written for *Progressive*. Author's Collection.

______. Interview with author. Washington, D.C. 28 October 1983.

Rauschenbusch, Walter. *Christianizing the Social Order*. New York: The Macmillan Company, 1917.

Reed, Roy. "Humphrey Found Decision Difficult." *The New York Times* (28 April 1968): 66.

Reuther, Victor. Interview with author. Washington, D.C. 18 September 1986.

Rielly, John. Memorandum to Hubert Humphrey. 13 May 1965. Humphrey Collection.

Ritter, Walter T. "Hustling Hubert Makes His Bid." *Saturday Evening Post* (25 April 1959): 38–39, 94–98.

Robb, Lynda Johnson. "Hubert Humphrey Remembered." *Ladies Home Journal* (May 1978): 107, 178, 180, 182, 189.

"Road Ahead for Humphrey." *U.S. News & World Report* (8 November 1968): 61.

Roberts, Paul [Rufus Phillips]. "A Program for Winning the War in Vietnam." *Pageant* (April 1965): 6–15.

Roth, Robert. "Few Have Served as Humphrey." *The Evening Bulletin* (4 May 1976): A7.

Rusk, Dean. Letter to author. 20 January 1984. Author's Collection.

______. Letter to author. 23 March 1984. Author's Collection.

Ryskind, Alan. *Hubert: An Unauthorized Biography of the Vice President*. New Rochelle, New York: Arlington House, 1968.

Sancton, Thomas. "Two Young Politicians." *The Nation* (12 March 1949): 294–95.

______. "The Great Debate." *The Nation* (26 March 1949): 350–52.

Schoen, Scott. "Hubert Humphrey: Can Minnesota's Errand Boy Make the Presidency?" *Human Events* (30 September 1959): 1–4.

Schrade, Paul. "Back Humphrey, and. . . . " *The New Republic* (12 October 1968): 20–22.

"Senator Humphrey Announces." *U.S. News & World Report* (24 January 1972): 50.

Segretti, Donald. Letter to Hubert Humphrey. 11 October 1973. Humphrey Collection.

"Senate Generals in Rights Battle." *U.S. News & World Report* (12 March 1964): 12.

Sherrill, Robert and Ernst, Harry W. *The Drugstore Liberal*. New York: Grossman Publishers, 1968.

Sherman, Norman. Interview with author. 28 June 1983. Washington, D.C.

Simmons, John. Letter to Hubert Humphrey. 23 April 1951. Humphrey Collection.

Smith, Dane. "FBI Probed Humphrey Links to Communists." *The Philadelphia Inquirer* (15 December 1975): 1A, 12A.

Solberg, Carl. *Hubert Humphrey: A Biography*. New York: W. W. Norton Company, 1984.

Stewart, John. Interview with author. Knoxville, Tennessee. 2 May 1985.

Stolley, Richard B. "Ev and Hubert: Heroes of the Historic." *Life* (19 June 1964): 36–37.

Szulc, Tad. "Humphrey Offers Policy Based on Spurring Red-Bloc Autonomy." *The New York Times* (13 September 1964): 1, 68.

Tang, Truong Nhu. *A Vietcong Memoir*. New York: Vintage Books, 1986.
"The Convention." *Newsweek* (7 September 1964): 16–31.
"The Historic Vote: 71 to 29." *Newsweek* (22 June 1964): 25–26.
"The Hubert Humphrey record." *U.S. News & World Report* (1 July 1968): 36–41.
"The Humphrey Image." *The New Republic* (21 March 1960): 3–4.
"The Liberal Flame." *Time* (1 February 1960): 13–16.
"The Once and Future Humphrey." *Time* (3 May 1968): 15–19.
"The People Around Humphrey." *U.S. News & World Report* (9 September 1968): 38–9.
"The President's Wise Selection." Editorial. *Life* (4 September 1964): 4.
"The Triumphant Ticket Whoops It Up and Saddles Up Way Down at the LBJ." *Life* (13 November 1964): 36–37.
"The Vice Presidency: The Bright Spirit." *Time* (1 April 1966): 21–25.
"They Finally Did It: They Busted the Big Filibuster." *Life* (19 June 1964): 32–35.
Thimmesch, Nick. "Look at All the Fun We've Had." *McCall's* (May 1977): 136–39.
"Threats Against Humphrey in '68 Bared." *The Philadelphia Inquirer* (8 December 1984).
Thompson, Kenneth. "The Ethics of Major American Foreign Policies." Reprinted from *British Journal of International Studies* (1980): 111–24.
Time. Special Vietnam issue (15 April 1985).
"Too Much Defense—or Not Enough?" *U.S. News & World Report* (15 October 1973): 76–80.
Truman, Harry. Letter to Hubert Humphrey. 12 December 1958. Humphrey Collection.
TRB [Richard Strout]. "Hubert's Shadow." *The New Republic* (2 October 1968): 1.
______. "Tribute to Hubert Humphrey." *The New Republic* (28 January 1978): 1.
Tyler, Gus. "The Case for Hubert Humphrey." *Progressive* (August 1968): 16–19.
Unsigned letter to Hubert Humphrey. 2 June 1946. Humphrey Collection.
"U.S. Officials Pondering Viet Policies." *The Washington Post* (29 August 1965): A18.
"U.S., Still the Land of Opportunity?" *U.S. News & World Report* 36–37.
Van Dyk, Theodore. Interview with author. Washington, D.C. 5 July 1984.
"Vice President Humphrey Presents Another Side of Vietnam Debate." *U.S. News & World Report* (14 March 1966): 71–75.
"Vice Presidential Sweepstakes." *Life* (8 May 1964): 94B.

Wainwright, Loudon. "Old Ev, the Good Wizard." *Life*, 29.
Walzer, Michael. *Just and Unjust Wars*. Basic Books, Inc., Publishers. New York, 1977.
Weaver, Warren. "Humphrey Joins Presidency Race; Calls for Unity." *The New York Times* (28 April 1968): 1, 66.
Weber, Max. *From Max Weber: Essays in Sociology*. Edited by H. H. Gerth and C. Wright Mills. New York: Oxford University Press, 1946.
"We Do Not Want a Group to Shoot Its Way into Power," interview with Hubert Humphrey. *U.S. News & World Report* (14 March 1966): 71–75.
Welch, Deschler. Interview with author. Doland, South Dakota. 13 September.
Weir, M. C. Letter to Hubert Humphrey. 1 May 1947. Humphrey Collection.
"We Work Together." *Newsweek* (9 November 1964): 30.
Whalen, Charles and Barbara. *The Longest Debate*. Cabin John, Maryland, Washington, D.C.: Seven Locks Press, 1985.
"When Attention Turns to the Vice President." *U.S. News & World Report* (18 October 1965): 37.
White, Theodore H. *The Making of the President, 1960*. New York: Atheneum Publishers, 1962.
______. "Memo to a Future Historian." *Life* (13 November 1964): 32–33, 44A–45.
______. "The Inauguration." *Life* (29 January 1964): 24–31.
______. *The Making of the President 1964*. New York: Atheneum Publishers, 1965.
______. *The Making of the President 1968*. New York: Atheneum Publishers, 1965.
______. *The Making of the President 1972*. New York: Atheneum Publishers, 1973.
"White House Honors Humphrey." *The Philadelphia Inquirer* (12 September 1984): 3A.
"Why Humphrey?" Editorial. *The New Republic* (19 October 1968): 1.
Will, George. "Humphrey Without Tears." *Newsweek* (23 January 1978): 88.
______. *The Pursuit of Happiness and Other Sobering Thoughts*. New York: Harper & Row, Publishers, 1978.
"Will the Real Hubert Humphrey Please Sit Down?" *Progressive* (July 1968): 3–5.
"Will West Virginia Stop Kennedy?" *U.S. News & World Report* (2 May 1960): 35–36.
"You Can't Quit HHH." *Reader's Digest* (August 1977).
Zimmerman, G. "Informal Visit with Hubert Humphrey." *Look* (20 October 1964).

Index